THE LIVES AND LETTERS OF AN EIGHTEENTH-CENTURY CIRCLE OF ACQUAINTANCE

For Sean and Stephanie, Joel and Wendy,
Noah and Matthew and Elena

The Lives and Letters of an Eighteenth-Century Circle of Acquaintance

TEMMA BERG
Gettysburg College, USA

ASHGATE

Published by
Ashgate Publishing Limited
Gower House
Croft Road
Aldershot
Hampshire GU11 3HR
England

Ashgate Publishing Company
Suite 420
101 Cherry Street
Burlington, VT 05401-4405
USA

Ashgate website: http://www.ashgate.com

British Library Cataloguing in Publication Data
Berg, Temma
The lives and letters of an eighteenth-century circle of acquaintance
    1.Clerk (Family) – Correspondence 2.Great Britain – Social life and customs – 18th century I.Berg, Temma F., 1943-
    826.6'08

Library of Congress Cataloging-in-Publication Data
Berg, Temma F., 1943-
    The lives and letters of an eighteenth-century circle of acquaintance / by Temma Berg.
        p. cm.
    Includes bibliographical references (p.   ) and index.
    ISBN 0-7546-5599-7 (alk. paper)
    1. English letters—History and criticism. 2. Letter writing—History—18th century. 3. England—Social life and customs—18th century. 4. England—Civilization—18th century. 5. Women—England—Social conditions—18th century. I. Title.

    PR915.B47 2006
    826'.50803552—dc22

                                                                            2005031629
ISBN-10: 0-7546-5599-7
ISBN-13: 978-0-7546-5599-2

Printed and bound in Great Britain by MPG Books Ltd. Bodmin, Cornwall.

Contents

Acknowledgments

This book would not have been possible without the help of many friends, colleagues, and relatives.

Les Deacon provided much background for the Clerke family. With him I visited Wethersfield, Castle Hedingham, and Brook Farm. He took me to Wethersfield Parish Church where members of the family worshiped and Hannah Clerke married Paul Henry Maty. He showed me the Clerke family memorial, which tells the melancholy story of Joseph Clerke, who had five sons, not one of whom outlived him. Deacon's biography of Charles Clerke, *In the Wake of Captain Cook*, with its wealth of information about English naval history and the sea-faring Clerkes, proved to be an indispensable resource.

And then, just when I thought I had filled in as many gaps as I could, Betty Rizzo, who lives in the eighteenth century, generously gave me many exciting new leads. I was able to learn much more about the Brathwaites, the Thorntons, and the Winstanleys. I saw just how intricately interrelated all the letter writers were. I learned that Mrs. Thornton was the wife of Bonnell Thornton, a prominent man of letters. I learned what happened to Sylvia's mother, Elizabeth Brathwaite, a character who until then had been invisible and presumed dead. When I returned to the British Library, I exhumed information about her affair with Major-General William Phillips. In the same day I read letters written by Phillips from his place of detention in the Colonies and letters about her husband John Brathwaite's incarceration in India. It was ironic that two of the men in her life should share such similar fates.

Elizabeth Lambert and Mary Margaret Stewart provided countless evenings of conversation about eighteenth-century life and literature. It was my habit to sit back and listen to their at once gossipy and learned exchanges. Their deep knowledge and endless encouragement helped me stay the course.

Many archivists and librarians assisted along the way. In particular, Bernard Nurse, the librarian at the Society of Antiquaries, was especially kind and helpful. A young man in the Oriental and India Office Collections in the British Library unearthed documents about Sir John Brathwaite that I would probably never have found (certainly not as quickly) without his generous assistance. The Essex Record Office staff provided important documents about the Clerke family and answered numerous questions. Miss Christine Reynolds, Assistant Keeper of the Muniments, Westminster Abbey, provided information about burial records and memorial plaques. Without the expert help of Susan Roach, Interlibrary Loan Specialist at Gettysburg College, I might never have found some of the documents I needed. Karen Drickamer,

Archivist of Special Collections at Gettysburg College, gave me much needed advice about exploring archives and creating TIFFs. Participating in Paula Backscheider's National Endowment for the Humanities Seminar on "Biography and the Uses of Biographical Evidence" enabled me to negotiate more successfully the complexities of English archives. I would also like to thank Ruth Perry, James E. May, Linda V. Troost, Brian Abel Ragen, and Jack G. Voller for their encouragement along the way. My research was also supported by several generous Faculty Development Grants from Gettysburg College.

And then there were the readers of earlier drafts. Charlotte Armster, Joel, Sean, Wendy, and Stephanie Berg, Anna Shannon Elfenbein, Philip Goldstein, Barbara Silverstein, Jane Tompkins, and the members of the Gettysburg College English Department Reading Group provided much thoughtful commentary and gave me much good advice, some of which I heeded and some of which I did not. Their incisive comments make this book better than it otherwise would have been. Any remaining faults are my own.

I have also incurred debts along the way to Loretta Cleveland and Joyce Sprague, who supported me in numerous essential ways. And to Erika Gaffney, for her steadfast and enthusiastic support of my project, and to Meredith Coeyman, for her gracious and meticulous editorial help.

And, last but not least, I would like to thank my husband, Mark Berg, who not only read the book but learned to live with ghosts.

List of Figures

Cover: T. Gainsborough, *The Mall in St James's Park*, 1783. Copyright the Frick
Collection, New York.

Preamble

What can be known will be collected by chance, from the recesses of obscure and obsolete papers, perused commonly with some other view.

Samuel Johnson, *Preface to Shakespeare* (1765)

It is not the profound, but the trivial, the homely, which grips the imagination of posterity and makes the dry bones live. The gossip of one age is the history of the next.

A.M.W. Stirling, *The Merry Wives of Battersea* (1956)

Preamble

The letters that serve as the basis for this book are real. They were written by people who lived and wrote in the second half of the eighteenth century. Nevertheless, these letters assume the shape of fiction and can be treated as a two-part novel. The first part—a domestic novel of manners, which we might title *The History of Lydia Clerke, Written by Others*—tells the story of Lydia Hammond's marriage to John Clerke, his improvidence and infidelity, and her subsequent distress. The second part—a blend of sentimental romance and picaresque, which we might title *The History of Sylvia Brathwaite, Written by Herself*—narrates the experiences of Sylvia Brathwaite, a young woman who comes to London, attracts the attention of many of the men she meets, including the Prince of Wales, and finally marries. Whether she lives happily ever after is up to you. "The adventure is something like a novel," writes Sylvia of one of her brother's escapades in France. The same could be said of many of the incidents narrated in these letters. They are full of fantastic and unexpected events. Although the focus of the narrative shifts from the first to the second novel, the same people circulate throughout, so it seems appropriate to bring the two books together under the title *The Lives and Letters of an Eighteenth-Century Circle of Acquaintance*.

I found the letters in the summer of 1993. I was preparing to write a new biography of Charlotte Lennox, the versatile and prolific eighteenth-century woman writer who is most famous for *The Female Quixote*, a book about a young woman named Arabella who perceives her quotidian real-life adventures as the stuff of the fantastic romances she reads until reformed by a learned Doctor, who convinces her that reading romances harms young minds. Looking for letters both by and about Lennox, I located two unpublished letters of hers in the Society of Antiquaries in London. Housed in a wooden box, they were part of a group of letters held together by a single sheet of folded paper.[1] Lennox's letters, which were addressed to a Lady Clerke, were, like her other letters, lively, literate, and legible. I read them several times before turning to the other letters, all of which seemed to be addressed to the same person, whose first name was Lydia. Tentatively I inspected them. They appeared tedious, the dull scribblings of dull women who had nothing better to do than to write long letters to one another. A few were written by men—a Charles

---

[1]   444/19, Cely-Trevilian Collection, Society of Antiquaries.

Clerke, a John Clerke, a T. Winstanley—but most were written by women. The largest number were from Sylvia Brathwaite.

Although at first I was not interested in the accompanying letters, gradually they exerted their spell. They might, after all, have more to tell me about Charlotte Lennox. I read them when I returned to London the following summer; I also transcribed a few of them. They were not hard to read but references were obscure and allusions uncertain. Who was Sylvia Brathwaite, the author of the largest number of the letters, and who was Lady Lydia Clerke, the woman to whom all these letters were addressed? Who was this absent center about whom the letters circulated? The initials of Lydia Clerke's name, I noted, reversed Charlotte Lennox's. I speculated about what possible significance this mirroring might have. The more I read, the more thrilling and inscrutable the letters became. It would take many years of extensive research in dusty old books, obscure reference works, and many record offices throughout England before their many allusions would become clear. Or, at least, a little clearer.

While the bulk of the letters were written by people who dwelled comfortably on the margins of history, others were written by people who gained some fame. The two letters from novelist Charlotte Lennox give us new insights into her domestic life and corroborate a growing suspicion that she was a good friend to women. In the letters of Susannah Dobson, a learned lady who entered the worlds of Frances Burney's diaries and Hester Thrale Piozzi's *Thraliana*, we obtain a vivid portrait of the intellectual woman's dis-ease with herself and gain new information about why Burney and Thrale might have so adamantly disliked her. Lady Clerke's letters also cast new light on Charles Clerke, the man who took over when James Cook was killed on their around-the-world journey. We learn not only about his maritime adventures but also about his domestic habits. Lydia's husband, John Clerke, also traveled far, and, before dying in Madras, became a good friend and supporter of Warren Hastings, the first Governor General of India. Thomas Winstanley was also a well-known figure. When Samuel Johnson sought comfort as he lay dying, he called on Winstanley. Feeling unequal to the task of comforting the great man, Winstanley refused to come in person but sent letters instead. According to witnesses, Winstanley's epistolary admonitions soothed Johnson and may perhaps have provoked a last-minute conversion experience. Altogether these letters cover much territory and have much to tell us about public and private life in eighteenth-century England.

Lydia Clerke's Circle of Acquaintance

In the interstices of my teaching life, I slowly and laboriously transcribed the letters. I was amazed and delighted by their contents. The two letters from Susannah Dobson tried my patience, for her cramped handwriting was nearly indecipherable. I wondered what her eighteenth-century acquaintances thought about her many foibles. I discovered that Sylvia Brathwaite was a reader of novels, a playgoer, and a heroine in her own right. Her poignant story could have come out of a novel by Lennox. Like the quixotic Arabella she perceived her world through the books she read: a young man in a park became Volpone; the actress Mrs. Abington became another "Capricious Lady," the title of a play in which she appeared; and Sylvia another "Victim of Fancy," the title of a popular novel; and her friend looked for his "Caroline," someone like the popular fictional heroine Caroline of Lichtfield. The letters from Charles Clerke gave me insight into life at sea. I read several contemporary accounts of his voyages and wondered if the image of him presented in James King's narrative of his last voyage with Captain Cook served Mary Shelley as a prototype for Walton, the frame-narrator/navigator of *Frankenstein*, or for Victor Frankenstein, her Promethean scientist/over-reacher.[2] When I read Charles Clerke's "death" letter, I felt as if I were receiving news about Frankenstein's death. The circle of Lady Clerke's acquaintance extended very far indeed, even to the edges of the known world, where the real and the imaginary crossed. The biggest surprise of all turned out to be the contents of the two letters not addressed to Lady Clerke. Written by Sarah Clerke, Lydia Clerke's sister-in-law, and addressed to "My dearest friend," they chronicled the death of Lydia.

As the many tales the letters told slowly unraveled—tales of wayward husbands and adventurous brothers and brothers-in-law, tales of loss and betrayal, tales of friendship and community, tales of youth and innocence and privilege, tales of aging and despair and poverty—I speculated about the person who saved these letters. Lady Clerke must have received hundreds of letters over the course of her life. Why did she save the particular twenty-nine she did out of what must have been a vast sea of correspondence? And, beyond Lady Clerke, who added the last two letters from Sarah Clerke to the collection and why? And, finally, how had these letters found their way into the Society of Antiquaries? According to its catalog, the letters once belonged to a Lady Vincent, a nineteenth-century woman who married in 1824 and died in 1876. It was her daughter Blanche who bequeathed the letters to the Society's library in 1915. What was Lady Vincent's relationship to the letters? How did she come by them? What did she believe she had found? Was it she who, with a graceful gesture, added the only two letters not addressed to Lydia Clerke as if to punctuate with a strong sense of an ending the stories the letters tell?

"Letter writing is a realm ascribed without question to women, and when chance has rescued from oblivion any group of their letters, social history has been thereby

---

[2]   James Cook and James King, *A Voyage to the Pacific Ocean Undertaken by the Command of His Majesty, for Making Discoveries in the Northern Hemisphere* (London, 1784) 3:254–5, 260–61.

enriched."[3] So wrote Myra Reynolds fifty years ago, and she was spectacularly prescient, for, in the fifty years since, there has been a remarkable resurgence of interest in women's letters and in what they have to tell us about the past. The Lydia Clerke letters are not unique in the access they give us. But, adding life and color to what were hitherto faded squares in the quilt of women's and men's collective history, they, along with the many other collections of eighteenth-century women's letters that have been examined over the past thirty years, illuminate our understanding of the "other eighteenth century."

An eighteenth-century letter reads differently than a modern letter, or even a nineteenth-century letter. Nevertheless, the Lydia Clerke letters will seem familiar as well as strange. When I read Ann Clerke's description of her aging parent—"our old Gent is in a strange way what we shall do with him I know not, neither sick nor well but his head alas his head declines every day"—I realized that her father suffered from the same debilitating disease as mine. I felt her pain and sadness and only wished I could write as poetically as she about the illnesses of aging. When I read Susannah Dobson's letters I discovered how radically unknowable the past could be. Her letters were long (even by eighteenth-century standards), circuitous, repetitive, full of abject humility and arrogant presumption, obscure, and, somehow, humorous. The strangest moment in her very odd letters (indeed, the strangest moment in all the letters) occurred just as she received notice of a letter from Lydia: "When your Letter came I was just pronouncing your Name with Awe. I had caught a Wasp and was violently busy in Squeezing out the Sting from its Tail and in Eyeing its clever and fierce Visage. I desired Johnson to help me as it was a Work of great Labor and Importance and was just saying, if my dear & beloved M[rs] Clerke was here I must not in her Presence do this—Down went all the things when your Letter came and the Sting half out and half in remains for further operation at my leisure Hours." What can be made of such a moment? Why did Susannah include it? What did Lydia Clerke make of it? What was I to make of it? And of its author? As it turned out, I was able to make much of her, and, in the process, learn to admire her, although always with a hesitation and an uncertainty as to who she was and what her intentions were. She remains the most inscrutable of Lydia's correspondents and her letters the most unreadable. After you have read her letters, you will feel the truth of Ann Clerke's description of her: "how different a manner of proceeding she has to every other creature that let a person be ever so much attach'd to her, it is impossible some times not to laugh at her expence." As with many eighteenth-century letters, Susannah Dobson's epistles were probably passed around and read by many people, who, as they sat down with one of her long sheets of tiny script, knew what to expect and both dreaded and relished her prolixity, tendentiousness, occasional insights, and

---

[3] Myra Reynolds, *The Learned Lady in England, 1650–1760* (Massachusetts, 1964) 31.

inadvertent humor. Like her contemporaries you will probably find her letters unintelligible, illegible (in the deepest sense of the word), and endless, but you will also find brief moments of heartfelt and passionate candor, which explode on the page, bursting through her convoluted sentences like small firecrackers in a night-time sky, and which reward the reader accordingly.

Organizing the Past

I could have organized the letters and the information I gathered about them and their authors in many ways. I could have written a chronological history or arranged the book by concepts and issues, but these structures would prevent the reader from knowing the letter writers as individuals and from entering into their different stories. It seemed best, for my purposes, to organize my commentary by letters and letter writers. It is the spectral presences behind the letters that most interest me. I want to raise the ghosts of the writers and give them substance. I want to let my readers know as much about them as possible. There are moments when I feel as if I know them well; then again, there are moments when I hardly understand them at all. Ingenuous and transparent, inscrutable and secretive by turns, the members of Lydia Clerke's circle of acquaintance inhabit a world in many ways like our own, but in many ways radically unknowable.

In the Foreword, "The Rise of the Novel, the Death of the Author, and the Lydia Clerke Letters," I consider the consequences of looking at historical documents as novelistic. The border between the real and the imaginary blurs and the notion of the author changes. In "The Letters, the Letter Writers, and Their Wor(l)ds," a brief overview of the historical background of the people who write the letters and of the many ways in which the smaller worlds of the letter writers intersect with the larger worlds of eighteenth-century England is followed by transcriptions of the letters and accompanying interpretive essays. In "Post/Crypt: Closing the Circle ... ," I look one last time at the difficulties inherent in separating fiction from fact and in bringing an archival research project to a close. I draw on one of Sylvia Brathwaite's letters, a letter about a ghost story, to dramatize the researcher's perilous and never ending quest. Sylvia's remarks about a nobleman who has learned to bring the dead back to life become a warning to the errant researcher: "He too has the power of raising from the Grave its Inhabitants how and by what means was but darkly Spoken. But so much they learned—the spirits having once been called had a perpetual Right to appear to the Person who so disturbed Them—& that they frequently did haunt the Beds and Feasts of These Noblemen." Like Sylvia's noblemen, researchers become haunted by the spectral presences they call forth. They want to ask more and more questions of the ghosts they have raised. They cannot rest until they have found the whole truth. And neither can the ghosts. Lastly, "Biographical Sketches of the Letter

Writers and of Persons and Places Mentioned in Them" and a "Chronology" are provided as appendices.

There were also, of course, decisions to be made about the best way to present the letters. Ideally, to preserve the arbitrariness of their sequence, I would have liked to publish them as I found them, loosely packed in a box. But this was not possible. I had to arrange them chronologically. I have done so, to the best of my ability, but the arrangement is sometimes arbitrary, for while some of the letters are dated, others are not, and it is not always possible to know which letter follows which. My most difficult decision was how to handle footnoting. After much thought, I decided not to footnote the letters. There were two reasons: first, there was my theoretical argument that these letters can be seen as forming a two-part novel; and, second, these letters are very unlike a traditional collection of letters. There are only thirty-one of them, they were written by nine different people; and the person who serves as the glue that holds the collection together did not write a single one. In a traditional collection the glue is the famous (or infamous) literary or historical person who pens the greatest number of letters; other letters are included primarily because they throw additional light on the great man or woman at the center. While such collections demand extensive footnoting, the Lydia Clerke letters lend themselves to a different treatment.[4] Therefore I present them as if they were letters in epistolary novels. However, because they are also real, information about the people, places, and events mentioned in them are provided in the headnotes that precede them, in the interpretive essays that follow, and in the appendices.

"Letters, as Janet Gurkin Altman reminds us, are both "literary artifacts" and "historical documents."[5] In order to read them, we need to deal with both their rhetorical strategies and their biographical and historical contexts. This is certainly true of the letters written by the women and men who form the circle of Lydia Clerke's acquaintance. Although only three of them—Charlotte Lennox, Susannah Dobson, and Thomas Winstanley—were published authors, they were all strong readers. And, like any group of strong readers, they drew on contemporary plays, essays, histories, and novels for images, metaphors, and interpretations of their lives. The women often saw themselves as heroines and the men around them as heroes or villains according to their treatment of the women dependent on them. The men were just as ready to see themselves as protagonists and antagonists, participants in

---

[4]   See Robert Halsband's "Editing the Letters of Letter-Writers" (*Studies in Bibliography*, 55 [1958]: 25–37) for a thoughtful discussion about editing collections of letters.

[5]   Janet Gurkin Altman, "Postscript: Epistolary Acts and Literary Careers in the Eighteenth Century: Permutations of Public Sphere and Private Persona among Writers," *Sent as a Gift: Eight Correspondences from the Eighteenth Century*, Ed. Alan T. McKenzie (Athens, 1993) 203.

dramatic tales of adventure, loss, and chicanery. If we want to read these letters as fully as possible, we need to understand both their literary and historical references.

During my many trips to England over the years, I absorbed the atmosphere of the letter writers' daily lives. I read the newspapers they read. I took the train and ferry to Gosport, where Lydia grew up, and walked to the Alverstoke Parish Church where she married John Clerke. I visited Brook Farm, the Clerke family home, and Wethersfield Parish Church, where they worshiped. In London, I visited the churches and parks frequented by Lydia and her acquaintance. I perambulated the various London streets and squares (Cavendish, Grosvenor, Kensington, Hanover) where they visited and wrote and read and re-read their letters to one another.

Most important, I too read and re-read what they had written. Fascinating and revealing windows on the lives of upper-middle-class English women and men, their letters encompass many worlds: "and in an hour I am making feathered headdresses or fighting at Pharsalia—thinking of the Life of our King and the death of Cato, or fifty things as unlike one another," as Sylvia ruefully and alliteratively observes. And yet, certain themes recur and patterns emerge: the importance of female friendship, especially the younger/older woman relationship; the predicament of the woman intellectual, her awkwardness and alienation; the sexual vulnerability of the young unmarried woman and her power of disruption; the economic and emotional instability of wives even in companionate marriage; the desirability, elusiveness, and corruptibility of paradise; and, most importantly, the centrality for women of writing and reading, sending and receiving letters. Letters were entertainment, bringers of news and information, providers of company and comfort, sites of intellectual and emotional satisfaction. They were the eighteenth-century person's soap opera, serial entertainment, escapist fare. They were also, as Alan T. McKenzie reminds us, incomparable gifts.[6]

While I want to believe that the themes I found in these letters emerged from my reading of them and from my deepening acquaintance with their writers and their contexts, and not from my own preoccupations, I know my readings of the letters and their writers were always already couched in terms of these themes, which, for the past thirty years, have fueled an abundance of literary and historical scholarship of the eighteenth century as well as of the centuries before and after.[7] Therefore, when I

---

[6]   Alan T. McKenzie, *Sent as a Gift* 16.

[7]   For example, Eve Tavor Bannet, *The Domestic Revolution: Enlightenment Feminisms and the Novel* (Baltimore, 2000); Emma Donoghue, *Passions between Women: British Lesbian Culture 1668–1801* (London, 1993); Jacqueline Pearson, *Women's Reading in Britain, 1750–1835: A Dangerous Recreation* (Cambridge, 1999); Betty Rizzo, *Companions Without Vows: Relationships among Eighteenth-Century British Women* (Athens, 1994); and Amanda Vickery, *The Gentleman's Daughter: Women's Lives in Georgian England* (New Haven, 1998).

discuss the letters and their writers, I deploy two procedures at once. I foreground the letters so that what they have to tell us about their writers and their worlds can emerge as unobstructed by my preconceived notions as possible. Alternately, I background them in order to bring forward the issues I want to discuss (friendship, companionate marriage, learned ladies, cannibalism, smuggling, etc.) and use the letters as evidence that these issues were indeed important in the eighteenth century. But, whether I am foregrounding or backgrounding the letters, I never forget just how completely the concepts and the letters construct one another.

I suspect that these letters could give and take context from other discourses, but I had to close the circle somewhere. I chose to focus on women's issues and, very briefly, on issues of empire. Focusing on women's and postcolonial issues has enabled me to see just how full of human frailty and nobility the eighteenth century was and how like and unlike ourselves its citizens could be. The Lydia Clerke letters are a microcosm, a tiny part of a very complex world and time; nevertheless, they give us insight not only into the eighteenth century but also into ourselves.

As L.P. Hartley so famously wrote, "The past is a foreign country."[8] We are still learning our ways around it.

---

[8]   L.P. Hartley, *The Go-Between* (New York, 2002) 17.

Foreword: The Rise of the Novel, the Death of the Author, and the Lydia Clerke Letters

By incorporating the knowledge deployed in reference to it, the archive augments itself, engrosses itself, it gains in *auctoritas*. But in the same stroke it loses the absolute and meta-textual authority it might claim to have. One will never be able to objectivize it with no remainder. The archivist produces more archive, and that is why the archive is never closed. It opens out of the future.

Jacques Derrida, Archive Fever (1995)

... I seem to call for a form of culture in which fiction would not be limited by the figure of the author. It would be pure romanticism, however, to imagine a culture in which the fictive would operate in an absolutely free state, in which fiction would be put at the disposal of everyone and would develop without passing through something like a necessary or constraining figure. Although, since the eighteenth century, the author has played the role of the regulator of the fictive, a role quite characteristic of our era of industrial and bourgeois society, of individualism and private property, still, given the historical modifications that are taking place, it does not seem necessary that the author function remain constant in form, complexity, and even in existence. I think that, as our society changes, at the very moment when it is in the process of changing, the author function will disappear, and in such a manner that fiction and its polysemous texts will once again function according to another mode, but still with a system of constraint—one which will no longer be the author, but which will have to be determined or, perhaps, experienced.

Michel Foucault, "What is an Author" (1969)

After having been advised to publish, a worthy friend called on me, and, speaking of the letters (part of which he had seen) said—"And pray what do you mean to call your Book, when finished—A Novel?"—I replied, "I do not know what to call it; for it is, and it is not a novel." "A very curious composition truly," said he, "It *is*, and it is *not*, is quite in the female style of contradiction!"—I was much obliged by his remark, which at once furnished me with a title, for which I had intreated THOUGHT in vain!—I then gave up all application to her, being fully persuaded (in a double sense of the expression) that IT IS, AND IT IS NOT A NOVEL.

Charlotte Palmer, It Is and It Is Not a Novel (1792)

Foreword: The Rise of the Novel, the Death of the Author, and the Lydia Clerke Letters

My argument that the Lydia Clerke letters form a two-part novel rests on three key points. First, novel readers have often experienced difficulty in separating fiction from fact, and novel theorists have repeatedly addressed this conundrum. In this Foreword, I look briefly at a truncated history of novel theory, beginning with Richardson and ending with Lennard Davis, to demonstrate how novel theory, and in particular epistolary novel theory, has long been engaged with questions of verisimilitude and the epistemological status of the letter. Davis provides eloquent and persuasive arguments about the fact/ fiction divide in both journalism and novels and brings us to a new understanding of that blurred border. Davis's arguments provide the foundation for my belief that the Lydia Clerke letters can be seen as fictional. And when we look at the way letters were used in journalism and novels and at the ambiguous "epistolary spaces"[1] created by the rise of the postal service during the second half of the eighteenth century, we can see just how squarely letters and early epistolary novels sit on the fact/ fiction divide.

Post-structuralism, the second support for my argument, and novel theory converge at the fact/ fiction divide. Post-structuralism has always challenged that opposition and asked us to look more closely at the institutional and discursive practices that give some people the power to name the real while taking it away from others. Post-structuralist theory also allows us to challenge romantic notions of the author. The author may not completely disappear but s/he recedes from view. In the novels composed by the Lydia Clerke letters, the author function changes.

---

[1] See James How's *Epistolary Spaces: English Letter Writing from the Foundation of the Post Office to Richardson's* Clarissa (Aldershot, 2003) for a fascinating discussion of the ways the rise of the postal system created what he calls "epistolary spaces." Epistolary spaces become the sites where public and private discourse merge: "In sum, epistolary spaces are 'public' spaces within which supposedly 'private' writings travel—at once imaginary and real; imaginary, because you can't really inhabit them as you can other social spaces—all meetings and incidents there are only metaphorical; real, because they were policed by a government ever more keen to monitor the letters that passed along the national postal routes" (5).

The third part of my argument rests on the existence of the Lady Clerke letters. While some may argue that the letters cannot form novels because there is no novelist, I would argue that perhaps there are too many. Many people assisted in the preservation and novelization of Lydia's letters: the letter writers, Lady Clerke, the unknown person who inserted Sarah Clerke's letters, Lady Vincent and her daughter Blanche, and me. Even so, not all my readers will agree that the letters are fictional. As testament to my own ambivalence, I use the third part of this Foreword to present arguments both for and against my own proposition. Ultimately, I affirm that the letters dwell precariously on the border between the real and the imaginary and, like Charlotte Palmer's 1792 novel, both are and are not novels.

The Rise of the Novel

Samuel Richardson is often credited with giving birth to the novel. After years of printing newspapers, reprints of earlier works, and other items that yielded him much profit, he was convinced to produce a work of his own, a book of familiar letters which might serve as models to "Country Readers." In the process of writing one or two letters from a maid to her parents narrating her successful resistance to her master's importunities, the novel *Pamela* was born:

> Little did I think, at first, of making one, much less two volumes of it. But, when I began to recollect what had, so many years before, been told me by my friend [the story of a beautiful and talented young woman who resisted all the snares set by her master and eventually married him], I thought the story, if written in an easy and natural manner, suitably to the simplicity of it, might possibly introduce a new species of writing, that might possibly turn young people into a course of reading different from the pomp and parade of romance-writing, and dismissing the improbable and marvelous, with which novels generally abound, might tend to promote the cause of religion and virtue. I therefore gave way to enlargement: and so Pamela became as you see her.[2]

Unlike his heroine, who resisted the temptations of her master, Richardson could not resist the tempting advice of those who encouraged him to enlarge his story. He went on to write a realistic epistolary novel, "a new species of writing" designed to counteract the noxious effects of contemporary romances. Richardson believed his novel *Pamela* was the harbinger of a new species of writing which buttressed the border between reality and fantasy and thereby promoted the cause of religion and virtue. Ironically, however, *Pamela* went on to serve as a prototype for endless numbers of romantic "Cinderella" stories which narrate the marvelous

---

[2]   T.C. Duncan Eaves and Ben D. Kimpel, *Samuel Richardson: A Biography* (Oxford, 1971) 89.

transformations of poor and beleaguered but virtuous victims into proud, happy, and wealthy victors. The romantic and the fantastical burgeoned; novels and novelists could not escape duplicity. As realistic as they might seem, still they stimulated the imagination and stumbled into romance. The epistemological status of novelistic discourse remained unstable. Scenes and characters were both real and unreal. Titles like *The Romance of Real Life* (by Charlotte Smith, published in 1787) and *It Is and It Is Not a Novel* (by Charlotte Palmer, published in 1792) underscore eighteenth-century awareness that the novel negotiated unplumbed waters as it sought to distinguish between brute fact and fantastical whimsy.

The rise of the novel, and of the epistolary novel in particular, has often been linked to women's increasing literacy. The letter and the novel of letters were ideal places for exploring, constructing, and expressing women's subjectivities. In *Women, Letters, and the Novel*, Ruth Perry attributed the rise of the epistolary novel to women's lack of economic viability and need for romantic compensation. Noting that between one and two hundred epistolary novels were published and sold in London during the early eighteenth century, Perry argues that "it is precisely the impotent suffering of the embattled heroine which produces the anguished consciousness that needs the release of writing letters."[3] The letter and the novel gave imaginary as well as real women new ways to analyze and reform their worlds. If we think of the eighteenth century as the century in which the sense of an autonomous self was growing, a self that could be written about, a self that could be engendered, a self that could be the subject of a biography, then we need to recognize eighteenth-century letters and epistolary novels as sites where selves could be identified, constructed, negotiated, mediated, narrativized. The rise of the novel and the letter, and in particular the rise of the epistolary novel, allowed women to name the real from their perspective.

In *The Story of the Novel*, Margaret Anne Doody reminds us that letter-writing has always been part of the novel. Letter-writing, she points out, is "one of the things novel characters do best, and do frequently—it comes naturally to them, like dreaming."[4] Likewise, Thomas O. Beebee insists on a long history and wide dissemination of the interweaving of the letter, the novel, and the letter-writing manual: "*Ars dictaminis* [letter-writing manuals], real correspondence, and fiction transmute vertiginously into each other," he concludes.[5] Richardson was not the only author caught in the dynamic created by the intersecting trajectories of real letters, fictional novels, and epistolary novels claiming to be real.

In *Women's Lives and the Eighteenth-Century English Novel*, Elizabeth Bergen Brophy examined the ways actual eighteenth-century memoirs, journals, and letters

---

[3] Ruth Perry, *Women, Letters, and the Novel* (New York, 1980) 22.
[4] Margaret Anne Doody, *The True Story of the Novel* (New Brunswick, 1996) 155.
[5] Thomas O. Beebee, *Epistolary Fiction in Europe, 1500–1850* (Cambridge, 1999) 28.

by women reflected novelistic situations. She concluded that because fictional stories matched the "real" ones found in letters and diaries, eighteenth-century novels were realistic and based on actual events.[6] The Lydia Clerke letters reverse Brophy's observations and force us to ask, How much do women's letters reveal that their writers were readers of novels and tellers of tales? Are the real tales people tell sometimes based on fictional ones? And how do we discriminate between the two?

Tracing the history of the separation of fiction from fact, Lennard Davis argues that during the course of the eighteenth century various political and cultural forces transformed a heterogeneous news/ novels print discourse in which there was "no real distinction between what we would call fact and fiction"[7] into the different genres of journalism, fiction, and history. As part of this process, the novel came into being "as a form of defense against censorship, power, and authority."[8] Davis's arguments add much to our understanding of the rise of the novel and of journalism, but because his study focuses on the different forms of print discourse, it necessarily overlooks the complex and highly volatile discourse of the eighteenth-century letter and its relationship to news and the novel.

In the eighteenth century many news articles were primarily composed of transcriptions of letters sent from ships after engagements at sea, or from far away after battles on land, or from nearby after local riots and other events. Letters conveyed news of public events, but, like novels, they were never uniformly real. Just as novels insisted on their verisimilitude even as they tilted toward the fantastic and romantic, just so the letter, sent from one real person to another and undeniably containing truth, yet employed rhetorical devices to relay reverie and supposition as well as fact. By constructing novels out of private letters, writers could ensure that their discourses remained both factual and fictive. Their stories could be both news from nowhere and news from everywhere.

Many factors were important to the rise of the novel—the rise of the middle class, the rise in the number of women readers and writers, the emergence of modern consumer culture, the need to distinguish fact from fiction.[9] However, without the

---

[6]   Elizabeth Bergen Brophy, *Women's Lives and the Eighteenth-Century English Novel* (Tampa, 1991) 267.

[7]   Lennard J. Davis, *Factual Fictions: The Origins of the English Novel* (New York, 1983) 51.

[8]   Davis 222.

[9]   The history of novel theory is long and convoluted and there are many theories of its origins and rise—Marxist, structuralist, feminist, cultural, psychoanalytic, postmodern, etc. I have limited myself to a few theories that look at the novel from the perspective of verisimilitude, the epistemological status of the letter, and the woman reader. For a wider history of the novel, turn to the January/ April 2000 special edition of *Reconsidering the Rise of the Novel*, which was dedicated to the memory of Ian Watt, author in 1957 of arguably the single most important volume of novel theory, *The Rise of the Novel*.

rapid growth of the English postal system, the novel might not have assumed the shape it did or taken off as swiftly.

The sending of letters has, of course, a long history. However, it was not until the seventeenth century that a series of "running posts" was created in England and postal rates set. In 1660, as part of the Restoration after the Cromwellian Revolution, Parliament passed an Act for erecting and establishing a post office. In the spring of 1680, William Dockwra set up a penny post. Primarily an urban service, it eventually became part of the government postal service, and revenue from the post office very quickly became an important source of money for wars and other governmental needs. By 1784 the volume of mail reached three million letters annually, not counting newspapers that went free, or the letters hidden in those newspapers in order to avoid postage. In 1763, five years before the first letter of *Circle* was written, the post office brought in £97,834; in 1795 it brought in £409,000; and, in 1815, when Sarah Clerke penned her two letters, receipts totaled £1,598,000.[10] The letter and the novel, and the conjunction of these two (the epistolary novel), shared an increasing visibility and saturation during the eighteenth century and became favored forms of discourse.

Titles of early epistolary novels suggest that the conjunction of the post and the novel was quickly seen as conducive to the reality of the imaginary. As early as 1603 Nicholas Breton produced *A Poste With a Madde Packet of Letters*. In 1692, Charles Gildon penned *The post-boy rob'd of his mail or, The pacquet broke open. Consisting of five hundred letters, to persons of several qualities and conditions. With observations upon each letter. Published by a gentleman concern'd in the frolick.* (Evidently opening other people's mail was not yet a crime.) Twenty-seven years later Gildon composed the equally complexly titled work *The Post-Man Robbd of his Mail: Or, the Packet broke open. Being A Collection of Miscellaneous Letters, Serious and Comical, Amorous and Gallant. Amongst which are, the Lovers Sighs: Or, the Amours of the Beautiful Stremunia and Alphonso the Wise, King of Castile, and Aragon, and Earl of Provence; with her Passionate letters to the King on his chusing another Mistress*. Gildon's two titles might be a way of gauging changing attitudes toward the complex interconnections among postal systems, epistolary novels, and truth. Just as the post-boy of the first title matures into the post-man of the second, just so insistence on the truth of the letters matures into ironic awareness of their

---

[10]   The following books contributed to my understanding of the rise of the postal system in eighteenth-century England: Kenneth Ellis, *The Post Office in the Eighteenth Century: A Study in Administrative History* (London, 1958); John G. Hendy, *The History of the Early Postmarks of the British Isles from their Introduction Down to 1840* (New York, 1905); John Peace, *A Descant on the Penny Postage* (London, 1841); Howard Robinson, *Britain's Post Office: A History of Development from the Beginnings to the Present Day* (London, 1953); Howard Robinson, *The British Post Office: A History* (Westport, 1948); Frank Staff, *The Penny Post, 1680–1918* (London, 1964); and Roy Wheeler, *A Postal History* (Hassocks, 1996).

fictionality. In his first title, the author may pretend to be one of the pranksters who stole the letters, but, in his second, his claims to authenticity quickly yield to the palpably unreal subtitle "The Lover's Sighs."

Over the past 15 years, there has been a shift in thinking about women's correspondence both fictional and real. The view of the letter as a site for the private revelations of the awakening self has been amplified. Building on the work of Lennard Davis and on Jacques Derrida's central insight in *The Post Card*—that the letter can stand in for all writing and its reversibility[11]—and on rereadings of canonical as well as marginalized epistolary novels and published correspondences, commentators have reshaped epistolary history. According to the new paradigm, epistolary novels and published correspondences realign the borders of the private and public, complicate our notions of what Michel Foucault called "the author function," create spaces in which heterogeneous discourses (the sentimental romance, the Gothic, the domestic novel of manners, the autobiographical memoir, the political tract, the philosophical treatise, etc.) circulate indiscriminately and blur any simple distinction between the real and the imaginary.[12] As Elizabeth Heckendorn Cook has argued, "The ways in which the letter saturated enlightenment culture makes it clear that studies of eighteenth-century epistolarity must begin by rejecting an anachronistic distinction between literatures of fact and fiction."[13] Like the letters in epistolary novels and in published correspondences, the Lydia Clerke letters dwell in the borderlands between fact and fiction.

From the eighteenth century to the present, authors have struggled with the slippery divide between fact and fiction. As a result, the novel has evolved over time and taken many shapes; likewise, theorists have defined the novel in many different ways and insisted on different defining attributes. However, as many definitions as there have been, all have insisted on one characteristic: the novel's form and content are linked to the root meaning of the word itself. The novel is always new. It is always

---

[11] See Jacques Derrida, *The Post Card: From Socrates to Freud and Beyond* (Chicago, 1987): "Perhaps they are going to find this writing too adroit, virtuosic in the art of turning away, perhaps perverse in that it can be approached from everywhere and nowhere, certainly abandoned to the other, but given over to itself, offered up to its own blows, up to the end reserving everything for itself" (223).

[12] Commentators who have contributed to this rich field of inquiry include April Alliston, *Virtue's Faults: Correspondences in Eighteenth-Century British and French Women's Fiction* (Stanford, 1996); Elizabeth Heckendorn Cook, *Epistolary Bodies: Gender and Genre in the Eighteenth-Century Republic of Letters* (Stanford, 1996); Mary A. Favret, *Romantic Correspondence: Women, Politics and the Fiction of Letters* (Cambridge, 1993); and Amanda Gilroy and W.M. Verhoeven, eds, *Epistolary Histories: Letters, Fiction, Culture* (Charlottesville, 2000).

[13] Cook 17.

changing. The two novels formed by the Lydia Clerke letters come at the end of a long line of novel interventions.

The Death of the Author

A product of its eighteenth-century context, *Circle of Acquaintance* also derives from post-structuralism. Post-structuralists insist on the difficulty of separating the real from the imaginary. The truth value of different discourses is not easily decided. All knowledge is fragmentary and situated. Truth remains elusive. What starts out as verity might end up as invented tale. Information slides into fable. Communication becomes fabrication as discourse constructs the world it presumes to describe.

Affirming (but not inventing) the deep intertextuality of the real and the fictional, post-structuralism refuses to privilege one discourse over another and alerts us to the incompleteness and situatedness of all knowledge. There are no totalizing gestures. Refusing to cut off discussion of any text or of any moment from the past, post-structuralism insists on the endless free play and supplementarity of meaning. Readers and writers add and peel off layers of interpretation to find there is no singularity of meaning. There is only nourishing and endless possibility. Like physicists, who use more and more powerful electron microscopes to discriminate smaller and smaller particles of matter and never reach bottom, researchers into archives probe farther and deeper into the past to answer questions only to find other and more perplexing mysteries. We do learn something new about the past but just as there is always a smaller particle to observe, there is always something missing in any story we uncover. There is always something more to be learned. There is always another angle of vision. Nevertheless, the endless supplementarity of reading thickens the texture of reality, or of what claims to be real, and enlarges our understanding of the past.

In its severest form, post-structuralist theory dismantles the opposition between history and fiction. Our search for truth becomes ever more difficult. As we ask more and more searching questions of the archive, we lose the old certainties we once found in historical documents. It becomes harder and harder to find solid objective truths in the written word. In *Archive Fever*, Derrida warns us that as the knowledge we gain engrosses the archive and thereby grants it authority, paradoxically that same knowledge weakens "the absolute and meta-textual authority it [the archive] might claim to have."[14] The archive can never be closed; our quest to understand documents from the past can never end. There will always be another document to challenge and change any reading of the past.

Reading the Lydia Clerke letters in different orders over the years has been a dizzying experience and has made me exceedingly conscious of how difficult it is to

---

[14] Jacques Derrida, *Archive Fever* (Chicago, 1995) 68.

understand the past on its own terms. As Ann Clerke remarks to Lydia, when comparing their different attitudes toward people of fashion, "there are many things we see in very different shades of light, or perhaps I may more properly say we View through very different opticks." If two people who were related and shared much could view the world so differently, how much greater are the discontinuities between a twenty-first-century reader and the eighteenth-century spectral powers she hopes to bring to life, or, at least, entertain for a short while.

More than any other post-structuralist concept, "the death of the author" has transfixed many with horror. To assail the individuality and autonomy of the author threatens our sense of self. To suggest that an author cannot control the meaning of her text undercuts our sense of control over the language we use. To give up the author's hold on his text forces us to give up our holds on our own lives and the various concepts we use to make sense of them. Also, to toy with the notion of the death of the author is, we are told over and over again, to privilege the reader/ critic in self-serving ways. The reader becomes more important than the writer in discovering the significance of the text. But the death of the author has never meant that the author does not matter, or that s/he disappears. The author matters very much. We want to know as much as we can about her. "The place of the one who writes must always be sought," observes Jacques Derrida, "even if it is not fixed."[15] But no matter how completely we search, we will miss much. The writer can never be completely understood. She moves away from us as we move toward her. The author and her words become the site of the many heterogeneous discourses which circulate through her, her age, and ours.

Circle complicates any simple notion of the author and creativity. Most of us want to believe that the author is the originator of the text s/he produces. In many ways, the eighteenth-century aided and abetted such romantic notions of authorship. The myth that works of art are born through individual acts of creation was supported by two increasingly prominent forms of eighteenth-century discourse: biography and the various arguments in support of authorial rights to copy. Biographers recorded the influences that created the great man, the great poet, the great writer/ philosopher. It was the biographer's duty to enshrine his subject and present him as the center of his age and to emphasize his uniqueness and the importance of his contributions to the republic of letters. This was Boswell's job as he wrote his compendious *The Life of Samuel Johnson* and in this he was only following in the footsteps of the great man himself, whose *Lives of the English Poets* set a standard for biography.

The flood of literary and legal discourse over the issue of perpetual copyright also contributed to present-day notions of authorship. As Mark Rose so lucidly and compellingly argues, "Copyright is founded on the concept of the unique individual

---

[15] Jacques Derrida, *Glas* (Lincoln, 1986) 107.

who creates something original and is entitled to reap a profit from those labors."[16] Who would want to deny an author her originality or her right to earn a living? But who is the originator of the two novels composed by the Lydia Clerke letters? Who deserves to reap a profit from their publication?

The Lydia Clerke Letters

One of the arguments against seeing the Lydia Clerke letters as novelistic is that there is no novelist here. But contemporary theory allows us to rethink the concept "author." As Foucault argues, "it does not seem necessary that the author function remain constant in form, complexity, and even in existence. I think that, as our society changes, at the very moment when it is in the process of changing, the author function will disappear, and in such a manner that fiction and its polysemous texts will once again function according to another mode, but still with a system of constraint—one which will no longer be the author, but which will have to be determined or, perhaps, experienced."[17] I believe that we did not have to wait for the twentieth century for the author function to change. It was changing even as biography and copyright law were constructing it in the eighteenth century. The novels formed by the Lydia Clerke letters become an example of Foucault's concept of another mode. Although individual letters were written deliberately by unique persons with different sensibilities, the collection as a whole was subject to different constraints. There was Lydia Clerke's "constraint." Saving some letters and discarding others, Lydia exercised great authority as she decided which of the hundreds of letters she received over a lifetime were worth keeping and which were not. There is no knowing for sure why she selected the ones she did. Perhaps she saved them because each in its own way struck her as an example of the romance of real life, of the ways in which life is and is not a novel. Perhaps she saved them because they were the pieces of her past she wanted to preserve. Likewise, we cannot know why someone inserted the two letters from Sarah Clerke, the only ones not addressed to Lydia Clerke. Did the anonymous donor see herself as fulfilling an "author function"? What effect did she intend to produce? Did she intend to produce any effect at all? Whether or not she intended it, the two letters she added give the collection its strong sense of an ending. They tell us that Lydia Clerke, the woman to whom all the other letters were addressed, is dead. And, of course, I serve an author function, insisting against all common sense that the thirty-one letters I found form two discrete but interconnected novels.

---

[16]   Mark Rose, *Authors and Owners: The Invention of Copyright* (Cambridge, 1993) 2.
[17]   Michel Foucault, "What is an Author?" in *Contemporary Literary Criticism: Literary and Cultural Studies*, Eds Robert Con Davis and Ronald Schleifer (New York, 1989) 274–5.

Haphazardly distilled from the endless circulation of epistolary and novelistic discourse that constructed and represented the eighteenth century, the "novels" I have constructed might just be products of my imagination. Some of my readers will insist that the letters are just letters and nothing more; they lack any novelistic qualities. These unsympathetic readers will judge my attempt to turn an ordinary set of letters into something extraordinary as an example of futile and self-interested interventionism. Sometimes I too am left with such an unforgiving assessment.

Nonetheless, *Circle* bears the marks of novelistic discourse—narrative suspense, text and subtext, rising and falling action, conflicts and resolutions, surprise, supposition, and surmise. It also includes many characters. Some are rounded so that we learn much about them; they have the capacity to surprise us. Others are flat and predictable; still others appear infrequently, remain unidentified, or serve as background to the trials and tribulations of the members of the Clerke family and the Brathwaite/ Thornton/ Winstanley clan. There is much exposition, sometimes elucidating, sometimes mystifying. There is some attention to setting and the events of the day, but the greatest emphasis is on character, evaluating one's own and others' actions, exhorting one another to behave well, and seeking affirmation that one has indeed behaved well. And, in the end, there is closure.

Most important, there is plot. The first twelve letters tell the story of Lydia Hammond's marriage to John Clerke. Alternately comforting and troubling her, her confidants tell us of Lydia's growing fears and her generous heart. We gain an intimate picture of the difficulties and joys of companionate marriage. In the seventeen letters that follow, we learn what it was like to be a young unmarried woman in Georgian society. Sylvia's letters are full of amazing amorous adventures. Her story ends when, in defiance of her family's wishes, she marries her "poor soldier." Unlike Lydia, whose story is told by others, Sylvia insists on telling her own story and giving herself her own happy ending.

Full of gaps and mysteries, replete with unknown beginnings and open endings, the Lydia Clerke letters are, like many novels and like life, discontinuous and contradictory. In the interpretive essays that follow the letters, I fill in some of the gaps, locate some of the beginnings, close some of the endings, and resolve some of the contradictions. We may not yet be able to answer all the questions raised by these letters, but we can answer many of them. We can see the ways in which the lives of Lydia and Sylvia and their friends and family touched upon larger events and how these larger events touched them. Though a small group of people, their experiences were wide. They were part of the bluestocking movement and the rise of the novel. They were also part of the Seven Years' War, the American War for Independence, the rise of English India, the expansion of the slave trade, and the circumnavigation of the globe. They were part of a century that moved from Enlightenment to Revolution, from hierarchy and subordination to democratic republicanism, from Johnson's common sense to Rousseau's sensibility.

The Letters,
The Letter Writers,
and Their Wor(l)ds

A Letter always feels to me like immortality because it is the mind alone without corporeal friend. Indebted in our talk to attitude and accent, there seems a spectral power in thought that walks alone—

Letter from Emily Dickinson to Thomas Wentworth Higginson (1869)

... and I have thought that many a complete letter writer has been produced from the school of the novelist; and hence, possibly, it is, that females have acquired so palpable a superiority over us, in this elegant and useful art.

Judith Sargent Murray, *The Gleaner* (1798)

I profess there is not a single word or expression, or thought in your whole letter, that I do not relish—not that in our Correspondence, I shall set up for a Critic, or schoolmaster, or Observer of Composition—Damn it all!—I hate it if once You set about framing studied letters, that are to be correct, nicely grammatical & run in smooth Periods, I shall mind them as no others than newspapers of intelligence; I make this preface because You have needlessly enjoin'd me to deal sincerely, & to tell You of your faults, & so let this *declaration serve* once for all, that there is no fault in an Epistolary Correspondence, like stiffness, & study—Dash away, whatever comes uppermost—the sudden sallies of imagination, clap'd down on paper, just as they arise, are worth Folios, & have all the warmth & merit of that sort of Nonsense, that is Eloquent in Love—never think of being correct, when You write to me—so I conclude this Topic ....

Letter from Samuel Crisp to Frances Burney (1773)

Chapter 1

Overview

Members of two families wrote the bulk of the letters in the Lydia Clerke collection. The joys and anxieties of the Clerke family fill most of the letters written in the 1760s and 1770s, while the Brathwaite/ Thornton/ Winstanley clan becomes more prominent in the letters from the 1780s and 1790s. Although the letters can be seen as two separate novels—one focusing on the lives of John and Lydia Clerke and one on the life of Sylvia Brathwaite—the people who write them are drawn together by many ties.

The Clerkes were a country people who owned land and supported charity schools. The Manor of Wethersfield was acquired by their ancestor, Dr. John Clerke, in the early seventeenth century.[1] Four generations later, a direct descendant, Joseph Clerke, lived on Brook Farm and still owned and managed the land. While Joseph's sons joined the navy, entered the Church, or pursued mercantile careers, his daughters stayed home. When he died, his daughters Ann and Sarah took over the management of his estates. He and his family, like many other Essex landowners, enjoyed a moderate prosperity, stimulated by the rapidly growing population in London during the eighteenth century. Although proud of his sons' achievements, Joseph must have been disappointed that not one of them became a farmer. His daughters became his inheritors.

Described as a Westmoreland country family in Betham's *Baronetage of England*,[2] the Brathwaites we meet in the Clerke letters spend most of their time in London or in distant parts. Unlike the Clerkes, who were plain people and seldom mixed with the aristocracy, the Brathwaites befriended dukes and duchesses, princes and prime ministers. While Sylvia might grow to dislike and distrust the aristocrats who encircled her, she also admired some of them. Praise and censure of kings, princes, and nobles fill her letters. Sylvia's grandfather (John Brathwaite, 1696–1740) owned a plantation in South Carolina and died on the return trip to England; her father (also John Brathwaite, 1739–1803) spent most of his adult life first in Gibraltar and then in India;[3] her brother Charles pursued a career in the service of the Duke of

---

[1] Cyril Hart, "John Clerke M.D.," *St Bartholomew's Hospital Journal* (February 1951) 34–5.
[2] Rev. William Betham, ed., *Baronetage of England* (London, 1805) 5:496–7.
[3] "Biographical Sketch of Major General Brathwaite," 0/6/9 MSS EurB 392, ff. 555–79, India Office Records, British Library. See also *The Record of Old Westminsters* 1:117.

Cumberland.[4] Protected by her aunt Sylvia Thornton and her grandmother Sylvia Winstanley, Sylvia Brathwaite lived in London and made a career of her coming out.

Many threads of affiliation bring these two families together. Susannah Dobson serves as a crucial link. Genealogies of the Brathwaite and Dobson families suggest there were long-distance familial connections between Susannah and the two Brathwaite sisters, Mrs. Thornton and Mrs. Armitage;[5] and, since in one of her letters to Lydia, Susannah credits a woman named Moritt with introducing her to Lydia, it might have been Susannah who introduced Lydia to Mrs. Armitage and Mrs. Thornton. In addition, Charlotte Lennox might have come to know Lydia through Susannah. Both Susannah and Charlotte were well-known writers and translators. Having met one another through literary connections, Susannah might have introduced Charlotte to Lydia. Or Lennox might have met Lydia through the Reverend Winstanley. According to Duncan Isles, Charlotte Lennox knew Thomas Winstanley in the 1770s, when her husband was employed by the Customs and the Lennox family lived on Tower Hill.[6] Then again, other literary liaisons provide a perhaps more logical connection. Both Bonnell Thornton (Sylvia Thornton's husband) and Charlotte Lennox were prominent literary figures in their day; both knew Samuel Johnson and formed part of his extensive circle. These connections might have first brought the Thorntons and Lennoxes together, and female friendship may have followed when Charlotte met Sylvia (Brathwaite) Thornton and Caroline (Brathwaite) Armitage. However they came to know one another, it is clear from the Lydia Clerke letters that Lydia, Charlotte, Sylvia, and Caroline were friends. Sylvia shared Lydia's letters with Charlotte (and probably vice versa); and when Lennox was arrested in 1778 on charges of disturbing the peace and assaulting a woman named Ann Brown, her bail was paid by Robert Armitage, Caroline's husband.[7] The more we learn about the people who form Lydia Clerke's circle of acquaintance, the more filaments we can discern drawing them together in an elaborate and strong network of mutual interests and acquaintance.

---

[4] See *The Correspondence of George, Prince of Wales 1770–1812*, Ed. A. Aspinall (London, 1963–71) I:224. In a letter to the Prince of Wales, dated 15 April 1786, the Duke of Cumberland remarks, "I shall be much obliged to you if you would use your interest with Ld Cornwallis for him to appoint Capt. Brathwaite of the 95 Foot my Equerry, who, having some business of consequence with his father, who is second in command at Madras, wishes to go to India, but there being no possibility of going to that country without an appointment, he is extremely desirous of being appointed his Aid de Camp, not only from the opportunity it will give him of seeing his father but also from the great advantage it will procure him in his military line."

[5] For example, the genealogy of the Brathwaite family that appears in Betham notes that a Frances Brathwaite married an E. Dobson.

[6] Duncan Isles, "The Lennox Collection," *Harvard Library Bulletin* 19 (1971) 179n.

[7] MJ/SP 1778, f. 29, Greater London Record Office.

The lives of Lydia Clerke's acquaintance not only intersect with one another, but they also connect with the larger world. *The History of Lydia Clerke*, the novel which focuses on the conjugal fortunes of John and Lydia, opens in the 1760s. The 1760s were, as Dickens was to write of 1775, the best of times and the worst of times. Britain's empire was expanding as was its economy. Not surprisingly, John Clerke's opening letter, sent from Paris and dated 20 November 1768, is filled with hope and buoyant expectation. John believes not only in his own future success but also in his wife's love. He contemplates many projects and is sure that eventually he and his wife will prosper. In that same year his brother, Charles Clerke, begins an around-the-world voyage with James Cook. While it is Cook's first such journey, it is Clerke's second. Having already served under John Byron, during his 1764 to 1766 round-the-world voyage, Charles undertakes subsequent trips with an insouciance as indomitable as his brother's.[8]

The 1760s also bring concern and disappointment. England begins to suffer the ills of imperial expansion—colonial unrest and wars. In 1768, John Brathwaite the younger, father of Sylvia, the heroine of *The History of Sylvia Brathwaite*, the second novel formed by the Lydia Clerke letters, returns with his wife (the former Elizabeth Browne) to England from the garrison at Gibraltar, where, according to his (probably mean-spirited) Westminster School biographer, he was removed from his post for issuing Mediterranean passes to individuals who were not British subjects. By 1769, he is on his way to India (without his wife). Once in India, Brathwaite prospers although his marriage falters and officially ends on 18 March 1777.[9]

The three letters that follow John Clerke's, one from The Reverend Thomas Winstanley and two from Susannah Dobson, give us background exposition as well as some rising action and introduce us to worlds much more insular, contemplative, and still than the masculine worlds of economic and military aggression. Educated at Westminster School and Oxford, Winstanley was also part of a world that rigidly excluded women, but as a clergyman he spent much time with his lady parishioners, arguing with them (as in the case of Mrs. Dobson), chastising them (as in the case of Mrs. Lennox), or praising them (as in the case of Mrs. Clerke). He officiated at the

---

[8]   The main sources for information about Charles Clerke were Gordon Cowley and Les Deacon, *In the Wake of Captain Cook: The Life and Times of Captain Charles Clerke, R.N., 1741–79* (Boston, 1997); the *Dictionary of National Biography; The Journals of Captain James Cook on His Voyages of Discovery*, Ed. J.C. Beaglehole (Cambridge, 1961); and Captain James Cook, F.R.S., and Captain James King, LL.D. and F.R.S., *A Voyage to the Pacific Ocean* (London, 1784).

[9]   The main sources for information about Sir John Brathwaite were *The Record of Old Westminsters* 1:117; *Journal of the House of Lords* 35: 36a, 68b, 69b, 94a, 96b, 174b; PROB 11/1398, Family Records Centre; and India Office Records (*Alphabetical List of the Officers of the Indian Army*, Eds Dodwell and Miles [London, 1838], 6–7, Madras Presidency), British Library.

marriages of all three of his step-children, thus not only metaphysically, but also literally drawing male and female worlds together.[10] Susannah Dobson's two letters, which were written in 1770 and 1771, give access to the world of the bluestocking movement which flourished toward the end of the eighteenth century.[11] Dobson not only writes about Elizabeth Montagu's *An Essay on the Writings and Genius of Shakespear*, which was published in 1768, but she also refers to Lord Kames's *Elements of Criticism*. She was a philosopher and a naturalist; in one letter we find her attempting to extract a sting from a wasp. She is a connoisseur of art, but even more, she prides herself on her friendships with women.

The 1770s proved to be a tumultuous decade for Britain as well as for the Clerkes and the Brathwaites. The American Colonies declared war. Britain faced threats from France and Spain. Invasion by these long-term enemies was a sporadic if not a constant fear of many British citizens, especially of those who, like Lydia Clerke and her mother Mrs. Hammond, lived along the Channel coast. British troops continued to engage with Indian armies in India, as did British speculators like John Clerke with native intermediaries. Knighted in 1772, John Clerke died only four years later in Madras.[12] His death threw Lydia's life into great disarray; she not only had to face the threat of poverty but she had to face the truth of her husband's infidelity. Three years later, Charles died of a consumptive disorder contracted while incarcerated in the King's Bench prison for his brother John's debt; he was buried at Kamchatka. At times feeling confined by, but at other times relishing, her simple life in the country, Ann Clerke feared for the safety of her sea-faring brother caught in aristocratic coils and of her friend and sister-in-law Lady Clerke, who lived with her mother near Southampton, close to the French and Spanish enemy. The only Clerke whose life seems to have steadily improved during the course of the 1770s was sister Hannah's.

---

[10]   The main sources for information about Thomas Winstanley were his *Alumni Oxonienses* biography (1590), the *Westminster Abbey Registers* (446n), PROB 11/1176, Family Records Centre, and the International Genealogical Index.

[11]   Three texts were particularly helpful when exploring the bluestocking movement: Myra Reynolds's *The Learned Lady in England, 1650–1760*, which was originally published in 1920; Sylvia H. Myers's *The Bluestocking Circle: Women, Friendship, and the Life of the Mind in Eighteenth-Century England*, which was published posthumously in 1990; and Ruth Perry's "Bluestockings in Utopia," which appeared in *History, Gender & Eighteenth-Century Literature*, ed. Beth Fowkes Tobin (Athens, 1994).

[12]   The main sources for information about John Clerke were *Biographia Navalis* (6:438–9); and *The Annual Register, or a View of the History, Politics, and Literature, for the year 1772*. Information about his dealings in India were found in the British Library, Hastings Papers. There is also a letter from Warren Hastings to John Clerke housed at the Society of Antiquaries (444/18, The Cely-Trevilian Collection). Cowley and Deacon's *In the Wake of Captain Cook* also proved helpful.

In 1775, at 40 years of age, she married Paul Henry Maty. One year later, her husband obtained his dead father's post of assistant-librarian in the British Museum. [13]

The upheavals that visited the Brathwaite family during the 1770s were as global and as shattering as those endured by the Clerke family. John Brathwaite discovered that his wife, Elizabeth, was committing adultery. He left India in July 1775 to return to England to initiate divorce proceedings. During the divorce trial, it was proven that Elizabeth gave birth to two children while her husband was in India and could not have fathered them. Although his identity never came out during the course of the trial, Major-General William Phillips was the father of Elizabeth's children. In 1776, Phillips went to America to serve king and country against the insurgent colonists. He fought briefly under Burgoyne, and was second-in-command when Burgoyne surrendered to the American troops. From 1777 until 1781, Phillips remained a prisoner of war. After four years of house arrest, he was finally released and allowed to return to duty in March 1781. Ironically, he died shortly afterward (on 13 May 1781) of a fever contracted during a series of raids in Virginia. Although in his will he left everything to Elizabeth, she rejected the Letters of Administration, perhaps because she had, soon after his death, married The Reverend Angus Macaulay. [14]

The 1780s continued to be a time of great tumult on public as well as private stages. While the American War pursued its course, the second Mysore War broke out in 1780 in India and continued until 1784. In February 1782, John Brathwaite, while commanding troops in Tanjore country, was attacked, defeated, wounded, and imprisoned. He did not obtain his release until April 1784, upon conclusion of peace with Tippu Sultan. [15] While her father was engaged with many struggles both financial and military, Sylvia Brathwaite lived in London under the watchful eyes of her aunt Mrs. Sylvia Thornton and her grandmother Mrs. Sylvia Winstanley, and spent many a season looking over marital prospects, falling in and out of love, eluding the Prince of Wales and other potential ravishers, and becoming more and more disillusioned

---

[13] See the *Dictionary of National Biography*, PROB 11/1150, Family Records Centre, and *Admissions to Trinity College, Cambridge* (London, 1911) 3:202.

[14] There were several sources for information about William Phillips's military career: *History of the Royal Regiment of Artillery*, Ed. Francis Duncan (London, 1874); the *Dictionary of National Biography*; Robert P. Davis, *Where a Man Can Go: Major General William Phillips, British Royal Artillery, 1731–1781* (Westport, 1999); PROB 11/1102, Family Records Centre; army records, Public Record Office; and letters written home while serving and imprisoned in the Colonies, British Library.

[15] The "Biographical Sketch of Major General Brathwaite," 9/6/9 MSS EurB 392, ff. 555–79, India Office Records, British Library, was especially helpful in obtaining information about Brathwaite's military career. For a first-hand account of his imprisonment in India, I read the *Diary of Col. Cromwell Massy, Late of Hon'ble East India Company's Service Kept While a Prisoner at Seringapatam Bangalore* (Higginbotham & Co., 1912). Reprinted in 1912 as a monograph, both diary and monograph can be found at MSS Eur B 392.

with aristocratic life. In 1789, she married Charles Parkhurst, an "honest soldier."[16] Eventually settling in Wales, she and her husband and son found unanticipated benefits in pastoral simplicity. When her father returned to England in 1802 and died one year later, he left her a handsome inheritance. However, it is possible that she never received any of it.[17]

With her two letters, Sarah Clerke closes the collection of letters as a whole. Confirming the death of Lady Clerke and filled with the *ubi sunt* lament of the only remaining descendant of Joseph and Ann Clerke, her letters leave the reader with the sense of an ending not only of a family but also of an age. The date of Sarah's last letter (the ultimate letter of the Lady Lydia Clerke collection) is 11 December 1816. By 1816, William Blake had published "Songs of Innocence" and "Songs of Experience," Samuel Taylor Coleridge had written "Kubla Khan" and Wordsworth his "Ode on Intimations of Immortality." Lord Byron had started "Childe Harold's Pilgrimage," Walter Scott had finished *Waverley*, and Mary Shelley had dreamt of Frankenstein toiling over his monster. By 1816, the English had defeated the French at Waterloo, and the Age of Reason had transformed into the Age of Romanticism. Haunting and elegiac, the two letters from Sarah Clerke express a sense of growing emptiness, sadness, loss and dissolution. A time of great hope and anticipation, of exploration and expansion, has passed. Exuberance has turned into exhaustion. Nonetheless, the stories of those times cannot be erased or forgotten. Traces remain.

Eighteenth-Century English Letters

Eighteenth-century Britons enjoyed the benefits of an excellent postal system. Within Britain, a letter took about two or three days to reach its destination. Overseas mail took longer, but it was dependable. Where possible, I have indicated locations from and to which letters were sent and dates on which they were sent/ received. Although some of the letters were marked with a stamped month and date, years were not always available so sometimes all we can accurately identify is a day of the month. However, using internal and contextual evidence (for example, the year that Harry Maty or the King of Prussia died), years can be given with some certainty to most of the letters. Dates inside brackets indicate conjectures. One of Sylvia Brathwaite's letters, Letter #21, was beyond conjecture and remains undated. I have transcribed the

---

[16]   International Genealogical Index.
[17]   John Brathwaite's will is 13 pages long. It is clear that he wanted to leave Sylvia a generous legacy. However. there are several marginal notes indicating that probate was delayed because of his son Sir George-Charles's early and unexpected death in 1810. Because Sir George-Charles died intestate, it would seem that probate was delayed until even after the marriage of his daughter, Frederica Emma Laura, who married in 1824.

letters as faithfully as I could. Although I have left in some abbreviations and oddities of punctuation, spelling, and capitalization, I have revised where necessary to ensure clarity. Words inside brackets indicate editorial interpolations of missing words or interpretations of illegible words. Although I have changed what might impede smooth reading (providing full stops at the ends of sentences and capital letters where necessary; eliminating long *f*'s; and breaking longer passages into paragraphs), I have, as Samuel Crisp advised Frances Burney, left in many of the dashes.[18]

I have provided brief prefaces to introduce letter writers and to explore the place of his or her letter(s) in the fictional worlds of *Circle*. Interpretive essays follow each letter or group of letters. I believe readers will get more out of the letters if they have an opportunity to read them before having all the background; they will then be able to see for themselves just how novelistic the letters are, how fanciful, how eloquent, how full of reverie and masked design, how full of humor, adventure, and incident. While several letters are treated individually, others are not. The two letters of Susannah Dobson, Charlotte Lennox, Sylvia Thornton, and Sarah Clerke are placed together as are all but one of the many letters of Sylvia Brathwaite. Reading these letters in succession will give the twenty-first-century reader a better sense of the narrative continuities and discontinuities of the collection as a whole, and of the novels that can be constructed out of them.

---

[18]   Letter from Samuel Crisp to Frances Burney (December 1773), *The Early Journals and Letters of Fanny Burney*, Ed. Lars E. Troide (Kingston, 1988) 1:320.

Chapter 2

John Clerke

... I was very sorry to hear of the Duke of Beauforts death. He was, what is very
unusual, a good Husband & a fond one to a reasonable Woman, it is common to see a man
humour a fantastical Woman & admire an artfull one, but it is not to see a Husband keep
up a passion for a woman whose character is as good & solid as the Dutchess of Beaufort,
& qui ne faisoit les valoir by tricks and hypocrisy.

Letter from Elizabeth Montagu to Sarah Scott (1756)

John Clerke (1734–76) was a career naval officer. He rose quickly through the ranks.
In 1748, he served as a midshipman aboard the *Lion*. In 1754, he served in the East
Indies under Rear-Admiral Watson. In 1761, he was promoted to the rank of post-
Captain. In 1771, he was appointed Captain to the *Prudent*. In 1772, he was knighted
and ordered to the East Indies, where he died four years later in Madras.

John's letter, sent from Paris in 1768, opens *The History of Lydia Clerke* at a
place long after most novels end, six years after the marriage of the hero and heroine.
Although his letter starts us at an unusual point, it serves well as an opening. We are
introduced to the two main characters, John the loving but errant husband and Lydia
the dutiful but neglected wife, and to the tensions in their marriage. John is reckless
and Lydia powerless to stop him.

1
From: John Clerke, Paris
To: Lydia Clerke, Gosport
Date: 20 November 1768

Your Letter, my very dear Girl, has fill'd my Heart with every tender Sentiment
that humanity can feel, And I this moment love and honor you, if possible, more than
the first day you bestow'd yourself on perhaps a very wrong headed, but not a bad
hearted Husband—Be of Comfort my worthy, my dear, my noble Girl, This long
Separation will have its advantages, and I doubt not but there is still Happiness in
store for us. My Peregrinations have been long and painfull, My Schemes manifold
and hitherto unsuccessfull—I have never forgot you, and if I have seem'd to neglect
you, it has been because I have had no good Tidings to give You. I was all the
Summer extreemly ill, but am very well at present, except now and then attacks of a
head ache which confines me twenty four hours more or less to the house. The Spring
carries me most undoubtedly to England, and believe me when I swear to you that you

can't possibly wish for our Common good more ardently than I do to see and embrace my dear Lydia.

With regard to a Voyage, I shall be very glad of one on many Accounts. The Physicians tell me unanimously that a Southern one will work a perfect reestablishment of my Health. All the Objection I can make then will be that of so soon leaving you again. Ld Rochfort's Continuance in the Ministry may be of Service, his Lordship and I are extreemly well together. You know my dear Friend the Repugnance I have to Obligations to a certain party, and weigh well I am sure the humiliating Circumstance of the other part of your proposition. I abandon however all Objections to the Pleasure of seeing you in ease and Peace. Act then as you think proper, and receive in advance the entire Approbation of your Husband of everything you may think necessary to do, and every Step you shall find à propos to take. This is the least piece of Complaisance you have a right to from me, for I never yet found a Confidence so well placed as in your self.

On the Subject of the Money, I have drawn on our Worthy Friend Ekins for a hundred Guineas wch you will remitt him forthwith, and I hope it will be the last I shall have Occasion for before my return. Therefore employ your Savings in whatever manner you please, and tell me if You have Occasion for Any thing that I can send you from France. I shall never execute any Commissions with so much Pleasure I assure you. I have still hopes of something clever during the Winter. If I am disappointed in my Prospects, the single one of seeing You soon after will more than compensate the Pains of my pursuit—Direct for Me à L'Hotêl de Londres, Rüe du Colombièr, Fauxbourg St Germains, à Paris.

Adieu! my dear, dear girl, believe you have a sincere Friend & tender Husband in J^n Clerke

Take Care of your Health, all will go well————

Husband and Naval Officer

John Clerke, like the Duke of Beaufort identified in Elizabeth Montagu's letter to Sarah Scott, is a good husband and blessed with a good wife. Although John writes his letter from Paris, he seems safe from artful women and attentive to his dear Lydia. However, there are hints that all is not well. While his epistle expresses sincere love and esteem for the companion he has chosen, his admiration is colored by his incurable roaming spirit and his equally incurable insouciance. Here is a man not unwilling to put marriage and financial security at risk. Here is a man not unwilling to endanger his wife and to squander her property. Here is a man not unwilling to spend long periods of time away from the woman he loves.

The Clerke family motto was *Ose et Espere*. Inscribed on the family dinnerware perhaps purchased in celebration of John's knighthood in 1772,[1] this motto suggests two inspirations for many of the episodes in John's life. He dared and hoped much, but, unfortunately, he was not very lucky. The close of John's letter—with its hopeful plea ("all will go well") and long dash—subtly suggests the obscure future into which he so willingly plunges both himself and his wife.

Born in 1734, John Clerke was the eldest son of Joseph and Ann Clerke of Brook Farm, Wethersfield, Essex. When he was thirteen years old, his mother died in childbed of her twelfth child. One year later, in 1748, John joined the Navy as a midshipman aboard the *Lion*.[2] Although it was not unusual for sons to join the Navy as young as John was, it was not common for first-born sons to do so unless the family was impoverished, which the Clerkes were not. Did John leave his home, soon after his mother died, to escape his father? Or, was it simply, as his letter suggests, that he was an adventurous spirit who loved to travel? Although John alludes to painful peregrinations, he does not anticipate returning home till Spring (at least four months later). Clearly, he enjoys being away from home and chose a profession which allowed him to rove far. During the course of his career in the Navy, he journeyed to America, the East Indies, and Africa.

On 19 April 1762, John married Lydia Hammond at Alverstoke Parish Church, near Gosport, Hampshire, where, on 25 December 1740, Lydia was born.[3] Her parents, James and Lydia (Isgar) Hammond, were Nonconformists, which may have displeased John's Church of England father. When, in 1768, John writes to his wife, "You know my dear Friend the Repugnance I have to Obligations to a certain party, and weigh well I am sure the humiliating Circumstances of the other part of your proposition," he perhaps refers to strained relations with his father, to whom Lydia would apply for help.

Throughout his life, John was as adventurous and free-wheeling in his business speculations as in his travels. In his letter, he refers to Lord Rochford. While John seems to admire the man, others might have warned him against such a dangerous liaison. Born not far from Wethersfield, at St Osyth Priory, Essex, on 17 September 1717, William Henry Zuylestein, or Lord Rochford, was a man possessed of dubious talents. He cast the deciding ballot against repealing the controversial American duties, and his personal extravagance was very great. In 1771, the *London Museum* coupled his portrait with the following legend from John Gay: "Man may escape from

---

[1]   F.W. Steer, F.S.A., "Stories in Porcelain: The Clerke Service," *The Essex Countryside* (April 1960): 146–7.

[2]   *Biographia Navalis* 6:438.

[3]   International Genealogical Index. I have also seen the parish record of Lydia and John's marriage (photocopy from the Hampshire Record Office). Her birth date was confirmed by a letter dated 3 September 1999 from Ian Edelman, Curator of the Gosport Museum.

2.1   A piece of the Clerke family Kien-Lung armorial china. Reproduced by
        courtesy of the Essex Record Office

2.2   Alverstoke Parish Church, where John and Lydia were married. Photo:
        Author's Collection

Rope and gun, but Infamy he ne'er can shun."[4] In 1768, the year in which he wrote his letter, John clearly expects much from his aristocratic acquaintance. And there are signs that Rochford did produce. In her first letter to Lydia, Charlotte Lennox believes Rochford helped John obtain his knighthood.

John's letter lets us and Lydia know just how carelessly he might expose her to financial ruin. He is not adverse to drawing on her resources to fund his speculations. He tells her that he has borrowed 100 guineas of Ekins and asks her to "remitt him forthwith." As if to atone for his business-like abruptness, he then tells Lydia to employ the rest of her savings as she pleases. While from the twenty-first-century perspective it would seem self-evident that Lydia might use her savings as she pleased, the rules of property in the eighteenth century were such that a woman's money was not necessarily her own. By eighteenth-century standards, John is generous. Once she married, coverture put an eighteenth-century woman's property (and person) in her husband's hands. Not until the second half of the nineteenth century, with passage of the Married Women's Property Acts, did married women gain legal control of their property and earnings. While some eighteenth-century wives were protected by marriage settlements, the fact that John dispenses 100 guineas of Lydia's savings without consulting her suggests that such was not her case.

There is other evidence that John was hopelessly and culpably improvident. He was careless not only with his wife's resources but also with his brother's life. In 1772, Charles became a guarantor of a £4000-debt of John's. Les Deacon and Gordon Cowley, Charles Clerke's biographers, underscore the exorbitance of such a sum when they note that the Admiralty bought the *Discovery*, a ship on which Charles Clerke sailed round the world, for £1895.[5] How John could have run up such a huge debt remains mysterious, and how he could have let his younger brother risk imprisonment as a consequence of it remains even more so, but it is undeniable that when Charles died in 1776, at the age of 38, it was as a result of the "disorder" he contracted while imprisoned for his brother's debts in the dank and unhealthy King's Bench Prison.

John escaped his debts by sailing to the East Indies, where he remained until he died in 1776. During his years in India, he became an associate of Warren Hastings. In his letters to Hastings, Clerke is the ingratiating, supportive underling: "I earnestly Hope and expect to See Your Constancy, and Perseverance Crown'd with Triumph, and Succeeded by fair Weather and Sun Shine."[6] He also sought to win privileges from Hastings. Five months before he died, he asked his superior to make him his intermediary with a certain "Nabob."[7] In return Hastings wrote a strong letter of

---

[4]   *Dictionary of National Biography.*
[5]   Cowley and Deacon 106.
[6]   ADD MS 29,136, f. 230, British Library.
[7]   ADD MS 29,137, f. 187, British Library.

recommendation: "I shall take it as a Favor if you will make him an Offer of this Service, & assure him from this Letter, if he requires such an Assurance, that there is no Man in India who possesses a larger share of my Confidence, or whom I would sooner recommend to his, than my valuable Friend Sir John Clerke."[8] Is Clerke's offer to act as intermediary between the Nabob and Hastings an attempt to get a share of the vast booty of the East India Company? Probably so, for John Clerke's financial speculations did not cease with his move to India. The world of the East India Company was vast indeed, reaching back even to Lord Rochford, who, according to John's last letters to Hastings, failed to come through with promised insurance money for lost ships.[9] Once again, the feckless aristocrat contributed to the younger man's losses.

While the movements of moneys and privileges in the volatile world of late eighteenth-century India are hard to trace, it is certain that John was ever hopeful that he would be able to leave his wife something. In fact, the only letter we have in Lydia Clerke's hand is an application to Hastings for help in carrying out "Dear Sir John's" plan: "Mr. Macpherson, (who is one of the more generous Minds that so warmly exerted their influence with the Nabob to procure those bonds I mentioned to you), has added to his former kindness the most friendly attention to my interest, and has written to the Nabob in very pressing terms in my favor and as he has the pleasure of being known to you is so obliging to me, as to write to inform you of the views he has to render the Nabob's bounty most effectual to my interest."[10] It would seem Lady Clerke's application was successful, for, as other letters in the collection confirm, her life after Sir John died was not poverty-stricken. Also, in her will, written in 1812, she mentions "a certain sum of nine thousand four hundred and twenty six pounds which has arisen from a debt heretaire due to me from the Nabob of Arest."[11] Ultimately, the widow received significant compensation.

Lydia Clerke's Widowhood and Remarriage

John Clerke died on 11 October 1776, in Madras.[12] After he died, Lydia wrote a letter to Mrs. Thornton which forgave him all his sins. According to Charlotte Lennox, this letter was unusually eloquent and compassionate: "Never did such natural and affecting eloquence flow from your pen before! it is your heart that speaks, and you

---

[8]   444/18, Cely-Trevilian Collection, Society of Antiquaries.
[9]   ADD MS 29,137, f. 275, British Library.
[10] ADD MS 29,141, f. 14, British Library.
[11] PROB 11/1563, Family Records Centre.
[12] ADD MS 29,137, ff. 369, 370, British Library. On 12 October 1776, James Wooley informed Warren Hastings of John Clerke's death "yesterday Morning about five o'clock."

speak <u>to</u> the heart so powerfully, that I wept as much at the third reading of your letter as I did at the first .... I forced it from Mrs Thornton in order to convert some of the infidels of the other Sex, who maintain that no woman was ever generous enough to forgive certain offences in a husband .... he is gone where falsehood, envy, and malice can neither aggravate his failings, nor rob his merits of their just reward." After his death, John Clerke's life became an open discourse among the women Lydia Clerke knew. As was common in the eighteenth century, a letter sent to one woman was read by many others. Copies circulated and reached audiences to whom the original letter was never addressed. Lydia's message of feminine fortitude and forgiveness in the face of male duplicity served as ammunition in the domestic revolution that occurred toward the end of the eighteenth century. Most important, judging Lydia a better wife than John a husband, Lydia's friends helped her deal with her grief and her losses.

If once her husband was dead Lydia was willing to forgive and forget his transgressions, it is much harder to gauge her behavior during the fourteen years of their marriage. What was their relationship like? We have been told by historian Lawrence Stone and others that the eighteenth century witnessed the rise of companionate marriage. Like those of so many of their contemporaries, Lydia's marriage to John must have been based on mutual attraction; they were, after all, willing to marry across religious lines and perhaps in defiance of parental disapprobation. But did their love last? How much did they share with one another? What were John's failings? Was one of them adultery? Whatever he did it deeply distressed Lydia. When she received a letter from Susannah Dobson full of insinuations about her husband's sexual misbehavior and her own vulnerability if she sought to retaliate in kind, she was perturbed by these epistolary intimations of his and her frailty. As a consequence, Lydia withdrew from Susannah. She also, as a consequence, held herself aloof from Ann Clerke, who insisted on remaining Susannah's friend. While the rift between Lydia and Susannah did not heal (as evidenced by the almost invariably satirical references to her and her eccentricities in several letters to Lydia), the breach between Lydia and Ann did eventually smooth over. Whatever she thought of her husband's behavior, however she learned to live with his misdeeds, she would not let his treachery interfere with her love for his sister.

Lydia remained a widow for fourteen years. Perhaps she remained single because her first marriage deteriorated so quickly. Perhaps she remained single because she was living with her mother Mrs. Hammond, who needed her care and attention. Perhaps she remained single because it was fourteen years before she met a man sufficiently attractive. Significantly, when she married The Reverend Joseph Townsend in 1790, she protected herself with a marriage settlement. In her will, she refers to her "dispensing power." Furthermore, she confirms that she may act as "if I were a feme sole [a single woman]." Not surprisingly, Lydia leaves the bulk of her estate to her husband should he survive her. Nonetheless she bequeaths generous amounts of money to many women of her acquaintance. Pointedly, in the case of

Charlotte Taunton, Lydia protects the inheritance from any present or future husbands: "[I declare the money] for her separate use free from the debts engagements or controul of her present or any future husband. I declare that her receipt for the same notwithstanding any coverture she shall be under." Lydia had suffered many financial stresses when married to John Clerke. Even though Joseph Townsend was a very different sort of man than her first husband, she built her second marriage on the firm foundation of a rational and fair marriage settlement, and she wanted to help the women closest to her achieve the same economic security she had finally gained for herself.

Cambridge-educated and Rector of Pewsey in Wiltshire, Joseph Townsend could not have been more unlike Lydia's first husband. Where John was reckless, Joseph was steadfast; where John was a man of action, Joseph was contemplative; where John went to sea for long periods of time, Joseph stayed home. According to his *Gentleman's Magazine* obituary, Townsend was gently satirized in Richard Graves's three-volume *The Spiritual Quixote: or, the Summer's Ramble of Mr. Geoffry Wildgoose, a Comic Romance*. Given that the novel was published in the same year that Joseph married his first wife Joyce Nankivell (1773), the novel may very well be a light-hearted tribute to them and their marriage, especially since it ends with a marriage between the hero, Wildgoose, and Miss Julia Townsend "solemnized at Mr. Townsend's in the Christmas Holidays."[13]

A more serious tribute to Townsend appears in a booklet compiled by three Pewsey parishioners, where Joseph is portrayed as genuinely concerned for the poor and progressive (he advocates the improvement of the highways). He is also granted great force of character:

> Taylor Dyke had received a large sum of money for some farm produce and lingered at the public house before going home to Manningford across Cow Ground and the Broadfields, where he was murdered. Footmarks were traced back to the village. On Sunday the Rector [Townsend] made everyone lay his hand on the corpse's face and swear his innocence. William Amor could not do it. He was searched and the murdered man's watch found on him.[14]

Lydia must have admired and dearly loved the gentle but stern and well-read man she chose for her second husband. In his will, he leaves her his books as well as his

---

[13] Interestingly, although the *Gentleman's Magazine*, November 1816: 477, believes Townsend is the subject of Graves's satire, Charles Whibley, the editor of a 1926 edition of the novel, believes the main character Wildgoose is meant to impersonate a Mr. Whitefield, whom Graves knew at Oxford.

[14] 493/84, Wiltshire and Swindon Record Office: a booklet prepared by Pat Beresford, Joyce Inge, and Vera Boaden.

furniture, his coach and the use of a house in Bath for her life, as well as a generous annuity.[15]

By all measures, her second marriage was happier. It lasted longer and was more egalitarian: husband and wife were closer in age (while John was six years older than Lydia, Joseph was only one), and they shared a love of piety, learning, and philosophy. Nevertheless, John was her first love. And when we learn from Sarah Clerke's letters that she might have kept his portrait, only bequeathing it at her death to her sister-in-law, we may assume that although their marriage eventually suffered deep rupture, Lydia still cared for John Clerke.

---

[15]   PROB 11/1587, Family Records Centre.

Chapter 3

Thomas Winstanley

"Mother of God!" said the friar, "is it possible my lord can refuse a father the life of his only, his long-lost child! Trample me, my lord, scorn, afflict me, accept my life for his, but spare my son!" "Thou canst feel then," said Manfred, "what it is to lose an only son! a little hour ago, thou didst preach up resignation to me: my house, if fate so pleased, must perish—but the Count of Falconara [must not lose his son]"—

Horace Walpole, *The Castle of Otranto* (1764)

Thomas Winstanley (1716?–89) matriculated at Oxford and took the degree of B.A. in 1737. He was a Prebendary of St Paul's and of Peterborough as well as Rector of St Dunstan in the East and of Llanevenarth in Monmouthshire, and held all these preferments until his death.[1]

Thomas Winstanley's letter provides important exposition. We learn from it that Lydia is unhappy. Clearly he is responding to a letter from her in which she asked him for advice and consolation. It is tempting to suppose that Lydia wrote to him about her disappointment in her reckless and improvident husband; it is also possible that she is beginning to suspect his sins are not just economic ones but also sexual. We cannot know for sure. We never learn the precise cause of her concern. Devastated by his own recent loss, the death of his only child, Winstanley cannot reflect directly on Lydia's affairs or offer her much comfort. Too self-devoted to serve as a sermon, his letter, nonetheless, partakes of that discourse and gives us some idea of the quality of his preaching.

2
From: Thomas Winstanley, London
To: Lydia Clerke, [Gosport]
Date: 20 April 1770
Dear Madam

I am sat down to write, and Compulsion as it were; having given the challenge myself, which you so condescendingly accepted. Had I not a more favourable opinion of your mind, I should almost be tempted to conclude that you had shewed me such condescension, merely to see how egregiously I could expose myself, when engaged in a correspondence I must be so unequal to. However, I am embarked; and must

---

[1] *Alumni Oxiensis* 1590; *Westminster Abbey Registers* 446n.

make as safe a voyage as I can: it will be a gainful one to me, though at the peril of my understanding. But no more of this: I will not seem to flatter.

You are a sufferer in this school of adversity, and wish to be assisted by the advice of your friends. Alas, Madam, you have applied to one of your friends, who is very unable to help you. I am a fellow-sufferer with you, and what adds to my affliction is, that my loss is irreparable. Is my loss a common one? Judge, when I tell you what I have lost. It is but little to say, I have lost my son, my only child too, whom I too much delighted in, at a time of life the most critical, just when he was arrived to manhood, healthy, vigorous, and promising length of days in his countenance: But such a son, excuse the partiality of a father, no, it is not partiality; the whole world, as far as he came within its knowledge, will say the same. Such a son, my dear Madam, as few, very few, have lost. So amiable and agreeable was he, that no one ever saw him, without being prepossessed in his favour. He had not as yet reached to the age of twenty one; notwithstanding he had the prudence of years, the gravity of the most respectable character, mixed with the pleasing vivacity, and the no less pleasing diffidence, of youth. How was he all piety to me and his fond mother! How was he all affection to his dear relations and friends! How was he all attention to his teachers and instructors! How was he all goodness and condescension to those who waited on his person! With what intense application, and advantage to himself, did he read and pursue his studies! With what modesty and reservedness did he partake of the pleasures of life! With what religious firmness and constancy did he bear his last, and indeed his first illness! What a glorious end did he make, serious and composed, taking a solemn farewell of us all, of me more especially, and preserving his innate vigor of mind, which never left him, no, not in the article of death! Such a son, and more than such a son, have I lost. O the time, the critical the unseasonible time, of his death! almost more bitter and affecting to me than even his very death itself! Just when he was about to be ripe for Academic honour; just when he was near the period of a finished education: just when he was going to repay us amply for all our anxiety, and to gratify our honest pride; to lose him then; Oh fatal and unrelenting stroke! What great and expected joy was changed into mournful sorrow on that sad occasion! Where must the doting father find a cure for the wound he received at this trying juncture? where shall he get a sufficient fund of spirits and resolution to prepare the necessaries for his funeral, to give orders for an honourable interment, and to follow him to his grave to see the last rites performed? All this I did, and more: and I glory in it, though it cost me very dearly indeed. Think then, good Madam, how miserably qualified I am to yield any one comfort in affliction. And yet, methinks, I have learned a good lesson in the school of affliction, if I could but teach it to others. I will see what I can do with you: for I have a great opinion of you, as a scholar.

In attempting to do you service, I will not treat you as I would do the generality of your sex: but I will call you to consider the peculiar talents you are blessed with, that heart of yours so disposed to every thing that is virtuous, and that mind of yours so stored with all that is rich and valuable. With such talents as you have, what pleasure can you afford to your friends, what entertainment have you always for yourself! If there is any happiness in contemplating the best of Beings; how exquisitely happy must you be, whose views of the Deity must be as far superiour to those of more moderate talents, as finite is below infinite! A good heart and a great mind have this singular advantage: wherever they are united, there is almost heaven upon earth. This advantage you eminently enjoy. I leave you to improve it at your leisure. A proper sense of it will do wonders in affliction.

It might have pleased God to have bestowed upon you great abilities, without a heart: and then these abilities might only have served to be as caterers to the passions, and to have entered you into life, as we say, with more taste and relish. But you are happy in being afflicted, as you have a heart that is good, and consequently can feel. How might you have been exposed to folly, had you not been placed in that situation, which perhaps you may think your misfortune. If your troubles have brought you nearer to God, if they have in any measure weaned you from the world and its vanities, well is it for you, that you have been in trouble. In this view, we must reverse the words of the Apostle, and say, that afflictions are not grievous, but joyous. We must feel, we ought to feel, it is virtue, as I may say, to feel; because feeling leads to virtue. Afflictions are meant to try us, to put our feelings to the test. If they find us callous, and as it were, insensible, they will find us in a state not much to be improved by them: or if they find us inclined to stifle them by pleasure and dissipation, they will find us equally indisposed to reap any benefit from them. To profit by our afflictions, we must feel them; and to profit by our feelings, we must rather indulge than suppress them. But of this perhaps too much.

Mrs Dobson, I presume, is with you: my best respects to her: if she will not see me herself, she will however be obliging by being the occasion of our seeing you soon. You give us hopes of it, and we expect it with pleasure. I often remember the conversation I had with Mrs Dobson, on the subject of our Lord's divinity; and I am sure I did not preach in favour of it the day after, out of any disregard I had for the opinion of that worthy lady. If anything was took amiss, it must be owing to mistake: for certainly I could not mean to offend where so much civility had been shewed. Pity it is that so good a lady & so capable, should err in so capital a point. Our Saviour must either be God, or he must be a creature. Exalt him as high as you please, he must be a creature, if he is not God. And how a creature can save us, or be more to us than Moses or Elias was, I am at a loss to conceive. There may be great mischief in not admitting our Lord's divinity: there can be no bad consequences arising from the belief of it. Christianity can easily be supported on supposition of his divinity: it will be a hard task indeed to defend it on supposition he was no more than man, however perfect.

I am, dear Madam, with the truest regards, Yours &c &c &c
T. Winstanley.

The Loss of a Son

The letter from The Reverend Thomas Winstanley conveys deep sorrow. Any reader would be moved by his distress over the loss of his only son. Overwhelmed, he cannot respond to Lydia Clerke's request for advice in the face of adversity until he has sounded the last note of his own pain. Reading Winstanley's words, one can only sympathize with his acute distress. Whoever has known either in her own right or through another the terrible loss of a child must acknowledge a grieving parent's claim on others' sympathy.

Thomas Ralph Winstanley was born in 1748 when his father was 32 and his mother Sylvia 34. He was his father's only child.[2] While his mother bore at least three other children (Caroline, Sylvia, and John) to her first husband (Col John Brathwaite),[3] she too deeply mourned and never forgot the son who died when he was not yet 21. In her will, she bequeaths a model of the day of Heaven (perhaps an imaginative representation meant to please a pious parent?) "given to me by my Dear Son" to her grandson George-Charles Brathwaite. She also leaves a "Gold pin with my Dear Tom's hair" to a Miss Crutchley and asks to be "buried in the Cloisters by my Dear Tom, my funeral as private as possible."[4] In his own will, Thomas also requested to be buried near his son.[5]

In May 1769, Sylvia and Thomas Winstanley's son Thomas Ralph was buried in the East Cloister of Westminster Abbey, where there is a monument to his memory.[6] Three months later, a eulogy "On the Death of Mr. Winstanley, late student of Trinity College, Cambridge," written by his father, appeared in *The Public Advertiser*:

---

[2] Information about Thomas Ralph Winstanley was found in *The Record of Old Westminsters*, 2:1014.

[3] Information about Sylvia Brathwaite Winstanley was found by looking at the documents about the men in her life. Also, since she is buried in Westminster Abbey there is a biography of her in the *Westminster Abbey Registers* (462n.).

[4] PROB 11/1328, Family Records Centre.

[5] PROB 11/1176, Family Records Centre.

[6] The monument to Thomas Ralph Winstanley can still be found in the East Cloister of Westminster Abbey. The white marble tablet reads, "Here is buried T R Winstanley,/ A youth, for gentleness of manners, simplicity and faith,/ Second to none, First, Admitted to Westminster School/ Then afterwards elected a King's Scholar, Captain of his contemporaries:/ Thence elected to Trinity College, Cambridge,/ Still chief of his fellows,/ Taken a little before with a bloody flux from the lungs,/ He died on 21st May,/ In the 21st year of his age, and AD 1769/ By all, alas, deservedly lamented.// If piety, transparent modesty, most spotless virtue,/ Considerable ability, shrewdness and innocence,/ If a courteous elegance and appearance be the sign of an honest mind,/ Charms of a young man and wisdom of an old;/ If these things have any nobility, or any lovable quality,/ That rightly, child, is all yours, that distinction is clearly for you." This transcription of the Latin was provided by Miss Christine Reynolds, Assistant Keeper of the Muniments, Westminster Abbey.

Say! to so lov'd a Vot'ry can the Muse
The Tribute of a mournful Strain refuse?
For him what Friends shall drop the tender Tear!
What Sighs be heav'd o'er his untimely Bier!
Whom Virtue, Learning, Piety, and Truth,
Sav'd not from Death's fell Stroke, in early Youth.
Each mental Charm was his; and in his Face
Smil'd winning Softness, join'd with manly Grace.
He shone well-skill'd in ev'ry Art polite,
In ev'ry useful Branch of Learning bright:
Was old in Sense, in Innocence a Child;
Serious, yet not austere; tho' grave, yet mild;
Neat, altho' plain, he borrow'd nought from dres';
Staunch Friend of Temp'rance, Foe to all Excess:
With filial Love his pious Bosom glow'd,
Rever'd his parents, and ador'd his God.
Such was Winstanley, such the Son we mourn,
From his fond Sire's belov'd Embraces Torn;
Just as the promis'd Fruit of Youth began,
Matur'd by Years, to ripen into Man.[7]

Although death at a young age was not uncommon in the eighteenth century, parents grieved long and profoundly. Winstanley's despair is real and deep.

Although his inconsolable misery sounds genuine in both his poem and his letter, there is a touch of mordant humor in his need to take us, and Lydia, through the entire litany of every stage of his suffering before he can offer solace in return. And when he does finally speak to her despair, he still cannot speak directly about the source of her unhappiness. He can only write in vague generalities. Of course, it is possible that Lydia did not give Winstanley the particulars she must have given Susannah Dobson, whose letters will be discussed in the following chapter. There are details one can tell a woman friend that one hesitates to tell a man friend, especially a man who is also a minister.

Whatever Lydia told Winstanley, he responds by insisting on the need for unhappiness in this world, and advising her that she is happy in her unhappiness, for she is blessed with "a good heart and a great mind" and can feel her pain sharply. Linking her unhappiness to his, he betrays a desire to continue indulging his own melancholy: "To profit by our afflictions, we must feel them; and to profit by our feelings, we must rather indulge than suppress them. But of this perhaps too much." With his concluding demur, Winstanley acknowledges his self-absorption, and the possibility that as he writes to Lydia about her affairs he is still concerned mostly with himself and his own grief. When he ostensibly urges her not to suppress her feelings,

---

[7] *The Public Advertiser*, 23 August 1769: 1.

he covertly permits himself to continue giving free rein to his sorrow. However, even as he succumbs to his need to justify his behavior, he suspects that it is "perhaps too much."

Winstanley's self-concern is not necessarily offensive. By displaying and enumerating his wounds, he participates in Lydia's sorrow. His pain makes him better able to help her. However, if we look at another extant letter of his—written 17 years later (in 1787) to Charlotte Lennox—we find a very different attitude toward expressing grief and despair. In his letter to the author, Winstanley abruptly insists she suppress her feelings: "Depend on it, you are upon good ground—only suffer not yourself to be perplexed about the Why and the Wherefore, of divine things. Be content that 'It is written'—though it surpasses your understanding to account for it."[8] His tone with Lennox is admonitory, almost accusatory. While he praises Lydia for her superior talents, good heart, and generous condescension in writing to him, he seems almost indifferent to Lennox's pain. And, if we consider the possibility that her anguish arose from the same source as his in his 1770 letter to Lydia, that is, in the loss of a child (her daughter Harriet), then his coldness becomes culpable rather than merely careless.

The date of Harriet Lennox's death is a mystery. Duncan Isles, who has exhaustively researched the possibilities, places it between April 1782 and March 1783. If the year (1785) I have given the Sylvia Brathwaite letter that mentions Harriet's dying is correct, then perhaps she died even later. In any event, it is plausible that, in 1787, when Lennox writes to Winstanley for advice and consolation, she still mourns the loss of her daughter and, in her pain, questions God's will. Winstanley responds curtly and unsympathetically, thereby becoming like the Friar in Walpole's *Castle of Otranto*, who preaches resignation to another although when he himself suffers a similar fate he is inconsolable.

There is a world of difference between Winstanley's two letters. While he comforts Lydia, he chastises Charlotte. While he urges Lydia to feel her distress, he urges Charlotte to forget herself and remember Christ. Why is Winstanley so reluctant to offer Lennox the same consolation he offered Lydia? It would not seem that his curtness with Lennox is simply a matter of not knowing her well, for he begins his note to her with a reference to Mrs. Thornton (his step-daughter) and her son Robert (the grandson to whom he will ultimately leave his sermons), suggesting that she is part of his circle of acquaintance. Nevertheless, he treats the aging author with much less deference than the young wife of the ambitious John Clerke. In 1770, Lydia Clerke was not yet a Lady, but she was a woman of consequence. When Winstanley tells her that he will not treat her as he would "the generality of [her] sex," he recognizes not only her special virtues as a woman but also her special virtues as a woman of some social importance. When Winstanley writes to Lennox in 1787, the

---

[8]   Isles 182.

author has not published anything for some time, her marriage is troubled, and, although she will publish *Euphemia* in 1790, she is only a few years away from asking the Royal Literary Fund for financial assistance, which will be granted and continue until her death. Winstanley might have hypocritically treated one woman more generously than the other because of her greater rank. Then again he might have admired Lydia for her scholarly and spiritual virtues and disliked Lennox. Or, perhaps, in 1787, he was too busy to take the time to write the kind of letter he wrote to Lydia in 1770. Or, seventeen years older and perhaps anticipating his own death (which would take place only two years later), he felt more deeply the rigors of his Christian faith.

Citizen and Husband

If we are tempted to characterize Winstanley's letters to Lydia Clerke and Charlotte Lennox as hypocritical or self-absorbed, other documents, in particular a sermon advocating tolerance of Jews and his last will and testament, complicate this picture of him.

Preached on Sunday, 28 October 1753, and published in that same year, Winstanley's sermon "On Occasion of the Clamours against the Act for Naturalizing the Jews" reveals a man capable of complex insight into the processes of assimilation as they were occurring in mid-eighteenth-century England. Defending himself against the charge that he was "a Jew and no Christian," Winstanley avers that he adheres to Christian tenets and seeks to assuage rather than foment public clamor against authority. The core of his argument is logical and acute. He supports the naturalization of the Jews because it will smooth the way toward their conversion. He calls upon Christians to manifest Christian charity so that Jews may see "the engaging nature of Christianity."[9] Winstanley saw that civility would be more effective than intolerance in bringing about the eventual conversion of the Jews. While as a Jew I might find fault with his assumption that Jews (or anyone else) need to be converted, I cannot find fault with his arguments about the consequences of tolerance. As history proves, tolerance does indeed facilitate the process of assimilation.[10]

Not only does Winstanley prove to be a man of conviction and intelligence in his only extant sermon, but, in his will, he proves a defender of women and a man of feeling. As already mentioned, he asks to be buried in the same grave as his son. In addition, he leaves his grandson Bonnell George Thornton the "classic authors" that his son-in-law (Bonnell Thornton, Bonnell George's father) had left in his will to

---

[9]   Thomas Winstanley, *Sermon* (London, 1753) 23.

[10]   According to Roy Porter, "The Act of 1753 legalizing the naturalization of Jews brought baying anti-Semitic mobs on to the streets: it was immediately repealed" (*English Society in the Eighteenth Century* [London, 1990] 101).

Thomas Ralph, a very apt return suggesting the care with which he made all his bequests.

One particular bequest tells us something about his relationship to his wife. In addition, it indicates how class might disrupt woman-to-woman bonding and how men might be the champions of women rather than their tormentors. As he brings his will to a close, Thomas mentions "poor Sarah Everit" and expresses his regret that he cannot leave her a "small Legacy" for fear it might "give offense." He wishes, however, that "she might be kindly noticed and respected by his family as a most attentive and faithful servant." Pointedly he adds, "at least to him." This brief and touching assertion suggests a very complex and perhaps long-standing domestic quarrel of some sort. Sylvia might have resented the attention her husband paid to the servant (or she to him); consequently, Thomas refrains from leaving the servant any legacy. But he mentions her and hopes that something can be done: "believing her from observation he could make to be as truly worthy a Woman in all respects as he ever knew as such he would commend her to the kind attention of her late [former] Mistress and her family a most acceptable tribute to his memory." It is clear that even in death he continues to mediate between the two women. Just as he returns the father's books to the son, just so he seeks to return Sarah to "her late Mistress."

But Sarah's former Mistress (and his wife, Sylvia Winstanley) is not easily appeased. Her intractable righteousness becomes evident when we look at one particularly remarkable request made by the husband and later unmade by the wife.

In his will, Winstanley leaves his share of stock jointly held with his wife to his two step-daughters "by even and equal portions to be possessed and enjoyed by them respectively and to their heirs respectively." The transfer of moneys is not to take place until his wife Sylvia dies. Significantly, he does not leave any money to his step-son John Brathwaite. He knows it is unusual to overlook the male child, so he explains his omission: "Col Brathwaite and his family were by no means forgot in this transaction but considered as amply provided for." The power of the usual pattern of male inheritance is indicated by the care with which Winstanley urges that his bequest to his step-daughters not be annulled. He prevails upon his wife to honor his decision when he circumspectly hopes "that their Mother the said Silvia Winstanley will leave her daughters the same at her death out of her own fortune as if no such bequest had been made."

Despite all his careful attempts to provide for his step-daughters, Sylvia Winstanley nullifies her husband's bequest when she writes her own will. She pointedly takes Thomas to task for trying to circumvent her first husband's will and directs the moneys diverted to her daughters back into their rightful channel, her son John: "whereas my late husband Thomas Winstanley did in and by his last Will dispose of the sum of two hundred and fifty pounds to my aforesaid two Daughters which sum was the sole right and property of my aforesaid son John Brathwaite as his proportion of the product of the Estate formerly sold in South Carolina ... [my trustees shall] deduct and retain from the respective shares arising and accruing to my said

two Daughters [250 pounds] ... to be paid to [my said son John Brathwaite] ... ."
Deliberately Sylvia Winstanley reverses her second husband's will, and preserves the
patriarchal succession that his generosity threatened. Sylvia Winstanley must have
been a very strong-willed woman.

A Religious Man

Winstanley cared deeply about religious questions and pondered them often and
thoroughly. In his letter to Lydia, he closes with a reference to an argument with their
mutual friend Susannah Dobson over the divinity of Christ. Since Susannah and her
husband Matthew were Unitarians, she must often have disagreed with Winstanley.
Nevertheless, he still speaks respectfully of her. He takes her seriously, "Pity it is that
so good a lady & so capable, should err in so capital a point." He offers once again
the compelling arguments he must have already used with Susannah, in the hope that
Lydia will repeat them to her and assuage any wounded feelings that might have
ensued from their discussion in person. In his 1787 letter to Lennox, Winstanley
continues this earlier argument, insisting even more firmly on Christ's divinity, and
enclosing for Charlotte's edification his reflections on the Sacrament of Communion.
Perhaps as he grew older and the spirit of the times more skeptical, he felt more and
more called upon to promote what he perceived as the essential point of
Christianity—remembering and reflecting on the centrality of Christ's divinity.

    Although Susannah, as a Unitarian, would have rejected orthodox Christology,
it is interesting that in one of her letters to Lydia, she nevertheless refers to Christ's
divinity: "The Picture at Olives is to please me one of the finest I ever saw, the child
beyond all description great, and there is another in the same Room of our Saviour
bearing his Cross which tho not an original struck me with extreme awe and
Admiration. The Subject so much greater than the other tho it must be confessed the
Expression of divinity & Benevolence wrought up so perfectly in the child Jesus
gives that Piece a more extensive Character then is generally to be observed in Pieces
of the same kind." Susannah's admiration of the child Christ's "expression of
divinity" suggests that she did sometimes believe in his divinity. Then again, she is
talking about a picture and what it expresses. Perhaps her comment is simply an early
example of that mingling of religious and aesthetic awe which became more common
in the next century. Then again, the ambiguity of her language suggests a deeper
ambivalence, and perhaps this is what encouraged Winstanley to pursue his argument
with her in hopes of bringing her to accept his way of thinking.

    Eighteenth-century religious attitudes were complex. We describe the period as
the Age of Enlightenment, as a time when entrenched religious attitudes were shaken
up and replaced by new progressive ideas. And this is, of course, an important part
of the eighteenth century. A new skepticism undermined traditional belief systems,
but religion did not disappear. In fact, not only did dissenting and Nonconformist

sects proliferate and the Roman Catholic Church remain a formidable competitor for religious adherents, but the Church of England fortified itself throughout the period.[11] Various philosophers might challenge many of the pieties but belief in a benevolent providence remained. Sylvia Brathwaite praises Rousseau repeatedly and Ann Clerke reads works which cause her to question the value of hierarchy, but both treasure the comfort they receive from traditional Christian affirmations of self-sacrifice.

Using the Lydia Clerke letters as a partial anatomy of eighteenth-century religious attitudes, we can see that religious language and habits of thought permeated eighteenth-century life. There are frequent references to the benevolence of providence, to the necessity of empathizing with and relieving people in distress, and to this world as preparation for the next. "Truth & Nature will sooner or later point out the folly of attaching ourselves to this World in such a manner as to weaken and diminish that Idea of and preparation for another," writes Susannah at one point; "On which every thing we can call or esteem real and Significant ultimately depends with respect to the best part of Us. That only Part which will survive all accidents from without or distresses from within and therin a tender sympathy attends us in pursuing our fellow creatures thro' the vicissitudes of human Life and a beneficial Turn of Mind much to be prefer'd as matter of Study as it enables Us to see beyond our own Glass, and ripens every bud of Benevolence & Compassion a kind Providence has implanted in our Hearts." The trials of this life multiply our virtues. We need to exercise as much good will as we can. Distresses and "trying Scenes" awaken our sympathy and develop our compassion for others. Twice Sylvia Brathwaite infers generosity of spirit when she learns that a lover quietly ameliorated the misfortune of another in such an inconspicuous way that she knew it was not done merely to impress her.

Benevolence and generosity toward the unfortunate were signs of a virtuous disposition. But even more important was stoic acceptance of one's fate: "[P]atience under inevitable evils, is not more an act of duty, than necessity," Lennox tells Lydia. "As to our selves," writes Ann, "we know if we continue in the World we must meet with changes & be they for the better or the worse I hope our spirits will be equal to them." We must resign ourselves to afflictions and accidents, death and illness, despair and doubt. To do otherwise is to question God's order.

The Lydia Clerke letters suggest that religion was central to eighteenth-century women's lives. While men, with the exception of those like Winstanley who entered the Church, did not express much religious sentiment beyond the occasional "God bless," women frequently drew on religious doctrine to support and cheer one another. Whether learned lady, woman writer, matron, spinster, or flirt, the consolations and explanations of religion were pivotal. Spiritual thoughts gave them

---

[11]   Gordon Rupp, *Religion in England 1688–1791* (Oxford, 1986) 49.

the hope and faith they needed to overcome poverty and troubles, pains and distresses, doubts and despair.

Thomas Winstanley and Samuel Johnson

Religious doubt and fear were ever-present in the eighteenth century. Many insisted on the impossibility of ever knowing the truth about God and His ways. Many wondered how, or if, God would reward us or punish us in the next world. Many wondered if there was a next world.

When Samuel Johnson lay dying and in need of spiritual consolation, Thomas Winstanley was called to his bedside. According to a letter written by The Reverend J. Sanger, Winstanley was afraid to meet the eminent author. He sent a letter instead: "Permit me therefore to write what I should wish to say were I present. I can easily conceive what would be the subjects of your inquiry. I can conceive that the views of yourself have changed with your condition, and that on the near approach of death, what you once considered mere peccadillos have risen into mountains of guilt, while your best actions have dwindled into nothing. On whichever side you look you see only positive transgressions or defective obedience; and hence, in self-despair, are eagerly inquiring, 'What shall I do to be saved?' I say to you, in the language of the Baptist, 'Behold the Lamb of God!' ... ." Sanger writes that Johnson asked to have Winstanley's words repeated and asked again to meet him. Again Winstanley felt unequal to the task; again he sent a letter "enlarging upon the subject of his first letter." Sanger believed Johnson's powerful reactions to Winstanley's words were signs of conversion in the Evangelical sense. In "The Rumor of Dr. Johnson's Conversion," a detailed study of this incident, Maurice J. Quinlan concludes that such was probably not the case. However, Quinlan does allow that Johnson may have, toward the end of his life, experienced "a general strengthening of his religious convictions."[12]

Quinlan surmises that Winstanley, who was nearly seventy in the last year of Johnson's life, "might very well have been in poor health" and felt unequal to the task of meeting with Johnson. But he also wonders about the accuracy of the account given in Sanger's letter and suspects that much exaggeration went into the account, and perhaps some fabrication. He finds the account "mythical." However, knowing Winstanley as we do from his letters to Lydia and Charlotte, and especially from his will, we might insist that this last incident reflects him accurately. Just as he feared to face his wife, he feared to face Johnson and hoped his written words of, in the one case, gentle persuasion, in the other, fervent consolation, would suffice.

---

[12] Maurice J. Quinlan, "The Rumor of Dr. Johnson's Conversion," *The Review of Religion*, 12 (1948): 254–61.

Quinlan may dismiss the possibility of Johnson's conversion, but he cannot diminish the power of Winstanley's voice (epistolary or otherwise). In fact, if we turn to William Roberts's *Memoirs of the Life and Correspondence of Mrs. Hannah More* we find more evidence of the strength of Winstanley's religious presence. Roberts refers to a passage in The Reverend Mr. Crabbe's memoirs of his father in which the son mentions the father's admiration for the sermons of Winstanley: "I give you a short abstract of a sermon preached this morning, by my favourite clergyman of St Dunstan's. There is nothing particular in it, but had you heard the good man, reverend in appearance, and with a hollow slow voice deliver it,—a man who seems already half way to heaven, you would have joined with me in wondering people call it dull and disagreeable to hear such discourses."[13] Although a picture at several removes, nevertheless Crabbe's words give us an image of the power of the man when in his pulpit.

---

[13]   William Roberts, ed., *Memoirs of the Life and Correspondence of Mrs. Hannah More*, 2nd edn. (London, 1834) 1:xxv–xxviii; 1:379–80.

Chapter 4

Susannah Dobson

There is hardly a character in the World more Despicable or more liable to universal ridicule than that of a Learned Woman. Them words imply, according to the receiv'd sense, a tatling, impertinent, vain, and Conceited Creature.

Lady Mary Wortley Montagu, *Works* (1710)

"Lady Cornelia," said Mr. Greville, "does not mix in company to converse, but to make orations. She will stun her female visitants of sixteen with learned gibberish; gives rules for epic and dramatic poetry, and cannot endure a comedy that is not within the law of four-and-twenty hours."

"Ah! if your charming friend," pursued Mr. Greville, looking at me (Can you guess who he meant, my dear?) "had been here, what a contrast might we have observed between true genius and an affectation of knowledge—elegant language, and pedantic stiffness, just sentiment and unintelligible conceit: when the other preached she would only speak; and, as some one justly observes, by making plain and simple answers to her riddles, and giving distinction to her confusion, she would have done at least the good office of expounding her to herself."

"A man makes a silly figure," said Mr. Harley, "in company with so learned a Lady, and her Amazonian friend. Talents so masculine, and so ostentatiously displayed, place them above those attentions and assiduities to which the charming sex have so just a claim, and which we delight to pay. Women should always be women; the virtues of our sex are not the virtues of theirs. When Lady Cornelia declaims in Greek, and Miss Sandford vaults into her saddle like another Hotspur, I forget I am in company with women: the dogmatic critic awes me into silence, and the hardy rider makes my assistance unnecessary."

Charlotte Lennox, *Euphemia* (1790)

I am on the Brink of confessing all to Dr Dobson, but his wife is *so odd*. I believe this nasty Bath is a Cage of unclean birds—Strange Stories are related both of that odious Mrs Dobson & charming Mr James; would I were away from them all.

Hester Thrale Piozzi, *Thraliana* (1784)

Susannah Dobson (1742–95) was a learned lady, a writer, and a translator. One of the few contributors to the Lydia Clerke collection to have earned an entry in the *Dictionary of National Biography*, she published a *Life of Petrarch* in 1775 and translated Sainte-Palaye's *Literary History of the Troubadours* (1779) as well as his *Memoirs of Ancient Chivalry* (1784). Her *Dialogue on Friendship and Society* appeared in 1777 and *Historical Anecdotes of Heraldry and Chivalry* in 1795, the year of her death. In her second letter to Lydia, she notes that she is "busy with my

History of Philosophy since I wrote last." However, the History was never completed. At least it is not included in any lists of works attributed to Dobson.

Probably born in 1742 in Toxteth, a present-day suburb near Liverpool, she married Liverpool physician Matthew Dobson in 1759. Two years later she gave birth to a daughter who died in her seventeenth year.[1] Another daughter, Susannah, is mentioned in her father's will but otherwise absent from the public record.[2] In 1770, Matthew became physician to the Liverpool Infirmary. Ten years later, he retired to Bath where, in 1784, he died. Eleven years later Susannah died in London.

If Winstanley's letter tells us Lydia was unhappy but never tells us why, Susannah's letters give us hints of what or who has come between John and Lydia. Several times Susannah expresses—in bad French—great concern that Lydia might have acted injudiciously when in France. Susannah fears that Lydia may have been too familiar with a certain gentleman and hints that Lydia acted in retaliation against her husband who had lost that place in her heart he once had. Susannah urges Lydia to exercise caution and insists, again and again, that she warns Lydia as a friend and not as a critic.

Susannah's letters provide unintentional satire. Constantly emphasizing her sincerity and solicitude, she nonetheless unwittingly reveals her prolixity and pretentiousness. She also spends much time elaborating her intellectual activities. Alternatively assertive and diffident, she mentions her many literary, philosophical, historical, and scientific endeavors. We also learn something about the mysteries of sexual identity in the eighteenth century when we try to make sense of Susannah's adoration of Lydia, her cool relationship to her husband, and her mysterious comings and goings once widowed.

3

From: Susannah Dobson, Liverpool
To: Lydia Clerke, At Mrs. Thornton's, in Orchard Street, near the Broad Way, Westminster
Date: 21 October [1770]

God be thanked my dearest friend for your Welfare and Safety. How oft have I invok'd his Protection and recommended to his Paternal Care my beloved Clarke. I Judged your Humanity would not suffer me to wait a moment you could help for the Account of your Journey. I doubted not your high Entertainment and am well pleased it so fully answerd your Wishes.

---

[1]   Ref 942 WAK 7(9), Liverpool Record Office: notes on Matthew and Susannah Dobson made by the antiquarian William Heaton Wakefield.
[2]   PROB 11/1128, Family Records Centre.

The Picture at Olives is to please me one of the finest I ever saw, the child beyond all description great, and there is another in the same Room of our Saviour bearing his Cross which tho not an original struck me with extreme awe and Admiration. The Subject so much greater than the other tho it must be confessed the Expression of divinity & Benevolence wrought up so perfectly in the child Jesus gives that Piece a more extensive Character then is generally to be observd in Pieces of the same kind. I have seen a very few pronounced to have Merit but of these none ever answer'd my Idea in respect to the Child but this. You who have seen many and some very capital ones will judge with more Truth of the Superiority given to this, but do you think the Virgin an expressive figure? To me she appear'd not so. Possibly Every thing in the Piece was artfully intended rather to give éclat to the child than produce two Subjects of equal Admiration as is frequently the Method with Capital Masters—

I had wrote only these lines when in came Mrs Armitage and teazd me with her Company all Morning. I was provoked but I did not show it, which was very moral behaviour considering the Employment in which I was engaged. She had a letter from Mrs Thornton the same day I had yours, and sets out for London on Sunday next. I have dined twice with Mama and deliverd your kind Message. She desires her love to You and is vastly glad to hear you are so well-arrived. Miss Polly, Mrs Johnson, and poor James take the freedom to rejoice at your Welfare, and my Children Skip about and beg their kind love. As for me I read from Morning to Night and dream from Night to Morning about you.

When your Letter came I was just pronouncing your Name with Awe. I had caught a Wasp and was violently busy in Squeezing out the Sting from its Tail and in Eyeing its clever and fierce Visage. I desired Johnson to help me as it was a Work of great Labor and Importance and was just saying, if my dear & beloved Mrs Clerke was here I must not in her Presence do this—Down went all the things when your Letter came and the Sting half out and half in remains for further operation at my leisure Hours.

I was much pleasd with many of Belfields Letters. The 2nd Vol is a lively Contrast to the first and from Gallantry and external dissipation we see him chang'd to the anxious & suffering Husband loving his Children beset with the Calamities of War and his Wife expiring in his Arms. But there are some reflections He makes in these situations & some descriptions worth ten thousand of the frippery fashionable Trifles which the first Vol. mostly abounds in, and indeed the whole is a very lively description of human Life in one class from the careless & idle Scenes of fashionable Youth to the Mature and reflecting. The trying Scenes that are often prepard by a Wise Providence to give that sincere & solid Turn so necessary to Unveil the truth, and place a Life to come in all its true Importance before Us. For however any may doubt for a time, Truth & Nature will sooner or later point out the folly of attaching ourselves to <u>this World</u> in <u>such a manner</u> as to <u>weaken</u> and <u>diminish</u> that Idea of and preparation for another. On which every thing we can call or esteem real and Significant ultimately depends with respect to the best part of Us. That only Part which will survive all accidents from without or distresses from within and therin a tender sympathy attends us in pursuing our fellow creatures thro' the vicissitudes of human Life and a beneficial Turn of Mind much to be prefer'd as matter of Study as it enables Us to see beyond our own Glass, and ripens every bud of Benevolence & Compassion a kind Providence has implanted in our Hearts.

The Memoirs of Brandenburgh entertaind me exceedingly and tho' so abominably ignorant as You justly observd of modern History, I was so lucky to meet there with a great Character I have read somewhere of: Lewis 14 & Cromwell, contrasted in a very admirable Manner with Frederick William that great and noble ancestor of the present King of Prussia, who is worthy of everlasting Fame for being the Father as well as the Hero of Brandenburgh. There is a great Similitude in the State of this author & Voltaire. I should have pronounc'd it his if I had not heard it was wrote by the present King of Prussia. You who so perfectly well know in this and every Subject both Works and Authors be so good to inform me whom you esteem to have been the Author of these Memoirs & whether you do not almost adore the Patroness of Leibnitz.

Why, my dear love, do you make any apology for making Use of me as a friend? Are you yet Ignorant that there is not that thing in the World if I know my own Heart that my poor Power could extend to I would not fly to do for any one in whom you was interested, much more hesitate a Moment to ask a few Questions of importance to such worthy People and I beg You will present our Respects and let them know we really have made as critical Enquiry as we could have done for our own child. But for this I should have sent my Letter a Post sooner. And as Mrs Alex has been so kind to assure us of not naming her Informers which in the D^r's Situation might be very Inconvenient shall frankly lay the Matter before You as we know it certainly to be. The Crossbys are a House where they do a great deal of business but it is the D^r and Mr Dobson's Opinion he will see business done to more advantage in Mr Daltera's Counting House—Mr Daltera is the person to whom M ʼWidens spoke before he spoke to Mr Crossby on this account as he had been apply'd to by his Brother in Law Mr Owen Brereton—Mr Daltera's business is Commissions and the Virginia Trade and very extensive. His Terms are for a Clark who enters for 5 years 3 hundred Guineas. But if Mr Alex chooses to see the Business of that House for one or 2 years, it will be a hundred Pound a Year. Mr Crossby's Business is the Commission Business, his Character as to Honesty is fair, and he is an orderly Family Man but not to appearances very bright. His wife is esteem'd the Major domo and She is a good sort of very Ungenteel Women in my opinion, but I think a good person enough, and he rather lowbred [than] otherwise. I should think it hardly a Place polite enough, tho' they are esteemed rich, for so genteel a Young Man to fix in. As to Religion it is hard to say. The Crossbys are, I believe, regular and good Church People and excellent French People, being extreme fond of good Dinners and fat Suppers. As to Mr Daltera's Religion I believe no one knows any thing about it. His character has been well spoke of since he was marry'd but he was a most dreadful Rake before that and I should think his Principles were rather doubtful but in business he is esteemed very clever. Mr Crossby is esteem'd a good Natured Man. What Mr Daltera's Temper is I dont know. He has several Clarks in his House; Mr Crossby lost one last year and whether he has more than one at present I cant tell. This is all I can collect for you. Hope it will answer your Wishes and assure You the D^r and I if the Young Gentleman comes shall have pleasure in showing him Every Civility possible either Public or private which I beg in that Case you will be so good to assure him of. As this affair had been named to Mr Daltera & my Brother Dobson whatever is said will be immediately thought to come from Us tho' Names should be omitted so must beg Caution as to Reasons given also to be used in what you and Mrs Alex shall determine upon if the Young Gentleman comes to either Place as in perfect dependance upon this we have been perfectly open and Sincere.

From Matters of Business I will proceed to Matters of Amusement—Last Thursday was our Assembly to which your poor heavy hearted friend repaired in her new Blossom Coulourd Negligee and all her bettermost things, her little heart ambitious to be thought something of after having been so highly honord by your love and persuading her self the very hearing of her Endeavour to become of some Acount would do something for her with you as it was expressive of her Gratitude for your friendly Admonitions—Admonitions she will ever revere & exult in as the strongest proofs of your love. Had not you occupied her fond Heart, her new Sack would have been made before, but where such a friend fill'd every Pore and Corner such Trifles could find no Room. Present at this grandee Meeting was all the Liverpool Quality to Solace themselves in Gazing at my Lady Molineux—her Ladyship was dress'd in White and Silver, the Pattern very Elegant, and appeard to me a very charming Woman. Her behaviour was elegantly affable to every one who had Visited her and Polite to all the Company. She had with her Mrs Penant our Member's Lady, whom, as I visit, when she came up to speak to me I was very near her Ladyship. I admired her extremely—Sr Frank stands to dance the Minuet with Lady Molineux. I did not greatly like her Minuet—Mr. Penant dancd Country Dances with her. She had on a diamond Necklace set to amazing advantage, Diamonds in her Hair, single dropd diamond Earings, Diamond Sleeve Knots, and Bare to her Stomacher, Her Hair in a sort of Toupee only with 2 curls on each side. Mrs Penant had on her Diamonds also which are esteemd very fine, a very large necklace, 3 drop'd Earings and [illegible word] in her Hair. She was General Warburton's Daughter, allied nearly to 2 dukes & will have a prodigious fortune. She is an exceeding good sort of Woman & pretty & he a most Worthy Man. One of their Seats is about 30 miles from Us, where they keep a Noble Table and do a vast deal of Good—Lord Molinox was in a Silver Tissue sort of Coat and french Embroiderd Waistcoat. Sir William Meredith, our other member, in a blue velvet of the ruff kind with a Silver Point Lace in it exceedingly pretty. Beside there were some Country Gentlemen and Gentlewomen great in their own Estates but not remarkable out of them; and as I mention'd before such a Concourse of Us Liverpool Quality to see this fine sight that we were ready to tread upon one an[other]. I own I did wish for you to have honour'd and Patronizd [our Assembly] but this was a favor I ought not to have Wish'd as such a crowd would have been as [irksome] to you as it was Amusing to Us dull Ignorant Country People, who see such fine things only once a year or twice. I doubt not my lovely friend but you have wrote to Mrs Ketsworth before this as her situation so strongly claims your tenderest attention; and as <u>such methods</u> of expressing your Interest in her interfere not with any minor considerations due to yourself.

For my own Part I so strongly feel the Minutest Circumstance that is connected with you; and my Idea of your Character is so enlarged that I disdain those fears reserves and hesitations in my language to you very incident to more common friendships. It was this perfect Idea of your Character and the tenderest feelings of my own Heart joind that led me to say what I did think of the utmost Importance relative to a certain affair, as I well knew that your own [calmness] of Temper led you to see and act envers autre sexe in that Brotherly and generous manner that would be very delightful if it could be done with safety. But, indeed my love, while customs and dispositions run in the [short run] you do this in the long run, will ever prove to have its Inconveniences, and when I heard you so amiably [express y^e] sentiment de regard vous avez sentir pour E-t en France et le Comportement dun certain Monsieur en Absence de votre Mari jai fremir en mons Coeur—particularly as I well knew it had been said in England more than once or twice Que quand vous este en France vous etiez extremement gai. Now this only seem'd to be spoke in the Sense of a very fine Lady and as of a Person who knew what a right they had to be sought and admired, yet I could not help feeling extremely upon hearing it, when I considerd how true a Right vous avez to a character infinitely superior, and how delicately vous este in all respects situated. Add to this que j'etoit bien assuré Votre mari avoit perdu ce place il avoit en votre coeur, et que vous reste pas insensible a les Douceurs que la Merite et quelque agreements peut Inspirer. Vous savez bien mon tres chere ecriture que c'est [question] seule la plus tendre Sentiment—that causes me to open my whole Soul to you. And I would have said something more than I did to you when present but I found myself too much agitated when ever a sorte de sujet was started to speak with propriety and you beaucoup trop agite d'encontrer. But, as I prize my Conscience and what appears to me the first Badge of Amity (or sacred & firm as I trust ours to be) above all things, I cannot refuse myself the doing a ce Temps Critique car je vous avoue que si aucune chose vous avez pers'wader d'aller a ce Place Publique avec Madame B—jaurois ete autant quel vous a respecter Wretched to ye very utmost Un plus grand imprudence en votre situation ne pouvait avoir este au Monde, and before Heaven and Earth si aucune Chose vous etiez Venu vous ne renvoir avoir apportée le moindre Vindication non envente.

[Dobson writes on three sides of the last page (which also bears the address). The following is at the top of the page:] Our Saviour when he commands us to pray we may not be led into Temptation does certainly imply that when we become so to others by their Vice and folly we ought to shun them or the possibility it may be even of meeting them as we would a Pestilence—and for that reason it appears to me we ought to avoid even lesser Instances of attachment—en consideration d un Nature des Hommes who have not refinement enough to bear it—and perhaps quand une homme est une fois en marriage however it turns out, son conversation avec Autre Sexe devoit estre bien gardée surtout si elle a les charmes de Personne et de Maniere; et si elle nest pas fort Heureuse en son sacré attachement. Vous est my most Beloved friend. Suffer me to speak all the Truth so perfectly calculated dinspirer de plaisir et les sentiments Interessant que sans doute souvent vous considerez comme les autres vous considere. You will find (and that we ought to do to be Worthy to regulate our actions accordingly with Judgement, but especially those whose betrayals are of so much consequence) Vous avez bien doccasion d exercer une grande Caution and that is not le voix of superstitious Reserve or of Seering Criticism but of the tenderest affection that ever resided in a human Breast and the truest Reverence that so many exalted Qualities must produce with a strong sense of your Influence & Power that dictates these honest Sentiments. All my aim all my desire is, God knows, to contribute to your Peace of Mind, and if I may but be so happy to produce in you that calm serene Temper without which we can not pursue our Business of Life with advantage as it respects another so I shall be abundantly gratified for all my care. The Quality & [impressions] your Mind is capable of are too great, my love, to be neglected in the smallest degree from the too rapid influence of any outward circumstances. The Cultivation of such faculties and the tranquilizing such a generous and amiable Heart should be your great aim. In my little & much narrower sphere I can say conscientiously this is my daily endeavour, and tho' I have had sad [Pollys] to encounter with and many Savage Matrons to subdue I despair not through a divine assistance and that Grace promised to the Sincere and Industrious to attain in time some better Disposition & Virtues more worthy your acceptance. And tho I well know I appeard barbarous to you [rest of sentence is hidden by tape].

[The following is at the bottom of the page:] This infinite Sympathy it is that whatever pain it cost me [rest of sentence is hidden by tape] but as wholly as my judgement and knowledge extended to the perfect friend and I thought this [the] time to do it before you Enterd on a Scene que pouvoit avoir d'un grand difficulty. And may that God [who is a] friend of Virtue assist you in all your Ways and cause all your Trials to prove the increase of your best Virtues and your quicker preparation for a Life where all folly and distress will be shut out for Ever. Soon must that Scene in whatever Shapes of Importance it may now appear close upon us both and then will all these things which in some way or other did not refer to that eternal one that is to succeed dwindle to yᵉ merest Nothings and only leave Us wondering how we could ever give them any great Weight with Us. And tho' to say these things are calld Preaching yet those who love their friends from the Soul and whose attachments are on the foundation of Immortality will ever rejoice to lift their Views with them to a Region where a true friendship and sincerity with all other Virtues will be rewarded and made Perfect. You can say I think I trust you feel that in the Bosom of Friendship you may repose your utmost Cares and that there is a Mansion however you may be circumstanced ever ready to receive & a Soul in it ever open to embrace You with all that concerns Your Interest. Therefore I beseech, my dear love, no poorer Ideas than I merit, no Tears that my love would be incapable of understanding, may ever cause you to hesitate one Moment in gratifying my ambitious Views for I cannot have, I have not a higher ambition in this world than to be in some small degree serviceable to you; and to be honor'd with your Preference. And I trust I shall find that if circumstances call for it, My humble advice will be accepted, My imperfections will be overlooked, and my abode accepted As the Mansion of Peace and tenderly dedicated to your Service tho' in all other respects [not] wholly unworthy. And whether such circumstances happen or not Your love will not require [regard] to stand my friend but will with the first Convenience direct its steps hither. What I feel for your loss no words can express. My Heart within me Melts. When I consider how far you've got from me and that what I am now saying will be 3 days eer it reach, but God is gracious. He will I trust guide and guard You. To him shall my daily Prayers & Hourly Ejaculations be lifted for your Welfare, and, Oh, write to me, I beseech you, with the first possibility as I know not what may happen to my feeling, my afflicted Heart. Adieu God Almighty bless You, Think of your poor absent friend with Candour & love & believe no love was more true or tender to you than y^t of your own S Dobson

[The following is in the last available space, adjacent to the address:] As they charg'd me wrong for your Letter I went to the Post House who repaid me and I mention it because they assured me that your Letters ought to have been refunded to you—and that it matterd not where the charge was laid on, the last post was obligd to refund upon seeing them—but they would not do it without they saw them, and that as they were not allow'd to open Letters they charg'd them at hazard, but that if the Letter was shewn the Money was obligd to be repaid. Your Letter has vex'd me so much I mentiond this. Pray my kindest Respects to your Valuable Sister and Comp^{ts} to Mrs. Thornton. Once more adieu my dearest best and most revered Love—Pray be very particular where I am to direct to you in your N[rest of sentence hidden by tape].

4
From: Susannah Dobson, Liverpool
To: Lydia Clerke, Gosport
Date: 10 January [1771]

Oh! my Love! my inestimable friend let me take up your Letter at the end rather than at the beginning and indicate my own Tenderness and Duty to you before I acknowledge the Excess of your Partial affection—I am convinced my Beloved Creature Letters are Unfaithful Dictators in any Points of Intricate Debate. Else could my Clerke have said her Dobson was severe to her! Good God! <u>Severe to my Clerke!</u> to one I love as my own Life nay even doat on with almost unequaled Tenderness. Severe to the friend whose Heart & Soul mine kindreds with beyond that of any other Being upon Earth!—yes— if to count the Tedious Minutes since her absence is to be Severe to her; <u>I am indeed Severe</u>—If to pray with unremiting ardour for her Peace <u>Serenity</u> & Virtue—If to make her next Heaven and my Duty the Object of my Hourly Contemplation, If to place her Example in those things my Capacity may aspire to & my Heart owns the high worth of, continually before my Eyes; if to anguish with all the Excess of Tenderness for a Reunion with so dear and embellished a character and to beg of Heaven to render me more deserving of its Preference, to perfect the Virtue and all the Sympathetic Joys of our Union, <u>to render it lasting as our souls</u>. and Endless as Eternity! If these unintermitting and United Employments convict me of severity then I am indeed severe to my Clarke! You have commanded me to be Silent however upon Subjects that caused this accusation; and <u>Obedience to you I prefer</u> to what I think I could say with Propriety at the close of it. And shall therefore only observe that as it was impossible to make any comparison in <u>thought</u>, much more in Word, between your feelings and those that arose from Vice—I accordingly observ'd as you will find upon a Review that I judged the Word Agrement could not be indiscriminately used for very different characters since Agrement or Wondering may be used to a Virtuous Mind but can never be an expression strong enough for a Vicious one—Most heartily shall I be glad for your sake and the sake of Virtue if your charitable hopes are or shall be realized; and well am I assured; (which as I have felt so I have even testified to you;) that I believe your Principles founded upon the Nicest Honor in <u>every respect</u>; and that <u>Rigid I may be or appear at least to you thro an Unfortunate and ill bred Manner. You are not les so</u> in every <u>active Principle</u> and have had proofs perhaps to give <u>incompatible with my Insignificance</u> and which are beyond even the most anxious tender and frank observations that <u>friendship of a first kind cannot always help making</u> with respect to Circumstances in which the Object it most loves is concerned and thus as you Desire Shall this and every other Subject you judge not proper for mutual debate be closed. And You as in all things <u>but one</u> You <u>ought to be</u> held my constant and revered Dictator, Dictator & kind Judge my Heart joys to be dictated by.

I have the Happiness to assure My beloved friend I have made a great progress in Health since I wrote last, and except a little Restless now and then at Night, am got charming well, and have been out very often among my Neighbours, who have been very kind in seeming desirous to have me again with them, and in receiving me upon the most sociable Terms. Your Tenderness, my dearest C, overcame me, or the mention of my designing an Act of Duty but very incompetent gratitude did you, but could I have express'd less toward a Person so dear to me, I must have been indeed devoid of all Sensibility.—Never could Flattery, my friend, coming from you fail to raise my Vanity but in the one light in which your last lines have presented it, Wherein you aim at humbling yourself Unjustly to do honor to your friend. But do not think because I have used a Sincerity about your character my view of your Superiority to all little feelings induced me to pursue & which in such Minds alone can answer the true Ends of Friendship. I did not feel at the same time what little right I had <u>as it respected myself</u> to point out the Ideas I had Entertaind of it, nor should right but the most perfect love on my Side & assurance of it on yours, lend the motions of Tenderness which urged me to enter into your whole Soul have tempted me so to do. And as it is impossible our love should be so poor as to be capable of Speeches. You will believe me when I say the continual review of my own character cannot but affect me in many instances with deep contrition of Heart, and that was you to enter its Secret Avenues, You would find cause to Sympathize with rather than praise its Owner. God forbid therefore that I should ever wound the cause of humanity; whether the feelings such a mature retrospect at Home ought to' give for others should despoil or Restate to revere its first loved friend and acknowledge that Superiority that can raise a very imperfect character merely for its Sincerity and Tenderness as you have done mine I well know in your <u>own Heart</u> as well as to <u>me</u>; and to <u>Others</u> as well as to <u>Yourself</u>. To confess our faults one to another is a precept of Scripture, but perhaps seldom to be practiced with Success but in the most tender friendships, but now I do think it is capable of greatly serving its Cause and heightening its affection, when done as must be with perfect sincerity. And tho I feel the excessive height of your Candour to be beyond every possible [Devotion] in me, yet the Manner in which you have expressd value for your own Soul for its affection to mine, in at once the most tender elegant and Heartfelt address, that a Human Pen could present to ye most beloved [Aspect], how then will my grateful Soul treasure it up in its deepest recesses & preserve it where the arrows of Time will I trust never never be able to reach it, or expunge one line of its dear contents—agreeable to what I have said above about confession of faults to those we love.

I must talk to you a little and desire you to assist me how to act in an affair that really lies heavy on my Heart when I reflect on it and which I mention freely to you because you have known it all. I have had no Letter from Moritt in answer to that I sent by you tho' I beg'd her so Earnestly & affectionately to send me one. So extreme a breach with a Person I have so dearly loved shocks my Nature—when I was ill it gave me extreme Pain; and I would not have died for the World without giving her some testimony of my affection and my hearty desire of her Welfare both here and hereafter. And I determin'd if it pleased God to spare me as he has graciously done, the utmost concessions on my part tho' more than the judgement I can honestly make of the affair might seem to require, yet should not be left untried to gain her to shew me a moderate kindness at heart as I hoped time and my heartfelt remonstrances would do something more. I told her in my last I would come to her if she would admit me, and that indeed I am determin[d] I will do. She cannot shut the Door against me I am sure, her humanity will not suffer her to do that. I am touchd to the very Soul by her Conduct and can hardly write for my Tears. Perhaps I was too hasty in my conduct to her & did not allow enough for her peculiar turn of Temper. I wish I had stay'd another Week with her tho it was so much against my Conscience as the time was fixed with my friends who were to go down with me, yet as She seemd so shock'd at my going that there had been umbrages so I think I ought to have done it, but she vexd me so much I was not Mistress of myself and, as I had no Nature but a vehement one wch thought itself wrongd to assist me, I acted with much too great Precipitation. I feel now I did and will readily own that very real Error but even my Tenderness for her shall never cause me to say the smallest nothing contrary to Truth or honor, and as I hold my connexion with You my dearest Happiness and most valuable advantage and Honor, so will I ever aver it to be so. She told me, she was sure when you and I met we should have a very real friendship, and added in my favor for your Minds are so alike so tun'd toward y[e] same objects—so superior to general objects, You are quite made for Each other. If so, I said, my dear Moritt, will it not make you happy to see Us united and such a degree of Happiness added to those you love? But you prize me too high when you speak of my connexion with Mrs. C any otherwise than thro her Condescension tho I must own I do feel a most ardent love for her in my Breast & not the fear you have often expressed. This and some other things like these pass'd. She went out generally before I came down to Breakfast and often I was alone for some time after; when I took the opportunity to go to M[rs] [Ketsworths] to talk with her about you; but it was plain that from the moment she saw my ardent attachment to you, she was unhinged in all her manner toward me; and as I thought this ridiculous and that I was not so destitute of Heart but I could love more than one Object, I was I believe often cavalier enough in my answer to her. The Point she went upon was that your Character was so much more distinguish'd than hers, I must love you better and this she could not bear. I could not deny your Character: I could not deny the feelings of my Heart. I could not deny that her conduct had weakened my Affection and herein [was] all the truth. Upon my Word I think I can honestly aver I felt no change to her but what her jealousy and doubt of me occasion'd and the anger did then and has since transported me a little on this acount and Vexation to think friendship should be so little capable of an enlarged way of thinking. Yet I have felt at times those returns of Tenderness for her that I doubt from her conduct she has not experienc'd for me. See her however I must; to settle as well as I am able our shatterd Union to mend—and tack it up at least if possible by the most humane and Sincere offer of kindness toward her that she will admit of; or that I can even force upon her. Tell me, my dear One, whether I shall send her another Letter from here or from London to let her know I am coming & take it to be somewhere in the way to

You and shall go as I come to you if you do not oppose it wth [yr answer] you will not unless you see some perticular Reason. I would fain come to you with a Mind as calm and conscious of <u>upright Actions</u> [& Christian] as I am able to bring, well assurd of your Unfailing Candour to its unwilling and Constitutional Errors. I dont know but I may come to London something sooner than I intended if my Health & the Weather will permit having a visit I must make to a Miss Barratt at Ham who was at Leverpool with me all last Winter an old acquaintance almost & must be [visited] in London. As for your Coming to London to meet me, no indeed my Dear Creature, that I will not permit. I shall come in my usual obscure Manner in the Stage and nothing but necessary affairs shall detain me a Moment from my Love. But, as I have Duties to observe, I think it better to discharge them before I come to you then have them upon my mind. My Brother too at Uxbridge must be visited either then or after, but I shall be so impatient to see you my love my friend I believe I shall defer that.

There are some folk also going from here in about 6 weeks with whom I would like to Stage it or Post it as they will and as I have received some Entertainment from their Characters I will make them known to you. They are two Germans, young Women and Sisters. They came here recommended to a Gentleman and Lady of my acquaintance who are very clever People. Their Father is dead and with him all their Expectations. They are from Berlin; he had a place at Court but saving no money his Children are obliged to go out in the World. And the younger was advised to come to England as a singer, and the other to be a Governess. Their Brother has now a good Place at Court and takes care of his Mother. The youngest has had 2 public Concerts here which were well attended—I was only at one of them, pleased those who had any Taste in Music very much. The others said they had rather hear any common Ballad than her fine Twirls as she called them, which indeed they were a much better Judge of. Her Singing is rather beautiful from Manner as it appears to me than from a great Compass of Voice, and her Piano and Base is particularly pleasing, and her Twirls as they calld the different Modulations of her Voice very happily expressd. I have had her several times at my House with different Parties and She has given us great Entertainment. To this is added as far as I am able to Judge a most cheerful and innocent Character, with Manners quite foreign & degagéè yet simple and artless. Her Sister is much older and appears a very sensible woman and well qualified for the Situation She proposes to Engage in. They have both a great deal of Conversation and very humble & modest deportment. Speak french very well and are Protestants. If I had not been going a journey and been fixed with a Servant I like I would have taken the oldest for Bessy and Sukey I like her so well. Perhaps I may some time hence if she is then at liberty. She would give them beside the french a little of that bon ton I am so wanting in my self. As they are People of Character they have met with a good deal of Civility here; and the youngest never having had the Small Pox has had an Invitation from the Lady & Gentleman above to be in their House to be Inoculated before she lives in London, where she is to sing in Public this winter. What an instance of Humanity is this in them both! but they seem as fond of her as if she was their own child. With this view they will stay here about 6 Weeks or longer, and probably I may then go up to Town with them. As they are so agreable and Entertaining I shall like it much. I have showed them every Civility in my Power & have real Compassion for this Situation and it is a great Pleasure to me to receive kindly every Stranger of Merit that comes here.

I mentioned before I had been a great deal out. My Mother took my Children into the Country with her and after my long confinement I found new Agreements in the Conversation of my friends and neighbours who were kind enough to seem rejoicd at my return into their World again; and to make really very much of me. So you see beside the Manifold Private ones, the public advantages occuring also from Sickness, in that it Causes such insignificant People as myself to Emerge for a moment from Obscurity, and by becoming a Novelty to be consider'd while they are so with kindness and attention by their friends and Neighbours. The choicest of these Hours I have spent with M^{rs} and Miss Atherton and with some authors we select for our Companions, particularly Chaucer, who engaged us in the most delightful manner the other day from 4 till Eleven, mixed with some excellent observations from Miss Atherton whose Capacity and Heart Improves upon my feelings. Every time she indulges me with a view of it—They were so kind to desire I would come to them on the footing of a Neighbour; and said they would not have any other Company but if I would introduce to them some of the dead or living whose merits I was acquainted with; it would be spending their time in the Manner they could wish and they was only sorry from having so large an acquaintance they could not so frequently as they wish'd devote their Hours in this manner when they met with Society who relish'd such Conversations. I have had, in Consequence of these assurances on their Part and a thousand kind things said by Miss Atherton that she hoped for the future we should be quite upon easy Terms together, so great pleasure in their Society and have given them to read Mrs Montague's Essay and have gone over part of it with Mrs. Atherton Myself. They are delighted beyond measure with it and study it line by line. It is a most elegant accurate and Masterly Performance—and if I can find time I will compare it with what Lord Kaim in his Elements of Criticism has said on this Subject; as I hear from a Gentleman reputed a very good Judge that Lord Kaim's Criticisms as they are in all respects Unequalled; so in reference to Shakespear particularly are most incomparable and judicious. Lord Kaim has been several times recommended to me, but I consider'd it as a Work far beyond my capacity, which was the reason I never sent for it tho it was in our Library, but I will get that Volume which contains the View of Shakespear & compare it with Mrs. Montague whose clear and Elegant observations will probably help me with more Ease to comprehend Lord Kaim. I should have told you when speaking of M^{rs} & Miss Atherton how highly they spoke of you & begd their respectful Comp^{ts} and I assure you my beloved friend I believe it owing to the impression they received in my favor from the kind of attention of such a Character as Yourself That I have receivd such marks of their civility and friendliness. But what Joys has not <u>your friendship</u> prepared for me! what honors has it not Led me to! Oh my Love! my Dear, dear friend when I reflect on the short moments which first cemented our Union, on the infinite Superiority of <u>your Mind</u>, on our distance from each Other, and on all the Circumstances that have surrounded Us, I ascribe to a good Providence that you have Ever taken part in my [felicity] and to your own Humanity that you have permitted me to indulge these feelings with a latitude which but for your Tenderness and Candour would have been the highest Presumption in me but You have overcome <u>as such Minds alone Can</u>, by your infinite Candour and love, Those distinctions <u>others must dwell upon</u>, and which but for your affectionate Heart would have forever bar'd me from a Union I hold the dearest to my Soul. This is a Subject delightful to indulge. It revived my drooping spirits some times when at their lowest ebb. And it gladdens and exalts every Hour of my Life; and raises a spark of ambition in me to become more deserving of your continued love and dear [friendship].

I have been several Times also at my own House, at hers; and some of her Neighbours in Company of a Lady who came about a Twelvemonth ago to reside here & whose manner and Deportment appear to me very amiable indeed. She married a Mr Fairfax of this Town now, but originally, I believe, from Ireland & the ancient Fairfax family, a Man of Family & very good fortune. She herself will have a great one, but that is a small Recommendation in comparison of that sweetness of Temper, Candour of Heart, and good Understanding she is said to possess. She had a reserve at first, as most Wise People have, that occasiond me ignorantly to think little of her, but I have found Beauties since in her Conversation & Manner I had no Idea of, and as it was my Place to seek her, being an Inhabitant, & finding her extremely Courteous upon more knowledge, I have endeavord to draw her out by the most Attentive Manner our Connexion was capable of. She has read a great deal: tho' her diffidence at first imply'd nothing like it; and this was ye Opinion of many beside myself, who have a Great Error in my Character in this respect wch I will freely confess to you. I have a mental aversion to Reserve naturally, and used to say foolishly, when I had reflected less than I hope I have since done, that Nothing could be worth so much trouble to get at: and that where People made such Rarities of themselves & their Talents they might as well be without them. But I have since discovered very <u>feelingly</u> this was an Opinion formd upon Ignorance and fixity of Mind, and the choicest Hours of my Life have been spent with, & my best pursuits and greatest felicity owing to, a Connexion with such Characters as were generally held by the Multitude to be very Stiff & reserved; and among the meanest of which multitude I must for <u>ever have</u> class'd; but for the assistance, Candour, and Tenderness of these great and dear and respected now, tho once slighted, characters.

[The following is at the top of the back page:] I hope for great advantages in Points of Philosophy when I come to you; but You must have great Patience at the [beginning], and I fear your Study will be too deep for me—You have the most Metaphysical Head I believe in the World not to say Female, and Morality is my highest aim and what my Capacity I take it is principally capable of and this Opinion strikes more feelingly upon me every day and from every new Research I attempt to make. I must now with what unwillingness your Heart will [testify] for me leave my dearly beloved C. Pray write soon very soon—The Time creeps on till I shall be reunited with my Love the Doctor who says he loves you monstrously (a fine thing truly!) looks as if he imagined I shall never come Home again or be able to leave my dearest C—how I shall indeed ever be able to leave You if I am once again bless'd in your Society I know not. But I will defer I could intent on Ideas and with True Gratitude to Providence for my present Prospects hope to indulge myself in the happiest View of them—I am truly sorry to find your amiable friend M^{rs} B is so poorly. I pray God she may get better if He sees it best. Pray my love to her and tell her my own sincere Wishes and Prayers are continually and sincerely hers. My grateful & most affectionate Respects to M^{rs} H & the Doctor's to You and to her and pray be kind enough to remember me to Miss Clark when you write, I would have given a great deal to have seen her again after your kind Introduction. Adieu my most beloved Creature may the kind hand of Providence guide, preserve, & guard you ever to your faithfull [friend] S Dobson

[The following is at the bottom of the back page:] And I have found the greatest Inconveniences in my own Life; to come from the want of a proper Reserve and Equality of Conduct, and my Words and Shews had Constructions put upon them, they were very far from deserving. But I must also add one thing in my favor, it has never been by those who were sincerely acquainted with my Heart, which has a Tenderness & I know it is incapable of injuring any tho its Conduct has sometimes been Hasty and Premature—I cannot imagine how Mrs. Campbell and Cathcart should think of making such a Woman as Mrs. Montague the Object of their Puerile Envy and Malevolence. Such a character as hers seem to me [soars] much above the reach of their Venom or the possibility of feeling the Influence of it. Poor [Miss] & Mrs. Duncombe might be perhaps taken off with Marks of Genius: but here they were greatly out of their latitude. I am sorry a woman so young & really gifted in some things as Mrs. C-C should be so wretched a character in every point of Heart and Principle. As for Mrs. C.t I ever considered her as a finishd Deceiver and so I often told M.t. whose attachement to her I never could account for, tho she is a sort of Woman that if I ever came Nigh I would behave with Civility to, from dread But not from Complacency. I hope she will not come over to see me when at your House, for I have no capacity to behave properly to such doubtful Characters & from Ignorance and the fear of doing wrong always exceed some way or other in my deportment to them—I have been very busy with my History of Philosophy since I wrote last and have wrote 3 and 4 Hours at a Time for my own as well as for Bessy's, and the Instruction and Entertainment it has given me has been very great. Boethius the author

I lent you is represented as he indeed was a bright high single star emerging from the thick darkness of that Period. Have you read his Work? You have never mentioned it to me in any of your Letters.

[The following is in the last available space, adjacent to the address:] Mr Alex has been in Cheshire with the gentlemen at whose House he is. Since he came here I have invited him 2 or 3 times when I have had Company I thought would amuse him. My mother's love and the children's. Adieu dearest Love Adieu
Wednesday Jany 10—

The Learned Lady

Long, abject, and effusive, Susannah's are the oddest letters in the Lydia Clerke collection. Employing a tiny handwriting on large sheets of paper, trying to convey more than is possible in one letter, one page, or one sentence; Susannah's words bleed into one another. Full of qualifying and parenthetical superscripts and subscripts and countless additions and corrections, as if she reread and revised her words over and over again before posting them, her letters are almost illegible. Meaning comes not from her sentences, which get tangled in the mazes of her syntax, but from repetition of certain words and phrases such as "sincerity," "tenderness," "candor," "friendship," "happiness." Constantly adding and erasing words and phrases to her already crowded page, she enhanced the complexity and density, but rarely the clarity, of her thought. Nevertheless, the peculiar turns of her style give us insight into the peculiar turns of her temper (or, to use another one of Dobson's phrases, give us entrance into the "Secret Avenues" of her heart).

In her letters to Lydia, Susannah writes about the many books she has read. She is proud of her accomplishments not only in Modern history but also in philosophy. A learned lady, Susannah eagerly presents herself as such.

The learned lady was on the rise during the eighteenth century. According to Sylvia Myers, in the late 1750s (when Susannah Dobson was coming to maturity), the different strands of female advocacy, wider social opportunities, and female aspirations to a life of the mind came together to energize the first generation of bluestocking women, which included Elizabeth Carter, Catherine Talbot, Elizabeth (Robinson) Montagu, Sarah (Robinson) Scott, Hester Mulso, and Lady Margaret Harley.[3] In her letters, it is clear that Susannah models herself on her more famous contemporaries. She gives her companions Chaucer and Mrs. Montagu's *An Essay on the Writings and Genius of Shakespear* to read. She hopes that Mrs. Montagu will help her understand Kames's *Elements of Criticism*, a work which she has always considered "beyond her capacity." Susannah's enthusiasm for the work of another

---

[3]   Sylvia Myers, *The Bluestocking Circle* (Oxford, 1990) 121–50.

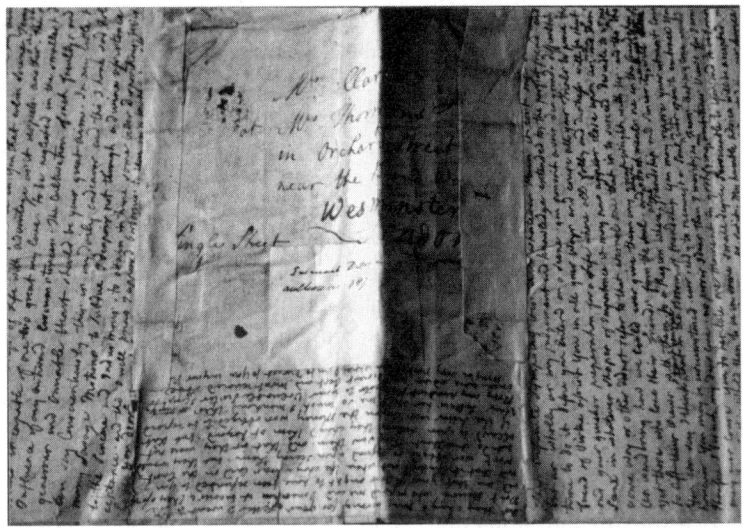

4.1   Letter #3 from Susannah Dobson. Detail. Photo: Author's Collection.
Reproduced by permission of the Society of Antiquaries of London

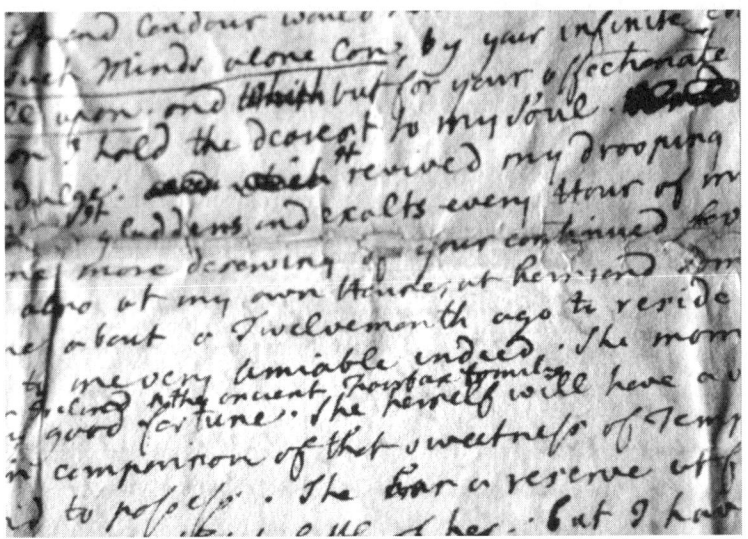

4.2   Letter #4 from Susannah Dobson. Detail. Photo: Author's Collection.
Reproduced by permission of the Society of Antiquaries of London

learned woman is heartfelt and sincere. Her generosity of spirit is admirable. Although she was never able to join Elizabeth Montagu's or Hester Thrale's more famous circles, she emulated them and sought, in her Liverpool world, to embody the spirit of intellectual inquiry and collaborative learning they modeled.

Although the learned woman was often admired in the eighteenth century, she was also severely satirized. Pictured as overbearing and slovenly, she was mocked for her pretentiousness and unpleasant physical appearance. There was much fear that an intellectual woman was an unnatural woman, a desexed woman, or worse, a masculine woman, a woman who did not know her place; consequently, she was scorned and reviled by both sexes. Susannah's circumlocutions seem to result partly from a misguided effort to ward off such scorn. She constantly minimizes her own accomplishments and disparages her own opinions as if to ingratiate herself with her reader: "I hope for great advantages in Points of Philosophy when I come to you," she writes Lydia; "but You must have great patience at the [beginning], and I fear your Study will be too deep for me—You have the most Metaphysical Head I believe in the World not to say Female."

Despite efforts to appear humble and diffident, she received much criticism for her conceit. Other members of Lydia Clerke's circle of acquaintance, in particular Mrs. Thornton and Sylvia Brathwaite, scorn her without pity. Mrs. Thornton stresses Susannah's insincerity and penuriousness: "Her conduct is such that every body in the house hates her. It would fill a sheet of paper were I to inform you of her dirt, meanness, deceit, and hypocrisy. She courts every person that has a Carriage, and sends to request to accompany them, and I suppose possibly pleads as an excuse, that she has lent hers to her rich friends." Mrs. Thornton's portrait of Susannah reaches epic Hogarthian proportions—"She has an old Grizzled Wig Which I suppose cost her two pence, it has been a Man's, Which she Wears of a morning to save a female one the colour of her hair. An Old Handkerchief coloured is tied ... "—as does Sylvia's last mention of her—"I have had a visit from Mrs Dobson with powder, false curls, lappets, black worsted stockings full of holes." While Sylvia emphasizes Susannah's untidiness and oddness, Mrs. Thornton's focus on her reluctance to use her "woman's" wig alludes not only to her frugality but also to her compromised femininity. An intellectual woman is an unnatural creature: "<u>our Friend</u> Dobson goes at Canterbury by the name of the <u>learned Pig</u>; is not it well named?" cruelly comments Sylvia in another letter. To be an intellectual woman was to be a freak.[4]

But Susannah was not simply the victim of a blind prejudice; there were rational causes for people's dislike of her. She was affected and loquacious, and her letters

---

[4] The maliciousness of the term "learned pig" deepens when we learn that such pigs actually existed. One such pig debuted in Dublin in 1783, and then, after touring the provinces, arrived in London in 1785 (the date I have given the Sylvia Brathwaite letter in which the reference appears). See Ricky Jay, *Learned Pigs & Fireproof Women* (New York, 1986) 9–27.

betray signs of stinginess: when she desires to use other people's things rather than her own; when she insists on being the visitor rather than the visited; when she frets about postal duties and urges Lydia to seek reimbursement for possible overpayments; and when, in order to get her money's worth out of the paper she has purchased, she fills it to overflowing. Moreover, dislike of Dobson extended beyond Lydia Clerke's circle. According to Frances Burney, Dobson was ambitious to get into Mrs. Thrale's circle, but the latter, "not liking her advances, has always shrunk from them."[5] So too did Burney, who, upon being introduced to Dobson, described her vain attempts to escape the bluestocking's gushing praises.[6] When Susannah confided that she made £400 with her life of Petrarch, Burney expressed amazement at the older woman's lack of tact.[7] Uncomfortable with the intensity and tenor of Dobson's conversation, she summed up Susannah's character thus: "[T]hough course, low bred, forward, self-sufficient, & flaunting, seems to have a strong & masculine Understanding, & parts that, had they been united with modesty, or fostered by Education, might have made her a shining & agreeable woman,—but she has evidently kept low Company, which she has risen above in *Literature*, but not in *manners*."[8] Although Burney's portrait is more balanced than Mrs. Thornton's or Sylvia's, it is still etched in acid. Dobson does not fit in. She is unnaturally masculine, immodest, and excessive in speech and action. Vulgar and probably not born to the class in which she now circulates, Dobson is guilty of what in *The Wanderer* Burney identified as "the unqualified bluntness of the curious underbred."[9]

While there is much in Susannah's epistolary logorrhea to suggest that she was not an easy person to like, and to help us understand Thrale's and Burney's reluctance to befriend her, it is important to remember that conceit and unnaturalness were staples of eighteenth-century portraits of the intellectual woman. As soon as a woman expressed intellectual pretensions, she was seen and treated differently. Thrale and Burney and the members of Lady Clerke's circle might have withdrawn from Susannah in an attempt to separate themselves from a woman who, it was believed, more clearly fit the prevailing contemporary stereotype, as defined by Lady Mary Wortley Montagu in her letters: "a tatling, impertinent, vain, and Conceited

---

[5] Betty Rizzo, ed., *The Early Journals and Letters of Fanny Burney* (Montreal and Kingston, 2003) 4:94.

[6] Rizzo, *Early Journals* 4:105–6.

[7] It may be unfair to note that when Thomas Lowndes offered Burney £20 for *Evelina*, her debut novel, she asked for 10 guineas a volume. According to Lars Troide, general editor of the most recent edition of Burney's journals and letters, "Fanny Burney agreed to the lower sum" (2:288n.). Perhaps part of Burney's contempt for Dobson was motivated by the huge disparity in the worth accorded their literary labors.

[8] Rizzo, *Early Journals* 4:106.

[9] Frances Burney, *The Wanderer* (Oxford, 2001) 606.

Creature."[10] Significantly, even the most highly praised learned women did not escape contamination. In 1782, Burney expressed her dismay that she has been included in a newspaper squib about "literary ladies": "Do you know they have put me again into the newspapers, in a copy of verses made upon literary ladies,—where are introduced Mrs. Carter, Chapone, Cowley, Hannah More, Mrs. Greville, Mrs. Boscawen, Mrs. Thrale, Mrs. Crewe, Sophy Streatfield, and Mrs. Montagu? In such honourable company, to repine being placed, would, perhaps be impertinent; so I take it quietly enough; but I would to heaven I could keep clear of the whole!"[11] Burney may admire the women with whom she has been compared, but even in such excellent company, there is much to fear. To be categorized as a learned lady was a fate to be avoided. And perhaps one way to escape that fate was to single out and separate oneself from other women perceived as more guilty of the crime than oneself.

Certainly this is what seems to be happening in the excerpt from Lennox's *Euphemia* which serves as one of the epigraphs to this chapter. In Maria Harley's account of the conversation between two of her uncle's guests (one of whom, Mr. Harley, she expects to marry), which she records for the benefit of her friend Euphemia, masculine dislike of learned women is presented in scathing detail. Lady Cornelia is accused of ostentatious display, of using "learned gibberish," of exhibiting "pedantic stiffness" and "unintelligible conceit," and of awing her hearers with dogmatic criticisms. Ominously, Maria Harley remains silent during the exchange, only recording her smug self-satisfaction when Mr. Greville looks at her approvingly as a "charming" girl by contrast ("Can you guess who he meant, my dear?" she coyly asks her friend Euphemia).

It is difficult to determine Lennox's position during this exchange. She might be satirizing learned ladies; or she might be looking askance at men who speak so complacently about what they do not understand; or she might be questioning Maria Harley's willingness to separate herself from "other" women. More than likely she was doing all three at once. Certainly Lennox understood the ways men use women against one another and just how completely women participate in their own subordination. When the men praise Maria for her charm, elegance, and "true genius" in the same breath with which they revile the earnest learned ladies, they use a very old ploy indeed. In his letter to her, The Reverend Thomas Winstanley tells Lydia she is better than most other women: "In attempting to do you service, I will not treat you as I would do the generality of your sex ... ." In one of her letters, Sylvia tells Lydia that her "poor soldier" believes she has a firmness few women possess, and she wholeheartedly agrees. It is difficult to resist such disarming masculine compliments. Lennox herself was accustomed to receiving them. Several times, Johnson compared

[10]   Robert Halsband, ed., *The Complete Letters of Lady Mary Wortley Montagu* (Oxford, 1967) 1:45. The passage comes from a letter to Gilbert Burnet dated 20 July 1710.
[11]   Charlotte Barrett, ed., *Diary & Letters of Madame D'Arblay* (1778–1840) 2:76.

her with other women and usually found her the fairest of them all. We will never know if Lydia, like Maria and Sylvia, congratulated herself on her superiority to her kind, or if Lennox congratulated herself on Johnson's compliments. Although in *Euphemia* she represented the mechanisms by which such preferences appear natural and reasonable, she also seems aware that such compliments divide women and disadvantage the learned woman. Still, in the *Euphemia* excerpt, she clearly prefers women like Maria Harley and Euphemia Neville to Lady Cornelia and Miss Sandford. Euphemia and Maria are her heroines; Lady Cornelia and Miss Sandford are objects of satire. Deeply engaged in the life of the mind, the translator of French memoirs as well as the author of a controversial study of Shakespeare, Lennox nevertheless used her novel to represent good men mocking intellectual, self-reliant women, thereby contributing to the eighteenth-century bluestocking's dis-ease with her own difference.

Preliminary to this satirical scene, we are given an even more dubious portrait of the two intellectual friends:

"But here comes the virgin huntress, with Mr. Greville on one side of her, and Mr. Harley on the other. I protest she does not accompany Lady Cornelia in the carriage, but mounts her steed with most masculine agility to escort her female friend. Her military riding-habit, the fierce cock of her hat, the intrepid air of her countenance, make her have the appearance of a very respectable guard. Ah! what a pity she has petticoats!" (2:162)

Clearly, the hero (and soon to be husband of the heroine of the novel) is disturbed by the woman's unseemly behavior. With the detail of "the fierce cock of her hat," Lennox subtly (or perhaps not so subtly) underscores the fears that men experience when confronted with what they perceive as the unnatural masculinity of a woman who prefers to ride on a horse rather than in a carriage and who wears pants rather than petticoats.

When Frances Burney first meets Susannah Dobson she describes her as dressed in a riding habit. This piece of information suggests that Susannah might even be the model for Lennox's Amazonian Miss Sandford, who "vaults into her saddle like another Hotspur." Although they must have known one another, for they were members of the same circle of acquaintance and both were learned women, Lennox makes no overt mention of Dobson in any of her extant letters. Perhaps in her unpleasant portrayal of the two learned ladies, Lennox covertly expresses her dislike of Susannah and other such ambiguous women and her desire to avoid contamination by association.

It is interesting that both Burney and Lennox use a riding habit to signify something out of the ordinary and in questionable taste. How out of the ordinary was it? The journals of Lady Mary Coke present a mixed accounting of such a sartorial choice. In a footnote, James A. Home, the editor of Coke's journals, argues that a riding habit was the usual morning dress of English ladies at this time (late 1760s/

early 1770s) whether traveling or not. Although a riding habit may have been common in the morning, Mary Coke declines dinner with a prince because she is so dressed. Also, when she meets in Turin the young Princess of Carignan on horseback, she finds her dress inappropriate: "She appear'd to me intirely in Men's Clothes, which I cannot reconcile with that delicacy which is so becoming in that sex." In a footnote to this entry, Home observes that wearing men's clothes was one of the charges against the Queen of Denmark, Caroline Matilda.[12] So, though sometimes deemed improper, queens, princesses, and even the very proper Lady Mary Coke wore riding habits. Such a sartorial choice could be represented as quotidian and ordinary or as extraordinary and injudicious transgression. Just as modern fashions evoke complex and contradictory responses in different people according to class and age and time of day, just so it must have been in the eighteenth century. Nevertheless it is significant how often wearing such an outfit was used to designate and deride the intellectual learned woman throughout the eighteenth and nineteenth centuries.

While the oddities of a male intellectual were also satirized, he was not as universally condemned as his female counterpart. In fact, his peccadilloes could become objects of veneration as well as humor. Samuel Johnson is a perfect example of this different treatment. Boswell's descriptions of him may read surprisingly like Thornton's description of Dobson, but his tone is not at all the same: "His brown suit of cloaths looked very rusty: he had on a little old shrivelled unpowdered wig, which was too small for his head; his shirt-neck and knees of his breeches were loose; his black worsted stockings ill drawn up; and he had a pair of unbuckled shoes by way of slippers."[13] Like Dobson, Johnson was often represented as odd, poorly dressed, stingy, and manipulative. Nevertheless, Johnson became the highly respected center of a vast circle, or series of circles, and went on to give his name to the age. Harry Maty, the Clerke brother-in-law who appears several times in the Lydia Clerke letters, may be accused of relying too much on art and too little on common sense, but he is always treated with humor and love. "Harry," Ann Clerke observes in one of her letters, "is a very honest fellow but a great oddity." Although his friends and family may have gently mocked him, they never reviled him.

Female Friendship

The women in Lydia Clerke's circle may have distrusted Susannah's excesses, but they were themselves autodidacts. Thoughtful, contemplative, spiritual, and even philosophical, they wrote eloquently and passionately about their own and others'

---

[12]   James A. Home, ed., *The Letters and Journals of Lady Mary Coke* (Edinburgh, 1889–1896) 3:305n.; 4:317, 317n.
[13]   James Boswell, *The Life of Samuel Johnson* (London, 1973) 1:245.

ideas. They were widely read and their letters expressive, often poetic. They commented on the books they read, on the conversations they heard, and on affairs of state, and freely condemned and praised princes, prime ministers, kings, and queens. Even Ann Clerke, buried as she felt she was in rural Wethersfield, read Newton (or, at least, read about his optical theories).

Why then did they feel such contempt for Susannah? Perhaps it was not so much her intellectual enthusiasms that offended them as the uncertain currents of her friendship. In her letters, we see a woman congenitally uncomfortable in relationships. She attributes her uncertainties to her lack of breeding: "She would give them beside the french a little of that bon ton I am so wanting in my self," she writes of a candidate for governess. She insists on Lydia's superiority to her in everything: "You who have seen many and some very capital ones will judge with more Truth of the Superiority given to this, but do you think the Virgin an expressive figure? To me she appear'd not so." And she defers to Lady Clerke on almost every subject: "You who so perfectly well know in this and every Subject both Works and Authors be so good to inform me whom you esteem to have been the Author of these Memoirs & whether you do not almost adore the Patroness of Leibnitz." She begins to sound very much like a woman who has moved up in class but not yet learned all the customs of the new country she has entered. She even, perhaps unconsciously, waxes satiric as she describes a crowded assembly to Lydia: "I own I did wish for you to have honour'd and Patronizd [our Assembly] but this was a favor I ought not to have Wish'd as such a crowd would have been as [irksome] to you as it was Amusing to Us dull Ignorant Country People, who see such fine things only once a year or twice." She not only accuses Lady Clerke of feeling superior to country folk, who are so dull-witted as to enjoy assemblies, but she also implies that Lydia is hypocritical, for, even if she claims to dislike such events, she still attends them; in fact, it is because she attends so many that they have become dull and routine for her. No wonder Susannah writes elsewhere, "I am convinced my Beloved Creature Letters are Unfaithful Dictators in any Points of Intricate Debate." She suspects that her words and intentions get away from her. She is better in person than on paper.

Susannah's ambiguous epistolary references reach a high (or low) with her allusions to Lydia's possibly indecorous behavior while in France. Distraught about her husband's behavior, Lydia must have written to her women friends for advice and consolation. Susannah responds by eagerly cautioning her friend against being too agreeable when in the company of a certain gentleman. Employing infelicitous French, Susannah urges Lydia to be more circumspect and to resist the "Douceurs" and "agreements" of men who have no right to admire her. She fears that Lydia may be tempted to commit sexual transgressions in a spirit of revenge against her husband, who has lost the place he once had in her heart. Susannah never states directly what John did to lose his place in Lydia's heart, but her emphasis on Lydia's sexual vulnerability suggests that his sin was sexual—perhaps adultery. Susannah fears that

Lydia might become guilty of the same sin in revenge. Susannah pleads with her friend not to entertain sentiments that might lead her astray. She is writing, she assures her friend over and over again, to save her soul. She apologizes for her directness and fears offending her friend, but she cannot restrain herself. Her friend is in danger; a true friend does her duty, even if she risks sounding censorious and consequently losing her friend.

Ascertaining the quality of Susannah's feelings for Lydia and the motives of her actions, especially in her first letter to Lydia, is not easy. Although she protests that she only desires to bring Lady Clerke peace of mind, she suspects her news will agitate rather than soothe. Just as her affirmations of humility begin to sound like perverse pride, so do her repeated calls for peace, calm, and tranquility begin to ring hollow. It takes her a long time to get to the subject of Lydia's dangerous French liaisons. She writes of many matters before introducing the subject, but her impending revelation is, whether consciously or unconsciously, clearly behind many of her preliminary and seemingly tangential remarks. When she describes the two volumes of Belfield's Letters and the change of scene from the trifles and dissipations of fashionable life in volume one to the anxieties and reflections of maturity in volume two, she anticipates the direction of possible changes in John and Lydia's life. And certainly, her ambivalence about broaching such a subject propels the narration of what is to my mind the strangest incident in the entire collection of letters: "When your letter came I was just pronouncing your Name with Awe. I had caught a Wasp and was violently busy in Squeezing out the Sting from its Tail and in Eyeing its clever and fierce Visage. I desired Johnson to help me as it was a Work of great Labor and Importance and was just saying, if my dear & beloved Mrs Clerke was here I must not in her Presence do this—Down went all the things when your Letter came and the Sting half out and half in remains for further operation at my leisure Hours." As Susannah prepares to thrust her own sting into her friend, her description of an encounter with a wasp comes to represent her misgivings about proceeding. While she might believe that her work is of great importance and must be completed, she yet worries that Mrs. Clerke will interrupt it in unexpected ways and cause it to remain suspended. The image of Susannah eyeing the "clever and fierce Visage" of the wasp as she removes its sting becomes a self-reflexive mirroring of such complexity that it would seem Dobson wants to take the sting out of her own tail/ tale even as she dips it in French venom.

Upset by Susannah's first letter, Lydia, in her response, must have accused her friend of severity. It is to this word and accusation that Susannah returns again and again in her second letter, even though Lydia obviously told her she did not want to return to the subject. Unfortunately, however, once Susannah has a bee in her bonnet (or a wasp by its sting) she will not let go. In her second letter, she repeatedly defends herself and insists on the rightness of her actions. It is possible that, in response,

Lydia withdrew not only from Susannah but also (briefly) from her sister-in-law Ann Clerke, who was unwilling to dump Dobson.

In many ways, Susannah's two extant letters to Lydia become a catalog of the varieties of women's friendships and falling outs. Susannah is capable of intense friendship as well as intense dislike. When she writes about Mrs. Fairfax, her new neighbor, Susannah demonstrates her willingness to work hard at friendships. At first reserved and unfriendly, Mrs. Fairfax subsequently revealed many "Beauties" in her "conversation & manner." Dobson also expresses a sophisticated understanding of the jealousies that can fracture women's friendships. She narrates in great detail the history of her relationship with "Moritt." Although Moritt brought Lydia and Susannah together because she thought they had much in common, she now believes that Dobson prefers Mrs. Clerke to her and, in retaliation, has closed her door against Mrs. Dobson: "it was plain that from the moment she saw my ardent attachment to you, she was unhinged in all her manner toward me." Dobson seeks Lydia's help in closing the breach; she does not want to lose either Moritt or Lydia.

Susannah not only works hard at holding on to the friendships she has, but she also behaves very kindly toward women who need her patronage. She writes about two German women left penniless by their father's unexpected death, who visit her neighborhood in search of employment. She not only considers accepting the older sister as governess to her daughters but she is full of praise for both sisters.

While most of Susannah's references to other women demonstrate compassion, friendliness, and unrelenting earnestness, there is her unmitigated dislike of the mysterious and very briefly mentioned Mrs. Campbell and Cathcart. Susannah vehemently dislikes these two women and expresses her fear that other women have not been as lucky as she to escape their artful hypocrisies. Miss and Mrs. Duncombe are, unfortunately, caught in the coils of their friendship along with "M.t." Although other women may be deceived by Mrs. "C.t." Susannah is not, and only appears to remain her friend out of fear. Consequently, she asks Lydia to help her escape running into her again, for "I have no capacity to behave properly to such doubtful Characters and from Ignorance and the fear of doing wrong always exceed some way or other in my deportment to them." Significantly, her strongest piece of evidence against Mrs. Campbell and Cathcart is their dislike and envy of Mrs. Montagu.

The unnerving complexities of her own life experiences may have led Dobson to write *A Dialogue on Friendship and Society*. Written in the form of a dialogue between Amanda and Aphasia, this book, published in 1777, presents an array of perspectives on friendship. At moments, it seems as if Dobson used the book to continue her argument with Lydia Clerke about the need for friends to be honest with one another: "The more perfect our friendship therefore is, the less blind shall we be to the errors of our friend, and the less willing to conceal them when they ought to be mentioned; but that secret charm which is spread over affection will not render such a liberty irksome as it must be in the common attachments of life."[14] Friends, she insists once again, warn one another against dangers. Elsewhere, another observation of Dobson's suggests that Mrs. Clerke never forgave the learned lady for her "severity": "Of this we may be sure, that those who cannot forgive a fault when it *has* been acknowledged; or who having allowed it was to be forgiven, are yet so ungenerous as to bring it again to view, are not only incapable of friendship, but must even be destitute of virtue and benevolence; and such a disposition is not only the most unkind and unpleasant, but it is also the most unserviceable turn of mind we can possess, in a short passage through a frail world!"[15] If at first Lady Clerke forgave Susannah for her severity in the "French letter," something remained unforgivable. Therefore, years later, Dobson used her dialogue on friendship to protest Lady Clerke's unjust severity toward her, as well as to promote her views of friendship, and to fortify her belief in her own righteousness.

Susannah's amiability makes another startling appearance in the historical record. In James Boaden's 1833 edition of Elizabeth Inchbald's memoirs, we learn that upon publication in 1791 of *A Simple Story*, Inchbald's first novel, Mrs. Dobson sent her a letter of appreciation. Inchbald answered the letter "immediately" and called upon Dobson, who presented her with an Aeolian harp. Drawing on Inchbald's papers (most of which are now hopelessly dispersed or lost), Boaden sums up their friendship: "she [Dobson] had a carriage at her disposal, and it was frequently at Mrs. Inchbald's service; but the elegant Troubadour was somewhat capricious, and perhaps expected from her civilities greater homage than her new friend ever paid to any body. They disputed sometimes over a table of delicacies, and the adorer of Petrarch became cross, and then cool; but the occasional clouds passed away, and the intercourse between the ladies was not interrupted by their rival pretensions to either beauty or wit."[16]

Boaden's narrative is remarkable on several counts. There is the surprising reappearance of a carriage. Knowing how bitterly Mrs. Thornton complained about Susannah's false promises of carriage rides, I wonder if Dobson really did lend her carriage to Inchbald or if she played the same trick on Inchbald that she did on Thornton. I also find it fascinating that Boaden emphasized Susannah's wit and beauty at the same time that he reiterated the difficulties of friendship with her. Though she was mercurial, Dobson was, according to Boaden, an important acquaintance for Inchbald: "Mrs. Inchbald, though at times she hardly felt secured of it, really possessed a very distinguished place among the friends of Mrs. Dobson. That accomplished woman died on the 1st of October, and Mrs. Inchbald received a ring, to be worn in remembrance of her. This acquaintance, with the frequent use of

---

[14] Susannah Dobson, *A Dialogue on Friendship and Society* (London, 1777) 127–8.
[15] Dobson 136–7.
[16] James Boaden, ed., *Memoirs of Mrs. Inchbald* (London, 1833) 1:293.

her carriage, and the constant invitation to her table, when in *the mood*, she owed to her best friend Mrs. Phillips, to whom she was proved to owe still higher obligations, during a long life."[17] After having read so many disparaging remarks about Susannah, it was encouraging to find that at least one commentator found her an accomplished and elegant woman whose friendship, however capricious, was worth keeping.

Both Boaden and Annibel Jenkins, Inchbald's most recent biographer, assume that Inchbald's friendship with Dobson began in 1791, when Dobson congratulated Inchbald on the publication of *A Simple Life*. There is reason to suspect, however, that their friendship began several years earlier. Boaden notes that Mr. and Mrs. Inchbald visited Liverpool from October to December 1776. While there, she read the "Man of Feeling" and the "Man of Nature," Valerius Maximus (in French), and Horace (in English). Given that Susannah Dobson lived in Liverpool at that time as the wife of a well-respected doctor and that she was the center of a thriving literary circle, I wonder if Inchbald and Dobson did not meet then. Is it not possible that Inchbald found a kindred spirit in Mrs. Dobson and became a part of her literary circle? As if to anticipate the negative consequences of such a possibility, which might turn Inchbald into a learned lady like Susannah, Boaden assures his reader that Mrs. Inchbald "neither felt nor fancied herself a commentator. She was sensible, not learned."[18] If it was problematic to be a learned lady in the 1770s and 1780s, it was even more so by 1833, the date of Boaden's tribute to Inchbald.

Lesbian Lover?

While other women were important to Susannah, Lydia seems to have been very special. Often Susannah addresses Lydia as one might address a lover. Susannah remains so focused on Lydia and other women in her letters that she mentions her husband only once: "The Time creeps on till I shall be reunited with my Love [Mrs. Clerke] the Doctor who says he loves you monstrously (a fine thing truly!) looks as if he imagined I shall never come Home again or be able to leave my dearest C—how I shall indeed ever be able to leave You if I am once again bless'd in your Society I know not." Oddly, rather than present her husband as jealous of her attention to her lady friend, she presents him as her competitor for the love of Mrs. Clerke.

There is other evidence that Susannah's relationship with her husband was not what it should have been. When I visited the Toxteth Chapel in Summer 2003, where Susannah and Matthew's daughter was interred upon her death in 1778 (and where, presumably, 19 years earlier they were married), I met two members of the congregation who kindly let me in to view the ancient building and, unasked, spoke

---

17 Boaden 1:352.
18 Boaden 1:73.

of the strangeness of the memorial to the Dobson daughter. Having recently found a translation of the epitaph in the *Transactions of the Unitarian Historical Society*, I agreed with their judgment:

> She is dead
> My beloved daughter,
> Elisa,
> My pretty, winsome, kind-hearted
> daughter is dead.
> Very simple she was and withal very intelligent,
> accomplished and well-read,
> pure in heart and spiritually minded,
> and she is dead.
> Farewell, dear Elisa, farewell!
> Always will you be regretted by your grieving father;
> regretted but, thanks be to God,
> not lost to me,
> for a happier day will dawn
> when I shall see you again, my daughter,
> and live with you for ever and ever.
> Matthew Dobson to his dear sweet and blessed
> daughter Elisa,
> who, at the age of seventeen
> and in the year of our Lord 1778,
> departed peacefully to heaven.[19]

While the inscription is not unusual in terms of its sentiment, its omission of any reference to Susannah, the dear departed's mother, suggests some uncommon circumstance. Perhaps the daughter died while her mother was away on one of her many visits to her women friends. Perhaps Matthew blamed Susannah for the death of their daughter. Whatever the cause of his pique, not only is Susannah excluded while on earth from remembrance of the dear departed, but when Matthew pictures himself with his daughter in the hereafter, he pointedly leaves out his wife.

How are we to construe Susannah's relationship to her husband? What can we surmise about their life together? What did he think about her friendships with other women? Did he find them odd? And how were such determinations made? And by whom? Did he find the language with which she addressed Lady Clerke excessive or not? How did Lady Clerke respond to Susannah's endless and effusive compliments? Why did Susannah offer them? What did she hope to gain with such extravagant epistolary paeans? Do they suggest that the relationship between Lydia and Susannah was more than friendship, at least on Susannah's part?

---

[19]   *Transactions of the Unitarian Historical Society* 237.

There has been, in recent years, much debate about the varieties of eighteenth-century women's sexuality. In *English Sexualities, 1700–1800*, Tim Hitchcock sees the eighteenth century as a period of transition which witnessed an evolution from "lascivious woman" to "romantic friend." He argues that "the rise of romantic friendship ensured that lesbianism remained an acceptable facet of female society." He would probably class Susannah's feelings for Lydia as romantic friendship.[20] Emma Donoghue, writing from a lesbian perspective in *Passions Between Women*, describes a wide range of practices and attitudes and questions the validity of progressive models. Affirming the need for flexibility when interpreting the long history of women engaging in sexual relations with other women, she points out that we are just beginning to decode the words earlier lesbians used to describe their activities. Rather than simply label women as "romantic friends" or "sapphicks," she prefers to emphasize how often the same woman could be seen differently by different people at different times.[21] As Judith Butler notes, "[T]here is no necessarily common element among lesbians."[22]

As has already been pointed out, Hester Lynch Thrale did not like Susannah. She saw her as odd, jealous, mad, violent, and inconsistent. In a footnote to her famous *Thraliana*, she accuses Susannah of nasty uncleanness: "The James Family & Mrs Lewis are the only People I am free with—yet I can't bear to tell even them the Truth—I am often on the Brink of confessing all to Dr Dobson, but his Wife is *so odd*. I believe this nasty Bath is a Cage of unclean birds—Strange Stories are related both of that odious Mrs Dobson & charming Mr James; would I were far away from them all!"[23] Given Thrale's almost obsessive concern with "unnatural" relationships between women, it is tempting, indeed obligatory, to see this tirade as referring to Dobson's sexuality.[24] Also, there is guilt by association, since elsewhere Thrale describes Mr. James, the man with whom Thrale links Susannah, as a Sodomite: "old Sir Horace Mann & Mr James the Painter had such an odd way of twirling their Fingers in Discourse;—& I see Suetonius tells the same thing of one of the Roman Emperors."[25] If the "charming" Mr. James is a sodomite, than what is the "odious" Mrs. Dobson? While Hester Thrale cannot settle on a term, she implies that Susannah's love of women is unclean, as unclean as Mr. James's love of men. When

---

[20] Tim Hitchcock, *English Sexualities, 1700–1800* (New York, 1997) 87.

[21] Emma Donoghue, *Passions Between Women: British Lesbian Culture, 1668–1801* (New York, 1993) 1–30.

[22] Judith Butler, "Imitation and Gender Insubordination," in *Inside/Out: Lesbian Theories, Gay Theories*, Ed. Diana Fuss (New York, 1991) 17.

[23] Hester Lynch Thrale, *Thraliana: The Diary of Mrs. Hester Lynch Thrale*, Ed. Katharine C. Balderston (Oxford, 1942) 1:595n.

[24] *Passions Between Women* 30; Donoghue describes Hester Thrale as "always on the lookout for sexual perversion."

[25] *Thraliana* 2:875n.

Mrs. Thornton complains in one of her letters about Susannah's secret assignations in London ("Unless she is engaged to a party at cards, she always goes to London, is set down at Hyde Park corner, and the Coachman at between ten and eleven waits at the corner of some street for her, but never hardly knows where she has been"), is she describing the activities of an eighteenth-century lesbian looking for companionship?

Thraliana also gives us insight into Matthew Dobson as a physician. He was trustworthy and treated his patients with gentle consideration. When Thrale wanted to marry Gabriel Piozzi, a younger man who was formerly a musician in her family, most of her friends and family were against the match. Dobson, on medical grounds, urged the return of Piozzi, whom she had sent from her at the request of her children and others. He declared to her daughter Sophia that her mother's life depended upon the return of Piozzi. When Thrale writes that she is on "the Brink of confessing all to Dr Dobson," to what can she be referring? Given that the note was written on 7 June 1784, perhaps she wanted to confess doubts about her upcoming marriage to Piozzi. Because Dobson supported her marriage and was on the fringe of her circle of acquaintance, Thrale might have felt freer to confess her hesitations to him, rather than to her unsympathetic friends and family. Then again, Thrale might have been ready to confess all she knew about Susannah to her husband. But that seems unlikely.

If we try to know "all" about Susannah we are surrounded with uncertainties. While the Thrale circle despised her, the Clerke circle was less condemnatory, at least at first. Ann Clerke cared for Susannah, and so did Lydia. But Lydia's feelings for Susannah must have been mixed. She was both repelled by and drawn to her. It is even possible that, in 1776, when Lady Clerke sought shelter against the storm of her husband's financial collapse, she accepted Dobson's open invitation to come to her. According to Lennox's first letter, Lydia was at Liverpool (which is where Susannah lived) at that difficult time. However, she probably quickly fled again as we learn from Lennox's perplexities about Lady Clerke's subsequent whereabouts: "I have been utterly ignorant of your motions, I thought you would have told me when you left Leverpool. I knew not that you were at Buxton I was in doubt whether you intended to come to town or not." Although Susannah wanted to console and thereby draw Lydia to her, her aggressive love drove the young and vulnerable widow away.

In the introduction to her ambitious study *The Renaissance of Lesbianism in Early Modern England*, Valerie Traub emphasizes the complexities of sixteenth- and seventeenth-century representations of lesbianism: "Rather than being organized through concepts of in and out, secrecy and disclosure, oppression and liberalism, the early modern representation of lesbianism is governed by tensions between visibility and invisibility, possibility and impossibility, significance and insignificance.[26]

---

[26] Valerie Traub, *The Renaissance of Lesbianism in Early Modern England* (Cambridge, 2002) 33.

Traub's use of the passive voice makes it difficult to locate the site of the tensions she describes. Are the tensions inherent in the representation? Or in the author or painter? Or in the early modern spectator/ reader? Or in the contemporary (twenty-first century) spectator/ reader who experiences the frisson of discovery ("Imagine my surprise!" as several researchers have expressed it) of something that might or might not be significant, visible, possible? While focusing on early modern England, Traub's arguments, however ambiguous, can help us navigate the currents of Susannah's inchoate sexuality. As we read and reread Susannah's words and the words written about her we discern a very complex system of images that resists our unraveling efforts. We must tease out the threads extremely carefully if we are not to destroy the fabric of the discourse altogether.

Dobson loved Clerke, there can be little doubt about that. She wanted to be a good friend, but with her wigs, handkerchiefs, endless letters, and equivocal flattery, she was not always likeable. The turns of her temper made friendship with her neither easy nor simple. A complex woman, a thoughtful woman, an aspiring and intellectually curious woman, she could also alienate others and render herself censurable. Uncertain of her status and her abilities, inscrutable and disagreeable, enthusiastic and warm, she remains a woman out of joint.

Chapter 5

Ann Clerke One

Physical surroundings were uncomfortable, overcrowded, unhealthy and, in winter, depressing. Visitors, William Pitt among them, were appalled at what they saw in rural Essex. A writer on life in north-west Essex in the 1770s returned again and again to the state of the houses, the roads and the villages themselves .... Some parishes lacked even a village street.

A.F.J. Brown, *Prosperity and Poverty: Rural Essex, 1700–1815* (1996)

Ann Clerke, Lydia Clerke's sister-in-law, is a younger sister of John Clerke. Born in 1738 and given her mother's name, Ann was the fourth child of Joseph and Ann Clerke to survive infancy. Eight years old when her mother died, she spent most of her life in Essex, living at Brook Farm with her father and her younger sister Sarah, and, as her father aged, caring for him in his decline. While we do not know when she died we know that she survived her father (who mentioned her in his will) but did not survive her sister Sarah (who died in 1818 and did not mention Ann in her will). The last notice of her in the public record can be found in the 1790 gamekeeper records for the Manor of Wethersfield and Codham Hall.[1] Ann was the responsible sister, the one who took care of everyone else, the one who served as the mediator when members of her family or circle of acquaintance quarreled. She witnessed her brother's wedding to Lydia Hammond in Alverstoke Parish Church in Gosport.[2] Warmth, generosity, steadiness, intelligence, and loneliness fill her letters.

Two of Ann Clerke's letters and Charles Clerke's two letters to Lydia form a subgrouping of their own. Written by siblings, an older sister and a younger brother, they are, not surprisingly, deeply interconnected, reflecting on similar topics from different angles and giving us insight into two very different worlds, a feminine world of cautious introspection and a masculine world of maritime adventure. As we shall see, when we read Ann's fourth and final contribution to *Circle*, the two worlds eventually converge in surprising ways.

Both Charles and Ann provide important information about the dynamics of the Clerke family as well as insight into the domestic tragicomedy in which they played significant roles. Unaware perhaps of the true causes of the deepening rift between John and Lydia, both Charles and Ann offer comfort and philosophical advice.

---

[1] Q/RSq4, f. 78, Essex Record Office.
[2] Photocopy of Parish Register, p. 216, no. 777, Hampshire Record Office.

In her first letter to Lydia, Ann finds herself caught between Lydia and Susannah. Ann hopes to repair their fractured friendship. Justifying her inability to give Susannah up, Ann tries, at the same time, to soothe her sister-in-law's angry feelings. She begs her friend to come down for a visit. Lydia would bring cheer to an otherwise gloomy household.

5

From: Ann Clerke, Wethersfield
To: Lady Clerke, at Mrs. Thornton's, in the Square, Kensington
Date: 1 February [1771]

Indeed my Dear Sister I have never deserved from you the disquietude your silence makes me suffer. How am I to account for it or what can I say. All I have now to ask of you is that you will (if this Letter finds you where I'm told you are expected at Mrs Thornton's) when you have paid your Visit to her come down into Essex where I have no doubt I shall convince you I have neither done, said, nor thought. any thing which ought to lessen me in your esteem. Nothing my Dear assure your self but what naturally occurs from the disagreeable circumstances with which I'm surrounded, & such as could [not] have created any disgust in your breast had not your imagination unkind to itself given them a source from a poison'd spring which you ought to have known my attachment to you better than ever to have supposed could have influenced me. You could not surely misconstrue what I said in my last. in regard to its being impossible for me to be so unreserved with you in regard to Mrs Dobson as I wish to be & always have been in all other respects. Need I explain the reason of this to you who know her so well, & how different a manner of proceeding she has to every other creature that let a person be ever so much attach'd to her, it is impossible some times not to laugh at her expence. But it would be unpardonable in me to communicate circumstances of this nature between two people so strongly prejudiced as you have lately been against each other. But let me beseech you, my Dear, to devest yourself of prejudice for a moment & impartially consider every perticular which has attended us. As to our first meeting you know & every circumstance which attended it, & every previous one which originated from yourself.

When I came down into Hampshire & found the terms you were upon, I was <u>well</u> aware disagreeable things might happen between us, & therefore was long diffident wither or not to pursue her acquaintance, for you well know my attachments are not of the mushroom sort. But, however disgusted you then seem'd to be with each other, it did not appear to me unlikely you might be very good friends again in time. What has occur'd since could neither be foreseen, nor thought of. I wish for both your sakes it could be for ever forgot. Nor should I despair of its being so were it not for the unkind offices of people fonder of promoting discord & hatred than peace & good will amongst their fellow creatures. But tho I must think more favorably of her than

5.1 Wethersfield Parish Church, where the Clerke family worshiped. Photo: Author's Collection

5.2 Brook Farm, where the Clerke family lived. Photo: Author's Collection

you perhaps think excusable from the unfortunate prejudices which have occur'd between you, this is no injury to you my Dear Sister. Consider my situation. How few amusements it affords me. Her Letters entertain me. She has treated me with the most assiduous attention & the fullest confidence by which she has created that kind of interest in my regard which a gratefull heart naturally wishes to pay where it thinks itself obliged. But you know her, you know me my Dear; let your own heart tell you the difference between this & that spontaneous affection which the heart only can give which neither can be purchased nor extorted. And then assure yourself you know as much as I can tell you of the Difference between my attachment to Mrs Dobson & you. Therefore let me once more entreat you not to add by this cruel silence to the disquiet of a Life in no danger of being too happy. But the only amends you can make me for what I have suffer'd must be by coming here that we may have a full explanation of all that is past. For without that I'm sure we are undone & this I can only have from yourself for I'm convinc'd by experience no third person can go between us without rendering us unhappy. I flatter myself you will have the pleasure of seeing your old acquaintance M^{rs} H [and] that from the present mood of all parties it will [have po]wer to render this house more agreeable [than] I had any reason to hope some time ago. Therefore [please] let me beseech you to think of coming as soon as you can. adieu God bless you & make you as happy as I wish you to be & believe me ever your truly affectionate, A Clerke

    Sat^{dy} night

    12, oclock   P:S my best Comp^{ts} to Mrs Thornton

Ann Clerke, Mediator

Essex experienced many changes during the eighteenth century. Most important was the great decline in the textile industry (during the 1740s, the period of Ann's youth). This loss, however, was offset by an advance in the agricultural trades, which must have encouraged her father in his many agricultural pursuits.[3] According to Essex historian A.F.J. Brown, Wethersfield was a "well-served village" with "four shops, two butchers, and a baker."[4] Nevertheless, Ann seems to have felt isolated. Her life, as she notes, was full of "disagreeable circumstances."

    In her first letter, written in the wake of a rupture between Lydia Clerke and Susannah Dobson, loneliness as well as the enduring and endearing qualities of her friendship come through clearly. She pleads with her sister-in-law to understand her situation ("How few amusements it affords me") and her unwillingness to give up

---

[3]   A.F.J. Brown, *Prosperity and Poverty: Rural Essex, 1700–1815* (Chelmsford, 1996) 22, 26–32.

[4]   Brown 37.

Susannah ("Her Letters entertain me"). She assures Lydia that her fondness for Susannah does not eclipse her love for Lydia. Caught in the middle, Ann tries to heal the breach not only between herself and Lydia but also between Lydia and Dobson. She does not want to lose either friend.

In order to protect both Susannah and herself, Ann chooses her words carefully as she negotiates the maze of conflicting interests in which she is caught. She explains to Lydia that she cannot speak as freely about Susannah as she did in the past, for to do so would widen rather than narrow the gap between them. She reminds her sister-in-law that it was she who introduced her to Susannah, a fact which is corroborated by Susannah in her second letter—"pray be kind enough to remember me to Miss Clark when you write, I would have given a great deal to have seen her again after your kind Introduction"—and that she hesitated becoming Susannah's friend. Because the woman was so peculiar, she anticipated that friendship with her would not be easy or untroubled. But because she believed Lydia and Susannah's friendship would weather the crisis it was then undergoing, she allowed herself to grow fond of Susannah and now does not want to reject her. She blames the intransigence of the present break on "the unkind offices of people fonder of promoting discord & hatred than peace and good will amongst their fellow creatures." Now that she has bonded with Dobson, Ann cannot give her up.

Ann's reluctance to give up Susannah suggests that despite her foibles, she could be a good friend. She could be amusing and attentive. Willingly sharing confidences and eagerly expressing interest in her friend's life and feelings, Susannah became a support on whom Ann leaned. Although she was not to every woman's taste, Mrs. Dobson won Ann Clerke's heart.

Ann may not want to give up Susannah, but she does not want to give up Lady Clerke either. She urges her sister-in-law to come to Essex so that "a full explanation of all that is past" might take place. She protests that no third party "can go between us without rendering us unhappy." She is right, for, as much as letters serve as third-party go-betweens, they can be duplicitous and unreliable. "Letters," as Susannah complained in one of her letters, "are Unfaithful Dictators in any Points of Intricate Debate." Every communication is fraught with peril. It can fail to reach its destination; it can be misunderstood upon arrival; it can circulate to unknown readers and have effects far beyond its original writer's intentions.

Chapter 6

Charles Clerke One

Tyrants, wicked Ministers, Conspirators, Inquisitors, nay Devils themselves, have had their several Apologists; and is a poor *Smuggler* a greater Monster than all these?

True Briton (1751)

I heard of the discovery of the American hemisphere and wept with Safie over the hapless fate of the original inhabitants.

Mary Shelley, *Frankenstein* (1818)

There is an air of truth apparent through the whole; and indeed, the author was so distinguished for his veracity, that it became a sort of proverb among his neighbours at Redriff, when any one affirmed a thing, to say it was as true as if Mr. Gulliver had spoke it.

Jonathan Swift, *Gulliver's Travels* (1726)

Charles Clerke (1741–79), Ann and John Clerke's brother and Lydia Clerke's brother-in-law, was, like John, drawn to the adventure and risk of a life at sea. The sixth child and fourth son of Joseph and Ann Clerke, Charles left home, at the age of 13, to make a career in the Royal Navy. After graduating from the Royal Naval Academy at Portsmouth, he joined the ship's company of the *Dorsetshire* and then the *Bellona*, frequently engaging with the French enemy. Once the Seven Years' War was over, Charles sailed on voyages of discovery. Under Commodore Lord John Byron, he made his first trip round the world (1764 to 1766). Two years later, he went around the world with Captain James Cook, sailing from 1768 to 1771. On his third (and Cook's second) voyage round the world, from 1772 to 1775, he sailed as second lieutenant of the *Resolution*. When he came home, he was arrested for his brother John's £4000-debt and sent to the King's Bench Prison where he contracted tuberculosis. On 10 February 1776, he was given the command of the *Discovery*, a ship which was to go with Cook's *Resolution* in search of a North-West passage. In July, after leaving prison, he went to sea. Just a little over three years later, on 22 August 1779, he died at sea and, seven days later, was buried at Kamchatka.

In his letters to Lydia, Charles presents himself as cheerful and affectionate. When he writes, on 19 May 1772, to tell her about his circumstances, he jests about his danger: "we've got into a Ship to go round the World, that wou'd not carry us safe to the Downs ... for I believe there never was such a Ship before upon the Seas, since Commodore Noah (who was the first Sea Officer of any kind of eclat that I ever heard of) to this present 19th of May 1772." Although he can find humor in his situation, it was indeed serious. The accommodations made for the naturalist Joseph Banks and his scientific equipment and entourage were destabilizing the ship; only after the structures were removed was the ship safe.[1] Angry that the ship no longer suited his needs, Banks outfitted another and invited Clerke to go with him to Iceland. Clerke declined.

From all accounts, Charles Clerke was a brave, humorous, generous, and well-liked young man. A complex human being, he was capable of great disregard of self, yet he was part of a movement of men and materials which took possession of large parts of the globe. To understand Charles Clerke is to understand a bit more fully this movement and the motivations of the men who risked their lives in quest of strange lands and exotic peoples. To read his words and the words written about him is to come face to face with the ambiguities of history.

In his first letter to Lydia he gives us insight into life in the navy. His ship the *Resolution* is not as resolute as it should be and he fears it may not be seaworthy. He also gives us more information about other sources of discord in John and Lydia's domestic life.

6

From: Charles Clerke, Resolution at Sheerness
To: Lady Clerke, [Gosport]
Date: 19 May 1772

Resolution at Sheerness Tuesday May 19/72

Doubt not but my very Dear Sister is much surprized she has not heard from me before; but don't accuse me of neglect my good Sis, till you've heard of our real situation—Major Sturgions (in Foots Minore) Marches and counter Marches, Orders and counter Orders, were but a joke to the confusd Sailings and Counter Sailings of the Resolution—

Have been in daily expectations of having it in my power to give you some absolute account of what was to become of us, but have been defeated in every scheme of that kind, till yesterday Morn: which brought us into Sheerness. In the first place my Dear Sister, we've got into a Ship to go round the World, that wou'd not carry us safe to the Downs; the Pilot absolutely wou'd take charge of her no farther, we've now got 12 leagues in 11 days, and the Pilot swore that his Carcass & character were in such jeopardy in Her, that he would go no farther; and is now gone up to the Navy Board to answer for his conduct in respect to her; which make no doubt but he very readily may, and acquit himself with honour; for I believe there never was such a Ship before upon the Seas, since Commodore Noah (who was the first Sea Officer of any kind of eclat that I ever heard of) to this present 19th of May 1772. The last

---

[1]   Cowley and Deacon 80–81.

18. The *Resolution*
Water-colour drawing by Henry Roberts

6.1   A reproduction of a watercolor by Henry Roberts of the *Resolution*, the ship
        on which Charles Clerke served as second lieutenant during his third voyage
        round the world. By permission of the Mitchell Library, State Library of New
        South Wales

time I had the pleasure to see my Dear Sis you know the Resolution was at Long Reach. We've left that place now 11 days. To be sure we've had rather a confusion of orders, and a little sailing backwards and forwards; but if 'twou'd have sav'd all our Lives, we cou'd not have got to the Downs, where we were order'd at our first sailing; tho' make no doubt but that some Vessels who sail'd at the same time with us, may have got 300 leagues off to Sea. Have sent an account to the Admiralty of the very extraordinary qualities of their good Ship, and they have ordered us in here, to make what alterations may be thought necessary; so hope and believe, we may have her transform'd into a safe and convenient Vessel: suppose our stay will be a fortnight or three weeks: will acquaint you as soon as I know, how we are to proceed, but intreat my good Sister to favour me with a few lines immediately upon the receipt of this; and tell me if any account is arrived from Madeira, of our Dear, good Knight. Do my Dear Sister, indeed you'll make me very happy. I shall be all anxiety 'till I hear from you. I know you're too good to keep me so did you know what I feel 'till your goodness relieves me.

Wrote my friend Banks an account of our Ship's demerits. He immediately apply'd for another, and believe has the grant of it if they cannot make this fit for our purpose. Hope they will, but we are at present at a great uncertainty what will be our destiny: shall know in a few days when you shall instantly be acquainted for I have a great deal to say to you. Indeed my Dear Sis I feel myself much hurt, least you shou'd think I've neglected by my silence that goodness which it ever shall be my principal study and endeavour to deserve; for my good, best friend I'm highly flatter'd and extremely happy in your friendship and affection; and will not be silent so long again if I only say what I must have said had I wrote a few days ago. My Dear Sister I'm all confusion, what I'm about can hardly tell, and what will become of me in 12 hours more, am sure I can't pretend to guess. I am &c &c: that must have been the purport of my letter Sis: and I was in daily & hourly hopes of having something more positive to tell you, but cou'd not 'till We came into Sheerness. Will certainly write again in a very few days, but my good friend write directly.

Peppin return'd the Wine to the Merchant at Calais again, so thank God there's no great loss there; tho' the Poor fellow was amidst numbers of perils and dangers with it, he has brought over three suits of fine Cloaths which are all very safe. He has been to see me onboard here, and will certainly wait upon you soon. Jack Wood has undertaken to get him to India. Poor fellow, he is to be sure a most unfortunate dog, but he was fortunate almost to a miracle in saving the Wine, but that was our Dear Johnny's fortune: Heaven grant good luck may ever attend the Dear Dear fellow; I wou'd ask, nor wish no more than his good benevolent heart deserves. <u>Oh my Dear Sis, we shall certainly see jolly days in Hill Street</u>. I enjoy it in prospect; God Bless him. To see him upon any Hill, or in any Street I'm sure wou'd make me exceedingly happy. No other Man on Earth gives me exquisite feelings, such grateful joys. Oh, the Dear fellow, how do I love him, but find my paper's out, so fare well for a few days, my Very Dear Sister and friend, pray write and make happy your unspeakably affectionate

        & obliged Brother
          Chas Clerke
You won't forget my proper Respects to Mrs Hammond

Smuggling

If Lydia wrote to her women friends about her growing suspicions of John's sexual dalliances, when she wrote to her brother-in-law Charles she expressed her concern about John's smuggling ventures. In his first letter to Lydia, Charles assures her that their "Dear Johnny's fortune [is saved]" and all will be well. Affirming that their "Dear, good Knight" will thrive, he urges Lydia to write him as soon as she knows anything about her husband, who is now in Madeira.

    According to Essex historian A.F.J. Brown, "the most blatant and least controlled form of crime [in Essex] was smuggling, which, particularly after the 1760s, became very profitable as a result of the higher taxes on spirits and some other commodities."[2] Smuggling occurred not only in Essex, but throughout England.[3] Graham Smith notes that from 1760 to 1780 smuggling reached unprecedented proportions and smugglers supplied regular orders as if they were legitimate merchants.[4] Tea, tobacco, brandy, wine, and other liquors, porcelain, and cloth (linens, calicoes, silk, and muslin) were traded. Many participated in the trade: not only the smugglers, but also all who sold clandestine goods (minor tradesman as well as large merchants who sought greater participation in the expanding global trade that came with imperial expansion); all who bought them (from the poorer classes who might purchase contraband at country fairs to the gentry and aristocracy who also purchased illegal goods in order to pay lower prices for luxury items); and landowners who allowed smugglers to use their lands and coastal borders. For many reasons, constables and military soldiers often turned away when they came across smugglers. Sometimes they were afraid of

---

[2]   Brown 148.

[3]   The following works contributed to my understanding of smuggling in eighteenth-century England: W.A. Cole, "Trends in Eighteenth-Century Smuggling," *The Economic History Review*, New Series, 10 (1958): 395–410; W.A. Cole, "The Arithmetic of Eighteenth-Century Smuggling: Rejoinder," *The Economic History Review*, New Series, 28 (1975): 44–9; Hoh Cheung and Lorna H. Mui, "'Trends in Eighteenth-Century Smuggling' Reconsidered," *The Economic History Review*, New Series, 28 (1975): 28–43; Paul Monod, "Dangerous Merchandise: Smuggling, Jacobitism, and Commercial Culture in Southeast England, 1690–1760," *The Journal of British Studies*, 30 (1991): 150–82; and Graham Smith, *King's Cutters: The Revenue Service and the War Against Smuggling* (London, 1983).

[4]   G. Smith 69.

retaliation; sometimes they were bribed. London was the chief market for contraband goods.

Historians, especially economic historians, argue about the extent and magnitude of the illicit trafficking, but all agree that it led to an increased consumption of luxury goods by all classes throughout the eighteenth century. Without the greater availability occasioned by lower prices, tea and tobacco and spirits might not have become as ubiquitous as they did by the end of the century. Smuggling was a significant economic activity; Paul Monod argues that it was "an alternative commercial culture."[5] Depending on a wide section of the populace and satisfying many people's interests, smuggling reached its apex in the 1770s, when the Clerke brothers were actively engaged in it, and did not disappear quickly. Although the Commutation Act of 1784, which lowered duties on many luxuries, contributed to the decline of smuggling as did the end of the American War of Independence, illicit trafficking did not entirely disappear until well into the nineteenth century.[6]

Smuggling seems to have been so widespread by the 1770s that one wonders why Charles writes in code. Because he does we cannot know who Peppin was (we are not supposed to know) although it is clear he returned wine to merchants at Calais (perhaps wine that he was unable to smuggle safely into England). Charles's need, in both his letters, to mask their activities suggests that smuggling was not as widespread or tolerated as some historians maintain. It was dangerous and sometimes one lost more than one gained. One could be arrested, fined, imprisoned. Charles takes Lydia's fears seriously and does all he can to allay them. Clearly he loved his sister-in-law and tried in every way possible to preserve and deepen the love she felt for her husband.

Charles apologizes repeatedly for not having written sooner, but explains he would only have filled his letter with uncertainties. He urges Lydia to look forward to the future when good luck shall have rewarded her husband's endeavors. He is confident that they will succeed: "<u>Oh my Dear Sis, we shall certainly see jolly days in Hill Street</u>." Charles was as confident as John that their smuggling endeavors would eventually succeed. Subsequent letters, however, prove the futility and fragility of these ambitions.

Imperialism in Action

J.C. Beaglehole, editor of the meticulous four-volume edition of Captain Cook's journals, beautifully sums up Charles's qualities: "Clerke was always cheerful, talkative, amusing, a generous spirit who made friends easily; tall, long-nosed, with a sparkling (and doubtless also roving) eye." He concludes, "it must be a difficult soul

---

[5]   Monod 180.
[6]   Monod 182.

who, reading [his] letters, does not feel his affection rise." In volume four of his work, a biography of Cook, Beaglehole praises Charles's handling of events in the wake of Cook's death. Reasoning that Cook was killed because he reprimanded a native in the midst of his people, Clerke refrained from retaliatory violence. In general, Beaglehole prefers Clerke to all of the other men on the journey, including Cook.[7]

In his dealings with the peoples he encountered on his journeys, Clerke was both prescient and prejudiced. Like most of the men around him, he arrogantly presumed his superiority as an enlightened European: "There are few Indians in whom I wou'd wish to put a perfect confidence, but of all I ever met with these [New Zealanders] shou'd be last, for I firmly believe them very capable of the most perfidious & most cruel treachery, tho' no People can carry it fairer when the proper superiority is maintained."[8] Animated by the spirit of his age, he could not help but see himself and his own kind as superior to the different peoples he met. Their habits were strange, their languages unintelligible, their responses unexpected.

When we look at contemporary descriptions of Clerke's and Cook's treatment of indigenous peoples, we see just how far Europeans were willing to go in their efforts to maintain a "proper superiority." In Lt Thomas Edgar Masters's *Journal of a Voyage undertaken to the South Seas*, we learn of extraordinarily harsh punishments meted out to natives for relatively minor infractions (or for what can be seen from our twenty-first-century perspective as misunderstandings resulting from cultural differences). On 24 June 1777, "Captain Clarke punished an Indian chief with 5 dozen Lashes for having stolen one Tumbler and two Wine Glasses during the time he was at Dinner with him."[9] Four days later, Captain Cook ordered even more severe punishments:

About 10 in the Morning three of the old Offenders who had ston'd our Centinels & Wood Cutters were taken prisoners—Captain Cooke punished one with 3 dozen Lashes, another with 4 dozen and the 3d with Six dozen Lashes—after this a strange punishment was inflicted on the Man which receiv'd Six dozen as Captain Cooke said that he might be known hereafter, as well as to deter the rest from theft or using us ill when on Shore—this was by scoring both his Arms with a common Knife by one of our Seamen Longitudinally and transversly, into the Bone—this the Man bore with all the Fortitude imaginable, as indeed they all did their punishments & but for all this they continued their insults and Thefts. Till the last day during our stay among these Islands, there were several things stole, but the greatest part, by application to Finou [a native interpreter], were restored again.

---

[7] Beaglehole 1:cxxxi; 2:xxxv; 3:lxxii; 4:674.

[8] Beaglehole 3:69n.

[9] ADD MS 36,528, f. 44: *A Journal of a Voyage undertaken to the South Seas on Discoveries by His Majesty's Ship Resolution and Discovery Captain James Cook and Cha^t Clerke Esq'rs Commanders*, Kept by [Lieut] Thomas Edgar Masters.

Even in an age known for the excessive brutality of its punishments, surely these actions were unusual. Masters must have thought so for he found the scoring of wounds to the bone "a strange punishment."

When he treated natives with appalling punishments for "barbarous" behavior, Charles participated in European efforts to justify appropriation and exploitation of "new" lands and peoples. But Charles, who also saw that European man brought disease, dis-ease, and chaos in his wake, was capable of imagining natives as superior to their European invaders and felt free to satirize his own kind. On 3 November 1766, he sent a letter to the Royal Society, via his brother-in-law Paul Henry Maty. It was subsequently published in the Society's *Philosophical Transactions* on 12 February 1767, under the title of "An Account of the very tall Men, seen near the Streights of Magellan, in the Year 1764, by the Equipage of the *Dolphin* Man of War, under the Command of the Hon. Commodore Byron." In it, Charles describes what happens when bellicose Europeans come upon a peaceful people: "The commodore [Byron] made a motion for them [the Patagonians] to go a little way from the water, that we might have room to land, which they immediately complied with, and withdrew thirty or forty yards; we then landed, and formed each man with his musquet, in case any violence should be offered. As soon as we were formed, the commodore went from us to them, then at about twenty yards distance; they seemed vastly happy at his going among them, immediately gathered round him, and made a rude kind of noise, which I believe was their method of singing, as their countenances bespoke it a species of jollity." Although the Europeans anticipated that they would be met with violence they were wrong. The Patagonians were peaceful. Rather than present arms they presented music. The only violence was the Europeans' readiness to use firepower against unarmed people.[10]

Clerke vouches for the truth of his story. He uses circumstantial and mathematical detail to give his report credibility. In his opening paragraph, he apologizes for his plainness, ascribing it to the presence of unembellished truth: "I wish I could embellish it with language more worthy your perusal; however, I will give it the embellishment of truth, and rely on your goodness to excuse a tar's dialect." His story may be plain and simple, but it is also filled with the marvelous: "They [the Patagonians] are of a copper colour, with long black hair and some of them are certainly nine feet if they don't exceed it. The commodore, who is very near six foot, could but just reach the top of one of their heads which he attempted, on tip toes, and there were several taller than him on whom the experiment was tried. They are prodigious stout, and as well and proportionally made as ever I saw people in my life .... The women, I think, bear much the same proportion to the men as our Europeans do; there was hardly a man there less than eight feet, most of them considerably more;

---

[10]   Charles Clerke, "An Account of the very tall Men," *Philosophical Transactions*, 57 (1767): 76–7.

the women, I believe, run from 7 ½ to 8. Their horses were stout and bony, but not remarkably tall; they are in my opinion from 15 to 15 ½ hands." Did Clerke's readers believe his story? Did he expect that they would? When the Royal Society published the tale, was its credibility enhanced or reduced? In *Far-Fetched Facts: The Literature of Travel and the Idea of the South Seas*, Neil Rennie notes that Horace Walpole likened the Patagonians found by Byron and his men to Swift's Brobdingnagians.[11] It is even possible that Mary Shelley knew of Clerke's report and used it to create Frankenstein's exceedingly tall, well-proportioned, black-haired monster. She might also have read some of the travel narratives of Cook's and Clerke's voyages in search of a North-West passage to create some of her novel's incidents and settings.

While Clerke's tall tale of tall men was unmistakably filled with fictional elements, there was truth in it too. He did travel to the Strait of Magellan, and he and his fellow officers did encounter peoples whose behaviors were unpredictable. Because real voyages could turn so easily into tall tales and fictions could be based on actual voyages, it is not always easy to discriminate between voyages in fact and voyages in imagination. People were thrilled by stories of distant places and oddities of human behavior. According to Percy Adams, the official journals of Byron, Wallis, Carteret, and Cook were runaway bestsellers. The public, or, to use eighteenth-century parlance, "the World" gobbled up these books.[12] If some people doubted the existence of tall men like the Patagonians, others did not. Especially in travel narratives the real and the imaginary became hopelessly entangled.

---

[11]   Neil Rennie, *Far-Fetched Facts: The Literature of Travel and the Idea of the South Seas* (Oxford, 1995) 78.
[12]   Percy Adams, *Travelers and Travel Liars, 1660–1800* (Berkeley, 1962) 38.

Chapter 7

Charles Clerke Two

And of the cannibals that each other eat,
The anthropophagi, and men whose heads
Do grow beneath their shoulders. This to hear
Would Desdemona seriously incline;
... and with a greedy ear
Devour up my discourse.

William Shakespeare, *Othello* (1604)

I have just received your letter, & laugh'd very much at Ld Strafford's idea of Mr Banks and Doctor Solander's having eat their companion. I did not hear they had been in any distress for provisions, & cannot suppose that choice wou'd have led them to such a meal.

Lady Mary Coke, *The Letters and Journals of Lady Mary Coke* (1771)

The ambivalence of colonial authority repeatedly turns from *mimicry*—a difference that is almost nothing but not quite—to *menace*—a difference that is almost total but not quite.

Homi K. Bhabha, "Of Mimicry and Man" (1994)

Written four years later, Charles's second letter lets us know he is still engaged in risky behaviors. He continues to defend the necessity and legitimacy of smuggling, and he has become friends with the notorious Duchess of Kingston. Moreover, he is imprisoned for debt as he awaits orders to set sail on his fourth and last voyage around the world.

In this letter, we also learn more of Charles's helpfulness (he is garnering votes for John Carnac, who was indeed appointed member of council at Bombay in 1776), and loyalty (he is visiting old family friends the Alexes and refuses to draw on his friend Kirkpatrick for money due him, even if it might help him settle with his creditors and escape prison). There is also a hint of anti-Semitism, for even if the second page of the letter is missing, we do know (from other letters) the origin of "the Philistines."

7

From: Charles Clerke, London
To: Lady Clerke, [Gosport]
Date: 11 April 1776

I'm quite asham'd my best friend to look at the date of your last letter. Indeed I frequently feel a sincere warmth of gratitude to Providence for giving you among your other Virtues such an abundant share of Benevolence and charity for your friends, for otherwise I fear I shou'd e'er this have been expung'd from that list in which it is my greatest happiness and ambition to retain a footing. Indeed my dearest Sis I'm perfectly and heartily sensible of your friendly indulgences and feel confoundedly <u>ugly</u> that I cannot render myself more worthy of them.

I hope long before this time our noble Cavalier has got possession of his Charcoal Dame with all her goods & Chattels. I know your idea of bringing the old Lass here and setting her in the right road to Heaven (Stockdale shou'd be her Pilot) but indeed my friend we must keep her among ourselves. We must not admit the Justice into the list, but upon good, firm, and well-bound conditions, for, between ourselves, was this <u>Disciple of Burn</u> once well establish'd with this diamond trim'd Queen (for objections I'm sure he wou'd have none) its by no means clear to me that either one of our [Foe's] would be a Pagoda the better for her.

I'm sorry this confounded distraction should thus keep perpetual War with us, for we must allow my Sis that a little distraction of our own has almost drove us under water and now the Devil has so manag'd it, that the distraction of others will not let us float again. But my dearest, best friend we must submit. Remember the old prescription: patience &c &c. Indeed it will do great things—God bless you, let not your noble heart be cast down; let us bear all cheerfully—for whilst you are easy I can never be unhappy. Indeed my Sis to see you cheerful, and the treat of a friendly smile wou'd rejoice my poor cast away heart amidst all the calamities this world cou'd possibly load it with.

I assure you, I was not idle in the business of our friend Mr Carnac. We are much oblig'd to your old acquaintance General Magra for the part he took in this affair at the instigation of your Ladyship. He procur'd us ten good Votes. Here has been the Allix's in Town. I stole as much of their company as I possibly cou'd. I need not tell you how much I honour them. They are now gone to Bath.

For God's sake, my Dear Sis, let nothing postpone your journey here past the 20th. My Bark begins to look too gay to stay much longer. I must set out I fear by the beginning of May.

Here are great preparation for the Dutchess of Kingston's trial and all the World is going to see her Grace shine at the Bar. As I found the attaining a Ticket was rather inconvenient I waited upon her Grace yesterday and beg'd to know if She wanted a fellow to swear any thing for her. She immediately accepted my services with many thanks, gave me my lesson, &c &c, so that I'm to be subpoen'd to set forth the excellencies of the good Dutchess's Character.

Here is Harry Matty and his Dear wife in Town, they both arriv'd on Wednesday night last. I've seen Kirkpatrick the other day—he's appointed Lieu^t Colonel—Governor of Fort Marlborough—and to a place in Council at Madrass. He swears he's not worth a shilling and I cou'd not find in my heart be the consequences what they may to deliver him into the hands of the Philistines, for we must remember, my Dear friend, the Origin of these [the second page of the letter is missing].

Truant Teller of Tall Tales

In his second letter to Lydia, Charles's tone remains insouciant, almost scattered. He jumps from point to point and can scarcely concentrate for more than one sentence on any incident. While some parts of his letter seem to suggest lack of mobility—"for we must allow my Sis that a little distraction of our own has almost drove us under water and now the Devil has so manag'd it, that the distraction of others will not let us float again"—others suggest he was able to move about the town freely. He tells Lydia he has been much in the company of the Alexes and has visited the Duchess of Kingston. There are many hints that he has great hopes of a windfall from John, and he pleads with Lydia not to interfere with their smuggling activities.

Lydia must have often pleaded with John and Charles to cease smuggling and adhere more closely to the laws of the land, and both brothers must have repeatedly assured her that everyone did it and there was no reason to "admit the justice into the list." The history of eighteenth-century English smuggling suggests that Charles is correct. Smith argues that many revenue officers "were in league with the smugglers, frequently seizing small cargoes just for effect whilst conniving at the landing of much larger cargoes."[1] There is, Charles insists, no right road to Heaven, for the justices are not honorable and would rather receive a bribe than the duties legally due them, so there is little incentive to give them either.

Charles is still confident that he and John will succeed in their ventures. Perhaps he even anticipates the money that will release him from prison. In the end, however, he seems not to have needed money to settle the debt for which he was imprisoned. The government, anxious to supply its extended forces with trained men, decided to grant military and naval officers special treatment. Depending upon a measure called "An Act for the Relief of Insolvent Debtors; and for the Relief of Bankrupts in Certain Cases," Charles anticipates release in time for a May sailing. He looks forward to serving as Captain of the *Discovery* and traveling again with Cook on another round-the-world voyage, this time in search of a North-West passage between the Pacific and Atlantic. Even while in prison, or "under water," however, Charles had remarkable freedom of movement. Clerke's biographers suggest that the "Rules of the Bench" afforded him much mobility. Under the Court's "Day Rules," a debtor, after giving his parole, was granted leave from prison during the day to transact his

---

[1]   G. Smith 65.

affairs, providing he was back by 9:00 pm. Charles obviously took much advantage of this concession.[2]

When Charles admits his eagerness to participate in the Duchess of Kingston's trial, which lasted from the 15th to the 22nd of April,[3] he makes it clear he is as willing to bend the truth as the next man or woman. Although the World declared her a scandalous person,[4] Charles was willing to attest to "the excellencies" of her character. Always skeptical about authority Charles looks forward to telling tall tales in high places. Like Lemuel Gulliver, another famous (though fictional) traveler, Charles was not adverse to telling improbable stories and leaving trails of irony behind him.

Did Lydia protest against his foolhardiness, or did she find humor in his tales of aristocratic chicanery? There are several hints that Lydia, unlike her sister-in-law Ann, was more amused than shocked by the scandals of the bon ton and the accommodating behavior of her brother-in-law. Sylvia also alludes to Lydia's fascination with fashion and the fashionable world: "I write to you about these People because I believe you like it." Like most of her epistolary companions, Charles wrote to inform and entertain Lydia, and she must have enjoyed his stories immensely.

Cannibalism

It is not easy to read Charles. As a narrator, he proves slippery, elusive, and sometimes unreliable. He is willing to look at the world, to use his sister Ann's words, through different optics. Because he is willing to look at things otherwise, he exhibits a cautious skepticism when encountering new peoples. While all around him men were finding confirmation that indigenous peoples ate human flesh, Clerke suspected that some of the demonstrations were flimsy:

> Our People have a strong Notion they [the inhabitants of Nootka Sound, near present-day Vancouver Island] are Canibals, which Idea took its rise from the following Circumstance: they brought on board frequently, among other Articles of traffick, some human Sculls and dried Hands, and one day a little Girl in perfect health, which they

---

[2]   Cowley and Deacon 122–3.

[3]   The full story of the Duchess of Kingston's trial can be found in *The Trial of the Duchess of Kingston*, Ed. Lewis Melville (Edinburgh, 1927). In the end, Charles did not testify on her behalf.

[4]   Secretly married to Augustus John Hervey in 1744, the duchess entered into a liaison with Evelyn, second duke of Kingston in 1750, and traveled abroad with him in 1765. In 1769, she married the duke. When he died four years later, his children brought forward the charge of bigamy in hopes of having his will disproved. The duchess was found guilty, but, pleading benefit of peerage, discharged.

wanted much to sell, and to enhance her Price, gave us to understand she was very good to eat; the Child I belive was 3 or 4 years old, the Price demanded for her a small Hatchet. They do make motions seemingly of having eat the parts from the Heads and Hands; but we are so perfectly unintelligible to each other that matters between us are very easily confused & misunderstood; however, this is the Argument for their being Canibals, whether they are or not, the Lord knows; I think here seems some Ground for suspicion, but in my opinion by no means a sufficient foundation to pronounce them such.[5]

Charles's caution is justified. The evidence, as he suspected, could be read very differently. The Englishmen assume the indigenous people bring body parts because they are leftovers; the parts serve as proof that the rest of the corpse has been consumed. But perhaps the natives bring body parts to the Europeans because the Englishmen will pay a good price for what would otherwise have little value. They may, in fact, suspect that it's the Englishmen who are cannibals keen to devour flesh. After all, for what other reason would they purchase body parts? As for the little girl, it is almost as if the people who hope to sell her have read Swift. If Europeans will purchase parts might they not also purchase whole bodies? Then again, the inhabitants of Nootka Sound might be trying to sell the girl for other purposes. Like their European customers, they might not be adverse to trafficking in girls and young women. As Clerke insists, on both sides there was much room for misunderstanding, and just as the Europeans misunderstood the indigenous people, just so the indigenous natives might have misunderstood the white men who came in ships, bought body parts, and took companions away sometimes never to be heard from again. The Europeans claimed they were taking these individuals to exotic places like England, but the natives might have suspected that their friends and family were going off to become dinner.

In an effort to bear witness to cannibalism, Charles participates in another equally ambiguous incident: "I [Clerke] ask'd him [a Maori native] if he'd eat a peice [of a skull] there directly to which he very chearfully gave his assent. I then cut a peice of carry'd [it] to the fire by his desire and gave it a little broil upon the Grid Iron then deliver'd it to him—he not only eat it but devour'd it most ravenously, and suck'd his fingers ½ a dozen times over in raptures: the Captain [Cook] was at this time absent."[6] Like the previous incident, this spectacle can be interpreted variously. It could be a scientific experiment; the ever empirical Charles wants to observe an act of cannibalism so he can be more certain that the practice of eating human flesh actually exists. However, as I read and re-read this journal entry, with its accompanying attention to detail and emphasis on precise observation, I began to suspect its recorder of irony. With its depiction of excessive gestures on the part of both the host ("and gave it a little broil upon the Grid Iron") and the guest ("devour'd it most ravenously,

---

5   Beaglehole 3:1329.
6   Beaglehole 2:293n.

and suck'd his fingers ½ a dozen times over in raptures"), I wondered what motivated this little piece of discourse. For whose delectation was the tale told? Whose appetite was it sharpening? When I learned that the Admiralty (the bureaucracy that oversees British maritime operations) read all seamen's journals upon their return from long-distance voyages in an effort to control dissemination of information, the possibility of intentional mockery increased substantially. Charles was fooling those anonymous, faceless readers at the Admiralty with spectacular tales of native behavior. He was playing a joke on them. I wondered if he succeeded. Did his readers indeed devour his story without reservation or did they see the tongue in his cheek?

If we turn to Cook's version of this same incident, we find an even more detailed account of a violation at once disgusting and abhorrent but also riveting:

> Tuesday 23rd. Calm or light airs from the Northward so that we could not get to sea as I intended, some of the officers went on shore to amuse themselves among the Natives where they saw the head and bowels of a youth who had lately been killed, the heart was struck upon a forked stick and fixed to the head of their largest Canoe, the gentlemen brought the head on board with them, I was on shore at this time but soon after returned on board when I was informed of the above circumstances and found the quarter deck crowded with the Natives. I now saw the mangled head or rather the remains of it for the under jaw, lip &c^a were wanting, the scul was broke on the left side just above the temple, the face had all the appearance of a youth about fourteen or fifteen, a peice of the flesh had been broiled and eat by one of the Natives in the presince of most of the officers. The sight of the head and the relation of the circumstances just mentioned struck me with horor and filled my mind with indignation against these Canibals, but when I considered that any resentment I could shew would avail but little and being desireous of being an eye wittness to a fact which many people had their doubts about, I concealed my indignation and ordered a piece of the flesh to be broiled and brought on the quarter deck where one of these Canibals eat it with a seeming good relish before the whole ships Company which had so much effect on some of them as to cause them to vomit. [Oediddee, a young Tahitian who joined the crew in September 1773 to serve as an interpreter and go-between] was [so] struck with horor at the sight that [he] wept and scolded by turns, before this happened he was very intimate with these people but now he neither would come near them or suffer them to touch him, told them to their faces that they were vile men and that he was no longer their friend, he used the same language to one of the officers who cut of the flesh and refused to except, or even touch the knife with which it was cut, such was this Islanders aversion to this vile custom.[7]

Like Clerke, Cook wants to see for himself, so, like any good scientist, he duplicates the experiment of his subordinate; however, when he records the results in his journal, he does not write ironically but with elaborate seriousness. A taboo has been violated

---

[7] Beaglehole 2:292–3.

and he needs to register his shock and sense of violation. He also needs to represent others as confirming his reaction, so he draws on Oediddee.[8]

Whether consciously or unconsciously, both Clerke and Cook bear subtle but compelling witness to European man's guilty hunger for "curiosities" and conquests. As Sara Suleri has warned, "the stories of colonialism—in which heterogeneous cultures are yoked by violence—offer nuances of trauma that cannot be neatly partitioned between colonizer and colonized."[9] Drawn (and loathe) to dabble (and trade) in body parts, scientists, seamen, and natives shared and deplored their own and each other's abhorrent impulses.

When Clerke and his companions returned to England after their experiences with the "cannibals" of New Zealand, their stories circulated everywhere. At a Royal Society dinner attended by Cook and James Boswell, held during the same week as the Duchess of Kingston's trial, the newly returned circumnavigator regaled his audience with tales of cannibalism. His empiricism convinced Boswell, the skeptical future biographer of Samuel Johnson: "He gave me a distinct account of a New Zealander eating flesh in his presence and in that of many more aboard, so that the fact of cannibals is now certainly known."[10] Reading both Clerke's and Cook's journal entries, we must conclude with Boswell that the event was "real." A Maori did eat flesh. But why did the Maori eat pieces of the skull? What significance did the act have for him? Was it a habitual act or a singular instance? Was there any convergence at all between his motives for his actions and the motives attributed to him by his observers? While some were convinced that cannibalism existed, others, like Lady Mary Coke, remained skeptical and treated stories of cannibalism as jokes. Many were unwilling to suspend their disbelief.

Like the intersections between the real and the imaginary, the intersections between colonizer and colonized need to be explored with care. As they encountered one another, Europeans and indigenous peoples constructed stories to explain the oddities of behavior they observed. But what they perceived as real was not necessarily so. Each perceived the other through different optics. Across huge cultural divides they imagined each other's realities.

---

[8] According to George Forster, Oediddee (or O-Hedeedee) "appeared to be of the better sort of people by his complexion and good garments" (*A Voyage Round the World*, Eds Nicholas Thomas and Oliver Berghof [Honolulu, 2000] 1:222). Thomas and Berghof note that the youth, "also known as Mahine, ... after visiting New Zealand, Easter Island, and the Marquess and playing a significant role as a cultural go-between in those places, ... abandoned the idea of going to England and left the ship at Raiatea in June 1774" (1:452n.).

[9] Sara Suleri, *The Rhetoric of English India* (Chicago, 1992) 5.

[10] James Boswell, *The Ominous Years, 1774–1776*, Eds Charles Ryskamp and Frederick A. Pottle (New York, 1963) 341.

Blackamoors and the Clerke Coat of Arms

It is hard not to like Charles Clerke. Cheerful, ironic, generous, always concerned about others, his brother, his sister-in-law, his friends, he comes across as unself-consciously admirable. However, there are those hints of clandestine trafficking in wine and other goods. And, as a member of the Royal Navy, Clerke was complicitous with and profited by the slave trade.

As we learn more about the history of the slave trade, we need to ask more questions of those who went before us. When Susannah Dobson talks about "the Virginia trade" in her letters to what was she referring? When she attends an Assembly she mentions Mr. Richard Pennant, a Member from Liverpool and a merchant prince who made a fortune in the slave trade.[11] According to Henry Smithers, although the slave trade came late to Liverpool, it was an important part of the city's commerce. Aware that the nineteenth century was not the eighteenth, Smithers, who published his book in 1825, bears witness to the horror of the trade but also to the attitudes of the century before: "[In 1765] 86 vessels traded with Africa that year and carried 25,720 Negroes! ... a mass of induced human calamity at that period scarcely considered as immoral."[12] Unlike Smithers, Susannah was not appalled by the source of her neighbor's wealth. Likewise, when Sylvia Winstanley writes in her will of her children's inheritance from an estate in South Carolina, she reminds us once again that English wealth was sometimes based on the sale of people as well as land and rice.

Charles also had his brush with the slave trade. According to *The Ipswich Journal*, when the *Bellona* (with Charles Clerke on board) captured the *Courageux* in August 1761, "700 men from St Domingo" were on board. The newspaper also reports that First Lieutenant, Mr. Male, with other officers and men, took possession of "the Prize" and received her 224 prisoners on board. We never learn what happened to the men from St Domingo. However, we do know that when an English ship captured an enemy slaver, its human cargo became part of "the Prize."

In 1761, Charles was only a 20-year-old Midshipman. He would not have benefited much from the capture of the *Courageux*. However, if we look at the exemplification of arms Joseph Clerke was granted on 24 May 1761, the same year as the *Bellona* incident, the relationship of the Clerke family to slavery deepens. The family's armorial is described as "Chequy Argent & Azure Two Chevronells Gules on A Canton Or, An Anchor & the Cable Sable, And for the Crest on a Wreath of the

---

[11]   Information about Richard Pennant was gleaned from the *Dictionary of National Biography* and from the Website Casglu'r Tlysau (Gathering the Jewels), a website devoted to Welsh cultural history.

[12]   Henry Smithers, *Liverpool, Its Commerce, Statistics, and Institutions* (Liverpool, 1825) 105.

Colors A Crown Naval Or thereout issuant A Negro's head proper."[13] Why would a family put a Negro's head on its coat of arms, and on its dinner plates (a Kien-Lung dinner service was ordered by Joseph soon after the family's coat of arms was officially recognized), if it did not symbolize something of importance? But what does a Negro's head signify? The only reference I could find to the meaning of a Blackamoor's head on a coat of arms indicates that it did not signify trafficking in people. According to seventeenth-century antiquarian John Guillim, a "Blackemore" head signifies the name of the bearer, as in the case of the "Coate-Armour of Humphry Blakamore of the Countie of Middlesex."[14] Guillim thus suggests that in the chivalric past, as in our postmodern present, sometimes a signifier refers only to another signifier, and not to an external referent. A Negro's head does not have to signify anything more than the name "Blackmore."

It is hard to tell how far back the Negro's head in the Clerke coat of arms goes. In 1741, it formed part of the scutcheon on a table-sized map of the Manor, so it was part of the family's coat-of-arms before Charles (or John) went to sea.[15] Interestingly, Brook Farm, where the Clerke family lived throughout the eighteenth century, is located near Blackmore End. So, are we then caught in a different linguistic loop? Does the head in the coat of arms refer to a place name rather than to a family name? But why would an English locale come to bear the name "Blackmore"? Does it indicate some long distant connection to the Crusades and to encounters with blackamoors in other lands and other times? Or, is the name just a name? In 1844, Mr. Alfred Hills, M.A., suggested a very different origin for "Blackmore": "As for Blackmore End, the word in olden days only meant dark and no doubt referred to the colour of the soil. Black occurs very frequently in place names .... so blackmore means the dark coloured swamp, and end is a meeting of roads." So the Negro's head might symbolize the color and quality of the soil.[16]

What most appeals to me about Charles Clerke is his love of words (he would have been delighted to learn about the multiple meanings of "blackmore") and his interest in the different peoples of this world. The Maori Chief in Nathaniel Dance's portrait of Clerke was, according to Cowley and Deacon, "the first known serious painting of a Maori chief and was reproduced by Dance from Captain Clerke's own drawing."[17] For over two hundred years, this painting has borne silent witness to

---

[13] *Miscellanea Genealogica et Heraldica*, Ed. Joseph Jackson Howard (London, 1888) 2:325.

[14] John Guillim, *A Display of Heraldrie* (London, 1638) 134.

[15] D/DFy P1 (from T. Skynner's survey of Clerke family estate, Wethersfield,1741), Essex Record Office.

[16] The *Halstead Gazette*, 18 August 1844: 22. In a letter to the author dated June 2004, Mrs. Cynthia Comyn, Genealogist at The College of Arms, concludes that "Mr. Hills was rather nearer the mark than John Guillim; within five miles of this house is a village called Blakemere and, in other villages nearby, farms named Blackmoor, Blackhouse and Blackbush."

[17] Cowley and Deacon ii.

27. Captain Charles Clerke, by Nathaniel Dance, 1776

7.1   A reproduction of a portrait of Captain Charles Clerke by Nathaniel Dance,
       1776. Courtesy of Government House, Wellington, New Zealand

Charles's at times respectful, at times skeptical encounters with the Other. While the Maori gazes past the Englishman, the Englishman looks into the distance. Enclosed in the same space, nevertheless their gazes do not meet. And, perhaps to ensure the Englishman's superiority, the Maori chief stands behind and slightly below Charles.

Charles's many stories about his encounters with others helped him make sense of an incomprehensible world. He could see himself as one in a long line of old tars, reaching back to Noah, who loved to tell wild tales. He could not wait to get on the stand and testify to the Duchess of Kingston's character and give evidence that would fool the judges. He delighted in telling tall tales about even taller men and men who ate each other. With cheerful irreverence, he told tales on and to the aristocracy, the admiralty, and authorities of all sorts. Finally, the story of his last moments and death became a narrative that traveled, as we will see, via copies of copies, to the widely dispersed homes of friends and family members and to generations of readers after that.

Chapter 8

Ann Clerke Two

Women were restricted in their ability to travel, confined to the company of their immediate neighbours in the locality, so that life must at times have been very lonely for them. They found in friendship with other women an outlet for their affections and a freedom absent in relations with the opposite sex. If this was true of all women, single women without husbands or children stood in particular need of friends and contacts with the outside world they so seldom ventured into.

Bridget Hill, *Women Alone* (2001)

In her second letter, which closely follows the last one from Charles, Ann Clerke expresses concern about her brother's behavior while in town. She fears his acquaintance with "the great" will prove harmful and affirms her preference for a simple and retired life. Sprinkled with references to members of her family and her Essex neighbors, this letter gives us more background into the lives of Lydia and John as well as insight into Ann's provincial life. We see a different side of Ann. Even as her brother prepares to set forth on his last voyage around the world to enter history, she challenges the pursuit of fame and glory. She can understand why men would value them but she believes they undermine Christian values and become "a modern apology for the Hierarchy."

8
From: Ann Clerke, Ely
To: Lady Clerke, Gosport
Date: 11 June [1776]
Dear Sister

The extreem hurry in which your last was wrote leaves me quite at a loss to guess what stay you intend to make in Town or even where to direct a Letter to you as you entirely forgot to tell me where your amiable Friend Mʳˢ Jackson lives. Your Gause & flowers I doubt not you found upon unpacking some of your Clothes after you wrote to me, for I think I'm very sure I saw you pack them up, & it is very certain you did not leave them here.

I want much to know whether you have seen Charles & when he expects to sail. It appears to me a great mystery how he has supported himself so long in Town, & I must confess I have some fears for him that nothing will effectually remove but the certainty of his being sailed. There is nothing more common than to see people live

& figure away in the World nobody can tell how or by what means, but I confess to you of all characters under the sun these are the last that a real honest mind can have any satisfaction in being c[on]nected with.

I was astonish'd to hear with what <u>pleasure</u> my F. [speaks] of C.C: great acquaintance & connection with people of Condition, rank, & fortune. You know my Dear Sister I live in a situation entirely obscured from the <u>glare</u> of <u>Human</u> Life & manners & [a] great part of my time is spent in the examination of my own heart & learning (at least endeavouring to learn) a just estimation of everything in this Life that offers itself to my observation. And what I have to beg of you my Dear Friend is that you will assist me in this darling study as I know I <u>feel</u> every moment that I'm in your Company that you have infinitely the advantage of me in point of knowledge. But there is nothing more dreadfull to my imagination than a head grown gray in Error, & I am guilty of a very great one if the connections Charles has form'd in Town among the great (some few excepted) will ever be of any real advantage to him. Anoth[er] thing I'm much inclined to fear is that he takes no sort of care of his health, for I was told the other day by a Gentleman who saw him in Town, about a month since, that he thought the gay Life he had for some time past led in Town full as injurious to his constitution as a South Sea Voyage could be if he might judge by the appearence he then made. I was in hopes you would have wrote to me when you had seen him.

As to the intrinsick Value of most things in this World I believe no two friends can more entirely agree in than ourselves tho it is certain my Dear there are many things we see in very different shades of light, or perhaps I may more properly say we View through very different opticks, Such as the Bon ton & its appendages, especially the article of dress. Tho to be injenuous could I meet with a fashion that would never change, no creature breathing has less objection to the being well dress'd. But I have been more inclined to envy at the sight of a spruce Quaker then upon any other occasion whatsoever, tho this is a mortification I very seldom meet with, for they like all the rest of the World are flying from all simplicity & originality & mixing with the herd of Copys of Copys & shadows of shades.

I [beg when you have read] Excellencies of the Christian Religion you'd let me know your opinion. [For my] own part I must confess I think there never was a B[ook] more likely to do real service to Christianity. I'm <u>afraid</u> [I do] not readily come into his opinion in regard to fame [courage] & false glory tho to me they appear strictly just as a man [of] the World [would think]. We must excuse him a little <u>fine drawing</u> [a conclusion] not I think strictly reconcilable with the principles before laid down, & may rather be call'd a modern apology for the Hierarchy.

I have a novel just brought me by my Friend Mr Cole (who came home last night & regrets much not having the pleasure of seeing you), Franklys Rambles. It begins well, let me know if you have seen it. I wish you'd write a few lines to my little Aunt when you have time. She'd be much pleas'd & really expects it. Madame Cole is the first person of taste I have met with since I parted from you. As a proof of it I can tell you she was in raptures with my French Cap at first sight. I gave your Ladyship the Credit of it immediately & indeed I should not easily have forgiven her supposing it produced by the brains of any less genius. If you see Mrs Thornton, tell [her] I respect & esteem her & however insignificant a being she may look upon me, if she knew how few people there is in the World that I pretend to say that to she would give me a greater degree of credit than I can otherwise have the least pretensions to, & as I Love every one that is beloved by you, the friend you are now with has no small share of my respect & good Wishes. Adieu, my Dear Sister, Love me as you are beloved by yrs A Clerke

A Woman Alone

Ann's second letter, like her first, reflects a thoughtful, troubled woman. Though she lived in an isolated and "depressing" country town, she rightfully insists that she has read widely and understands the ways of the world. In her second letter, she expresses deep concern about her brother Charles. While his letters to Lydia are cheerfully insouciant about his prospects, Ann is anxious about them. Charles is her younger brother; when she writes about him (and probably to him) she adopts the disapproving tone of the indignant older sister. She wishes he were at sea where he would fare better.

Ann most likely did not know about her brothers' smuggling ventures. Both Charles and John might have preferred to keep this information from their father and sisters back home. Nevertheless Ann suspects Charles's dealings with the aristocracy are more dangerous than any South Sea voyage. Much in the Lydia Clerke letters supports Ann's fear that members of her class (people of the middle to upper-middle classes) were not safe when they associated with those above them in rank. John's relationship with Lord Rochford contributed to his ruin, Sylvia Brathwaite risked seduction and betrayal every time she went to an opera or dinner party, and Charles Clerke landed in prison, if not directly due to his own aristocratic connections, at least indirectly due to his brother's.

The Lydia Clerke letters and eighteenth-century discourse in general overflowed with contempt for the empty formalities and mindless dissipations of courtly and urban life. Repeatedly, Georgian men and women expressed their preference for the pleasures of a simple country life. The young Sylvia Brathwaite, in particular, uses this language with great enthusiasm and ingenuity. She speaks so often of her dislike of the fashionable world that one begins to suspect that such an attitude was itself fashionable. According to Amanda Vickery, more often than not genteel protests against aristocratic excess were just empty platitudes, which people felt compelled to repeat: "By far the most overworked dualism drawn on in discussion of leisure and culture was that of fashionable worldliness versus philosophical retirement, a 'hurry' versus peace, the gaudy town versus the rural glade." Such beliefs were simply conventional commonplaces, Vickery suspects, not heartfelt convictions.[1] While this may have been true for some, it was not true for Sylvia and Ann. They are sincere. Sylvia does not marry for money or rank; she marries for love and companionship and uncomplainingly suffers the consequences. And Ann also lives her life according to her convictions. She remains in Wethersfield, sequestered in her rural home, and watches fearfully as her brothers and sister-in-law suffer the consequences of engagement with the wider world. In the eighteenth century, the aristocracy was extraordinarily powerful, and undeniably many of its members abused their privileges. When Rousseau urged a life in nature without distinctions of rank, his ideas did not enter a vacuum but were received by a world deeply disturbed by aristocratic excesses.

One of the more controversial issues in recent discussions of eighteenth-century women is the question of their complicity in patriarchy. They did not, according to some modern commentators, protest the inequalities between ranks or genders, but accepted the world as they found it. Rather than argue against the ways of the world or try to change them, they preferred to work within the limits of their lives to challenge institutions subversively if at all. Betty Rizzo argues that although women protested against particular injustices (for example, slavery) and engaged in charitable works, the first general protest against hierarchy did not come until William Godwin's *Enquiry concerning Political Justice*, which appeared in 1793. What women wrote and experienced, Rizzo concedes, may have contributed to the formation of Godwin's philosophy, but women did not question the hierarchy per se. They preferred to emphasize their sensibility as their badge of moral superiority and to pride themselves on their powers of endurance and resignation.[2] Lawrence Stone is convinced that, throughout the eighteenth and nineteenth centuries, women who obeyed unquestioningly far outnumbered the few who protested.[3]

Like many of the women she knew, Ann stoically accepted what she could not change (early deaths of loved ones and the diseases and distresses of old age), but she did protest against what she perceived to be harmful inequities. In her second letter, she refers explicitly to questions of hierarchy and, considering who her brothers were and the lives they led, squarely challenges it: "I [beg when you have read] Excellencies of the Christian Religion you'd let me know your opinion. [For my] own part I must confess I think there never was a B[ook] more likely to do real service to Christianity. I'm <u>afraid</u> [I do] not readily come into his opinion in regard to fame

---

[1]   Vickery 282.

[2]   Betty Rizzo, *Companions Without Vows: Relationships among Eighteenth-Century British Women* (Athens, 1994) 23.

[3]   Lawrence Stone, *Road to Divorce: England, 1530–1987* (Oxford, 1990) 363, 378.

[courage] & false glory tho to me they appear strictly just as a man [of] the World [would think]. We must excuse him a little <u>fine drawing</u> [a conclusion] not I think strictly reconcilable with the principles before laid down, & may rather be call'd a modern apology for the Hierarchy." Ann argues that since the author she has just read stresses the excellencies of the Christian religion and thus does much good, he contradicts himself when he privileges fame and courage. Christianity, if correctly understood, does not support hierarchical class systems, not even those based on fame and courage. Christianity, and especially the Quaker sect (whose simplicity obviously attracted Ann), stressed Christianity's leveling spirit. All are equal. Though Ann admires much in the author's work, she questions his willingness to defer to fame, courage, and glory, but understands that, as a man of the world, he could hardly do otherwise; however, in so doing, he constructs "a modern apology for the Hierarchy." At this point, Ann's words come remarkably close to the language of egalitarian feminism, a language which, some would insist, was not born until the nineteenth century.

In *The Domestic Revolution: Enlightenment Feminisms and the Novel,* Eve Tavor Bannet distinguishes between two strands of eighteenth-century feminism —egalitarian and matriarchal—and concludes that because the matriarchs (women like Hannah More, Jane West, and Maria Edgeworth) were successful in veiling their own feminism and trivializing and demonizing their more radical sisters (women like Catherine Macaulay and Mary Wollstonecraft), a Great Forgetting followed the domestic revolution that occurred between 1750 and 1800. Nevertheless, the revolution was real. Women brought about great changes during Ann's lifetime.[4] And Ann, a thoughtful and wide reader who was prepared to challenge the modern hierarchy, was one of them.

Ann must also have been a deeply religious woman. When she notes that Quakers no longer dress or behave as their beliefs suggest they should, she expresses her fear that the age is losing its best self. Gordon Rupp, author of *Religion in England, 1688–1798,* agrees with Ann that there was a falling off among Quakers: "By the middle of the eighteenth century, though there were plenty of humble people in their [the Quakers'] ranks, there were enough who were comfortably off and prosperous to arouse some criticism."[5] Likewise. A.F.J. Brown notes changes in Quaker behavior: "As the century progressed, even Quaker meetings had to report a weakening of self-discipline."[6] Ann preferred simplicity and sincerity, but both, she rightly feared, were disappearing.

---

[4] Eve Tavor Bannet, *The Domestic Revolution: Enlightenment Feminisms and the Novel* (Baltimore, 2000) 195–223.

[5] Rupp 150.

[6] Brown 119.

Chapter 9

Charlotte Lennox

... The affair of Miss Bowes is but too true. A wretch who is a member of Parliament & calls himself a Gentleman, sent a man who is a famous pimp at the Cardigans head into this Country to ingratiate himself with Miss Bowes's footman, & to tell him he shd have a reward of twenty thousand £ if he wd help to carry off the young Lady; that the person who was to marry her was a member of Parliament & wd make a great figure in the H: of Commons this sessions; this footman, you must know, is lover to a Woman who was nurse to the young Lady, & now attends her as a servant. These two persons pondered on this proposal why they did so I can not tell, but however 5 days after it had been made they acquainted Mrs. Bowes with it. She in a fright told her steward, her steward in a fright seized the man of the Cardigan head, & in a fright sent him to the justice the justice in a fright sent him to the house of correction, which I hope may tend to the amendments of this wicked fellows morals but cannot serve any other purpose whatever for he will not confess who sent him into ye Country, nor what he was to do, had this footman been ordered to appear to acquiece, the whole design wd have been unfolded now all they learn from ye letters in his pocket is that Mr. H— is the person who sent him into this Country & ye errand to run away with Miss Bowes by help of her footman, but whither by fraud or violence is not clear. & all that is certainly known is that ye first letter of ye member of Parliaments name is H. It seems there is a Gentleman who is a sort of an adventurer who has been seen in London with this fellow whose name so begins & is also a member of Parliament. It is imagined the servants were to carry this young creature by force, & that ye adventurous lover wd have so married her perhaps abroad, & have trusted to his agrémens & ways of making himself agreable for her submitting to be his wife, but she is a girl of sense & spirit, & I think he wd probably have been hanged for his pains. Mrs. Bowes & Miss Bowes made me a visit since I came hither, she is really a fine girl, lively, sensible, & very civil & goodnatured.

Letter from Sarah Scott to Elizabeth Montagu (1763)

Prove, therefore, that the Books which I have hitherto read as Copies of Life, and Models of Conduct, are empty Fictions [proposes Arabella], and from this Hour I deliver them to Moths and Mould; and from this Time consider Their Authors as Wretches who cheated me of those Hours I ought to have dedicated to Application and Improvement, and betrayed me to a Waste of those years in which I might have laid up Knowledge for my future Life.

... It is the Fault of the best Fictions [asserts the Doctor], that they teach young Minds to expect strange Adventures and sudden Vicissitudes, and therefore encourage them often to trust to Chance ... the Order of the World is so established, that all human Affairs proceed in a regular Method, and very little Opportunity is left for Sallies or Hazards, for Assault or Rescue; but the Brave and the Coward, the Sprightly and the Dull, suffer themselves to be carried alike down the Stream of Custom.

Charlotte Lennox, *The Female Quixote* (1752)

Charlotte Lennox (1729–1804) is, without question, the most famous of the letter writers. Born Charlotte Ramsay in Gibraltar in 1729, she spent 1739 to 1742 in the colony of New York, where her father was stationed.[1] In her second letter to Lydia, she marks the death of her father as a turning point in her life: "I have been a wretch since I was thirteen years old when I lost my father—adversity is habitual to me." Upon her father's death (in 1742[2]), she was sent to England to live with a rich aunt. However, upon her arrival in London, she learned that her aunt was insane and/ or dead. Left unprotected and alone in London, she was patronized by the aristocratic Rockingham/ Newcastle/ Finch circle and the literary Samuel Johnson/ Thomas Birch circle. Her first book, *Poems on Several Occasions*, appeared in 1747, the same year in which she married Alexander Lennox. Her first novel, *The Life of Harriot Stuart, Written by Herself*, appeared in 1751, and her most acclaimed novel, *The Female Quixote, or, The Adventures of Arabella*, followed in 1752. Her most controversial work, a critical survey of Shakespeare's plays in which she found Shakespeare's revisions inferior to the original romances on which they were based, was *Shakespear Illustrated; or The Novels and Histories, on which the Plays of Shakespear are founded Collected and Translated from the Original Authors with Critical Remarks* (1753). She also wrote plays, translated memoirs, and edited *The Lady's Museum*. Supported in the last years of her life by the Royal Literary Fund, she died penniless on 4 January 1804.

Lennox's letters provide the story of John and Lydia with its most dramatic moments. John's letter opens the story with the hero and heroine married and confounded by the exigencies of domestic life. The ensuing letters from Winstanley, Dobson, and Ann and Charles Clerke give us exposition and rising action, humor and pathos. We get a better understanding of the problems—sexual, financial, legal, familial—facing John and Lydia. In Lennox's letters the narrative comes to a crisis and achieves resolution.

Lennox's first letter is dated 10 August 1776. Lydia clearly is in deep distress. By the time Lennox sends her second letter, dated 16 June 1777, John Clerke has died

---

[1]   The date and birthplace of Charlotte Lennox have not yet been unequivocally established. Miriam Small (1935) and Gustav Maynadier (1940) suppose that she was born in New York City in 1720. Philippe Séjourné (1967) moves her birth date forward to between 1727 and 1729 (143) and argues that she was not born in the American Colonies. Duncan Isles (1970) suggests Lennox was born in 1729 or 1730 in Gibraltar, where her father was then stationed.

[2]   WO 64/10, f. 39, Army List of 1745, Public Record Office. This Army List gives the career of John Ramsay. He is listed as an Ensign in the Coldstream Regiment of Footguards on 3 August 1703, as Lieutenant on 1 September 1706, and as Lieutenant Captain on 23 April 1729. On 30 December 1738, he becomes one of four captains in a company at New York. The document also notes Ramsay's death on "13th February 1741/42."

(on 11 October 1776) and Lydia has weighed his failings against his virtues and found peace.

9

From: Charlotte Lennox, Tower Hill
To: Lady Clerke, Buxton
Date: 30 August [1776]

Oh my dearest Lady Clerke what a letter have you wrote me! how shall I comfort you, how shall I comfort my self—I feel I have philosophy only for my own misfortunes—yours depresses me quite—believe me I neither feign, nor exaggerate—I am overwhelmd with your affliction—I can think of nothing but you, and ever since I have received your letter I have not been able to speak a civil Word to any body—peevish, quarrelsome, and out of humour with my self and every thing about me—good god! what a reverse—you have known nothing hitherto but prosperity—how severely must you feel this stroke—I have been a wretch since I was thirteen years old when I lost my father—adversity is habitual to me—but you—oh my dear friend my heart bleeds for you—what an affecting picture do you draw of your present situation—wandering alone—wishing to seclude yourself for ever among the rocks that surround you—but my dear friend you shall not while I have life, live in a cottage alone—I will accompany you in any retirement, I will join my pittance to yours, and your dear society would perhaps make some sparks of genius again and enable me to enlarge our little income by my pen—such is the wish of friendship—oh that Mr. L would allow me some thing yearly that I might put this scheme in execution—that abominable Lord Rochford—what can he say for himself—is he not trustd to finish his own Work—why did he encumber you with a title and why draw you in to impoverish your self to fit out your husband for his fatal expedition—I could stab him—alas! my dear Lady Clerke amidst so many solid causes for affliction, I am likewise tormenting myself about one which indeed compared with the rest is trifling and yet I feel it sensibly—you tell me you are going to your old lodgings because you suppose I have not a spare bed as I did not mention it—Good God! my dear friend, how could you serve me so—I have been utterly ignorant of your motions, I thought you would have told me when you left Leverpool. I knew not that you were at Buxton I was in doubt whether you intended to come to town or not—I have dispatchd My Nurse to Painton Street with directions to find out if you have absolutely engagd the Lodgings, and if you have not, to tell them that it was a mistake—and that you are to be with me—I have likewise ordered her to await your arrival on Friday and to attend you here—could I have hoped that this letter would have reached you at Buxton before you left I would have sent it to the post—but I have but this moment got your letter this is Monday evening; and you are to set on Wednesday, and nurse tells me you would not get my letter in time—Mr.

Lennox this moment tells me that if I send my letter now, you will get it before you leave Buxton, I have not a moment to lose—I will send it away—remember my dear Lady Clerke you must come directly here—I shall die with grief if you go to a lodging. For heaven's sake spare me this mortification—adieu my dearest friend I must not add another word for fear of delay

Yours ever and entire[ly]

[Gr]eat Tower hill   CL

[Au]gust 30

10

From: Charlotte Lennox, Nottingham Street, near Marybon Church
To: Lady Clerke, Gosport
Date: 16 June 1777
My Dear Lady Clerke

Mrs Thornton indulgd me with the perusal of a letter from you on a late melancholly event—I say indulged me, for although my eyes streamd at every line, I would not have exchanged the sweetly painful emotions I felt, for the broadest mirth of unfeeling prosperity. Never did such natural and affecting eloquence flow from your pen before! it is your heart that speaks, and you speak to the heart so powerfully, that I wept as much at the third reading of your letter as I did at the first—I freely confess to you that I have this letter now in my possession. I forced it from Mrs Thornton in order to convert some of the infidels of the other Sex, who maintain that no woman was ever generous enough to forgive certain offences in a husband. That unaffected display of the most tender, the most generous sentiments that ever warmd a human breast, does you so much honour, that they ought not to be conceald, and form the noblest apology for the mistakes of the dear Object of your regrets, since no one can doubt for a moment, that he who could inspire so pure and constant a passion in such a heart as yours, must have possessd many, and great Virtues. And let it be your consolation that he did possess them and that he will now reap the full benefit of them—for he is gone where falsehood, envy, and malice can neither aggravate his failings, nor rob his merits of their just reward. You say your health is impaird, I fear it will be more so my dear friend, if you continue to give way to grief—amiable as that grief is, you ought to suppress it, when its effects are likely to be so fatal—patience under inevitable evils, is not more an act of duty, than necessity—"we are all (says a certain philosopher) born with a heavy log to which we are chaind, but he who takes it up, and carries it, feels less inconvenience than he who drags it along." I hope this letter will find you on your return from Wales, in better health, disposd to admit company, and to enjoy tranquility, which while you were continually fluctuating between hope, and fear, was not to be expected.

I ought to make you an apology for not letting you know of my removal from Tower hill—I can not palliate, nor disguise the truth, therefore I will honestly own, that not having received any answer to two or three letters which I wrote to you—I thought I owd so much respect to my self as to be silent for the future—I am here at Marybon where I have the greatest part of a pretty house, in a very pleasant situation—Your Harriet is with me, and one maid makes up all my equipage—My dear little boy is always with me from Saturday, till Sunday evening, when he returns to the Academy, of which, young as he is, he is the ornament, and delight—As I have a spare bed chamber Mr Lennox is here, as often as his business will permit—he has an apartment near the Custom house, and for the present supplies my expences—but how long he will be able to do it I cannot tell, for the American War has greatly reduced his income, while it has left him the same habits of expence—My sufferings were so great during the last twelve month that I resided at Tower hill, that I was reduced to a most deplorable state of health, and this added at least ten years to my looks, as every one who saw me could easily perceive.

I thank you my dear Lady Clerke for your subscription, and for what you mention concerning Marmontel's book—my necessities will I fear oblige me to take up my pen again, but I doubt much whether I can bear any sort of study, my nerves are so much affected by the continual agitation of my mind for so long a time: besides I am likely to be engaged in a War with [the] booksellers—who have venturd in [defi]ance of an act of parliament to prin[t a] new edition of Sully's Memoirs, [which is] now my sole property—Doct[or Johnson] has been with me on this occa[sion and] pointed out to me what measu[res I need] to pursue—I believe I shall not find it difficult to find Lawyers who will serve me without fees—but Lord Camden is the person who could do me most good, and him, I am afraid I hav[e lost him]. Garrick who brought [Lord Camden] to visit me at Tower hill, [is now] very much disposed to be [angry with me]. I have disobligd Garrick [by not giving] the comedy of Old City Manners to him, as he hopd, and even in an artful way requested I would—he has been my enemy ever since and doubtless will prevent Lord Camden with whom he is very intimate from being of any use to me. Harriet begs I will leave room for her to write a few lines to you whom she truly dotes on—my best compliments wait on Your Mama—I am my Dear Lady Clerke ever

Yours affectionately
C. Lennox

direct for me at No. 7
Nottingham Street, near Marybon Church

[Harriet's message to Lady Clerke is written on the back of her mother's letters; brackets indicate holes in the paper and possible missing words:]
My Dear Lady Clerke
My ma[ma tells me]
to say I love you but not to [say how much]

that would require a whole [page and not]
leave space enough for me [to sign myself]
    [Your F]aithful
          Henrietta-Holles Lennox

Charlotte and Lydia

In Lennox's first letter, we learn that John has suffered a devastating financial mishap. Lydia fears penury. Lamenting John's "fatal expedition," Lennox insists Lydia come to her and take up residence in her house so that they might live together and support one another emotionally and financially. By the time Lennox writes the second letter, John is dead and Lydia is no longer in danger of impoverishment. As her will explains, she received a substantial sum from a Nabob. She now has the wherewithal to purchase a subscription from Lennox. Not only has she arranged her financial affairs but her emotional affairs are also in order. In a letter to Mrs. Thornton, Lydia has reflected on her marriage, summed up John's virtues and vices, and, in the purity of her passion, forgiven him much. Charlotte has read this letter, admired it, and "forced it from Mrs Thornton in order to convert some of the infidels of the other Sex, who maintain that no woman was ever generous enough to forgive certain offences in a husband." Because Lennox writes indirectly, we cannot know for sure what is the unforgivable offence in a husband Lydia now forgives, but with Susannah Dobson's epistolary innuendoes in mind it seems likely that the transgression was sexual.

Lennox's concern for Lydia is unaffected and touching, her sympathy spontaneous and moving. Perhaps she expresses herself so candidly because she sees her own domestic situation mirrored in Lydia's. Both women were married to improvident men, and there was very little they could do to protect their financial security, for even their own money was not their own. Although in her second letter Lennox speaks of Sully's *Memoirs* as "my sole property," it was actually her husband's. Under eighteenth-century coverture (and until passage of the Married Women's Property Acts in the nineteenth century), a woman's earnings were her husband's property. Not only is she unable to spend even her own earnings without her husband's consent, but she must watch helplessly as he wastes his own. Lennox knows from bitter experience the helplessness of Lydia's position, and her epistolary eloquence is real and passionate.

Charlotte and Lydia not only shared the insecurities of volatile domestic situations, but each also sought the consolations of female friendship to ease the pains of her predicament. The existence of the Lydia Clerke collection proves just how completely Lydia depended on her women friends. While she enjoyed receiving and rereading letters from the men she knew (as witness the existence and preservation of letters from her husband, Thomas Winstanley, and Charles Clerke), clearly it was letters from women like Ann Clerke and Sylvia Brathwaite (whose letters outnumber those of anyone else in the circle) that she most treasured. Female friendship was also vitally important to Charlotte Lennox. Although Janet Todd praises *Clarissa* as "the century's most acute analysis of female friendship,"[3] the accolade might just as fairly go to *Euphemia*, Lennox's last novel.

Euphemia portrays a relationship between two women, Maria and Euphemia, that is not only heart-felt and enduring but exemplary in its sororal parity. Moreover, the two heroines (already a significant deviation from the usual pattern of a single and singular heroine) are very like Lydia Clerke and Sylvia Brathwaite. One heroine, Euphemia, is, like Lydia, older and married, sadder but wiser. She writes to the younger woman, Maria, who, like Sylvia, seeks guidance in her choice of a husband.

Euphemia not only reflects the relationship of Lydia Clerke and Sylvia Brathwaite; it also reflects that of Lydia Clerke and Charlotte Lennox. Like Euphemia and Maria, Lydia and Charlotte support one another. While Lennox offers philosophical advice and emotional support, Lydia offers literary advice and monetary encouragement. In an intervening letter that we do not have, Lydia must have suggested to Charlotte that she translate one of Marmontel's works. Lennox agrees that she will have to "take up [her] pen again," but doubts that she can undertake such an arduous task as translation. Lydia has also bought a subscription to Lennox's works and Lennox thanks her accordingly.

Euphemia enabled Lennox to emphasize the centrality, vitality, and urgency of female friendship, which was, both in her fictions and in her life, essential and elusive. "Female friendship," observes Janet Todd in *Women's Friendship in Literature*, "was a fascinating and inspiring theme in the eighteenth century."[4] However, as important as friendship was to women, fractures occurred. Women do not always like one another; jealousies and competitions interfere. Sylvia Brathwaite makes fun of Susannah Dobson's ridiculous outfits and intellectual activities, while Sylvia Thornton mocks her stinginess and ambiguous sexuality. Susannah Dobson dwells on Lydia Clerke's misfortunes to the point that her concern borders on smugness. Eventually Lydia Clerke distances herself from Susannah, possibly as a consequence of her long-winded intimations of John Clerke's guilt and Lydia's sexual vulnerability. While we might understand her rejection of Susannah, we must question her neglect of the gentle Ann Clerke upon her refusal to cast aside Susannah. Women can be very hard on one another. Nevertheless, rather than see the volatility of these women's relationships as evidence of their inability to make firm and lasting bonds, we can view it as signifying the importance of friendship for eighteenth-

---

[3]   Janet Todd, *Women's Friendship in Literature* (New York, 1980) 413.

[4]   Todd 359.

century women. Friendship was so important that even the slightest instance of discord or malice could rupture it.

In Lennox's letters to Lydia, we see how brittle the tie between women can be. In her first letter, Lennox sincerely and enthusiastically offers to help Lydia in any way she can. She wishes she had money of her own so that she could share it with her friend. She implores Lady Clerke to come to her house. Yet, from the tenor of Lennox's second letter to Lydia, it would seem that Lady Clerke was repulsed by Lennox's first letter. She did not answer it in a timely manner, and Lennox interpreted this hesitation as rejection: "I can not palliate, nor disguise the truth, therefore I will honestly own, that not having received any answer to two or three letters which I wrote to you—I thought I owd so much respect to my self as to be silent for the future." Even two hundred years later, the hurt Lennox felt at what she perceived as rejection by Lydia registers distinctly. Why did Lydia delay responding to Charlotte? Perhaps the slight was unintended. Perhaps someone else closer to hand offered protection and in the bustle of all her comings and goings she postponed responding to Lennox. Perhaps the slight was intended. Perhaps Lydia found Charlotte's eagerness, particularly her image of their living together in a cottage alone, disconcerting. We cannot, in the end, know for certain how Lennox's letter affected Lady Clerke, or why she put off answering it. But it is clear that by the time Lennox wrote her second letter, the relationship was reaffirmed. Lydia must have finally sent a letter (or letters) to soothe Lennox's bruised feelings. Lennox's second letter alludes to what Lydia might have offered, and Lennox accepted, as a reasonable excuse for the gap in their correspondence: "I hope this letter will find you on your return from Wales, in better health, disposd to admit company, and to enjoy tranquility, which while you were continually fluctuating between hope, and fear, was not to be expected." Lydia's vacillating emotional state interfered with her ability to be the friend she usually was. Lennox not only excuses her friend but finds fault with her own expectations; she should not have expected Lydia to be otherwise than distracted.

Protecting Younger Women

Female friendship was important to women not only as they weathered marital difficulties, but also as they tried to protect young women like Sylvia Brathwaite from harm. When Sarah Scott writes to her sister Elizabeth Montagu about "the affair of Miss Bowes," she presents an example of the terrible hazards a young girl faced.[5] Her unequivocal assertions—"The affair of Miss Bowes is but too true"—and final return to the norms of genteel women's visiting habits—"Mrs. Bowes & Miss Bowes made me a visit since I came hither, she is really a fine girl, lively, sensible, & very civil &

---

5   Box 29, MO5754, Montagu Papers, Huntington Library.

goodnatured"—attest to the reality of what admittedly sounds like the plot of a novel, in fact the most famous novel of the period, Samuel Richardson's *Clarissa*. Published in 1747, *Clarissa* tells the story of an ambiguous seduction/ abduction. An immediate bestseller, it served as a model for numerous novels that followed, including Lennox's *The Life of Harriot Stuart,* published three years later. Perhaps Richardson's novels as well as those of some of his imitators were in Scott's mind as she represented the reactions of the various characters and rhythmically repeated "in a fright" as if to turn her story into a fictional one. She knew that her story might be seen as just another of those outrageous fictions about which women were constantly being warned in the eighteenth century. But by ending her story as she did, with a peaceful return to normalcy, she underscores its truth to lived reality.

Although her mother was able to protect her in this instance, in the end Miss Bowes encountered troubles from which her mother could not extricate her. In 1767, four years after Scott's letter, Miss Bowes married John Lyon, Earl of Strathmore. Quickly widowed, she once more became the prey of fortune hunters. In 1777, she married Andrew Robinson Stowey, an Irish adventurer. He "proceeded to squander her fortune, indulge in sexual exploits with servant girls and beat his wife as a punishment for her very existence." The full story of their marriage and divorce can be found in Jane Cox's *Hatred Pursued Beyond the Grave.*[6] A fictional version can be found in William Makepeace Thackeray's novel *The Memoirs of Barry Lyndon, Esq., by Himself.* Like the life of Lydia Clerke, the life of Miss Bowes slips easily into fiction.

Although eighteenth-century women were constantly warned against reading fiction, for it aroused the emotions and fostered unnecessary fears, Lennox used her fictions and plays to argue that women do indeed suffer alarming assaults, such as the one Miss Bowes barely escaped. The vulnerability of the young girl forms the subtext of nearly everything she wrote. It is present in all her novels from *Harriot Stuart* to *Euphemia*. It is present in her criticism of Shakespeare, where she faults him for weakening and trivializing the women characters he found in his predecessors' texts, and in her play *The Sister*, where a young man traduces a young woman and even urges his friend to take sexual advantage of her only to learn in the end that she is his long-lost sister. He closes the play with an eloquent plea to men to treat all women as sisters. And it is most completely and complexly present in *The Female Quixote*, her second and most famous novel. Naive and yet extraordinarily insightful (like her even more famous Spanish predecessor), Arabella, the heroine of the novel, believes the romances she reads are true and, as a consequence, turns the mundane experiences of her ordinary life into sensational fictions. She insists that a new gardener is a disguised nobleman hopelessly enamored of her and undertaking menial labor in order to be near her. She lives in constant fear of abduction and rape. As the novel ends, she

---

[6]   Jane Cox, *Pursued Beyond the Grave* (London, 1993) 28–35.

engages in a debate with a deeply learned and serious-minded Doctor who is brought in by her friends to "cure" her of her "affliction" and to reduce her dependency on the intoxicating flights of fiction. The Doctor tells Arabella that life is not as full of danger and passion as novels would have it. She seems, in the end, to acquiesce to his view of the world. However, it is questionable just how much she capitulates. Although she agrees with the good Doctor that it is wrong to provoke men to commit "Violence and Revenge" for the sake of proving their love, she does not actually ever agree that fiction is empty.

Like her heroine Arabella and her friend Sarah Scott, Lennox found real life to be full of incidents as amazing as any found in fiction. It is hard not to suspect that Lennox uses *The Female Quixote* to poke a little fun at the sacerdotal complacency of the good Divine. While the Doctor would empty life in order to empty fiction, Arabella, Scott, and Lennox insist on the fullness of both. Sometimes terrible and unexpected things do happen to real people, and especially to young women, who spend their lives subject to the unreliable protection of husbands, fathers, and brothers. Mrs. Scott's sober narration of such an amazing episode about real people, whom she knew and with whom she exchanged visits, assures us that outrageous acts were committed against young women not only in fiction but in fact, and Lennox's irony in both her novels and plays affirms time and again that young women need to be warned against men just as much if not more than they need to be warned against reading novels.

Lennox's most poignant example of a young girl's peril, in fact, occurs in a "real" letter rather than in a fictional text. Written to her husband, it represents their daughter Harriet as exposed to serious danger. Mr. Lennox wants to send their daughter to a convent in France, a situation perilously close to one encountered by Lennox's fictional heroine Harriot Stuart. Lennox wants to keep their daughter closer to home:

I have talkd with Mr. Johnson, and other persons of good sense and experience, upon the expediency of sending Harriet to Boulogne for her education—and they are all of opinion, which they supported with very good reasons, that a Boarding school here, will be equally advantagious, equally cheap, and is liable to fewer inconveniencies than a convent. Their reasons have convinced me, and that is the cause that they will never convince you—therefore I submit to your despotick will, with this condition only, that I go with her, and see her settled—this point I never will give up—the next thing to be considered, is what necessaries must be provided—I will give you a list of what cloaths and Linnen are usually sent even to the cheapest schools Half a dozen frocks—she has two already; a dozen pr of stockings—she has four pr but they are old; half a dozen night caps—she has one; four under petticoats—of this article she has none but rags; Morning gowns—of these she has four which I think is enough; Three quilted caps with lace borders—of these she has none; a dozen shifts—of these she has five new ones, three not made up—the others are rags; a handsome Skirt, to wear on Sundays; All the skirts she has had, for more than

THE

Female QUIXOTE;

OR, THE

ADVENTURES

OF

ARABELLA.

In TWO VOLUMES.

VOL. I.

The SECOND EDITION:
Revised and *Corrected.*

Mrs C. Lennox

LONDON:

Printed for A. MILLAR, over-against
Catharine-street in the *Strand.*

M. DCC. LII.

9.1 Title Page from the second edition of *The Female Quixote*. From Author's
Collection

two years past, have been made out of my gowns—she has two of these now, but more than half worn out and only fit to wear in common.[1]

Lennox's tone as she enumerates her daughter's scanty wardrobe reflects her desperation and despair. She cannot provide even the necessities for her daughter. How can she begin to exercise control over what will happen to her? She cannot stop her husband from willfully removing their daughter to a French convent. She can only insist on seeing her settled. Lennox knew from personal experience the dangers young women traveling alone confronted and how powerless mothers could be in their efforts to protect their daughters. When Scott ends her narration with Miss Bowes safely and securely by her mother's side, she, like Lennox, insists on the mother's right to confront and defeat threats, real and imagined, to a daughter's virtue. But, with her rhythmic acknowledgment of the hazards a mother ran in a world controlled by unpredictable footmen, stewards, justices of the peace, and members of Parliament, Scott too concedes the limits of a mother's power.

In her letter to her husband, Lennox goes on to suggest a school about four miles from Gosport, which would be preferable for many reasons, not least of which because of its proximity to Lady Clerke. Hoping to keep her daughter closer to home and under Lady Clerke's protection, Lennox tells her husband that Lady Clerke has promised to "supply the place of a mother to her—that she would see her every week or fortnight, take her home to her Mama's house during every vacation, and write me regular accounts of her health, her improvements and her behaviour." As a further inducement Lennox tells her husband that Lady Clerke has already mentioned Harriet in her will, and that, considering Lady Clerke's situation, their daughter would be "in fortune's way" as well as in virtue's way under her care.

Mothers and Daughters

Charlotte enthusiastically nurtured a relationship between Lydia and her daughter. "Your Harriet is with me," she writes in her second letter. It was natural that she wanted these two people to know and care about one another; it must have pleased her to think that if anything should happen to her there was another woman who cared deeply about her daughter's welfare. "Harriet begs I will leave room for her to write a few lines to you whom she truly dotes on," Lennox remarks just before sending her compliments to Mrs. Hammond, Lady Clerke's "Mama." Lennox might have hoped that an emphasis on the mother/ daughter bond across the generations would ensure Lydia's continued interest in Harriet.

---

[7]   Isles 426–7.

Undeniably Lydia Clerke cared about Harriet, and Harriet's words to her express a sincere regard in return. Did Lennox tell her daughter what to write? or did she watch proudly and silently as her daughter penned the delightful note that now exists? If she did indeed supervise the construction of her daughter's note it becomes just another sign of her maternal solicitude and belief in the power of female friendship. Harriet's words are gentle and loving, and it is not hard to imagine that they deeply moved Lydia, whose tears may have worn the holes in the paper that now make reading the young girl's words so difficult. Rereading Harriet's note over the years, Lydia must have wept often, indulging in the sorrowful feelings brought on by bittersweet memories of a promising girl who died young.

In 1777, when she writes her amiable message to Lady Clerke, Harriet is twelve years old and under her mother's protection. Just one year later, at the age of thirteen, she is arrested, along with her mother and a woman named Hannah Davis, for disturbing the peace. Indicted in the county of Middlesex as "wicked and evil disposed persons and Riotous Routers and disturbers of the peace," the three women are accused of causing a great tumult "in the Dwelling House of one Nicholas Hancock" where they assaulted one Ann Brown.[8] One of the strangest documents I came across, this indictment confounded me; I could not understand why a thirteen-year-old girl along with her mother and a third woman would engage in riotous assembly. Perhaps her age of thirteen years should alert us to another reading of this incident. Like her mother, who, according to her first letter to Lydia Clerke, was thirteen when her father died, Harriet was also thirteen when she encountered a potentially extremely dangerous situation.

Laetitia Hawkins, a young contemporary of Lennox's, refers to this incident in a book of anecdotes. From her point of view it betokens Lennox's brutality, which she sees as like Samuel Johnson's: "The matter is indeed set even by his [Johnson] having decreed the palm of excellence in female authorship, to his favourite Charlotte Lennox whom I remember waiting at Hick's-hall, till a trial came on before my father and the other justices;—a trial in which it must be confessed she had some concern; for it was an indictment preferred by her maid against her, for beating her! It came out that a battle had taken place between 'the Female Quixote,' and her solitary domestic. How the legal question was decided, I have, I regret to say, forgotten:—it gave me an opportunity of seeing the illustrious lady, and at a safe distance."[9] Hawkins writes many years after the event, so her memory may be faulty as well as incomplete. Nevertheless, her animosity and jealousy come through clearly and her representation of Lennox as a wild amazon ready to pick fights with hapless innocents is certainly supported by the wording on the indictment drawn up against the author, her

---

[8]   MJ/SR 3358/9, Greater London Record Office.

[9]   Laetitia M. Hawkins, *Anecdotes* (London, 1824) 1:331.

daughter, and Hannah Davis. But is the incident as unequivocal as the indictment and Hawkins suggest?

If we turn to other legal documents (dated 1782 and 1789) from the same Middlesex record office, we find that Ann Brown may not have been Lennox's maid. In 1782 and 1789, a woman named "Ann Brown" was charged with luring men into rooms to relieve them of their money and watches while they slept.[10] The Ann Brown in Lennox's indictment might have been the same Ann Brown identified as a pickpocket-prostitute in the other two court documents. If both Ann Browns were the same woman and remembering that Harriet Lennox was, at this time, thirteen years old, might we not see Charlotte Lennox and Hannah Davis (perhaps Lennox's maid?) as rescuers of a young girl who had been taken to Nicholas Hancock's house for illicit purposes? This possibility is admittedly far-fetched, but trafficking in women has a long and underground history, and it is not implausible that Lennox was indeed acting like her most famous heroine, rescuing a young woman (her own daughter in this case) from a situation she perceived as dangerous. Whether or not it was actually dangerous we cannot know, but it could have been. In *Hatred Pursued Beyond the Grave*, Jane Cox presents the seventeenth-century case of a prostitute named Lucy Hungate, who was indicted at King's Bench for abducting a young girl.[11] In *English Sexualities*, Tim Hitchcock notes that the average age of a prostitute in the eighteenth century was between 15 and 25.[12] While Hawkins prefers to see the rescue as an example of Lennox's brutality, it can be seen as an example of her tireless and perhaps futile battle to protect her imperilled daughter from the snares of this world.

We do not know whether Harriet Lennox ever went to school, either in Gosport or in France. We learn, in Sylvia Brathwaite's letter about ghosts, written in 1785, that she is dying: "Harriot Lenox is supposed to be dying—poor Thing—I believe latterly she has been amiable—Her Ilness is lingering—her sense good—and I trust she will think properly." Sylvia's words are harsh. Had Harriet been less than amiable? Was she headstrong? Are we making too much of Sylvia's words if we speculate that the undated "school" letter was provoked by some sort of improper thinking on Harriet's part? Given the fact that she is thirteen when the ambiguous Middlesex incident occurs, it is possible to surmise that as she reached her difficult teenage years, she became impulsive and unruly. With this possibility in mind, we can offer still another reading of the incident. Perhaps Harriet was not kidnapped by Ann Brown after all. Perhaps she was seduced. Or, fretful about her parents' restrictions on her movements and sexually curious, she might have gone freely and willingly to the home of Nicholas Hancock. Like many adolescent girls, Harriet was probably moody, sometimes sweet and loving, but, at other times, rebellious. Did the threat of school

---

[10] OB/SP 1782 Ap/41, OB/SP 1789 Jy/24, Greater London Record Office.

[11] Cox 87–93.

[12] Hitchcock 95.

send her into the streets for adventure? or, did her dangerous adventures cause her parents to seek out an appropriate school?

We know so little about Harriet. All that remains of her are her words, fragile and fading, on the back of her mother's second letter to Lady Clerke. It seems appropriate that the last mention of Lennox's daughter in the Lydia Clerke collection appears in a letter about ghosts.

If 13 was a difficult age for Harriet Lennox, it was also a difficult age for her mother. Charlotte Lennox's biographers often point out that the fictional adventures of Harriot, the eponymous heroine of *The Life of Harriot Stuart*, derive from her author's actual experiences. "Lennox," Margaret Anne Doody contends, "allowed others to believe that the novel was autobiographical."[13] Like her heroine Harriot, Lennox was thirteen when her father died and she sailed from America to England in the hope that her mother's family would help her and her financially straitened family. The family connection proved useless to both Harriot and Lennox, but both received unexpected help from strangers. As already noted, two different circles of acquaintance—a circle of wealthy women which included the Duchess of Newcastle, Lady Cecelia Isabella Finch, and Lady Rockingham; and a circle of up-and-coming literary men, which included Thomas Birch and Samuel Johnson—patronized the young Charlotte Ramsay. In *The Life of Harriot Stuart*, she represents the first circle when, perhaps unfairly, she satirizes Isabella Finch in the fictional "Lady Cecelia," who, at first, befriends the hapless Harriot and promises her a position at court, and then turns against her when she is falsely accused of attacking the family tutor (who actually first sexually assaulted her). Many people held this fictional portrait of Finch against Lennox. Lady Mary Wortley Montagu bristled in a letter to her daughter the Countess of Bute: "I was rouz'd into great surprize and Indignation by the monstrous abuse of one of the very, very few Women I have a real value for. I mean Lady B[ell] F[inch],who is not only clearly meant by the mention of her Library, she being the only Lady at Court that has one, but her very name at length, she being christen'd Caecelia Isabella, thô she chuses to be call'd by the Latter. I allwaies thought her conduct in every light so irreproachable, I did not think she had an Enemy upon Earth. I now see 'tis impossible to avoid them, especially in her Situation. It is one of the misfortunes of a suppos'd Court interest ... even the people you have oblig'd hate you if they do not think you have serv'd them to the utmost extent of a power that they fancy you are possess'd of; which it may be is only imaginary."[14] Whether Finch was hypocritical and self-absorbed, as Lennox represented her, or the blameless victim of heartless satire, as Lady Montagu protested, or, more likely, something in between, the story of Harriot's predicament attests to the ease with which a women's story can be distorted to suit different purposes.

---

[13] Margaret Anne Doody, "Introduction," *The Female Quixote* (Oxford, 1989) xix.
[14] Lady Mary Wortley Montagu 3:8.

Women's stories are not easily re-membered. Both men and women prefer his story to hers. In *Harriot Stuart*, the tutor's story of the eponymous heroine's aggressive attack on him easily supplants her story of his sexual assault on her. The patriarchal judicial view of Lennox's actions seems more rational to Laetitia Hawkins than Lennox's view of herself as the rescuer of women in peril. It is not easy to present the woman's point of view; it is easier to dismiss it. When Arabella, in *The Female Quixote*, hears the shady history of Miss Groves's seduction, she transforms it. Rather than agree that the mother of two children born out of wedlock is a wicked woman, she would rather traduce the man as a cowardly seducer who vilely abandons the woman who loves him. But few are willing to accept Arabella's version of Miss Groves's history. In her handling of Arabella's unusual (and often feminist) explications of the stories she hears, Lennox suggests that women need to listen more carefully to each other's stories.

As much as Charlotte and Lydia shared—difficult marriages, a desire to protect vulnerable young women, and lives that slipped easily into fiction—there were important differences between them. One of the most significant must be their different experiences of mothering, both as mothers and as daughters. Lennox left her mother behind when she came to London at the very young age of 13. Chances are she never saw her mother again. Catherine Ramsay died in New York in 1765, the same year that Harriet Lennox was born. While Charlotte lost her mother just when she probably needed her most, Lydia was lucky enough to have her mother with her during the most trying times of her married and widowed life. Almost every letter to Lydia asks after Mrs. Hammond. We do not know when Mrs. Hammond died, but it is likely that it was only after her mother passed away that Lydia felt free to marry Joseph Townsend and move to Wiltshire.

Not only did the two women have very different mothering experiences as daughters, but they also had different experiences as mothers. Lydia and John had no children. However, when Lydia remarried, she became the step-mother of six children, four sons and two daughters. In Sylvia's last letter, she recommends a chaperone for Lydia's daughters, thus suggesting that Lydia had the means to protect and care for the step-children she acquired by marriage to Mr. Townsend. Lennox was not as lucky; she had few resources and little help in caring for and promoting the interests of her two children. As already suggested, her daughter died young. In addition to Sylvia's terse comment in her "ghost" letter, there is a memorial poem in Lennox's own hand "On Henrietta Holles Lennox 17," which speaks movingly of an early death: "And take a lesson from this early grave ... /In youth and beauty mark how vain to trust." Duncan Isles believes the existence of the poem confirms the fact of Harriet's death at 17.[15]

---

[15]   Isles 428–9.

Lennox's second child, George Louis, born six years after his sister, also seems to have come to a lamentable end. As a young man, he demonstrated great promise; he published poems and short stories in such magazines as the *British Magazine and Review*, the *Edinburgh Weekly Magazine*, the *Hibernian*, the *New Novelist's Magazine*, and the *Weekly Entertainer*. In her second letter to Lydia, Charlotte crows: "My dear little boy is always with me from Saturday, till Sunday evening, when he returns to the Academy, of which, young as he is [six years old], he is the ornament, and delight." Unfortunately this early promise did not last. The next reference to him, found in Lennox's 1793 letter of application for assistance to the Royal Literary Fund, suggests that his father lured him into illegal activities and that he consequently had to flee England: "I see an only child upon the brink of utter ruin—driven as he was first to desperation by a most unnatural father; and then deserted, and left exposed to all the evils that may well be expected from the deceitful circumstances he is in."[16] Of course, this letter may include fictional elements. Looking at Lennox's elaborations ("The last ship that will go to America till next March, will sail in a week—the money for the passage must be paid before he goes on board, and the very lowest terms that are offered, are out of my reach") and taking into account the letter's replication of fictional difficulties encountered by the son in Lennox's 1790 novel *Euphemia*, it is possible that Lennox drew on her fiction to dramatize her need for financial assistance and to create a sense of urgency. However, she pleads with such passion and conviction that I sometimes doubt my own skepticism: "I would preserve him if I could," she exclaims, her voice full of authentic parental anxiety. Perhaps Lennox used the real-life situation of her husband and son to feed her fancy when constructing the events of *Euphemia*. Whether life became fiction, or fiction fact, we cannot know. Nor can we know for sure if Lennox's efforts on behalf of her son were successful.[17]

Lennox's experiences as daughter, mother, and wife were far more difficult than Lydia's. While Lydia died with a loving husband beside her and probably some of her step-children in attendance, Charlotte died alone and poor in Dean's Yard, Westminster, on 4 January 1804, and, according to Nichols's *Literary Anecdotes*, "lies buried with the *common soldiery* in the further burying-ground of Broad Chapel, undistinguished even by a headstone to say where she lies."[18]

Altogether, Charlotte's life was much harder than Lydia's. While Lydia led a peaceful existence, spending most of her life in Gosport or Southampton before moving to Pewsey, Wiltshire upon her marriage to Townsend, Charlotte's life was peripatetic, almost frenetically so. As a child, she moved from the American Colonies

---

[16]   BM, Microfilm M1077, Reel #1.
[17]   See Berg, "Getting the Mother's Story Right: Charlotte Lennox and the New World" for a fuller explanation of these arguments.
[18]   John Nichols, *Literary Anecdotes of the Eighteenth Century* (London, 1812–16) 7:435.

to England, and as an adult, she moved many times from one end of London to another, often fleeing creditors. She struggled ceaselessly to keep a roof over her head, to earn a living, and to care for her children.

A Woman Writer

Lennox's main source of income throughout her life was her work as a writer, and, in the course of a 50-year career, she produced a formidable bibliography: a book of poems and occasional verse, seven novels, two books of criticism (*Shakespear Illustrated* and *The Greek Theatre of Father Brumoy*), four translations from the French, three plays, and a periodical, *The Lady's Museum*, which ran to eleven numbers. In 1752, 1775, and 1793, she circulated proposals for new editions of her work by subscription. Lydia Clerke probably purchased a subscription in response to the 1775 proposal.

Although a successful writer, Lennox encountered many difficulties. In her second letter to Lydia, she writes about one of her many wars with the booksellers. She and her publishers were quarreling over plans to reissue Sully's *Memoirs* without consulting or remunerating its author. Lennox counts on Dr. Johnson's and Lord Camden's help, but fears her old friend and antagonist David Garrick will do more damage than the other two men can do good.

The eighteenth century was a time of great change in the book trade. As the patronage of the wealthy declined, the power of the booksellers grew and acts of Parliament were necessary to regulate the trade. At the beginning of the century, on 1 April 1710, The Act for the Encouragement of Learning came into force: a book published prior to that date, was given to the bookseller for 21 years; if the book was published after 1710, as Sully's *Memoirs* was, then the bookseller was given a copyright for 14 years but could renew his copyright for another 14 years with the author if s/he were still living. In 1774, in a landmark case, Donaldson v. Becket, the House of Lords voted against perpetual copyright, effectively ending the booksellers' stranglehold on the book trade. The booksellers protested and a relief bill designed to provide booksellers with an additional fourteen years of copyright was proposed.[19] It was perhaps with this relief bill in mind that Dodsley decided to reprint *Sully*

---

[19]   There is a wealth of material about eighteenth-century British copyright law. Particularly helpful to me were Mark Rose, *Authors and Owners* (Cambridge, 1993). A.S. Collins, *Authorship in the Days of Johnson: Being a Study of the Relation between Author, Patron, Publisher and Public, 1726–1780* (London, 1927); John Feather, *A History of British Publishing* (London, 1988); Benjamin Kaplan, *An Unhurried View of Copyright* (New York, 1966); and Martha Woodmansee and Peter Jaszi, eds, *The Construction of Authorship: Textual Appropriation in Law and Literature* (Durham, 1994) were also helpful.

9.2 "The Nine Living Muses of Great Britain: Portraits in the Characters of the Muses in the Temple of Apollo," by Richard Samuel, 1779. Charlotte Lennox is on the right. National Portrait Gallery, London

without consulting Lennox. However, the bill was defeated, and Lennox correctly concludes that Dodsley is acting in defiance of Parliament in reissuing the work without consulting her. Although in her letter Lennox fears she will lose her battle, it would seem that she won, or that, at least, she and Dodsley compromised, for two editions of the *Memoirs* appeared in 1778, one identifying her as the author and the other not, and no new printings of Sully's *Memoirs* appeared until 1805, a year after Lennox's death.

Copyright may have been the issue that most frustrated Lennox as a writer, but she also cared about her reputation. She hoped her fame would last. In a brief, undated letter to Johnson, she urges haste for she fears she will soon be forgotten: "as it is of great consequence to me to have the book presented to His Majesty, before I am quite forgot, the sooner you begin to deal with Mr. Strahan the better."[20] Though ultimately her fame was fleeting, in her own day she was declared a genius. Her books were important; her ideas and images, particularly that of the female Quixote, circulated widely; her learning was celebrated by her contemporaries. In 1779, she was included as one of "The Nine Living Muses of Great Britain" by painter Richard Samuel.[21] Nonetheless, during the course of the nineteenth century, she almost disappeared from literary history, eclipsed by the many literary men of her day. We could accept this occurrence as a normal adjustment in literary appreciation: gradually and over the course of time, the best writers rise and the second-rate fall. Modern literary theory, however, suggests that literary history and the fluctuations of authorial reputations are not such rational processes. Prejudice, chance, and intentional oversight complicate matters. If Lennox was forgotten, overlooked, or mentioned only briefly (usually in a footnote) in most nineteenth-century and early twentieth-century histories of the Age of Johnson, it might have been as a result of forces unrelated to literary value but more a consequence of the way women's roles play and re-play in history. While men are usually treated as independent and autonomous, women, more likely than not, are treated as appendages of the men they knew. Lennox's obscurity perhaps partly results from the intense spotlight focused on Samuel Johnson, her friend and colleague. In biography after biography (even those focusing on Lennox), she is pictured as gratefully receiving the patronage of the established and twenty-years-older writer.

Nevertheless, at least once, in a 1754 letter to Lennox from Mary Jones, a poet and occasional writer who lived in Oxford, Lennox moves to the foreground while Johnson fades into the background. She becomes the luminary, he the satellite: "And now I'm got among the celestial Signs, pray, where is that Meteor, that Rambler, that.

[20]   Small 53.
[21]   The other eight were Elizabeth Carter, Anna Laetitia Barbauld, Angelica Kauffmann, Frances Sheridan, Catherine Macaulay, Hannah More, Elizabeth Montagu, and Elizabeth Griffith.

shew'd himself in our Hemisphere last Summer, & has never been heard of since, except among the Transactions of the Literati? If he is often at your Elbow (a Situation he had the Confidence to boast of to me) I should be oblig'd to you if you'd make my Compliments to him. He's so restless a Companion, that twas impossible to take my Observations of him, with any Accuracy, in his Company; but now he's got Abroad, & exhibits himself fairly to the Eye, I doubt not of contemplating his Magnitude with the greatest Satisfaction."[22] It is refreshing to see Johnson, the Rambler, boasting of his friendship with Lennox and dropping her name into a conversation in order to magnify his importance in another woman's eyes. Presenting himself as Lennox's confidant reflected glory on him.

If we look at what both Lennox and Johnson produced by 1754, the date of Jones's letter, her perception becomes not simply contrary but also insightful. While Johnson had published much by 1754, Lennox had published more. Johnson's translation of Lobo's *A Voyage to Abyssinia*, his poems "London" and "The Vanity of Human Wishes," and his *Life of Mr. Richard Savage* had appeared; his Plan for *A Dictionary of the English Language* had circulated; Garrick had produced his tragedy *Irene*; and the *Rambler*, his periodical, had appeared every two weeks for two years, from 1750 until 1752. He had also, for several years, composed the "Parliamentary Debates" in the *Gentleman's Magazine* and contributed to his friend Hawkesworth's *Adventurer*. Meanwhile, Lennox had published *Poems on Several Occasions*, two novels (*The Life of Harriot Stuart* and *The Female Quixote*), translated *The Memoirs of the Duke of Sully* and Voltaire's *Siècle de Louis XIV*, and produced *Shakespear Illustrated*, becoming, as Margaret Anne Doody notes, "the first woman to produce a scholarly work on English literature, and the first feminist critic of a major author."[23] It is not necessarily a misconstruction to reverse the values we have conventionally given Johnson and Lennox. Johnson was older and achieved greater importance eventually, but Lennox was a widely known and successful author who perhaps reached larger audiences than Johnson in their own day. She was as much his

---

[22] Isles 42–3. Mary Jones's *Miscellanies in Prose and Verse* was published by Dodsley in 1750. With her playful irony, she strikes me as, like Lennox, a precursor to Jane Austen: "Wit mixt with Good-nature, and corrected with good Manners, is certainly an agreeable Qualification, and many times an useful one too. But as 'tis generally manag'd, I reckon a Tooth-drawer, or a Corn-cutter by far more useful Members of Society. Nay have heard some of our Male-Critics positively assert, That she who can make a Pudding, or a Pye, has a much better Title to their Approbation, than she who can make a Pun or a Preamble of an Hour long" (299). In their 1755 edition of *Poems by Eminent Ladies*, editors Bonnell Thornton and George Colman the Elder describe Jones as "the daughter of the late Mr. Oliver Jones, of Oxford. She is now living; and the reader will readily agree that Oxford is deservedly called the Seat of the Muses while this ingenious Lady resides there" (254).

[23] Margaret Anne Doody, "Shakespeare's Novels: Charlotte Lennox Illustrated," *Studies in the Novel* 19 (1987): 307.

peer as his protégée. According to Norma Clarke, "Mrs. Montagu may have been 'Queen of the Blues' but Charlotte Lennox, crowned queen at the Devil tavern by her peers, was the reigning monarch of the booksellers in the 1750s."[24]

If it is with great difficulty that contemporary literary critics see the woman as equal to the man, it was just as difficult, if not more so, for the citizen of the eighteenth century. Women were judged as a category apart from men. Even Johnson, as much as he praised Lennox, always did so in reference to other women: "I dined yesterday at Mrs. Garrick's with Mrs. Carter, Miss Hannah More, and Miss Fanny Burney. Three such women are not to be found: I know not where I could find a fourth except Mrs. Lennox, who is superiour to them all."[25] Women might be geniuses but they were not comparable to men. Lennox felt this disparity deeply. In her novels, plays, and essays, there is much evidence of her discomfort with the ways women in general, and women writers in particular, were treated.

The Lady's Museum

In *The Lady's Museum*, a dialogic compendium of history, natural science, poetry, fiction, and philosophy, Lennox gives us perhaps her most complete and complex subversion of the many complacencies of her day. While the explicit texts of many of the periodical's articles suggest that women are triflers and happiest when they submit to their natural inclination to trifle, ironic subtexts argue that women sometimes want to be taken seriously and that perhaps even the Editor herself—despite her many claims to Trifler-hood—has purposes other than merely to divert and please her readers. Using a series of personae—"Parthenissa," "Perdita," "Penelope Spindle," and "Mrs. Trifler"—and declaring herself to be the self-proclaimed daughter and granddaughter of triflers, Lennox produces a discourse so polysemous that it is hard to tell where she stands: "if we poor women furnished our minds with moral and historical truth, and took pains to acquire the true principles of taste and criticism, we should be very apt upon this supposition to discern the deficiencies of our admirers in these articles; and from a total dissimilitude of manners and pursuits, grow quickly disgusted at each other, and to risk our establishments for the sake of accomplishments no longer respected."[26] If we carefully peel back the layers of irony in this "letter to the editor," we are left with the inescapable conclusion that men are not the lords of creation they claim to be. While it is in women's economic interest to defer to men, such deference is fragile and false. It only lasts as long as women remain uneducated. If they were to furnish their minds

---

24 Norma Clarke, *Dr. Johnson's Women* (London, 2000) 118.
25 Boswell, *The Life of Samuel Johnson* 1:510.
26 *The Lady's Museum*, January 1761: 641–3.

"with moral and historical truth" and "acquire the true principles of taste and criticism," they would soon learn how deficient their male counterparts were. Women dare not better themselves, for then they would not be able to stay with the men they admired and chose in their ignorance. Husbands and wives would grow dissatisfied with one another. Husbands would become less solicitous; wives might lose their homes. And, as Lennox's last clause suggests, once women were accomplished, the accomplishments they struggled so hard to obtain would lose value. What men (and women) respect in men, they do not as readily respect in women.

Lennox's sentiments were enthusiastically echoed in "To the World," an anonymous introduction to a 1761 edition of Susannah Centlivre's works: "Be it known that the Person with Pen in Hand is no other than a Woman, not a little piqued to find that neither the Nobility nor Commonality of the Year 1722, had Spirit enough to erect in *Westminster-Abbey*, a Monument justly due to the Manes of the never to be forgotten Mrs. Centlivre, whose Works are full of lively Incidents, genteel Language, and humorous Descriptions of real Life, and deserved to have been recorded by a Pen equal to that which celebrated the Life of *Pythagoras*."[27] Protesting against the poor treatment Centlivre's work and reputation received earlier in the century, the self-declared female author pointedly seeks a woman writer like Anne Dacier (the French classical scholar) to indite the biography of the now deceased Centlivre, thus implying that a male writer would not do the job as well. The anonymous critic goes on to castigate the ways in which men promote themselves and one another: "Some Authors have had a *Shandeian* Knack of ushering in their own Praises, sounding their own Trumpet, calling Absurdity Wit, and boasting when they ought to blush; but our Poetess had Modesty, the general Attendant of Merit. She was even asham'd to proclaim her own great Genius, probably because the Custom of the Times discountenanced poetical Excellence in a Female. The Gentlemen of the Quill published it not, perhaps envying her superior Talents; and her Bookseller, complying with national Prejudices, put a fictitious Name to her *Love's Contrivance*, thro' Fear that the Work shou'd be condemned, if known to be Feminine." Because, unlike her male counterparts, she did not promote herself, Centlivre is forgotten even though her works were popular and revered in her day. The anonymous author would like to believe that conditions have changed and that women are no longer unfairly treated. She does not want to "reproach the present Age for the Sins of their Fathers." So she points out how much better things are. Men are not ashamed to own their dependence on and collaboration with women writers: "A pleasing Prospect I've lately had, *viz.* the Work of the ingenious Lord *Corke*, and the not less ingenious Mr. *Samuel Johnson*, who have took pains to translate a large Part of Father *Brumoy's Greek* Theatre, and were not ashamed that their Labours should be joined to those of Mrs.

---

27 Mrs. Centlivre, *The Work of the Celebrated Mrs. Centlivre in Three Volumes* (London, 1761) 1:vii–x.

Lennox." She goes on to hazard that since now men willingly admit women have souls, it may not be long before they also admit women can write poetry equal even to Pope's.

I begin to suspect that Lennox was the anonymous author of "To the World," which was published in the same year as the last number of *The Lady's Museum*. The sentiments in the Centlivre introduction are not unlike those in Lennox's periodical. Both are full of complex and multilayered ironies. Both vigorously protest women's unnatural and disadvantageous subordination. Likewise, both the anonymous author and Lennox insist that women's political as well as literary abilities are equal to men's. My strongest piece of evidence, however, is the stress the anonymous author places on Mrs. Lennox, the only living woman writer identified by name in the piece. When she advertises with detailed particularity the collective translation of *The Greek Theatre of Father Brumoy*, it is easy to imagine Lennox slyly giving her friends a hint as to the identity of the writer, thus adding another layer of self-reflexive irony to her text. Since within the text she stresses women's tendency to minimize their own achievements, she can hardly promote herself directly. However, even as she playfully professes anonymity and frets about a woman writer's need to behave with ladylike propriety, she shamelessly promotes a recently published work.

Both *The Lady's Museum* and "To the World" overflow with provocative ironies. Writing anonymously and subversively allowed Lennox to transgress boldly. Without fear of ridicule, she could vehemently and covertly wield her pen against all the injustices that threatened her livelihood and her future fame. She might even have had a quixotic hope that her words would, either in her own day or some time in the future, reach ears that heard.

Chapter 10

Ann Clerke Three

Never had perhaps so great a naval force been assembled on the seas. Never any by which less was done.

The Annual Register (1780)

Written on 7 September 1779, three years after the death of John Clerke and 16 days after the death of Charles, Ann's third letter to Lydia is brief and solicitous. She does not mention the recent death of her younger brother; it is unlikely the news would have reached her yet. Even if it had, the danger Lydia faces overrides any other concerns. French and Spanish ships threaten to invade Gosport, where Lydia and her mother live. Rhetorically balanced between anxious concern and comic relief, Ann's letter opens with an earnest reference to the "general alarm" and ends with humorous descriptions of her sister Hannah's and her brother-in-law Harry Maty's peculiarities. There is an elegiac tone to this letter. A generation is growing older yet things are not getting better. War, loneliness, old age, and foolishness haunt the human condition.

11

From: Ann Clerke, Wethersfield
To: Lady Clerke, North Street, Gosport
Date: 7 September 1779

Where shall I find you my Dear Sister in this time of general alarm. I'm at a loss where to direct to you but think a direction to Gosport the most promising chance of my Letter finding you some where, & I beg you will let me have a line from you as soon as this reaches your hand. For tho there are few people trouble themselves less about publick affairs then I do I cannot help being anxious about these french & spanish Fleets when I read in the papers that it is supposed they will make an attempt upon Portsmouth & that all the inhabitants of Gosport are preparing to abandon there habitations. But I hope no part of this news is true or at least that Sir Charles Hardy being at Spithead will secure your part of the Kingdom what ever depredations may be made by the enemy else where, but I shall hope that the almighty who blew with his wind & scattered the invincible Spanish Armada will again find means to deliver us from the invasion of these perfidious Gauls. But I never met with any occasion in the course of my Life before, I can truly say, that made me wish so much for a House of my own that might afford you & your good mother an asylum till these troubles are past, of which what will be the event God only knows. The people about us seem under great apprehension but as I cannot at this distance judge what <u>real</u> cause there is for disquiet & various reports prevail, I determine to hope the best while hope is left.

Mrs Maty is still with us, her health I think is much mended since she came to us. But it is a great misfortune to both her & her Husband that they can have the advice of Physicians for nothing. I'm satisfy'd they would have both better health if they would listen less to art, & use plain reason & common sense in the preservation of their health. I expect they will stay with us till the latter end of this month & by that time we shall all be very glad to part, for indeed if it was not for the amusement the Dear innocent Child affords me I'm afraid my patience would scarcely be sufficient for the occasions Mrs Matty gives me to exert it, for she is indeed the most, the same woman at seven & forty that she was at seventeen as one can possibly imagine a woman to be. I don't mean as to person but mind & manners. Harry is a very honest fellow but a great oddity, & my Father not less, so that I am often at a loss how to act between them. He hopes you received your parcel safe by the Gosport stage. The Wind blows very high tonight, I wish it may disperse the Enemy's fleet, but I beg & intreat you will let me hear from you immediately & believe me with the sincerest affection yours A Clerke

M^r & Mrs Maty desire their kindest Comp^ts to you, & I beg you will remember my most affectionate wishes to Mrs Hamond. I shall be very anxious to hear from you on her account, for as to any great anxiety & apprehension there is no saying what effect it may have upon a woman at her time of Life. As to our selves we know if we continue in the World we must meet with changes & be they for the better or the worse I hope our spirits will be equal to them. But old age & infirmities naturally wish for rest & quiet, & are consequently distress'd at the appearence of trouble. Do me justice to Mrs Williams & family. God bless & keep you & all you Love. Adieu. I will write to you again as soon as I can get any information where you are—

Master and Commander

When Ann writes to Lydia on 7 September 1779, she has good reason to be concerned about her friends in Gosport. Invasion and bombardment are imminent.

In 1763 the Peace of Paris brought the Seven Years' War to an end. Although the British opposition claimed the Peace was too lenient on France and Spain, the French felt humiliated and, in a spirit of revenge, had long been planning an invasion of England. Gosport, directly across from Portsmouth, was an important part of the French invasion plan. According to A. Temple Patterson, "An attack on the Isle of Wight would be made first, followed by one on Gosport, from which Portsmouth and its dockyard could be bombarded and destroyed."[1] Because their ships had been plundered and their territories invaded, Spain was eager to join with France and declared war on 16 June 1779. In the meantime, the British navy was in disarray. When Keppel resigned the command of the Channel Fleet in March 1779, it proved hard to find a successor. Finally Vice-Admiral Sir Charles Hardy, the Governor of Greenwich Hospital, volunteered. Sixty-four and in poor health, he had not commanded at sea for nearly 20 years. He was an unlikely hero.

At first, Hardy disappointed many. He did not take decisive action. He procrastinated, cautiously avoiding the enemy rather than boldly engaging with them. However, in the end, this strategy proved successful. On 31 August, Hardy passed the enemy at Land's End in the fog and decided to draw them as far as he could up the Channel before risking an engagement. Reaching Spithead on 3 September, he planned to obtain reinforcements, land the sick, and replenish his water supply. Unbeknownst to him, sickness was spreading on the enemy's ships and on 1 September the enemy fleets had been ordered to return to Brest. Although Hardy's plan of withdrawal eventually won the day, throughout the month of August there was much fear of bombardment. On 17 August, the *Ardent*, on its way down the Channel to meet Hardy, mistook the enemy fleet for his, sailed right into it, and was compelled to surrender. On 18 August, the enemy's fleet could be seen about six leagues out from Plymouth Sound. According to the *Hampshire Chronicle* of 23 August, "Cries of distress and fright arose from women and children; all business ceased and shops and houses were shut up." On 28 August, an article in the *Ipswich Journal* claimed that "[t]he French fleet has been seen off the coast of Cornwall. It is believed they will not be able to maintain their situation, nevertheless, 700 miners are brought in to dig entrenchments along the shore." When Ann writes, she expresses the apprehension that was in the air not only in Essex and Hampshire but in all of England.

The Matys and Unsung Miltons

Ann does not want to minimize her friend's fears, but she does want to cheer her up as well as offer sympathy, so once she has expressed her dismay at the current military situation, she returns to more familiar and more amusing matters. She finds humor in Hannah's girlish ways. Just four years earlier, in 1775, Hannah married Paul Henry Maty, a man who was nine years her junior. Perhaps she believed girlish ways minimized the unusual disparity in their ages. Ann not only finds humor in her sister's childishness but also in her brother-in-law's eccentricities, in particular his over-reliance on new medical treatments. An assistant-librarian in the British Museum and

---

[1]   A. Temple Patterson, *The Other Armada* (Manchester, 1960) 49.

a member of the Royal Society, and, by 1779, its foreign secretary, Harry Maty undoubtedly enjoyed easy access to the latest medical theories of the day. And, as we all know, sometimes too much medicine can be a bad thing. Certainly Ann believes so. Nevertheless, Ann finds humor in the Matys' dependence on science and in their uncritical and irrational acceptance of all its methods and findings. Although impatient with their frailties, she yet loves them both and welcomes their visits and the diversions they bring, even though her own common sense and simplicity are very much tried in the effort it takes to entertain them and she is always glad when they leave.

In tune with the currents of eighteenth-century thought, Ann carefully evaluated every situation of which she became aware and used her experiences and knowledge to gain a deeper and more philosophic understanding of the world and her place in it. Although she did not blame the narrowness of her lot and the limitations of women's lives in general on the existence of an onerous and pervasive patriarchy, there is evidence that even if she did not always use our modern vocabulary, she did not suffer gladly the unfairnesses of patriarchal power. In this, her third letter to Lydia, she writes, "I can truly say, that made me wish so much for a House of my own that might afford you & your good mother an asylum till these troubles are past." In this brief mention of her dependence we can perhaps hear a deeper note of anguish. Forced to live in her father's house, she does not have the wherewithal to protect the people she loves. Also, in the letter about Charles's aristocratic acquaintance, she expresses disapproval not only of Charles but of her father: "I was astonish'd to hear with what pleasure my F. [speaks] of C.C.: great acquaintance & connection with people of Condition, rank, & fortune." Joseph Clerke must not have been an easy man to live with, especially after his wife died. As he grew older and lost his mental abilities but retained his physical strength (a condition we now identify as senile dementia), he must have become more and more unmanageable. After her brothers sailed away to exotic places and her sister Hannah moved to London to live with her husband, leaving her home alone with an aged parent and her younger sister Sarah, Ann must have sometimes felt frustrated by a world which constricted and burdened her in so many ways and so willingly left her behind.

Although she may have sometimes felt buried in Wethersfield and wished she could escape family obligations, Ann's mind ranged widely and deeply. In her letters, she muses about many things. Without ever sounding pompous or didactic, she ponders the world's virtues and vices. Her voice is eloquent, her style both graceful and forceful. Time and time again her words slide effortlessly into the rhythms of poetry: "let your own heart tell you the difference between this & that spontaneous affection which the heart only can give which neither can be purchased nor extorted"; "But I have been more inclined to envy at the sight of a spruce Quaker then upon any other occasion whatsoever, tho this is a mortification I very seldom meet with, for they like all the rest of the World are flying from all simplicity & originality & mixing with the herd of Copys of Copys & shadows of shades"; "The Wind blows very high tonight, I wish it may disperse the Enemy's fleet"; and the very poignant close to the letter that narrates Charles Clerke's death and burial at sea: "our old Gent is in a strange way what we shall do with him I know not, neither sick nor well but his head alas his head declines every day." Though she rarely left Essex, Ann's spirit soared freely. When late eighteenth-century poets imagined unsung Miltons, did they ever suspect the existence of women like Ann?

Chapter 11

Ann Clerke Four

"It is now impossible to proceed the least farther to the Northward upon this coast (America); and it is equally as improbable that this amazing mass of ice should be dissolved in the few remaining summer-weeks which will terminate this season; but it will continue, it is to be believed, as it now is, an insurmountable barrier to every attempt we can possibly make. I [Charles Clerke], therefore, think it the best step that can be taken, for the good of the service, to trace the sea over to the Asiatic coast, and to try if I can find any opening, that will admit me farther North; if not, to see what more is to be done upon that coast; where I hope, yet cannot much flatter myself, to meet with better success; for the sea is now so choaked with ice, that a passage, I fear, is totally out of the question" ... and though he [Clerke] knew, that by delaying his return to a warmer climate, he was giving up the only chance that remained for his recovery, yet, careful and jealous to the last degree, that a regard to his own situation should never bias his judgment to the prejudice of the service, he persevered in the search of a passage, till it was the opinion of every officer in both ships, that it was impracticable, and that any farther attempts would not only be fruitless, but dangerous ... I [James King] will not endeavor to conceal the joy that brightened the countenance of every individual, as soon as Captain Clerke's resolutions were made known. We were all heartily sick of a navigation full of danger, and in which the utmost perseverance had not been repaid with the smallest probability of success. We therefore turned our faces toward home, after an absence of three years, with a delight and satisfaction, which, notwithstanding the tedious voyage we had still to make, and the immediate distance we had to run, were as freely entertained, and perhaps as fully enjoyed, as if we had been already in sight of the Land's-end.

> James King, *A Voyage to the Pacific Ocean Undertaken, by the Command of His Majesty, for Making Discoveries in the Northern Hemisphere To Determine the Position and Extent of the West Side of North America; its Distance from Asia; and the Practicality of a Northwest Passage to Europe* (1784)

Putting a period to the life of Charles Clerke, alerting us to the decline of patriarch Joseph Clerke, and reminding us, through metonymic contagion, of the death of John Clerke, who died three years before his younger brother, Ann Clerke's fourth letter brings the domestic novel of manners of John and Lydia and the maritime adventures of John and Charles to a poignant close.

12
From: Ann Clerke, Wethersfield
To: Lady Clerke, Southampton

Date: 20 March 1781

My Dear Friend

Herewith you receive the Letter I promised in my last. That to Mr Banks is as follows

Resolution at Sea

18th Augst 1779

My ever Honourd Friend/

The disorder I was attack'd with in the Kings Bench Prison has proved consumptive with which I have Battled with various success although without one single day's health since I took leave of you in Burlington Street. It has now so far got the better of me that I am not able to turn my self in my Bed, so that my stay in this World must be of very short duration; however, I hope my Friends will have no occasion to Blush in owning themselves such, for I have most perfectly & justly done my Duty to my Country as far as my abilities would enable me, for where that has been concern'd the attention to my health which I was very sensible was in the most Imminent danger has never swerved me a single half mile out of the road of my Duty, so that I flatter my self I shall leave behind me that character it has ever been my utmost ambition to attain which is that of an honest faithfull servant to the public whom I had undertaken to serve. I have made you the best Collections of all kinds of matter I could that have fallen in our way in the course of the Voyage, but they are by no means so complete as they would have been had my health enabled me to pay more attention to them. I hope, however, you will find many among them worthy your attention & acceptance. In my will I have bequeathed you the whole of every kind; there are great abundance so that you will have ample choice. I must beg you to present my warmest & most affectionate Comp^{ts} to Dr Solander & assure him I leave the World replete with the most social ideas of his much esteem'd & ever respected Friendship—I must beg leave to recommend to your notice Mr Wm Ellis one of the Surgeons mates who will furnish you with some drawings & accounts of the various Birds which will come to your possession. He has been very usefull to me in that service in that perticular & is I believe a very worthy young man, & I hope will prove worthy of any services that may be in your way to confer upon him—The two clerks of the two ships Mr Wm Dewar & Mr Greg^y Bentham have I believe been very honest servants in their stations & having by Capt Cooks & very soon by my death lost those to whom they look'd up for protection are I fear destitute of friends. If it should be in your power to render them any Services, I flatter my self they will be worthy of such attention. If I should recollect anything more to say to you I will trouble my Friend Mr King with it who is so kind to be my amanuensis on this occasion. He is my very dear & perticular friend, & I will make no apology in recommending him to a Share in your friendship as I am perfectly assured of his being deserving of it, as in that also of the worthy Doctor's.

Now my Dear and Honoured friend I must bid you a final adieu, may you enjoy

many happy years in this World & in the end attain that fame your indefaticable industry so richly deserves. These are most sincerely the warmest & sincerest wishes of your <u>Devoted, affectionate,</u> & <u>departing</u> servant <u>Charles Clerke</u>
Note. The words with the <u>mark under</u> them were his own hand writing. This was written the 18th of Augst. On the 22^d he expired & was Buried agreeable to his perticular desire at Parakitca some distance from the Harbour of St Peter St Paul which thay were just entering at the time he died, of which Capt Williamson sent me the following account—

To Mrs Tompson—

Dr Mad^m

'Agreeable to your desire I send you an account of the manner in which our old 'Friend Charles was carried to the Grave. It was on the 29th of Augst 1779 we paid our 'last tribute of Duty & regard to our old Friend & Capt with all the decency & respect 'we could in the following manner. The Ships & boat with their Colours half up, the 'Corps was put into his own Boat. The Crew in their white shirts & black Caps, their 'oars reversed, their Heads reclined, & [their arms] resting on their oars on each side 'the Coffin, were the Bearers. The Boat was towed on shore by another, the Cap^{ts} 'following in their Boat, the Lieutenants after them. Then followed the midshipmen 'after, the ship's company bringing up the rear. [The] Boat began to move, each ship 'began [to follow]. The Corps was received on shore by the officer & his Party 'who preceeded it to [shore], Captains & officers following in the order they came on 'shore when the procession began to move. After the Landing, each ship began to fire 'minute gunns, the coffin was cover'd with a Union Flag, his Sword drawn & laid 'across the Coffin the Drums muffled, & the french Horns playing the dead march. 'The funeral service was read by Mr. Lan, our surgeon, at the end of which there was 'three discharge of small arms from the marines. At the first discharge the ships 'ceased firing the minute Guns & at the last hoisted their Colours close up: the 'officers were in their Uniforms with Black Crape on their arms—

The writeing this has cost me some tears, as I dare say the reading will do you, some people will perhaps think we had been as wise to have spared our selves such an unavailing regret which this retrospect must occasion but I'm persuaded it will be agreeable to you. I therefore determined to send it you.

I saw your old acquaintance the Hickfords today. They inquired after you, they are upon a visit at a Clergyman's House in this neighbourhood. They seem very well & in good Spirits, & I hope will take us in their way tomorrow as they travel this way to another Gentleman's House thay are going to spend some time with, but their spirits & chearfulness are realy surprising considering the circumstances every one hear supposes them to be in, but I hope the World is mistaken, & that they have some private dependance which supports them without those apprehensions of poverty which must otherwise overwhelm them. Adieu my Dear yours affectionately A Clerke

Sister Sally desires her Love to you & Lady E Morley who has been with me this week desires her Comp^{ts}—our old Gent is in a strange way what we shall do with him I know not, neither sick nor well but his head alas his head declines every day—my kind Love to your Mother

March 20th 81

Shadows of Shades

According to King's narrative of Cook and Clerke's last voyage, both men behaved with extraordinary courage and self sacrifice.[1] Emphasizing Clerke's determination to go on despite terrible weather and deteriorating health, King turns the young navigator into an over-reacher in the tradition of Mary Shelley's Frankenstein and his fellow traveler Robert Walton. Like the scientist Frankenstein, Clerke risks his health in his quest for knowledge and brings on his own early death. Like the navigator Walton, he searches for a North-West passage, returns home with great reluctance, and writes letters to his sister (and sister-in-law).

While in *Frankenstein*, we only have Walton's letters to his sister, in *Circle* we have some of the letters Charles's sisters wrote to one another. This gives us a different perspective on the navigator/ over-reacher. We see what Walton anticipated would happen but avoided by returning home—the sadness and longing of those left behind and the ways in which women valued the maritime accomplishments of loved ones.

An intricate, mysterious, and melancholy braiding of different voices, Ann's fourth letter opens with a few words of cursory introduction: "Herewith you receive the Letter I promised in my last. That to Mr Banks is as follows." Then we have Ann's transcription of a letter originally sent to Joseph Banks. Dictated by Clerke during his dying moments, the letter was recorded by James King and then forwarded to Banks. This part of the letter affectingly expresses Clerke's hope that he has done his duty. Clerke also urges Banks to befriend three men who might otherwise be left without protection in the wake of his and Cook's deaths. King's transcript of Clerke's words is then followed by a "Note," which tells Lydia that the underscored words "Devoted, affectionate, & departing servant Charles Clerke" were written in Charles's own handwriting. This note is then followed by a transcript of an account by Captain Williamson of Charles Clerke's burial at sea.

Since Ann is sending Lydia a copy completely in her hand, it makes sense that she marks the words written by their brother, for if she did not, Lydia would have no way of knowing which words were written by Charles. It is less clear why Ann does not tell Lydia how copies of Banks's and Williamson's letters reached her. Did Joseph

---

[1]   King, *A Voyage to the Pacific Ocean* 3:260–61.

Banks send her a copy of King's letter to him? or did King? Williamson's narrative also seems to have followed a circuitous route. Ann's explanatory note tells us that "he [Charles] expired & was Buried agreeable to his perticular desire at Parakitca some distance from the Harbour of St Peter St Paul which thay were just entering at the time he died, of which Capt Williamson sent me the following account—" Thus, at first glance, it would seem that Captain Williamson sent his narrative to Ann or to the Clerke family, and Ann copied it in order to send it on to Lydia. However, the first two words of Williamson's letter—"Mrs Tompson"—suggest otherwise. The letter must have first gone to Mrs. Tompson, who sent a copy to Ann, who is now forwarding a copy of a copy to Lydia.

The unusual trajectory of this part of the letter might explain Ann's use of quotation marks. She punctuates Williamson's narrative with an inverted comma at the beginning of each line, an eighteenth-century convention which usually denoted the incorporation of another person's spoken or written words into one's own discourse. Although such a device is often used in newspapers, books, and official letters, it is rare in personal letters. When Charlotte Lennox uses quotation marks to indicate the words of "a certain philosopher" in one of her letters, she uses only one set to mark the beginning and end of the commonplace; she does not place an inverted comma at the beginning of each line. Why does Ann feel compelled to distinguish Captain Williamson's words so completely? Even more strange, why does she do so with Williamson's text and not with King's since both were written elsewhere and to others and inserted by her into a letter meant for still another? Did Ann perceive King's words differently than Williamson's? Were King's somehow private because they included Charles's last spoken and written words, while Williamson's letter crossed over into the world of public discourse? And, therefore, she needed to set off his words with inverted commas?

Both King's and Williamson's texts circulated widely, passing from reader to reader, copyist to copyist. Versions of their narratives can be found in Beaglehole's compendious edition of Cook's journals, among Joseph Banks's papers, and in King's three-volume edition of Cook's and Clerke's last voyages on the *Resolution* and *Discovery*. Ironically, Ann, who strove for simplicity and directness throughout her life and shunned copies of copies and the shadows of shades, found herself, in 1781, as she wove different discourses together, caught in the epistemological trap of her age and enmeshed in the ambiguities of discourse.

Chapter 12

Sylvia Brathwaite

There is nothing more common than to hear *youth of modern honour* and *fashion* use this argument for female seduction:

"Why, such a plan, no doubt, would have been disgraceful and infamous to have attempted upon a woman of *rank* and *fashion!*—but to an ordinary girl, and below one's rank, Lord! where's the harm? ...

... I consider those below me as born to be subservient to me; and I think there is no harm in seducing a girl that is not entitled to expect me for a husband. If she allows liberties in such expectation, she is a fool: if she keeps her own secret, and manages well, she has a chance of getting a husband suitable to her."

Gentleman's Magazine (1788)

Sylvia Brathwaite, a charming young girl full of acute and telling observations about fashionable society, is the ingénue of the second novel constructed by the Clerke letters. Much like Harriot Stuart, the eponymous heroine of Charlotte Lennox's first novel, she imagines that every man she meets (including the Prince of Wales, the future George IV) desires her. Young and old, married or single, propertied or propertyless, English or from another country, all are attracted to her. In the end, she marries Mr. Parkhurst, a poor but gallant soldier, thereby losing her family's, and especially her father's and grandmother's, approval and financial support. In her last letter, which can be found in Chapter 14, she, like Charlotte Lennox, worries about her husband's extravagance and crows over her son. Her sexuality, what Vivien Jones called a woman's "potentially anarchic power," has been successfully contained and channeled into marriage and motherhood.[1] At this point, her story ends.

Sylvia's letters signal not only the start of a different story with a different heroine but also the beginning of a different genre. Because she spends so much time describing her many romantic encounters, her letters can be seen as sentimental romance. When we add the two letters from her aunt Mrs. Thornton (which can be found in Chapter 13) to Sylvia's novel, her story turns into sentimental romantic tragedy. We learn the sad consequences of her decision to marry against her family's wishes. When we read the only letter we have from her as a married woman, then her story becomes domestic comedy. While her aunt may mourn what her niece has lost, Sylvia believes she regains paradise.

---

[1] Vivien Jones, *Women in the Eighteenth Century: Constructions of Femininity* (London, 1990) 58.

Finally, Sylvia's heterogeneous discourse fits still one more category—the picaresque. Realistic, episodic and autobiographical, picaresque novels conventionally focus on low-life male characters who serve a series of tyrannical masters and end either in the "new world" or in the galleys. Upper-middle-class and female, Sylvia is not the usual picaro. But her iteration of the oppressiveness of her master—the tyrannical fashionable world to which she is subject—supports the parallel to the pessimistic picaresque, as does the episodic nature of her many amorous conquests. From beginning to end, the same story recurs. It recurs so often that it becomes extremely difficult to separate one story from another. When she writes about her "soldier," we do not know if she is referring to Banastre Tarleton or to Charles Parkhurst or to someone else whose name we will never know. And even as she declares for Parkhurst she feels the pull of another man's attractiveness. Sylvia's story, like that of the typical picaro, could continue indefinitely. Her final choice of Parkhurst seems arbitrary, for, even in her last letters as an unmarried woman, we are not sure if she will choose him or Harry Greville. Although she suspects Greville is toying with her, there are moments when she believes he loves her and might be serious. Also, like most picaresque novels, her story concludes ambiguously. Is Sylvia in a new world of her own making or is she doomed to poverty and misery?

Sylvia's letters contain a large cast of characters. We meet many members of the English aristocracy: the Prince of Wales (to become George IV in 1820) and Maria Fitzherbert (the Catholic commoner he married in an illegal, secret ceremony); the Prince's dissolute uncle, the Duke of Cumberland and his wife the Duchess of Cumberland, the former Mrs. Anne Horton; the Duchess's notorious brother Colonel Henry Laws Luttrell and her sister Lady Elizabeth Luttrell; the "Old Countess" Lady Ferrers; and Lady Elizabeth Craven, whom "the World" believed had eloped to Paris with her footman. We also learn about political leaders like William Pitt, Hyder Ali, and Frederick, King of Prussia; players like Mrs. Abington, Mrs. Siddons, and her younger brother John Philip Kemble; as well as novels (*Victim of Fancy, Caroline of Lichtfield, Vathek*) and writers (Shakespeare, Jean-Jacques Rousseau, Laurence Sterne). We watch the antics of the many men who loved her, among them Casamajor, who, if he is the John Henry Casamajor who served over 40 years in the East India Company identified in a *Gentleman's Magazine* obituary dated 23 January 1815, kept his promise to her and never married. Most important, we meet Sylvia's family—her aunt Mrs. Thornton, her grandmother and grandfather Winstanley, and her cousins Robert and Bonnell George Thornton and Whaley Armitage—and her circle of acquaintance—Thomas Boothby Parkyns and the young woman he married, Elizabeth-Ann James, and her mother Lady James; Sir Yelverton and Lady Peyton and Mr. Calvert, Lady Peyton's son by her first marriage to Felix Calvert; Mary Robinson (the writer, actress, and ex-mistress of the Prince of Wales) and Colonel Banastre Tarleton (returned from the war in North America); and many others.

Because the narrative in Sylvia's letters is endlessly accretive and arbitrarily cut off, her letters were extremely difficult to arrange chronologically. I would have liked to put the letters that begin "Dear Lady Clerke" ahead of those letters addressed "My dear friend," for logically she should progress from a more formal to a less ceremonious form of address. However, logical progression does not always help when working with Sylvia's letters. As she herself acknowledges, "[I have an] aversion to writing a regular story." Nevertheless, there were ways to sequence her thoughts. If I took into account the shifts in her attitude toward "Volpone," I could place the letter in which she was attracted to him ahead of the letter that expressed her disenchantment with him, a different but possibly still deceptive logical progression. The sequence of other pairs of letters was less ambiguous. The letter that mentions news of her father's safety had to precede the letter in which she gives a fuller account of how she obtained the information, presumably in response to a request from Lydia for more detail. Likewise, when Sylvia alludes to "a tale of spirits—from an Old German officer," Lydia, in her returning letter, must have asked for the story in full, and Sylvia obliged. Other letters were easy to place because they referred to independent events (John Philip Kemble's first season in London, Whaley Armitage's entrance into Cambridge, the deaths of Harry Maty and the King of Prussia, the publication of *Vathek*) for which years are available. Letter #15, which defied even approximate dating, was slipped in where I thought it fit smoothly.

Although sequencing Sylvia's letters was a difficult task, her story is not at first glance a complex one: the tale of a young girl searching for the perfect man and at risk of preferring the wrong one. As season after season passes, we witness her many different reactions to the men who pursue her. Several women plead with her to be careful—her aunt, her grandmother, her friend Lady Clerke. At first nothing seems unusual in her story. Even the absence of her mother can be explained: she's dead and that's why Sylvia lives with her aunt. Although a likely explanation, it turned out to be wrong. Sylvia's story is much stranger than that. It is, in fact, as strange as fiction.

To read Sylvia's letters is to enter the "real" world of an eighteenth-century epistolary novel.

13
From: Sylvia Brathwaite, London
To: Lady Clerke, Southampton
Date: 22 October [1783]

Why must my heart that longs to be with my dearest Friend to sooth her hours of sickness and amuse those of returning health be confined to the dull cold language of a letter yet so it is. But, no, my beloved Friend, my heart even now is with you. Tis in your keeping. Recover to take care of it. Tis a little Pilgrim of a short journey yet much sorrow that sought full many a time a resting place. Invited by kind looks and fair words to take shelter, it <u>used</u> to believe them, till coldness or falsehood turned the Wanderer trembling away. At last it came to you—wearied and sad—on you secure it rested as the Poor Bird escaped from Peril sits singing on the Branch of some Noble tree. Let not the Branch break oh heaven. The Bird will fall with it and shall sing no more. Write to me—tell me you love me so well that you will take care of yourself. I have much to tell you. Even all my thoughts and actions for some months—but paper is tedious and We shall meet again. Fancy and Friendship shall deck Old Time with flowers, and pleasure throw her mantle over him as he passes. Imagination in her many coloured Robe shall sit between us raising with her wand a thousand fairy Visions, such as Shakespear saw. We will drink of the Waters of oblivion from the fair hand of charity, forgetting or forgiving. Modest Mirth and civil sincerity shall dwell with us. You smile. Or, perhaps like Me, you shake your head and sigh. How would the Wise Ones, the Sir Oracles of this World, smile contempt on my Ideal Fabrick. Let them smile. Tis We are Wise, for if this world be made of passing shadows—he alone is Fool who sets his heart on substance.

Talking of Fools put me in mind of the Fool flap and that put me in mind—of our Wise Man. One morning in the Spring on a Sunday—I was with a Lady in Kensington Gardens—I was walking down the Green Walk—when at the Garden Gait—stood a tall lean pale Figure in black—leaning pensive and frowning on his untasselled cane—in one hand hung suspended a handkerchief. No wight it was Volpone—I walked quicker—(Not that I intended it) but I walked quicker. A fine Fool met me in a motley Coat—the fine fool stopped me to tell me ten thousand Nothings—Volpone darted across the Green and was lost in shade—I was provoked—the fine Fool was not a little surprised to see any Woman provoked by whose side he walked—he bowed and left me—this [the] only time I have ever seen Volpone.

Miss James is going to be married to Perqins, one of the Duke of Cumberland's Equerys—he is a genteel young Man, his Father a Baronet of large Estate in Nottinghamshire. My Brother will be Equery in his room to his Royal Highness, I believe. We have got a new Player in Town—Brother to Mrs Siddons—a very good Actor, very hansom—a Countenance expressive—an elegant figure—pleasing Voice, graceful action—and great judgement. I never remember the stage so pleasing as this Winter. Mrs Siddons, Kemble, Henderson, and Shakespear's plays—have made me a Rake—I am going tonight to see Mrs Siddons in Calista.—write to me dear Friend or some how let me know how you do—My best respects to Mrs Hammond—and Compts to Mr Mrs Matty if with you

I always enquire but have no India News for Lady Peyton. None but the praise of Mr Calvert and that cannot be News to her. My best Compts to Sir Yelverton. Is he coming to town? My Grandmother's kind regards attend you. My Aunt is better. Adieu Yours affectionately

Sylvia B_____

14
From: Sylvia Brathwaite, London
To: Lady Clerke, Southampton
Date: [1783]
My dear friend

You are very naughty to make me apologies when you give me advice and I am half affronted with you. As to the Royal Party—you shall have a full true and particular account of it—and then judge. In the first place I made it my particular request that I might dine there, when the Prince did not. A day was accordingly fixed when the Duke and P_____ were to dine with Lady Melbourn. My dress was pretty—it was of Italian tiffany over white Satten, the sleeves large, fastened with beads and grass green satten, The ornaments all grass green, a hat of crape and blond with beads and a white willow feather round the crown at the back of my head within, round my hair a long wreath of black and white velvet [aureoles]. I had bracelets of ribbon with cut steel [matter] which my Brother gave me. I never, I think, looked so well. When I arrived at C_____ House I found the Duke at home—who came up and saluted me—a compliment only paid to Countesses. The Duchess took my hand and seated me upon a sofa next her—and then whispered—the Prince dines here—He has this moment sent to say He would. I was sorry—In came his Royal Highness—with a Grace unequalled—made me a gracious bow—and whispered to my Brother and then led the Duchess in to dinner—I had just time to say to Capt Luttrell—sit next to me—He smiled and replied—what a compliment but I see you are afraid of the Young Lion—I wish it may be so, but The Highnesses will do as they please. There were two chairs at the top of the table. The Duke took one—The Prince the next but one—I looked grave—and stood hesitating—Luttrell held my hand—Come M^d, said the Duke. You must let go, Luttrell, said the Prince, and Luttrell let go. I walked round and took my seat. The Duchess sat near the bottom, Mrs Parkyns on the other side. You are grave said the Duke. The Prince looked earnestly, but said Nothing—was very attentive—very amusing—but did not much address Himself to me, till turning suddenly—He said, All the World, M^d, have drunk champaign but you and I. Will you allow me to order two glasses? If your Royal Highness will excuse Me I shall be obliged. He looked piqued, every Body stared, my Brother frowned. It seems it was never done before. <u>People always</u> do as the P bids them.

I looked very grave. They began to talk Polliticks. The P____e spoke well. He turned to Me. Do you think with me, M^d? Perfectly Sir. Then help me, dear M^d, to convert Capt Luttrell—He look's as if you had absolute power over Him—assist me—speak half what you look—and tis done. You do me a great deal of honor Sir—but tis a subject that perhaps I have no business to ever think about, much less to make Converts supposing I had power. The Prince made me no answer, but smiled at my Brother and said, ah Brathwaite [a line of text is obliterated by tape]. I was puzzled as to what the Duke said. I do not relate it because I suppose you only interested about the Prince. He then told me a very droll story, softly, and begged me to repeat it, which I did not do—but He succeeded in making me laugh and the gaiety was so universal that I could not be grave. When the dessert came, He took part of a pine apple—and presented me saying—to the Fairest. Was it not so the Shepherd on Mount Ida said? None Sir, said I, thank you—Venus was conscious she deserved the apple. She allowed, M^d, Paris to be a judge [said the Prince]. But what, Sir, if she had not desired the prize? Why then she deserved it more. Miss B, said Luttrell is thinking Ill be sworn of the fatal apple in Eden. I thank you, Sir, said the Prince, frowning—the simile does me much honor.

The Conversation then went to Ireland, and Mrs Sawbridge. The Duchess spoke eloquently. I said Nothing. The Duchess rose to go. Stay, said the Duke, a little with us. Nay go, said the Prince; we will follow you. We went—and in about five minutes the Prince Came in alone—gave us each a dish of Coffee—then, turning to me, asked if I had seen the Picture of his Sisters. I said yes. Do you think me like Augusta? I think all of them like your Royal Highness. You flatter Me; I am vain of my Sisters and as fond of them as Brathwaite is of you. Then, turning to the Duchess, He said—Madam have you in France a dress like this of Miss B's—or was the Idea stolen from Ephegenia in Aulis—tis well I was not the Priest—There would have been no sacrifice—but that of a heart. Do you think the Gods would have been propitious? I looked earnestly at Him and replied, No Sir, when in public characters, private feelings get the better of the Public good, the Gods are never propitious. My Brother came in. Brathwaite, said He, your sister is teaching me to be a Prince. The rest came in—and the Duchess and I conversed a long time about Southampton. She told me if I could enquire out a House big enough for them she would go there next summer—the Prince sung—and sung with taste but has but an indifferent voice. He then talked about Musick, poetry, and plays—they laughed at him for having wept at seeing Mrs Siddons—He spoke feelingly—and rather sensibly—talked to me of dress—Fêtes—and Shops—and amusement—I spoke as if indifferent to all—He talked of Beauty and Grace—I answered it was all in imagination and there could be no standard. He seemed mortified and soon after went—but came up to me and said good night—I will remember all you have said—or rather taught me.

Twice since I have been asked but, finding the Prince was to be there, pleaded a cold—and have only called upon His Royal Highness of a Morning. I have literally told you what passed—He was simply and finely dressed—his voice, his air, his Eyes—are seduisant—but He is less hansom than He was—and I think in Person much inferior to many of his suite. He left me where he found me—with my heart still true to my poor soldier—Still without a wish to please in a circle He was not. As to Him, to my great surprise He told me smiling he heard I had been introduced to the Prince—but I find it was properly by the Duchess—your Brother's line makes it necessary, and your good sense will see a Prince without his George and Garter. I would trust you in the Island of Circe—you have a firmness few women possess. He is agreeable and hansom, but He will amuse without engaging you. He speaks of your Beauty and coldness—and your fame can receive no further addition—He does you Justice—and has made even me his friend.

I thank you for consulting the Winchester Sibil about me after the day I dined. My going abroad was never mentioned. They come back to stay—next May. I have been disappointed about Money—and am more obliged to you for your offer than I can find words to express—but my good Friend all things are for the best—if I had money I should go into Publick. If I went into Public I should see and of course be well acquainted with the Prince—Tis best as it is— and I have enough to pay what I owe to M^r W— . Tell Sir Yelverton not to doubt me—I wish for his good opinion—and tho he does not know me I would have Him be generous—and make me a present of it. I gave Him mine too—My compliments to Lady Peyton. I will enquire about what she desires—I shall send you a Cap which I hope will please you. There are but two of them in England—one the Duchess of Devonshire has and the other Lady Dungannon, but she has never worn it. They bought them of my own Milliner Devise. Coloured satten hats, with black snake trimming at the edge, are worn and black bonnets bound with velvet. I have one and think it pretty but have seen no dressed hats but these for the back of the head. The new colour is Green—and foil trimmings much worne, the Cloaks white satten with Fox skin—long but not wide, the handkerchiefs still very large—the Robbins very deep and with four falls.

The day after I arrived in town I sent your letter to Mrs Matty with my compts and that I would call very soon. My Servant brought in answer that they were very well but not at home. He left the letter. Such a Cap as the one you bought of Harper are much worne in black crape—My affairs are at present in a confused state. The first Report I heard from M^rs W upon My arrival was that T— was going to be married—This must be false—Never did I see him so much a Lover. He had sent it seems to beg to speak with my Brother—which Charles evaded and left England without seeing Him—except in Company—this my Brother told me—but T— has never hinted—he has relieved the distress of a poor wretch in the most generous way—and when I taxed Him with it—supposing I only guessed at it—denied it. I hear Him abused every day—

M^r C— has worried me with letters—still I sent them unanswered—He still Corresponds with my Grandmother—She reads with apparent pleasure—but his letters and her answers are profound secrets. My Brother has done with Him—but has taken it in his head Luttrell likes me (who by the by) has a good fortune—and this pleases Him—I am obliged to M^r L— for some very hansom behaviour upon a very awkward occasion and for the Most unbounded Praises of Me to the Duchess—He is very pleasant—and detests all the parade of C------- House

15
From: Sylvia Brathwaite, London
To: Lady Clerke, Southampton
Date: Undated
My Dear friend

I send you back the Coat—which has [to] be detained for the Book—I have enquired at every shop possible for Your trimming. None have ever seen it—Hamilton in St James Street say if you will give them a pattern they will make it.

I have dined twice at Cumberland House—both times sat next the Prince at dinner—His behaviour was attentive without levity—his conversation very animated, rather sensible, and often witty—his manner much beyond any I have ever seen—I really believe He never behaves Ill but when the Women begin—the Duchess is very charming, wonderfully informed, and pleasant—the Duke worse than I thought Him—

So much for my honors—they charm but little—I am still tormented by C_____j_____ who is almost Mad—and I have hurt T_____y foolishly—to please those who do not deserve it—his pride—his Coquettry are over—and He is all I wish—Accident has revealed to me such an Act of benevolence of his to a poor old Woman that he has won my heart a second time—but he has made Me Miserable. In Consequence of the way I spoke of Northy, he has sent Him a Message to Desire he would never call upon or bow to Him. It was rash and foolish and if it ends in fighting—I shall go mad—I cannot get any Money and want it more than ever—My Aunt T is pretty well, write to me soon. I have hardly a moment's time to write and fear you will not be able to read it—both the Miss Browns go to India. Parkyns and M^{rs} are gone to the south of France. He looks dying— [I fear] She is good for nothing—best compts to M^{rs} H—

                            Yours affectionately
                            S B—

16
From: Sylvia Brathwaite, London
To: Lady Clerke, Southampton
Date: [1783]
My dear Lady Clerke

It has often been an observation with me that sorrow presents her Cup always full to the brim—as if fearful that joy should mix one drop of balm to sweeten the potion. While joy incautious presents her cup half empty—open to receive any mixture Grief may fling in. Such has been my case. Last week I had the delightful news that my dear Father was well in Hyder's Camp—in a tent near his own, had been permitted to send to Madrass for his own Servants to attend him—and had been desired by Hyder to write to the Governor and Council of Madrass on some Public business—scarse had I rejoiced in this news when your letter came and I found that my dear friend was Ill and dispirited and that perhaps she did not come to town—Why am I not with you at this time? We would forget the World—We would raise an Ideal Kingdom—Fancy should adorn it with Inhabitants of her own Creation—There should be no rank but that of merit—no laws but those of honor—No marriages but of love—no cont[ribu]tions but in generosity—the souls of All our favorites should live again—Rouseau should rise again the child of nature and sensibility, Rouseau who felt more than Stern feigned—whose writings never called a tear where the Author had not shed a hundred—Sidney should charm another World—Our Essex should awake without those few faults that cost him so dear—& our Mary should rise unblushing cleared of all the guilt envy heaped upon her—in such Ideas we would pass the hours—and enjoy all that Mortality may ever know. Ficticious happiness! My heart, my mind is with you—I am sorry you have lost your Italian Friends—but why think you shall meet no more! are they sworn never to see this Country again? If they had found nothing worthy of observation or productive of amusement in England—yet having known you—and having been admitted to your friendship, they will not want a cause to draw them here again. I wish I had seen them, my Grandmother is always happy to see those who she knows I wish to see—being your friends would have made her receive them with double pleasure.

What a finished Wretch is Volpone. Silly sheep that we were to be led by such a Pastor and not led by the silken cord of flattery thru verdant Vails and flowry meads—but by the hard chain of contradiction and reproof—over Rocks and rugged paths—but his crook is broke—and his Pipe shall no longer allure me. I am charmed with the name your friend has given to Warwick but am inclined to doubt his reformation. Poor Miss Anley: I am sorry for her—she had not sensibility to excuse her even. You have given me to my young Bard—perhaps you thought my praises of him seemed as if I had given myself but if so—it was an Ill seeming, for tho I love him—tis as I love Scipio, or Epaminondas And I had rather be his Sister than his Wife.

I have made many enquiries after Lady Peyton's son but have met with no one very lately come from the settlement he is at. But all unite in praising him which with his merit is extraordinary—and I attribute it to his being in another Country—so that they speak as truth undefiled by Envy dictates. He is, I find, continually speaking of Lady Peyton and with all that warmth of affection that proves how much happiness his return will give her.

You bid me tell you the Conquests of my eyes. They are not worth telling. That ridiculous Mr. Turner has at last given tongue to his folly, offers 3 thousand a year—is refused—tells me he is worth more—he protests he loves me and will never be got rid of. I have been lately very much in Public—have a train of danglers—the agreeable I fear—the others I hate. The characters of the Chief are as follows. First a Man of faschion, Old Family, about 8 and thirty, well looking, sensible, very artful, comes under the title of my friend—advises me against every Man I know—watches me—is angry if I talk too much to any Gentlemen in Public, reads to me—tries every method to discover if I am the least attached to him—depends on his fortune and family and the expectation of a Title. Tells me he likes me—but at the same time hints that he is not to be made a fool of. The second—younger, hansomer, a Man of the World in all but his sentiments, in them very excentrick and very obstinate. Flatters well, is attentive, avoids being tiresome, is not the least Jealous. The 3^d—about 3 and twenty, a goodnatured Coxcomb, without an Idea beyond the erudition of Christie's Catalogue & Fortrells list of running Horses, vain assuming, noisy, and impertinent. The 4th is one who unencouraged comes. A married Man, a Man of high faschion, good sense—elegant manners—great accomplishments, much sensibility—perfect respect, distant attention, and timid gallantry. Him I avoid and pity. Married when he returned from his tour of Europe to a Woman of Quality—hansom and good tempered but with a mind uncultivated. And a Nature almost at War with sensibility. She is sick of his conversation and ridicules his feelings. He treats [her] with perfect complaisance, gives up his house and time to a Set of People he despises. His Wife is fonder of me than any one, which is unlucky as she is for ever making partys for me, but as yet I do well. I do not pretend to see thru his intentions, nor in truth do I believe he wishes I should. For he takes pains to conceal what I wish I did not observe.

You bid me write you some thing about the gay World. What can I tell you? That Lady Craven is gone off with her footman. The gay World is all a scandal, and with too much reason. There are a hundred new plays—a revived play of the capricious Lady pleased me much—Mrs Abington is wonderfully great in that character. Tis the best piece of acting I ever saw, or perhaps it is her real character. The stage is in perfection. Mrs Siddons has inspired the other players. I send you enclosed a poem of Fielding's on seeing her act Countess of Salisbury. I think it as well written as anything I have seen.

What do you think of Pitt? Has Rome or Greece ever produced a finer character? In what a confused state are our National councils, and how bright does Pitt shine forth amidst the corrupted statesmen and false Patriots who surround Him. He will resign—I always thought him too good for a Minister. I saw Young Asgill at the Opera a few nights ago and was glad to see him because he was unfortunate, for I believe he has no particular [merit]. Tarleton is forgotten, he lays his Laurels at Perdita's feet, and she had rather have gold than glory. I am impatient to hear from you again. If it is but one line, write that I may know how you do, and tell me if you are better.

When does Sir Yelverton come to town again? Present my Compts to him, and tell him if he comes and does not call upon us I will wish all the Ill things I can think of. First that he may be out of your favor and that he may read his favorite Mary defamed in every Book he takes up, and that the faschion of stooping may grow more universal [so] that upright People may be considered as Monsters—and that elegance and goodbreeding may be considered crimes in which case he will be found remarkably guilty, and, as my last wish—may he make the tour of Europe and visit Rouseau's tomb with no Companion but Mrs Kinderrly.

I am writing on my knee. The clock is struck five and tis so dark that I rather <u>feel</u> than see what I write. Heaven keep this scra[tching from] the Eye of Misses who write Copper plate. And a very good thing too—many a foolish Idea has been set off by a fine hand, as a bad Book sells by a good binding. I am at this moment in expectation of a party to tea. I have been writing all day—but have no merit in it—because writing to you is one of the greatest pleasures I know, except hearing from you. They are come—Adieu for a few hours. S Brathwaite

17
From: Sylvia Brathwaite, London
To: Lady Clerke, Southampton
Date: [1783]

My Dear Lady Clerke is always all goodness to Me—a thousand thanks for your letter—I am sorry, very sorry tis written in a way that convinces me your spirits are very much depressed. Why, so are mine. They have had a hundred trials lately. I rejoice that you have found a friend in Mrs Irvin—I had once the pleasure of meeting Her at a Mrs Cummings in Charles Street, Cavendish Square—She then struck Me as a charming Woman.

We have had upon the whole pleasant news of my Father—the adventure is something like a Novel. My Brother was sent by His R Highness to get a House at Aise—He found none proper—the Duke de Crillon offered His Hotel at Avignon. Charles set off to prepare it and on the road met a Carriage attended by Blacks. The Idea struck him that they might be East Indians who had come over Land—He stopped the Carriage and enquired the Names of the Gentlemen. Was answered, Mr Brodie (my Father's Agent and particular Friend). Nothing could exceed the joy of Both—Mr Brodie said He had received letters from my Father since His being Prisoner in which He spoke gratefully of the good treatment He had received—and of his being in perfect health. Mr Brodie has been very long on His way home—He says My Father's circumstances are good—and His affairs in Honest hands. This from my Brother, and, at the India House about a week ago, upon the Subject of Commander in Chief being debated upon, some of the Directors (who think the <u>form</u> of Justice necessary) mentioned some of their own Servants in opposition to General Sloper, and One of Them was my Father. All this is good—and I am Thankful—but my heart is afraid to believe good tidings least it should be disappointed. With respect to Thornton, he left me in great agitation, but said He would never see me again unmarried—this He did not keep to, but has engaged himself to a Miss Greens. She has 300 a year and eight thousand pounds—is about nineteen, short, fat, brown, ugly, and vulgar, but perfectly goodtempered, Not wanting in natural sense, and distractedly fond of Him. His Mother objects to it very much but the Matter is fixed—and in opposition to <u>My wishes</u> I am Now in the House with Him—He Melancholly and as fond of Me as ever—but quite determined to Marry—I am very sorry for Him—

And now to another history—how much I wish I could talk to you. Casamajor—my Noble Generous Indian—I have made wretched—He loves to Madness—My friends approve. Five whole days has He spent at my feet in tears and I weeping with Him—but still refusing—I told Him I had no heart to give—He offered to marry me still; time, his attention would teach Me to give him my heart—I went to the play—He of the party. He was seized with a shivering fit—burst into Tears—was carried out—My God what I have suffered—I esteem him of all Men the most. I still see him—See him <u>Now</u> an uncomplaining Wretch, hear and love Him. Finding No hopes, He said my happiness was dearer than his own. If <u>fortune</u> was the obstacle to my giving my hand where I had bestowed my heart—he intreated me to Consider Him as a Father—and to allow Him the only happiness He could Now ever hope for: that of seeing Me happy. He is going to India—begs he may take leave of Me—He will kill Me I believe—I grow thin, pale, and haggard. I can neither Eat or Sleep—still the Image of the once happy Casamajor haunts Me—made miserable by Me—I look at him as a fond Mother does on a sick Child—He sees it, presses my hand—Starts and says I give you pain my Sweet Saint—I will go and <u>wander</u> in the World without You—His Friends look at me as if I had murdered him. We are thought Mad with Romance—Casamajor alone knows why I refuse Him—He is almost More than Mortal. Had I known him four years ago I had been happy in making Him so, but fate has decreed I should be unhappy Myself and make others so—how much do I wish for you—tho when you was last in town my friend—I had hardly a moment to open my heart to you—you will naturally wish to know who it is who has possession of this little heart—and you shall [letter torn here].

18
From: Sylvia Brathwaite, London
To: Lady Clerke, Southampton
Date: 19 December [1784]
My Dear Friend

Enclosed is a letter for Mr Anstey—I have already recommended Him warmly to My Father. How I grieve for you—what you must have suffered with poor dear Mrs Hammond. I rejoice that she is better—yes, my Friend, with truth I declare your joys and sorrows are mine and ever will be—how you talk of Philosophy—do you? do you indeed feel it—No—

Nor Peace Nor Ease that heart can know
   That like the Needle true
Turns to the touch of Joy or Woe
   But turning trembles to.

How you praise Me and all for what. I have obeyed the dictates of my heart—Not fallen the victim of a Temptation that did not charm Me—I have not been false to My own hopes and attachments—I have been true when I had not power to be false. I am still Ill—My Cough allows Me no rest. I am to be bled—be not uneasy. Tis not a consumptive cough, it will soon be well.

I am in good spirits—I am contented. My Gallant Soldier is what I ever thought Him—Noble, humane, generous—and unsuspecting—as his hopes grow better, in point of fortune, his love grows humbler—They all abuse Him—vices they can find none—but He is a Fool—is a Fop—is Ill bred—is a mere Soldier—I hear, I bite my lips but say Nothing—He may be all the Family are pleased to say—but I cannot see it—Therefore to me He has Them Not. But I tell you everything without reserve—He is young—passionate—and in high spirits. He thinks I must be His—He forgets His former distance, talks with the wildness of a young Man's passion. A melancholy and unsuccessful Lover is easy to manage, but this Swain is a plague to Me. He behaves upon the whole well—but is upon his knees five times in an hour. If I look cross—there He remains begging forgiveness. If I but smile tis over—He sighs, trembles, lets go my hand, takes up his hat and runs away. I cannot marry Him yet—at least I must have my own fortune first—I find fault. He answers, when you are angry, how can I go? and when you smile, I dare not stay. He is a little in disgrace for all this—for the last time I saw Him alone—we parted with my saying, Go, I am not angry with you—I hate affectation. You are in spirits—you are a Young Man—when ever I meet you in Company, I will distinguish you, but for a time we meet no more alone. I have kept to this—He looks humble and sometimes angry—I am however right—He is hansome—I like Him and therefore must be a little strict.

The first moment I am allowed to go out I will see Miss Poynes' Caps—your Cap is worn except in full dress—worne in the Stage Box at the play. I have heard from Miss Roberts the history of Miss Moody's wedding—Make My Compts to Sir Yelverton. Tell Him I am very, very, much obliged for His good opinion and will endeavour to keep it. Do the Thomases go to France? If I had any Interest with Mr Pitt, I would give it all for a Place for Mr Thomas—He has the feelings of a Creature rarely seen Now—a British Gentleman.

I am glad you like the Prince. I hope better from Him than the world in general—and as far as a cool wish for his happiness—He stands well with me—I had tickets for a Concert last week—my Swain was with me. I had Them in my hand. He looked at them—You will shine M^d—the Prince will be of your suite. He is always there. Do you think He will join me? I am sure of it. I will lay you a wager he does not and I flung them in the fire. This is the second Concert I have lost by H— R— H—

I will write to you soon again I wish your Lottery Ticket success—my respects to M^rs H— Adieu—you are very good to write me so long a letter. Yours with truth and affection. SB

19

From: Sylvia Brathwaite, London
To: Lady Clerke, Southampton
Date: September [1785]
My Dear Lady Clerke

My Brother will I believe remain in Town. I shall therefore not have the pleasure of seeing you again at Southampton this year. London is stupid beyond all description and the weather miserably bad—by way of amusement I am learning to Ride—and they tell me am very successful—yesterday I mounted a Charger and sat his kicking and jumping vastly well—I am very envious of all the People who are to see Mrs Jackson—and if she comes to town—I shall bribe Her Milliner that I may be permitted to carry home a Cap—for see Her I must unless you will make Interest that I may call in my own character. My Brother dines and spends every day—and this trio remains unbroken unless by my Grandmother or Capt Luttrell who now and then makes a fourth, but we do not want Entertainment—Charles has been a great while at Rome—and very much a[t] the Court of Naples & from His situation admitted of all the private Parties, and He is, I give you my honour, at least as amusing as More's Travel's. And He has brought a tale of spirits—from an Old German officer that is enough to prevent one's ever sitting five minutes alone again. All these things—My performances on Horseback—Triquette—& learning to play at Chess—amuse us tolerably tho the shutters are closed of every House—and a lean faced Housemaid stitching in every parlour window. I hear you are <u>very fine</u>, have got the duke of Northumberland, and for six weeks, besides four or five Lords. The Duke's star I hope shed the most animated lustre on Hayne's Ball Night. He is I think very well looking and has a Nose that one should be civil to without knowing it was His Grace. And yet when I think He is a Peircy, I find Him quite horrible—in short if one wanted to draw the Peircy—it would be impossible to find a Model.

I am writing you a strange letter—but this is one of those days when the bridle hangs unheld upon my Fancy—and in an hour I am making feathered headdresses or fighting at Pharsalia—thinking of the Life of our King and the death of Cato, or fifty things as unlike one another. We have no news in Town—but the Duke of Milan & His Duchess. My Brother goes to them for an hour every Evening—and likes them very much. The <u>duke is a miracle</u>. He is come to see Men and manners—does not regret the time of year—for, says He, there are Operas, plays, Fetes, and <u>persons of Faschion</u> in all Countries & it is not these I come to See—the Duchess is a sensible, well proportioned, black Eyed, Illdressed Woman. The Ladies with Her—One a

Princess, Her dame d'honeur—is young, lively, and hansome—these People are taken no notice of—but by the Prince and he has no House to ask them to—the King and Queen asked them to a Concert at Windsor—gave them no Supper afterwards and let them sleep at an Inn—Brunswick thou art a goodly Name—in most vile keeping.

I am Come to the End of My paper—as a Lover does to the end of His walk without knowing it, and like Him can only Stop and Sigh an adieu to Her whose I am with real affection.

My Aunt is Much the same—M^r W better a great deal. My best respects attend Mrs Hammond—I wish much to know how you do—and for you sake rejoyce in the cold weather.

20

From: Sylvia Brathwaite, London
To: Lady Clerke, Southampton
Date: 30 October [1785]

Surely our letters my good friend will be Belle letters among the <u>Gomnes</u> since we are equally under the dominion of gloom—at this moment Illness adds to mine. I am not able to fetch one breath out and have a cough that tears my breast to pieces—but no more of this.

I will do all I can about your Protegee. I have already written to a Lady who has Interest with Sir Joshua Reynolds and have some hope of success. I need make you no assurances because you know I must be Interested when you are—and of themselves Youth, Poverty, and Genius are strong recommendations.

You ask me so earnestly for my story of the Ghosts that notwithstanding My aversion to writing a regular story—and the absence of my Brother which prevents my giving You one of the Names—begin it—The story was told to Charles by a Man of sense faschion, and of a middle age—besides my Brother were present their Royal Hignesses, their Chaplain, several English Gentlemen, and some French Men of quality—and Lord Beauchamp. Earl Hertford's son is now gone to the Relater of the tale to enquire into it and to see the <u>Spirits</u>. The Count's name who told it I have forgot—but as soon as my Brother returns from the Lodge—you shall have that also.

A Company of German, French, and Prussian Noblesse amounting to fifteen in number falling into Conversation upon the real existence of Ghosts & Phantoms, One of them, a German of good faschion—said that they certainly did Exist for <u>He</u> could raise them—bringing back the dead—to Mortal Society again & constrained to answer questions. All doubted. <u>He</u> persisted and offered, if they had courage, to convince them—to which the Duke of Courland agreed desiring the Experiment might be tried at His Palace. The next night was fixed and the Company invited. The duke ordered the Captain of his Gaurd to see the Room cleared and searched &, after they were all In, to be with the Men of his Gaurd Sentinels at the door, Suffering none to Enter.

They all stood together, except the Sorcerer, who bid them be still—He spoke a few words in a language they could not understand—and presently an Old Man of small stature appeared on His Right hand to whom He bowed—and received a bow in return. Then turning to the Company—this, said He, is my Familliar—now say who among the dead shall appear—but to save trouble Name some one who was generally known to the Company—they consulted & the Duke of Courland desired the Sight of a Marechal of France who had been dead about ten years—in a few Minutes a Figure arose shrouded wan and without Eyes or nose—the Duke undismayed said, This may be any One, for no feature remains to tell. Speak then to Him, said the German, speak—He will answer. Spirit, said the Duke, do you Remember what passed between us in the Bois de Boulogne, for none living but Myself do know it. Yes, replyed the Spectre, We were hunting—and separated from the Company—We quarelled & by the laws of honor should have fought—but being long Friends & now alone We agreed to make it up and never for our Fame's sake tell it. I dyed six weeks after. After this the Duke was convinced—but several More appeared & Many questions were asked, some that offended the Ghosts who all seemed angry. At length the Old Man turned to the German—and said aloud—Haitez-vous—vous avez abusé votre pouvoir. The Spirits vanished & the little Old Man. The Sorcerer appeared Confused, and besought them to meet Him the next Evening at the Entrance of a Wood near.

They met—Gentlemen, said He, I have indulged your curiosity—My Fate is perhaps near—You heard the Old Man—He is my Friend and therefore spoke in the Gentlest way He could—all may yet be well—wait Here—and what ever noise you hear—None advance to the Wood. He went in. They heard the noise of arms—He came out—I have hope, said He. I must return again. Do as before—but I have hope. He reentered the wood—a confusion of voices was heard—and soon the Report of a Pistol. They waited—He returned no more—They went into the Wood after some hours and found him shot to all appearance by Himself, his pistol being near his Right hand. Two of the party put Themselves to death the week after—The Wife of the Relater of this story, who was one of those present, requested the Duchess to ask no more about it, as, she said, Her Husband was always Ill and haunted after telling the story—He too has the power of raising from the Grave its Inhabitants how and by what means was but darkly Spoken. But so much they learned—the spirits having once been called had a perpetual Right to appear to the Person who so disturbed Them—& that they frequently did haunt the Beds and Feasts of These Noblemen. Further, that any one who would say from his heart—My God I abjure Thee—oh devil I worship Thee should see a Familliar & possess this power. This is as well as I remember the story—if Lord Beauchamp sees them at his Return we shall know better. [His] wife is so impressed with horror that she says she will receive Him [only] if He Succeeds. The Idea on her part is Natural but they are [happ]y & in all probability she will forgive Him. So My Tale—read it, and smile at Macbeth—tell Me if your head is not filled with fancy raised Specters, Your lights burning bleu, and the fatal winding sheet rolling round your Candle. Our Prince believes the tale and like another Ulysses wishes to speak to these poor disturbed spirits. For me, I pity Them—that are denied Rest even in the Grave—and give a doubting Credit, and a fearful belief. Read this to Miss Palmer—when you see her—but, dear friend, on the whole be careful to whom you tell it. Weak minds may be hurt several ways by it.

The Duke & Duchess are gone to day from town till after Christmas, & my days of state are put off—Her Royal Highness has this time behaved to me with the most gracious and Familliar kindness—&, for the sake of shewing Me particular kindness, put by all state and walked with me down Pall Mall that She Herself might present Me to Her Sister Lady Elizabeth, of whom knowing but little I must say but little. She has neither her Sister's Grace or Sweetness but has wit—& a certain manner—which pleases many. The Duchess is always telling ye she was not allways Royal, Lady Elizabeth never forgets she is Sister to a Princess—You will I know be sorry to hear that Harriot Lenox is supposed to be dying—poor Thing—I believe latterly she has been amiable—Her Ilness is lingering—her sense good—and I trust she will think properly—Mrs Irwin has been very often to see Me. She lives very properly—<u>our Friend</u> Dobson goes at Canterbury by the name of the <u>learned Pig</u>; is not it well named? Lady James is going soon to Bath—they say a heart covered with a Red Ribbon is offered to Her Ladyship and Rank is her Object.

You see I write like a good child. I am best on paper, but I think as my health grows worse my spirits are better. I congratulate on the hope of seeing Mrs Jackson so soon. I am sorry you are so Unhappy—but you was made to be so—My respects to Mrs Hammond and wishes for better health. Adieu my dear Friend. Yours most affectionately <u>SB</u>

21
From: Sylvia Brathwaite, London
To: Lady Clerke, Southampton
Date: [1785]
My Dear Friend

I should have written to you before but have been very much employed in real business, money business, which I have at last got—My Guardian and My Father's Agent has chose to fling up the business—and I have been at no small trouble to find another Agent fit to take it. I have ten thousand disagreeable things to do—but will not plague you with them—I have had a bad cold—and have got my cough again—I am behaving vastly well—had a Box to see Mrs Siddons, found the Prince was to have the other Stage Box—and did not go—a Gentleman a few days ago brought me tickets for a Concert His Royal Highness always goes to—and which He had asked Me to subscribe to—I refused; pray praise me—alas I have no merit—The Prince is to me—No better than a Prince in gingerbread. My <u>Prince</u> is chose and must reign for ever. The King has given His Father a Regiment of Guards—and the Son is I believe now the Youngest Field officer in the Army, and the Most fortunate. He has a few airs—is proud, somtimes, but very Humble after. In short, the Tons have promised Me to Him this Year, and better pleased will I be in a Cottage, when He flings a brace of Partridges at my feet, than should our Future King place his Crown There.

And now for Lady Peyton's Cloaks—white sattan trimed with Fox—or black with 3 capes and arm holes—short cloaks are not worne, but if worne are best in white—I have sent once to Miss Poynes, she was then not returned—I will go there tomorrow—Mrs Ironside and Her sister drink tea with me this Evening—My Aunt T is pretty well, Bonnell I really believe going to be married to Miss Lycester. Robert still in France—Whaley gone to day to Cambridge to be entered—I have hardly a Moment. M^{rs} W keeps her room, I keep the House. Have to look over and settle all the business about the Agent & my Father. A great deal left Me to do for My Brother. All My acquaintance come to town—Court Mourning to Make—a Mad Lover to avoid, a Melancholly one to hear—and a favored one to please—but still I find time to scratch a letter to you. I will write you a longer letter soon. Never do I pass a day without thinking of you. Remember me to M^{rs} H— When you can, write to Me—always believe me—most affectionately

　　　　　　　　Yours S B＿＿＿＿

Mrs Dobson goes next summer to France --------------

22

From: Sylvia Brathwaite, London
To: Lady Clerke, Southampton
Date: 18 October [1786]
My dear Friend

I have promised to write to you often and will if possible keep my promise but I have my doubts about my letters. I feel like a Spider who has finished his Web. I seem to have done all I have to do—My heart beats heavily and my Spirits March to its dull tatoo. Nothing amuses me and yet I seek amusement with wonderful avidity—nay but few things Interest Me—in that I am an old Woman and seem to have lived my time—perhaps tis want of health gives this sensation—but I feel a gloom within I fear no Sun shine can remove—I have no hopes—no wishes—and think only of the day before Me as a thing I must get through. I am caressed and surrounded by <u>the World</u>—and they are to Me no better than a Mob—who stifle and keep me from better Views—this dear faschionable circle for which the vulgar sigh—what is it? The Old are deceiptful and wicked—the young Wanton & Ignorant. The women without Modesty—the Men without tenderness. I pity them—they pity Me—They rally me—I give them the Victory. I yield them the Crown, I have no Shame in the defeat. But yet I am a slave. I hear all the principles of my soul, all my sentiments, ridiculed and profaned. I never defend them, I am silent. I give up my God—or My friend—tamely, for tis My Lord Duke, or the Countess who spoke. This is my life and will be more so. My opinions remain unshaken—and my heart disdains the placid smile on my face. I will, however, endeavour to learn what I can of these people—at least I shall see characters and if I get spirits this will amuse Me—they begin already to be distressed to attack Me—they say—You are a little Indifferent—We ask all the People we suppose likable—and you distinguish none—come tell us who is your Favorite that we may grow fond of Him for He must be pleasant. Thus the <u>Women</u>. Then the Men—they say, with Infinite Ease, you keep us in doubt. Chuse sombody—you make us Idle—and We lose time—determine for Somebody. Proudly I reply—return to your <u>Useful</u> occupations—I will do what is quite as well, Namely determine for <u>Nobody</u>.

This is my Society, blessed Group. Yet it is Necessary I should distinguish some One of these <u>fine</u> People and the <u>very</u> <u>happy</u> Man this winter will be Harry Greville—I have told Him you are vain—you think I have sense—your vanity is to be taken notice of by women of sense—you know—I <u>know you</u>, You know my heart is beyond your power—I think you amusing—I will dance with you—You shall be of my Parties at the opera—you shall be my <u>Flirt</u>. But the moment you talk of Love We are No More acquainted. This perhaps surprises you—but my good Friend it must be—this will keep other Men from paying me attention, and yet not leave me unattended—and he has no heart—and will like the plan vastly. Lady James is going to Bath—she <u>perfectly adores Me</u>. I have dined with Capt Bromfield—He came in Her suite. We are good Natured People—love me, love my dog. I met the other day with a very Sensible Man in the Navy who belongs to the Duke of C— a Capt O'Hara. He is a Gentleman & has read. We stole in a Corner & talked of Books—but were <u>horribly</u> afraid of being overheard by the Company. We luckily escaped and it passed for a <u>strange</u> flirtation—but this Man is a Gamester—they <u>all are something</u>. I have bought Caliph Vathek—The Genteel Men say it is <u>foolish</u>—the Genteel Woman say it is a pretty story but very Improbable—and there ought to be more about Nouronihar in it—I have seen the Duke of Bedford but will pass no opinion about Him yet, but that He is hansome and has the air of Noblesse. The Duke of Dover has just won sixteen hundred pounds of His Grace at Newmarket—<u>Every Body thinks it very clever & damned good</u>. I don't think about it Much—

To day the Prince & the fair Fitz return to town for the Winter. My Brother finds her not charming—but He is difficult—She is certainly a sweet Woman Malgré tout. They say she was <u>kind</u> to the Cardinal de Mohan once—I have good authority—but yet there is something in her face says no to Wantoness and even now she sins with dignity and in his Highness has no small Excuse for Error. I hope He will be

Constant, for if He leaves her she is More Undone than Anything on Earth. He says, If She ceased to please Me—I <u>think</u> I am bound to Her in honor—and May his honor remember it. He will go no More to Court, but will live in a Corner of His Palace—with a splendid Retinue of Menial Servants but no Officers of State, but will never be unattended. The Number who Love his Royal Highness for Himself will keep Him in a Crowd—I saw the Minister yesterday—and tho a Minister He is a <u>Man</u>, for he laments unfeigndly the death of His Sister Lady Esther Elliot.

I write to you about these People because I believe you like it, as you bid Me tell you News. My Brother has had a letter from the Governess of the Princess Royal of Prussia. Never was King so revered, loved, & lamented. She says all the New officers of State, those who rose by his death, wept at his Burial—She speaks with great respect of the New King—the will of his late Majesty was a very odd one—and too Masked as to his <u>Religious</u> system—but He speaks most hansomly of the Queen and gives a Number of small tokens of love one would not have expected from the roughness of his Character. The Lady who writes this to my Brother is a Woman of the most ancient Faschion and much good sense. She says—as a proof that death is indeed the Conqueror of Conquerors our superb King is no More—Prussia is in tears. The soldiers weep like women—thus says the Countess.

The Age has lost its most conspicuous character, and not one crown Now circles a Son of Fame—Greatness has methinks lost a limb—it will not easily recover; and yet, till He died, I never much revered the King of Prussia. His private Life is already forgot—and His Public is only remembered. The Bad Man is sunk in the Just Beneficent King—& the brave & Successful Soldier. As far as I can learn of Courts & Kings, France is the best Man. He is Not a Comet—but He is a star of Mild & benevolent lustre. Tis his custom often to say—I will do so and so—Can I? Certainly Sire. But is the Money in the Treasury? No, but the People! it will be furnished immediately. Not at all, replies the King; I will let it alone. I will call upon them for my Use & their advantage but never for my pleasures. This Man is surely great in the Eye of Reason, and tho Fame should never sound Him—the blessings of millions will be heard in an Ear—beyond that of Europe & his People. The Queen is most unamiable—all the Emperor's sisters are ambitious, wanton, & designing, & ready to sacrifice every duty or tie to their Brother and the glory of the House of Austria.

I should have Much pleasure in Conversing with you—My Brother's situation has given Him free Entrance into all the foreign Courts, and as [for] Royals, they have been much behind the Curtains. Above all People, the King of Naples seems the most curious—it is his custom when he rises to go in his shirt into a Balcony in View of all his People—here after gaping some time He calls for his Clothes and dresses thus in Public. He, too, poor Man, is married to a Sister of Germany, who Governs the Nation—but this greives Him little, His whole delight being Boar hunting. The present Politicks of that Court are obliging all the Nobles to live at Court. The Feudal System consequently already wanes and will ere long be quite destroyed. The

Chateaux are deserted and the Person of the Baron unknown upon His own Estate in order to live splendidly. [The tena]nts are [wret]ched &distressed—Luxury [has] innervated the Great Man—and poverty the poor One—so that Tyranny finds no [bar]. The Court is dull—no hansom women well receive[d], no galantry allowed, the queen being very Jealous and her vengeance dreadful when called forth. Her own society select in her Apartments gay & dissolute—but no Public appearance of Sports or Shews. The King treating her with such homage as to stand and bow as she passes to go to the play. She sits in Council always—the King seldom & but a short time.

I have written you a Mighty long letter about Kings and Queens—and perhaps have said very little worth knowing but I write as I should talk. Let me hear from you dear friend—& for my sake take notice of Miss Palmer—she is afraid of your abillities & very diffident of Her own. She would love you dearly if she dare.
Adieu Yours Most truely S B—
My Aunt T— is but Indifferent.

23
From: Sylvia Brathwaite, London
To: Lady Clerke, Southampton
Date: 12 January [1787]
My Dear Friend
I have now very little time to write—the World are come to Town and my Mornings are very Much devoted to Italian and the Riding School. Cumberland House is always gay and full of Company, but People of Faschion are not my People, and I every day grow more fatigued with my active Idleness. The Duchess is a Star among the circle—she has sense—Information, benevolence, and grace—but she is obliged to shine on all alike. The Men are all very disagreable, not one natural character, & they only feign unpleasant Ones. I am born, I believe, to be discontented—for I hate a [words obliterated by tape]. Young Women, I know, Envy Me—They are all tormenting Me to be presented at St James's. I have positively refused. I trust my father will yet be kind and not place me forever in a Court. I will have a Court of my own, one day. My Ministers shall be my Friends. My Courtiers honest Villagers. I must be Interested to be happy—and these gay, titled, glittering People do not Interest me. They would make a pretty dessert but they will not do to feed intirely upon—and my head and heart are starved. Our Prince I still like very well, generous, open, goodnatured, Graceful, gracious, humane, & accomplished. As a private Man He would be very pleasing. His manners to the fair Fritz are tender, respectful, and delicate—of his Sense perhaps it may not be powerful—but his Information has not been small—& his Memory is wonderful. I think as a King I could venture to prophecy that He will protect the arts—and be gentle in His way—merciful in His punishments and very liberal in His rewards—Great I do not

think he will ever be—but we must remember the brightest Fires <u>burn</u> as well as shine and in short the time of Heroes is past. The last died in Prussia.

London is full of Foriegners, Venetians in particular—and we have a <u>Roman</u> Senator il Principi Besonico—a sensible worthy Man—and I am pleased to see the real attention and civility We pay these unwise Strangers who quit the Land of Sunshine, song, dance, Softness, arts, & Science to Freeze with us—in gloom—and dull imitations of the perfections they have left behind. I tell the Senator, He takes England as a bitter to give new sweetness to Italy. I am to sup in a few days with the Tripoli Ambassador. My Brother tells Me He is pleasant. As to News we have very little, but that Both Secretaries of State are likely to go out. Lord Camarthen not contented—Lord Sydney with the Post office, which will please Him. But I believe you do not care about these things—I am you know a Party Woman—Your friend Mrs Jackson is very well—She is the best Informed Woman I have met [in] a long while. [We are] already very good Friends—I hear of [you] now and then—and, you see, never wait for letters from you but write when I have time—I am very anxious about you—and your situation—Books I can say little about. I have just finished a tour thro' America—but cannot say Much of it. I hear you are moved, I hope, for the better. I will [remainder of letter is missing].

24
From: Sylvia Brathwaite, London
To: Lady Clerke, Southampton
Date: 13 February [1787]
My Dear Friend

I write to thank you for your letter for I really have not time to tell you anything that would amuse you. Up all Night and asleep all day—My head is Either stupid—or filled with a repetition of the Puppet show of the past Evening, where R^t Honorable's without honor and Excellencies without Excellence dance in My Brain. This and the <u>unfelt</u> labours of the Toilet mark My hours—what then shall I tell you—why to read the Victim of Fancy. It is a New Novel, and is Either well written—or perhaps one <u>Victim</u> of Fancy loves another. <u>I am not spoilt yet</u>. I sit over a Faro Table—as I would by a Malignant Fever—I tremble with its symptoms—and shudder at the Infection. As to lovers I have enough—One a Friend of Mine—I wish you knew Him. He has the heart and Person of a Walstein. He hopes in vain to find a <u>Caroline</u>. For the rest, they [are] <u>Men</u> of faschion without any character to describe them by—Greville, they say, for once Means honorable—He is agreable—& fascinating—but, why I cannot tell, My heart is unmoved. I neither wish Him honorable & sincere or even think about Him.

Col T—I have seen—still He loves—His Wife is at the point of death. She dies of a broken heart. Poor Maria—thy wrongs are mine—May He love on—and may it be mine to Revenge your death. He has treated Her with cruelty and Contempt—they say He is Mad—He talks reasonable and well. How I pity Her—I view Her as one who has drunk of the Poison that was mixed for Me—every angry thought is dead—God forgive the Husband and receive the Wife. I could Nurse Her—I could weep over Her—it seems My Name has tipped the dart of Many an Arrow that has stung this Sufferer's heart. But No More of this.

Parkhurst alone can stand a chance—He has a heart—He is gone to Lyons—and has more of my good wishes than any here who like me—but I shall love No More I fear. I was so rudely waked from my dream of Love—that I can dream no more—I write to you from My Soul. I conceal Not a thought—but I must finish this—I was up all Night at Almack's. I am going out to dinner—the Prince and I are very good Friends—I am grown a Stateswoman and trusted with secrets. I like Him sincerely and He Me—His Constancy to the Fair Fritz pleases Me. He never talks even in the way of common Galantry, but is Condescending enough to advise Me if He sees Me with any Body He thinks not proper. Poor Maty but No Man was fitter to die—I am sure you felt a great deal. My Aunt T is ill—the rest of the Family well—I have had a visit from Mrs Dobson with powder, false curls, lappets, black worsted stockings full of holes. They do not agree, I hear, at Kensington. God Bless you, My dear Friend—write to Me when you can & believe Yours with the truest affection

25
From: Sylvia Brathwaite, London
To: Lady Clerke, Southampton
Date: October [1787]

You praise me so hansomly for writing to you twice in a short time that you see I am induced to deserve again your praises. I was much diverted with your Party at Mrs Thomas's—but, my dear friend, you was not made only to live in Societies to laugh at—I supped with Lady James the Night she arrived in town. We met at the Old Countess Ferrer's—Her Ladyship was very gracious—indeed she <u>now</u> must be—for we live all like one Family. Mrs Parkyns expects every day to lay in—She seems much altered, & My Brother Confirms my observation—attentive to Her Husband, simply dressed, and watching every look of Her Mother. I hardly knew again the Silly Flirt of last year. Parkyns is better but looks Ill—He seems grown very fond of Her. We must live very Much together as we all meet undressed & Sup two or three times a week at Lady Ferrer's—and next month their Royal Highnesses come over—This as far as it keeps my Brother here does well—but for Me I shall be sick to death with it. I like the Duchess but nothing interests Me in the circle. The Women are foolish—the Men treat me like a Fool. And I look around, if my Brother quits the room for a moment, with distress, like a Creature left alone among its Enemies. I have been unwell lately—and I find being in Spirits too great an Exertion—and yet I am so accustomed to it that when in Company I always resolve to be so. I hate forms and with Royalty these are very necessary. I am in Company always—but my heart is always alone—I am Sick of Myself—and find Nothing to like. I have taken up a Melancholly Idea, that Nothing can make me happy—Rank—power—wealth, love, health, Friends—not all could make me happy—I have lost the taste for happiness and tho apparently gay I am the Soul of gloom & Ennui—I can cry with Hamlet Man delights Not Me, Nor Woman neither. And yet I dress, laugh, and talk with earnestness of every Trifle. Like a slave of Custom I do this—and Othello's occupation done.

Of Parckhurst I have very slightly spoken to my Brother—We once have quarrelled & never again can speak upon Such Subjects. For the Young Man, He has as Much of my pity as Another had of my love. I never Saw a Lover before, I am convinced, and if Sense, tenderness, strong feelings, perfect generosity, total forgetfulness of Self, Strong passion, & corrected Manners might Speak for love and gain it—He would have it. He sought my heart when another had rudely flung it from Him—He asked my pity when I felt what it was to love in vain—to this may be attributed the pains I took to avoid hurting Him—had I known this Man five Years ago—it had been better, tho Even then—the other without half His qualities or Graces would without <u>seeking</u> have won Me. So then, My Friend, Heaven's Ganameed—and Earth's Anthony—England's Harry Greville does not charm you, nor me, for what does Harry want! He wants a heart. The Youth has marked Me for His triumphs, but No, tis not seducing powers that win Me. I heard, Saw, and never Sighed.

We have very little News except about Newfounland Fisheries and hear Pitt has made a woeful blunder—but I cannot care about Fisheries—pray remember Me to Sir Yelverton & Lady Peyton—I am unfortunate in never meeting with them at Southampton—my Compliments to Mr Haynes. I am in debt to him for more civility that my Rank or Situation required, and if my Rank and Situation allowed it would gladly give it Him back. Miss Palmer has a thousand amiable qualities and is More a Child of Nature than one often sees, I like Her very much and wish you would, for, as it is, one lives like a Flower in a Garden of weeds. I shall have much pleasure in seeing Mrs Jackson, in seeing any Friend of Yours. As to public Places this winter, I have great doubts if my health will allow it. At present it would not. I wish much you could see my Brother. He has not one atom of a Fop remaining I think. Next Spring He has determined to Enter the Prussian Army for six months. I respect this Intention as it has Not a Shadow of amusement in it. Often have I sighed that Court had spoiled Him—it did for a time—but Nature breaking through—He is once again all that a Young Man should be. Poor Bonnell goes on sadly I mean in <u>Nothingness</u>—if the Emperor Titus wept a lost day what torrents should He shed for a lost Life—Thus I talk <u>who</u> live as Insignificantly Myself.

When you can, let me hear from You—but never when it hurts you. I will write to you as often as I can, but somtimes the <u>People</u> I hate take up so Much of My time that I have none for <u>those I love</u>—and often lately my mind is too Confused to allow me to write at all. Greville has just left Me—and almost against my better knowledge made me believe he has feeling.

I shall this Winter be able to give You a just character of the Prince as I shall be Much in his Society—One Thing I will tell you M^{rs} F is fallen with Me—She is no <u>Rosamond</u>—and the Prince has wept and knelt for what other Men with half His Graces have won easier. But this to Yourself—or at all Events <u>not from me</u>. My Respects to Mrs Hammond—Adieu, my very dear Friend, I am at the bottom of my paper—even such a page is Life and so full as <u>this</u> of Nothing—Yours Ever

Sylvia Brathwaite

26
From: Sylvia Brathwaite, London
To: Lady Clerke, Southampton
Date: 31 March 1788
My Dear Friend

I am very sorry my letter was so Ill timed & far from wondering you were angry, I rather wonder you are good enough to forgive me. You are now better and Summer on its way. Nature will present you with objects lively and Interesting—the Smiles of Nature are catching & the uncorrupted heart Smiles with Her. I am very sorry for the situation of Mrs H. With most People the debt to Parents goes <u>unpaid</u>, but you are now returning ten fold the Cares she bestowed on you in your Childhood. Heaven is pleased with this return of duties, and tho Rousseau's works may have little power when offered at the Throne of Grace, great shall be the hopes of that Being whom an Aged Parent shall present loaded with blessings. Go on then cheerfully. Lead her gently through this World—and receive its admiration till she sinks peaceful to a better World and prepares for you your reward.

I have been much hurried with an unpleasant adventure at the opera. A Man I believe <u>Mad</u> chose to be in love with me, followed me, & flung his arms around my waist. Fear made me fly. Unfortunately the Prince stopt my flight and knew the Cause—went up, was going to beat the Man—went out in the Street to call my Carriage & carried me out leaning on his Arm. It was in vain I intreated. He is young, active for Women, and enraged when they are Ill treated, & He forgets how much <u>harm</u> He may do by being interested. It is much talked of, and M^{rs} T seems angry with Me. All this is very Unlucky because I have escaped everything of this kind as yet. The Prince has, I believe, a friendship for me—but knowing my Ideas till Now has ever avoided anything the least particular.

Remember me to Mrs Jackson if she is still at Southampton—[and] give My best Compts to Sir Yelverton and Lady Peyton. Mrs Hulse told Me she had met them in Hertfordshire where they had the goodness to mention Me very kindly—I live among a <u>fine World</u> so bad that the praise of good People is doubly sweet. <u>Quite</u> <u>forgive me</u> & believe me affectionately

Yours SB

A Young Marriageable Woman

Seventeen eighty-three, the year in which *The History of Sylvia Brathwaite, Written by Herself* opens, was an exciting time for Londoners, especially young women. The theater was spectacular. Sarah Siddons was in her second year at Drury Lane and her brother John Kemble in his first. "The stage is in perfection," enthuses Sylvia in one of her letters. The novel was on the rise, and circulating libraries provided women and men with the latest novels at affordable prices. Reading and talking about books was an important part of London life. Fashion was gaining in importance. Magazines devoted to spreading information about new dress designs proliferated. Women spent much time arranging and admiring their costumes. Politics was rousing and rowdy as the Prince sided with the Whigs; aristocratic as well as genteel society followed the ups and downs of such political celebrities as William Pitt and Charles James Fox and the ins and outs of parliamentary debates and maneuvers. Most important for young women, the American War had ended and the city was full of returning soldiers prepared to enthrall listeners with tales of military exploits. It is no wonder that Sylvia mentions "poor gallant soldiers" in so many of her letters. First attracted to Col Banastre Tarleton, she later flirts with Harry Greville, and then finally marries Charles Parkhurst. All were military men.

Filling her letters with her sometimes humorous, sometimes distressing, sometimes perilous amorous encounters, Sylvia took a long time deciding whom to marry. An exhilarating sexual freedom, absent from the older women's letters, pervades her epistles. She freely chastises and restrains her many lovers. She not only checks her more ordinary lovers, but she also tutors the Prince. In an early letter, from 1783 (#14), she describes a Royal Party as a scene of subtle but earnest intrigue from which she emerges as victor. Although the Prince singles her out for flattery and assiduous attention, she remains steadfastly cautious. She refuses to drink champagne with him, and when he offers her part of a pineapple she refuses again, leading Col Luttrell to observe that "Miss B ... is thinking ill be sworn of the fatal apple in Eden." When the Prince tells her that were she Iphigenia at Aulis, "[t]here would have been no sacrifice—but that of a heart," and asks her if the gods would have approved, she warns him that the Gods are never propitious "when in public characters, private feelings get the better of the Public good." Once she has disciplined the Prince, she appears to relax and enjoy his company but nonetheless she ends her narrative of the evening by emphasizing her incorruptibility: "He left me where he found me—with my heart still true to my poor soldier."

BEAUTY *in* SEARCH *of* KNOWLEDGE.

London. Printed for R. Sayer & J. Bennett, Map, Chart & Printsellers N.º53 Fleet Street 30.ᵗʰ Dec.ʳ 1782.

12.1   Unknown, "Beauty in Search of Knowledge," 1782. Mezzotint. Courtesy of the Lewis Walpole Library, Yale University. Like many other eighteenth-century women, Sylvia patronized circulating libraries

As a young, unmarried woman Sylvia had tremendous power to discipline and punish, to choose and reject. She could even tell the Prince to curb his personal appetites if he wanted to preserve the public good. Why should she give up such power? Certainly before doing so, it behooved her to decide carefully. Writing out her adventures, her likes and dislikes, in her letters to Lydia helped her make up, and delay making up, her mind.

From Sylvia's point of view, there was little incentive to make a final decision. There was much more reason to defer her decision indefinitely, flirting and testing, encouraging and dismissing lovers at will. She enjoyed dangling her train of lovers: Mr. Turner with his 3,000 pounds a year, the Man of Fashion of Old Family, the Man of the World, the Coxcomb, and the Married Man. However, while she might enjoy her deferential lovers, others assailed and weakened her. Mr. Casamajor pursues her from the beginning to the end of her letters. Deeply upset by his inability to accept her rejection of him, she fears for his life and her own health. Her cousin, Bonnell Thornton, also pursues her. Twice he is engaged to others (a Miss Greens in Letter #17, a Miss Lycester in Letter #21), in order, she believes, to revenge himself on her for her indifference, but he continues to torment her, making it difficult for the two of them to live in the same house. "Volpone" unnerves her. Describing him as a "tall lean pale Figure in black," she at first feels drawn to him and is disappointed when a fool "in a Motley Coat" stops her in her path and proceeds to monopolize her so that she can only watch helplessly as Volpone disappears from view. Nevertheless, in her second letter about him, she lets Lady Clerke know that she has rebuffed him. She cannot understand why she let herself be led by the "wretch" for so long, since all he did was offer her contradiction and reproof.[2] Being a young, marriageable girl was not always easy.

While we might laugh at some of Sylvia's exaggerated actions and reactions and dismiss them as trivial nonsense, we should keep in mind that she was preparing to marry a man for life, and that this man would have almost absolute control over her person, her fortune, and her future. Understandably it is hard for Sylvia to decide whom to marry. She knows that if she chooses the wrong man she risks making an irremediable mistake. Like Betsy Thoughtless, in Eliza Haywood's 1751 novel of the same name, Sylvia wants to hear all the different proposals that might be offered her before making up her mind. While some might view such behavior as "thoughtless,"

---

[2]   While we cannot know for sure who Volpone was, it is possible that he was a member of the Fox family. In Book II of the *Female Spectator*, Eliza Haywood uses the pseudonyms "Lindamira" and "Vulpone" (with a "u" instead of an "o") when narrating the elopement of Caroline Lennox and Henry Fox. While the story originally appeared in May 1744, Sylvia might have read a later collected edition of Haywood's periodical. Although Charles James Fox is a likely candidate for Sylvia's "Volpone," his portly figure would hardly fill her description of "a tall lean pale figure in black." I am indebted to Mary Margaret Stewart for this reference.

Sylvia knows (and, I suspect, Eliza Haywood would agree) that such careful deliberation is preferable to accepting the first likely proposal.

Sylvia wants to be sure she is making the right decision. In a late letter, from 1787 (#25), she lists the characteristics of a good lover: "Sense, tenderness, strong feelings, perfect generosity, total forgetfulness of Self, Strong passion, & corrected Manners." But the heart is not always rational and sometimes gives itself to the wrong person. Even so, Sylvia never loses sight of her most important criterion: unostentatious charitableness. More than once she mentions that a lover performed an unheralded act of kindness. She wants a generous man with a truly good heart who will spontaneously and secretly give to others; she does not want a selfish tyrant who will only pretend to be kind in order to win her.

Whom Sylvia loved and who loved Sylvia is not always easy to determine, but the stories of the various men's protests, demands, and lures are well worth the telling. Interestingly, Lennox's commentators often find her fictional character Harriot Stuart's many love affairs incredible; however, if we look at Sylvia as an actual person (which she indeed was), we must accept the notion that such repetitive and endless amorous encounters were indeed possible, in fact expected, in the fashionable world of eighteenth-century society. Whether or not all of Sylvia's lovers were actually in love with her is impossible to tell, but certainly she believed they were. In fact, given the expectations of her world, she could not have seen the many men circulating around her otherwise. They had to conform to the role of hapless admirer or ruthless rake or boorish sober citizen. If they failed to fit any of these categories, they probably ceased to exist for the marriageable young woman.

An eighteenth-century woman was expected to declare for one of her beaux by the end if not of the first season at least by the second or third.[3] To take overly long to decide was costly for the family; it was much more expensive to live in London than in the country. However, Sylvia deferred her decision for a long time. Perhaps she felt freer to take longer because she had an aunt (Mrs. Thornton) and grandparents (Mr. and Mrs. Winstanley) who lived in London with whom she could stay while her father served in India and her brother at court. Perhaps she took longer because she was unhappy with the selection she was offered. Perhaps she took longer because she was aware of her vulnerability and wanted to choose carefully or had friends (for example, Lady Clerke) who urged her to be sure before she declared for anyone. Or perhaps she was one of those women who, as Amanda Vickery wickedly suggests, preferred to make a career of their coming out.[4]

---

[3]   In the eighteenth century (and on into the nineteenth) the aristocratic and genteel classes broke the year into two parts. Part of the year (the summer) was spent in the country, but during "the season" "the World" migrated to London.

[4]   Vickery 82.

While not all genteel families spent the season in London, those with marriageable daughters usually did. From the point of view of the marriageable daughter, "the season" was a marriage market. Women attended balls and assemblies, dinner parties, the theater, and the opera, in order to meet eligible young men; hopefully a woman was chosen by a man of whom she and her parents might approve. If we use Sylvia's letters as a guideline, a young girl's preferences mattered. A predicament like the famous fictional heroine Clarissa's (whose family sought to force her into marrying the disagreeable Solmes) was much less likely by the time Sylvia reached her late teens in the 1780s. Fathers and brothers and aunts and grandmothers might be unhappy about a young woman's refusals and ultimate choice, but they could not force her into marriage. Nevertheless, while a young girl was not to be forced or rushed into marriage, her family could exert tremendous pressure. Sylvia's brother supports Luttrell's attentions because he is wealthy (obviously Sylvia's family was unaware that Luttrell was married), and her grandmother corresponds secretly with Casamajor, Sylvia's most persistent suitor. Also, the family vehemently disapproves of her "Gallant Soldier."

Sylvia was not a duchess or an heiress (although eventually her father accumulated a large fortune). She was, we can assume, "an ordinary girl" of her upper-middle-class world, what Amanda Vickery identifies as a gentleman's daughter. But, as much money and privilege as she had, she risked losing it if she took the wrong step. Completely aware of her exposed situation, she knew how hard it was to discriminate between wily seducers and potential husbands, for deflowering her was, as "Belzebub" admits in the *Gentleman's Magazine*, the goal of many of the young men she met. She needed to tread carefully, for whatever she did or did not do, she would be blamed for any subsequent loss of respectability.

The World

Throughout her letters, Sylvia expresses vehement dislike of the aristocratic world in which she moved. She had much reason to distrust it. Due to her brother's profession and ambitions (he served as an equerry to the Duke of Cumberland[5]), she was drawn into the world of the Duke and Duchess of Cumberland and spent much time at Cumberland House. Their world was indeed treacherous. Henry Frederick, the Duke of Cumberland, was an uncle of the Prince of Wales. His marriage to Mrs. Anne Horton, a commoner, was one of the circumstances that led George III to introduce the Royal Marriages Act of 1772. According to E.A. Smith, a biographer of George IV, the Cumberlands encouraged the Prince's drinking, took him to brothels, and

---

[5]   A. Aspinall, ed., *The Correspondence of George, Prince of Wales 1770–1812* (London, 1963–71) 1:224n.

introduced him to gambling. The Duchess, Smith asserts, was "addicted to coarse language and behaviour."[6] The King forbade his son their company. Smith believes their influence was short-lived, and diminished after 1782/83, but Sylvia's letters suggest that this was not the case.

Like the Cumberlands, Colonel Luttrell had a dreadful reputation. Nevertheless, Sylvia is positively impressed by him. She notes that she is obliged to him "for some very hansom behaviour upon a very awkward occasion and for the Most unbounded Praises of Me to the Duchess." Luttrell, she concludes, "is very pleasant," and, like her, "detests all the parade of C------- House." Although Luttrell was a rake, he does not seem to have ever lost Sylvia's favor. Perhaps when with her he behaved well. Sylvia also admires the Duchess. In Letter #23, she describes her as "a Star among the circle—she has sense—Information, benevolence, and grace—but she is obliged to shine on all alike." If the Duchess often used coarse language, she must have refrained from doing so in Sylvia's presence. Sylvia's unqualified respect for her suggests that, once again, we must be careful when listening to judgments about women. Smith might have overlooked the Duchess's good qualities in order to elevate the Prince. The worse her behavior, the more his misbehavior could be attributed to her bad influence (and that of others).

The Duchess's sister, Lady Elizabeth, does not win Sylvia's favor: "She has neither her Sister's Grace or Sweetness but has wit—& a certain manner—which pleases many. The Duchess is always telling ye she was not allways Royal, Lady Elizabeth never forgets she is Sister to a Princess." Lady Elizabeth Luttrell is a different sort of woman from her sister. Sylvia finds her arrogant and unnatural. Perhaps she would have appreciated the end given her by A. Aspinall, the editor of George IV's letters: "On the death of her sister she was thrown into gaol. There she gave a hair-dresser £50 to marry her. Her debts then becoming his, she was discharged. She went abroad, where she descended lower and lower, till, being convicted of picking pockets at Augsburg, she was condemned to clean the streets, chained to a wheelbarrow. In that miserable situation she terminated her existence by poison!"[7] Such a stranger-than-fiction ending must owe something to the inventiveness of rumor and the desire to give an unpleasant person the poetic justice of an unpleasant ending.

Sylvia also begins to dislike the Duke. In Letter #15 she declares that he is "worse than I thought him." In that same letter, she criticizes the Prince, and, like Smith, blames his behavior on the women around him: "I really believe He [the Prince] never behaves Ill but when the Women begin." Her attitude toward the people she meets in Cumberland House grows more and more dismissive. In Letter #22, she laments, "I am caressed and surrounded by the World—and they are to Me no better than a

---

6   E.A. Smith 17–18.
7   Aspinall 1:224n.

Mob—who stifle and keep me from better Views—this dear faschionable circle for which the vulgar sigh—what is it? The Old are deceiptful and wicked—the young Wanton & Ignorant. The women without Modesty—the Men without tenderness." Others might envy her, but Sylvia knows her life is not enviable. Despising the aristocrats with whom she must associate, she knows that while there might be some pleasure in aristocratic company, it is short-lived and dangerous.

At one point, Sylvia tries to gain some control over her life in a corrupt society. Cynical and tired of the endless solicitations of the men around her, she tells Lydia, in a letter written in 1786 (#22), that she has decided to select one man as her "flirt" in order to keep others away. She selects Harry Greville because his "vanity is to be taken notice of by women of sense." She believes her heart is safe, for both she and Harry know what they are doing, but affairs of the heart do not always go as planned. In the same letter that first mentions her future husband by name (#24, written in 1787), Sylvia begins to believe Greville has feelings for her: "Greville, they say, for once Means honorable—He is agreable—& fascinating—but, why I cannot tell, My heart is unmoved." Later, in Letter #25, even as she declares for Parkhurst, she cannot deny her feelings for Greville. Reading between the lines, it almost sounds as if Sylvia settled for Parkhurst on the rebound from Greville: "He [Parkhurst?] sought my heart when another [Greville?] had rudely flung it from Him—He asked my pity when I felt what it was to love in vain—to this may be attributed the pains I took to avoid hurting Him—had I known this Man five Years ago—it had been better, tho Even then—the other [Tarleton?] without half His qualities or Graces would without seeking have won Me. So then, my Friend, Heaven's Ganameed—and Earth's Anthony —England's Harry Greville does not charm you, nor me, for what does Harry want! He wants a heart." Reading this heartfelt summary of her perplexing love life, we cannot know for sure which man is meant at each point. There may even be other men whose names never appear in the letters we have. But it does seem clear that the fickle and irrational heart sometimes prefers the wrong man. Harry Greville threw away her heart. Parkhurst picked it up. Still she is inexplicably attracted to Harry.

While in this vacillating state, Sylvia has another ambiguous encounter with the Prince, underscoring how dangerous it was for her to continue deferring her decision. In her narrative of the "Royal Party," Sylvia wins the day and remains, even after her extended and sexually charged sparring with His Royal Highness, unsullied and unperturbed. After her second encounter, which takes place five years later, in 1788 (Letter #26), she sounds frightened and even angry. The Prince may have successfully rescued her from a madman, but in throwing his arms around her waist and carrying her to her carriage, he puts her at a different sort of risk. When a woman leans on the Prince's arm, she is "much talked of." Sylvia writes to Lydia as if to defend herself from the recriminations of her aunt who "seems angry with Me." She assures her friend that until now she has "escaped everything of this kind as yet." The power and range of the young woman is real but also precarious. One false step could be fatal.

Did this misadventure accelerate her decision-making process? Perhaps. Or, her feelings for Greville might have changed. Or, Parkhurst's passion might have won her over. Or, she might have grown weary of her own indecisiveness. Or, she might have feared another such mishap as befell Casamajor, who could not accept her rejection: "I told Him I had no heart to give—He offered to marry me still; time, his attention would teach Me to give him my heart—I went to the play—He of the party. He was seized with a shivering fit—burst into Tears—was carried out." His pain and suffering deeply upset her: "He will kill Me I believe—I grow thin, pale, and haggard. I can neither Eat or Sleep—still the Image of the once happy Casamajor haunts Me—made miserable by Me." With such consequences attendant upon her hesitations, she must decide. In the end she chooses Parkhurst, and, in her last letter, lets us know that she not only married Parkhurst, but married without her family's consent. She chose her heart's preference rather than the World's.

Fallen Women

Perhaps because she well knew how much she risked every time she entered the World, the theme of the fallen woman becomes a *leitmotif* in Sylvia's letters. From beginning to end, she muses about the sexual proclivities of the women around her. Delighted when her "poor soldier" tells her that she has a firmness few women possess and believing herself incorruptible, she sometimes judged harshly other women who lacked her self-control. In Letter #16, she castigates "Miss Anley" who "had not sensibility to excuse her even." While she can laugh at Lady Craven, who the World believed had run off with her footman, she cannot escape metonymic contagion when, in almost the same line, she goes on to remember "the capricious Lady," the title of a recent play, and to doubt the honesty of Mrs. Abington who played the title role: "'Tis the best piece of acting I ever saw, or perhaps it is her real character." Wildly contaminating, women's sexuality cannot be contained. In such a slippery world, it is no wonder that Sylvia sometimes used the defensive mask of self-righteousness to separate herself from her own sexual vulnerability.

Three interpolated tales illustrate Sylvia's fascination with fallen women and let us see how observation of the real-life experiences of the women around her helped her read her own story. First we have the potentially tragic, but happily ended tale of the James/ Perqins/ Parkyns ménage; then, the sometimes romantic, sometimes satiric story of the Prince of Wales and Maria Fitzherbert; and, last, the pathetic story of Banastre Tarleton and Mary Robinson.

The James/ Perqins/ Parkyns tale begins in Letter #13, where we learn that Miss James is about to marry "Perqins"; in Letter #14, the marriage is a fait accompli: "The Duchess sat near the bottom, Mrs Parkyns on the other side." In Letter #15, Mr. and Mrs. Parkyns are bound for the South of France; Sylvia tells Lydia that he is dying and she good for nothing. But, in Letter #25, Mrs. Parkyns, along with her mother Lady James, is transformed: "I supped with Lady James the Night she arrived in town. We met at the Old Countess Ferrer's—Her Ladyship was very gracious—indeed she now must be—for we live all like one Family. Mrs Parkyns expects every day to lay in—She seems much altered ... attentive to Her Husband, simply dressed, and watching every look of Her Mother. I hardly knew again the Silly Flirt of last year. Parkyns is better but looks Ill—He seems grown very fond of Her." Her earlier misbehavior forgiven and forgotten, Miss James, or Mrs. Parkyns, becomes a virtuous woman. About to give birth, she has evolved into a model wife and daughter attentive to both her husband and mother.[8]

While Mrs. Parkyns earns Sylvia's respect, the reverse happens in the second narrative. Sylvia begins by expressing admiration for Maria Fitzherbert, but ends by condemning her. Sylvia can understand the temptations the widow faced when the Prince declared his love for her, but she cannot suppress a reference to her less than virtuous reputation: "She is certainly a sweet Woman Malgré tout. They say she was kind to the Cardinal de Mohan once—I have good authority—but yet there is something in her face says no to Wantoness and even now she sins with dignity and in his Highness has no small Excuse for Error." Did Sylvia know the open secret that Fritz was married to the Prince on 15 December 1785? And, if she knew that, did she know the marriage was illegal since the Prince was underage and she a Roman Catholic commoner? Whatever she knew, Sylvia tried to overlook the ambiguities of their relationship. "His manners to the fair Fritz are tender, respectful, and delicate," she writes in one letter; "His Constancy to the Fair Fritz pleases Me," she writes in another. However, Sylvia's tolerance of their irregular union gradually fades and, in her final reference to the couple, she emphatically castigates the Prince's cast-off mistress: "One Thing I will tell you M^{rs} F is fallen with Me—She is no Rosamond —and the Prince has wept and knelt for what other Men with half His Graces have won easier. But this to Yourself—or at all Events not from me." Unlike Rosamund, who, confined in her labyrinthine bower, remained true to Henry II (until she was poisoned by his wife Queen Eleanor, as some legends will have it), Fritz's affections cannot be confined. It is interesting that in this case Sylvia's severest rigor is reserved for the woman and not the man. Fritz is fallen, but not the Prince. The inconstant Prince proved his mettle when he remained steadfast for as long as he did. If he has finally proved unfaithful, it is Fritz's fault. She is responsible for her own downfall.[9]

---

[8]   The Reverend William Betham's *Baronetage of England* confirms that not only did Thomas Boothby Parkyns and Elizabeth-Anne James marry, but they sired five children (3:46–7). Although Betham records that they married on 16 December 1788, according to the International Genealogical Index, they were married on 24 December 1783, at St Mary's Marylebone Parish Church, London.
[9]   See E.A. Smith's *George IV* for a fuller discussion of the affair.

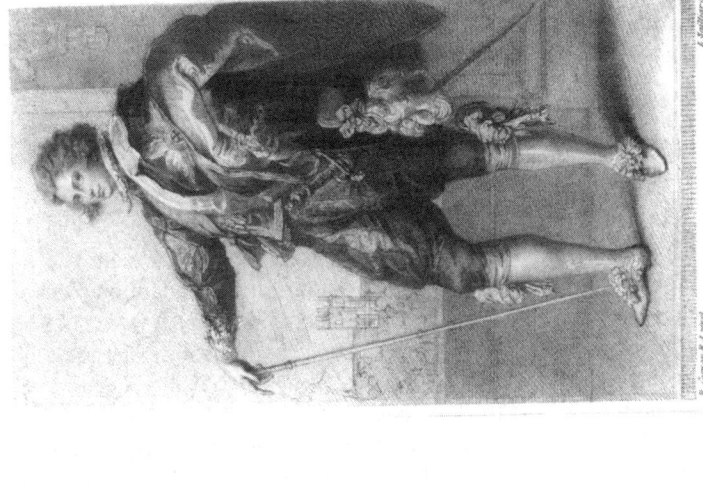

12.2 Maria Anne Fitzherbert by John Condé,
     after Richard Cosway, 1792. National
     Portrait Gallery, London

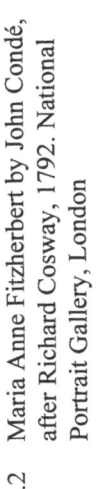

12.3 George IV by Louis or Lewis Saillar (Sailliar),
     after Richard Cosway, 1787. National Portrait Gallery,
     London

In the story of Banastre Tarleton and Mary Robinson, Sylvia finds the clearest depiction of her own alternative fate. If Tarleton had not turned to Mary, Sylvia believes, she might have become the unhappy wife of a scornful man.[10] In Sylvia's telling of the tale, Mary Robinson, otherwise known as "Perdita," a sobriquet which resulted from playing Perdita in *Florizel and Perdita*, an eighteenth-century revision of Shakespeare's *The Winter's Tale*, and from playing Perdita in real life to the Prince's Florizel, Mary is at first presented as the archetypal fallen women but in the end redeemed as a sentimental tragic heroine.

Returned from the war in North America, Tarleton at first directs his addresses to Sylvia. At least I assume that he is the "T—" referred to in her second letter (#14, written in late 1783): "The first Report I heard from M^{rs} W upon My arrival was that T— was going to be married—This must be false—Never did I see him so much a Lover."[11] Then, in Letter #16, he turns his attentions to Mary: "Tarleton is forgotten, he lays his Laurels at Perdita's feet." When Tarleton shifts his attention from Sylvia to Mary, Sylvia at first takes out her disappointment on the new woman in his life rather than on the inconstant soldier/ lover and angrily accuses the actress of greed: "she had rather have gold than glory." It is not clear what Sylvia means when she accuses Mary of preferring gold to glory, but she might be referring to Mary's desire to claim the bond the Prince promised her when they were lovers. Sylvia might have seen Mary as spurning Tarleton (and the "glory" of *her* poor soldier) for a financially rewarding reunion with the Prince. In a letter written in 1787, Sylvia gives us the conclusion of Tarleton and Robinson's affair: "Col T— I have seen—still He loves—His Wife is at the point of death. She dies of a broken heart. Poor Maria—thy wrongs are mine—May He love on—and may it be mine to Revenge your death. He has treated Her with cruelty and Contempt—they say He is Mad—He talks reasonable and well. How I pity Her—I view Her as one who has drunk of the Poison that was mixed   for   Me—every   angry   thought   is   dead—God   forgive   the Husband and receive the Wife. I could nurse her—I could weep over Her—it seems My Name has tipped the dart of Many an Arrow that has stung this Sufferer's heart. But No More of this." It is now several years later. The bold young cavalier and the

---

[10] It is uncanny how much Sylvia's story resembles Mary's. Both entertained at different times and in different sequences the attentions of the Prince, Charles James Fox (if he is the "Volpone" mentioned in two of Sylvia's letters), and Tarleton. Both were attracted to "the prince, the politician, the action hero," as Paula Byrne identifies the triad in *Perdita: The Literary, Theatrical, Scandalous Life of Mary Robinson* (New York, 2004) xvi.

[11] According to Paula Byrne's thorough biography of Mary Robinson, she and Tarleton were lovers as early as Spring 1782 (179). Obviously Sylvia did not know this. Perhaps her grandmother did. Byrne also places Tarleton in France from September 1783 to March 1784. Sylvia's letter suggests Tarleton returned to England in late 1783. My surmise is that Tarleton acted the lover with Sylvia in order to fool his mother, who disapproved of his relationship with Mary and threatened to cut off all financial support if he did not leave her.

12.5   Sir Banastre Tarleton by Samuel William Reynolds, after Sir Joshua Reynolds, 1782. National Portrait Gallery, London

12.4   Mary Robinson by John Keyse Sherwin, 1781. National Portrait Gallery, London

avaricious actress have changed places in Sylvia's heart. Her sympathies are no longer with the man, who still loves her, but with the woman. Disgusted by his indifference to his "wife's" suffering, Sylvia finds Tarleton's love for her appalling rather than gratifying. If she could, Sylvia would use his tenderness for her against him in retaliation for his scornful treatment of Perdita/ Mary.

As she tried to make sense of Mary and Banastre's story, Sylvia might have lacked important information. For example, it seems that she did not know that Mary was born Darby and secretly married to Thomas Robinson on 12 April 1774. Given the notoriety of Mary's life, such ignorance would seem unimaginable, but when Sylvia prays, "God forgive the Husband and receive the Wife," it appears as if she did not know of the earlier marriage, or, if she did, she believed it was dissolved and that Mary and Banastre were wed. Or, perhaps, she was just being polite, or politic. Whatever Sylvia knew about Mary, in the end she saw Mary as the victim she might have been. Portraying the older woman as the suffering sentimental heroine of a tragic romance enabled Sylvia to present her own story otherwise. Her story was not tragic. She was a victor, not a victim.

Sylvia's Novels

Sylvia, it cannot be repeated often enough, was at risk. She was sexual prey. To avoid betrayal, she needed to rely on all available discourses. Not only did she draw on the stories of the real women around her, but she also drew on the lives of women in the novels she read. While some of her contemporaries might condemn novels as corrupting time-wasters, she knew they were a vitally important resource. They helped her name and negotiate the sexual (and psychological) dangers she faced.

While all of Lydia Clerke's women friends were well-read, it is Sylvia's reading that we come to know most intimately (perhaps for as serendipitous a reason as the sheer abundance of her letters). In one letter, she quotes from Frances Greville's "A Prayer for Indifference," a poem which, according to Roger Lonsdale, was "the most celebrated poem by a woman in the period" and frequently published from the 1760s onwards.[12] (Did Sylvia know that the author of the poem was Harry Greville's mother? Given how much she knew about the literature of her day, she probably did.) Elsewhere, Sylvia presents a delightful account of the engendered contemporary reader-response to *Vathek*. While the men find it "foolish," the women find it "a pretty story but very Improbable" but still they want to know more about Nouronihar. To express the power of the imagination Sylvia draws on Shakespeare: "Imagination in her many coloured Robe shall sit between us raising with her wand a thousand fairy Visions, such as Shakespear saw." Despite the fact that reading Rousseau was linked,

---

[12]   Roger Lonsdale, ed., *Eighteenth-Century Women Poets* (Oxford, 1989) 190.

in many eighteenth-century minds, with seduction and illicit sex,[13] Sylvia freely used him to support her dislike of the fashionable world. Like him, she wants to live in a natural world, where rank and inherited distinctions no longer matter. The only qualification in her esteem of him comes when she compares his contributions to Lydia's and decides that daughterly dutifulness outweighs metaphysics: "and tho Rousseau's works may have little power when offered at the Throne of Grace, great shall be the hopes of that Being whom an Aged Parent shall present loaded with blessings."

As Sylvia penned her many letters to Lydia, did she ever see herself as writing the novel of her life, or, at least, of her amorous life? Perhaps so. Certainly as she composed her narratives, she drew on novels as models. If her retelling of Mary Robinson's story draws on sentimental romance in general, her Royal Party letter draws on Frances Burney in particular. Real-life events become fictional situations as Sylvia shapes and comes to understand her own story. Two novels in particular—*Victim of Fancy* by Elizabeth Sophia Tomlins and *Caroline of Lichtfield* by Élisabeth de Montolieu—helped Sylvia name the real from her perspective. Mentioned in the same 1787 letter in which she first identifies her future husband —Charles Parkhurst—by name, both novels center on heroines who are great readers and who reflect often on their favorite pastime, sometimes defending it, sometimes blaming it for their confusion and pain.

In *Victim of Fancy* the heroine Theresa Morven has found the *ignis fatuus* of the perfect lover in the author of *Sorrows of Werter* and, believing such a perfect novel could not have been written by "a dull German" but must be the product of a "son of Britain," she sets out on a journey to find him in Bath. In the course of events, a friend of her brother's falls in love with her and decides to engage someone (his brother) to impersonate Goethe so that she might be cured of her fancy. Eventually Theresa learns of the deception. Angry at first, she later realizes "all the force of my capricious preference, and all its ingratitude" (Letter XXXVII). Caught between two deserving brothers (both brothers are now hopelessly in love with her), her health suffers and, in the end, she dies. Obviously this novel alerted Sylvia to the dangers of dangling different lovers and taking too long to decide whom to marry.[14]

Did reading this novel help Sylvia make up her mind to marry Parkhurst? Perhaps. In Letter XIV, Theresa's aunt gives her niece (and by extension the reader of the novel) important advice: "A little less ardor and more moderation in your expectations had secured you from this." Did Sylvia take this lesson to heart? The novel was

---

[13] Jacqueline Pearson, *Women's Reading in Britain 1750–1815: A Dangerous Recreation* (Cambridge, 1999) 74, 79.

[14] The full text of this novel can be found online, at the Chawton House Library and Study Centre website. I use Roman numerals to identify letters from this novel, in order to distinguish them from Sylvia's.

published in 1787. Sylvia married Parkhurst on 25 April 1789. And, as already noted, in the same letter in which she alludes to the novel she first identifies Parkhurst by name: "Parkhurst alone can stand a chance—He has a heart—He is gone to Lyons—and has more of my good wishes than any here who like me—But I shall love No More I fear." It is conceivable that Tomlins's book helped Sylvia reduce her expectations and find satisfaction, despite lingering regrets, in a man who loved her even if she did not love him in return.

When Theresa ponders the dilemma of Ruth, a young woman who declares her love to the man who pursues her only to find herself subsequently deserted, the fictional heroine gives Sylvia another important lesson:

> How often are women branded with affectation and insincerity for rejecting the affection to which their hearts are sensible, and assuming coolness when they scorn to feel it; yet, when they give way to their native candour, it is thus [to be deserted] they must expect to be rewarded. (Letter XXXVII)

Tomlins may not use the term "double bind," but she describes the concept. Sometimes when confronted with two alternatives, a woman is caught in a bind; whichever option she chooses, she loses. As Ruth's fate warns Sylvia, a woman will be accused of flirting if she denies her love; but, if she declares her love, she risks desertion. By declaring her love, a woman loses power; she is too easily won. Sylvia suspected this when (as early as 1784) she wrote, "I like Him and therefore must be a little strict." Better to flirt and cool a lover's ardor, even at the risk of being accused of insincerity, than express it and lose him.

If Tomlins's book helped Sylvia reach a decision about whom to marry and confirmed her belief that women sometimes needed to act like coquettes, then Montolieu's book helped her understand the extent of her danger in aristocratic society and the necessity of marriage as a safe asylum.

Montolieu's novel tells a beauty-and-the-beast fable of a young woman named Caroline who marries, against her own wishes and in deference to the wishes of others, a disfigured young man—Count Walstein—whose inner beauties she learns to love. This story would not seem to have affected Sylvia although she does note its effect on one of her lovers who has "the heart and Person of a Walstein [and] hopes in vain to find a Caroline." Affirming that though this lover is noble like Walstein, he will never find the woman he wants and deserves, she thus notes her own inability to love a man who is worthy but unattractive. While this situation does not seem to perturb her, another tale, marginal to the novel, might have deeply distressed her.

The story comes toward the end of the first volume. It is told to Caroline by Baron Lindorf, a man with whom she has fallen in love subsequent to her marriage to the Count, and thus a potential seducer. The Baron initially hesitates to tell her the story; he knows it will condemn him; finally, however, he does, for it will help her understand her good fortune in being the wife of the Count. The story focuses on a young woman named Louise and her brother Fritz, who serves as a companion/ valet to the Baron. Hoping to gain advantage with his master, Fritz urges a liaison between his sister and the Baron. When the Baron hesitates, Fritz tells him that he would rather his sister became the mistress of a great man like the Baron than the wife of a rustic who would not appreciate her. Conflicted about seducing the young girl, the Baron reveals his heart to his friend Walstein. The Count entreats him to flee temptation. It would be wrong to seduce a lovely young girl. Besides, Walstein tells Lindorf, Louise loves a villager named Justin. Ever the plotter, Fritz convinces Lindorf that the Count lied about Justin because he too loves Louise. When Lindorf next sees Louise and the Count, he challenges the Count to a duel. The Count shoots in the air, but Lindorf wounds the Count, disfiguring him for life.

It should be clear why such a story might impress a young woman like Sylvia whose brother served in the household of the Duke of Cumberland. Even in her letter about the Royal Party, written four years before the novel, Sylvia notes her brother's frown when she refuses to drink champagne with the Prince. What did she make of his frown? Why did she note it? Did she ever wonder if he was concerned that her refusal to drink champagne might hurt his career? Did she compare him to the fictional Fritz and suspect him of—to use another modern phrase—trafficking in women in order to gain advantage with his superiors? As Sylvia grew increasingly unhappy with court society, did she ever blame her brother for her inability to escape it? It does not seem so. Most of her references to him are warm and loving. Although she did at one point fear for him—"Often have I sighed that Court had spoiled Him—it did for a time"—in the end she insists that he has escaped contamination: "but Nature breaking through—He is once again all that a Young Man should be." He is her protector: "And I look around, if my Brother quits the room for a moment, with distress, like a Creature left alone among its Enemies." Growing more and more disenchanted with aristocrats and their ways, Sylvia depended on both her brother and her novels to help her evade her enemies and know who were her friends.

Sylvia's Mothers

Sylvia's ability to avoid the many snares that beset her probably also owed much to her unusual situation of being well mothered. Many feminist literary theorists have written about the lack of mothers in fiction and the positive consequences of such a situation for the typical heroine. She is freed from many of the restrictions that beset the typically mothered young woman. Sylvia's story suggests that while it may be advantageous to be motherless, it is not always so. Sometimes young women need to be protected. And if a woman lacks a biological mother, it behooves her to find substitutes.

Three mother substitutes guided Sylvia from girlhood to womanhood. Lydia Clerke was the loving mother in whom she could place her complete trust. Her aunt Sylvia Thornton was the caretaking mother whom she strove to please. And her grandmother Sylvia Winstanley was the unbending matriarch who never forgot a wrong done her.

Although we do not have Lady Clerke's letters to Sylvia, we can imagine that they were full of advice to the younger woman. Lydia served Sylvia not only as surrogate mother but also as mentor. Sylvia could tell her "everything without reserve." Lydia is the older but wiser woman and very likely cautioned Sylvia to be prudent as she dealt with her various admirers: "I will remember all you have said—or rather taught me," she assures Lydia. And sometimes Lydia praised her when she emerged unscathed from dangerous situations. Sylvia received such praise in a delightfully self-deprecating way: "How you praise Me and all for what. I have obeyed the dictates of my heart—Not fallen the victim of a Temptation that did not charm Me— I have not been false to My own hopes and attachments—I have been true when I had not power to be false." Lydia encouraged Sylvia in her adventures, for they afforded much amusement and were the sign of Sylvia's independent spirit. The younger woman must have reminded her of herself when she was young and with the world before her. The two women nurtured one another: while Lady Clerke comforted Sylvia as she suffered the attentions and inattentions of her many admirers, Sylvia comforted Lady Clerke when she was ill or distraught about her mother's increasing frailty. And when she tore Sylvia's Letter #17 in order to keep the secret of who possessed Sylvia's heart, Lady Clerke protected her young friend into the unknown future. Just as Lydia would "naturally like to know" whom Sylvia loved, so would we, but now we will never know.

Like Lydia, Mrs. Thornton cared deeply about Sylvia. She too hoped to protect her niece from those who might harm her. Fearful that her niece's reputation might be permanently damaged by the Prince's actions or by those of others, she carefully supervised Sylvia's comings and goings. While Sylvia may have sometimes chafed under her aunt's persistent gaze, she probably also appreciated and depended on her aunt's love and concern.

Her grandmother, Mrs. Winstanley, is harder to read. In Sylvia's letters, she comes across as both autocratic and affectionate. At one point, Sylvia notes her grandmother's love of both Lydia and herself: "I wish I had seen them [Lydia's 'Italian friends'], my Grandmother is always happy to see those who she knows I wish to see—being your friends would have made her receive them with double pleasure." However, more often than not, her grandmother seizes every opportunity to control the situation. When Tarleton returns to London and Sylvia falls under his spell, her grandmother quickly warns her against him, and just as she hoped to keep Sylvia and Tarleton apart, she tried to bring her niece and Casamajor together, going so far as to carry on a clandestine correspondence with him. "She reads with apparent pleasure—but his letters and her answers are profound secrets." Although Sylvia can see that Casamajor's letters please her grandmother, she cannot see his words. Her grandmother chooses to keep his thoughts to herself.

Sylvia resists her grandmother's efforts to control her and marries the man she prefers. In return, her grandmother never forgets this piece of insubordination. In her last will and testament, written in 1791, two years after Sylvia married Parkhurst, Mrs. Winstanley leaves the bulk of her estate to her grandchildren, to be divided among them "share and share alike," with the proviso that "all such of my female grandchildren surviving me and who now are or may hereafter become married are secured and kept entirely free from the Management and controul of their present husbands." Not only does Mrs. Winstanley protect Sylvia's bequest from her husband, but she also leaves Mr. Parkhurst a gift with special metaphoric significance: "[M]y Box with friendship on the Lid I give to Mr. Parkhurst. It broke I believe the very day his friendship ceased to me. I return it with a full forgiveness for all ye affliction he and his Lady have given to me."[15] When she gained a husband, Sylvia lost a grandmother.

Why did Sylvia's mothers, especially her aunt and grandmother, monitor her behavior so strictly? While at first I saw their precautions and distrust as the ordinary concerns of solicitous parents, when I discovered who Sylvia's mother was I knew the source of their anxiety. They were afraid the daughter would take after her mother.

Who Was Sylvia's Mother?

The answer to this question brings the various threads of Sylvia's story together. Her mother is the fallen woman whose fate Sylvia struggled throughout her life to avoid.

Sylvia's mother Elizabeth Browne married her father John Brathwaite on 13 April 1761.[16] Soon after, Mr. Brathwaite joined his regiment at Gibraltar, and Mrs. Brathwaite followed. Four children were born in Gibraltar: Henry-Pulteney and John died as infants; Sylvia and George-Charles lived to adulthood. Elizabeth and John returned to England in 1768. One year later (in August) John sailed to India to assume his post as Major in the East India Company's forces stationed at Bencoolin. This time Elizabeth did not accompany him, perhaps an early sign of marital discord. In July 1775, after they had spent six years apart, John returned home to initiate divorce proceedings. According to testimony at the trial, Elizabeth gave birth to two children,

---

[15] PROB 11/1328, Family Records Centre.

[16] *Journals of the House of Lords* 35: 94. During the divorce trial of Elizabeth Browne and John Brathwaite, Thomas Winstanley testified that he married them at St Margaret's Church, Westminster, on 13 April 1761.

a boy and a girl, while John was in India and could not have fathered them.[17] The identity of the father of the children born illegitimately was never disclosed during the trial, but other documents point toward Major-General William Phillips as the father.[18] Altogether Elizabeth and William produced four children. While we do not know when their love affair began, given that four children resulted, it must have begun very soon after John left for India in 1769 (perhaps even before), since, by September 1777, Phillips was in North America participating in the Battle of Stillwater. While under house arrest near Charlottesville, Virginia, Phillips frequently wrote home asking for help in regaining his freedom. His letters reveal strong feeling for the woman he left behind. Several times he mentions letters to or from "our friend." When he believes he may soon be released in order to succeed General Haldimand, he asks if he can first return home "as I should not incline to take upon me so serious and important a Service without a previous consultation with his Majesty's Ministers."[19] Perhaps Phillips also wanted to marry and bring over Elizabeth Browne and their four children? Or just see her again before his next military engagement? Whatever the subtext of his letter, if there was one at all, he never did return home. He died 13 May 1781, and, one year later, on 20 June 1782, Elizabeth married again. Like her daughter, Elizabeth attracted men. Unlike her daughter, she did not protect her virtue.

Was Sylvia trying to understand her mother as she considered the various temptations and capacities for resistance of the less than virtuous women she knew, both real and imaginary? What, after all, did she know about her mother? When did she learn the truth about her? She was a young girl when her mother left home four times to bear another man's children. Did she notice her mother's absences? During the trial, only two births were presented as evidence of adultery. According to witnesses, both babies were subsequently sequestered in the country. Elizabeth obviously tried to hide the evidence of her adultery both before and during the trial. What, if anything, did she tell her daughter? And what were Sylvia's emotional reactions?

---

[17]   *Journals of the House of Lords* 35:94. Walter Farquhar, surgeon, testified that Mrs. Brathwaite twice applied to him for help in arranging "a private lodging, a nurse, and a midwife." A son was born in 1773, a daughter in 1775. Farquhar claimed he never learned who the father was.

[18]   In his will (PROB 11/1102, Family Records Centre), William Phillips left everything of which he stood possessed to Elizabeth Browne. But addenda to the will note that "Elizabeth Macaulay formerly Browne (Wife of the Reverend Angus Macaulay) the Universal Legatee named in the said Will ... renounced the Letters of Admin with the sd Will annexed ... ." Robert P. Davis, Phillips's biographer, also identifies Elizabeth Browne as the mother of William Phillips's children (34).

[19]   ADD MS 38,215, ff. 155,156, British Library.

12.6 Letter #22 from Sylvia Brathwaite. Detail. Photo: Author's Collection. Reproduced by permission of the Society of Antiquaries of London

12.7 Marylebone Parish Church, London, where Sylvia Brathwaite married Charles Parkhurst and where Elizabeth Browne married Angus Macaulay. Photo: Author's Collection

We do not know how much time Sylvia actually spent with her mother or where Sylvia and her mother lived once John Brathwaite left for India. Did her mother continue to live in her husband's home? While, on the one hand, court records make it clear that Elizabeth acted in secrecy when giving birth to her illegitimate children, which might suggest she was still living in her husband's home, we also learn that during the 1770s John Brathwaite not only purchased a Cornetry in the Dragoons for his son George-Charles, but also educated his daughter "under the Eye of [his] Sister at a very considerable Expence."[20] Such an action would suggest that John already distrusted his wife and sought to protect his daughter from her bad influence. Mother and daughter were most likely separated when Sylvia was very young. Born between 1763 (her brother George-Charles was born 3 December 1762) and 1768 and perhaps placed in her aunt's house before her father's removal to India, Sylvia might have been as young as six years old when she became her aunt's ward.

When her parents were undergoing divorce, Sylvia was near that dangerous age of 13. What was she told? by her mother? her father? her aunt? her grandmother? She never once mentions her mother to Lady Clerke. Was she angry that her mother left her? Did she take her father's part? Did she ever meet her mother again after the divorce? While William Phillips served king and country in North America, Elizabeth Browne waited for him in London, residing not far from her daughter. When she remarried, in 1782, the ceremony took place in St Mary's Marylebone Parish Church, which is where, a mere seven years later, Sylvia married Charles Parkhurst. Surely their paths must have occasionally crossed. Did Sylvia know about her mother's four children by Phillips? Did she ever meet any of them? According to Robert P. Davis, Phillips's four children turned out well. After their father's death, they were befriended by the Cornwallis family and although Elizabeth renounced the Letters of Administration of her lover's will, which left the bulk of his estate to their four "natural" children, they did eventually benefit from their father's inheritance.[21] Did Sylvia resent that while her mother's sons by Phillips went on to pursue successful military careers, her own husband's career floundered? What, in short, did Sylvia know?

---

[20]   HLRO, HL/PO/JO/10/7/520.
[21]   Davis 34.

Chapter 13

Sylvia Thornton

At Margate, aged 42, Mrs. Anne Emelinda Foster. She was grand-daughter to Henry Masterman, esq. of York, and legal heiress to his whole fortune, being his son's only child. Her first husband was Mr. Skinn, an attorney; her second, Nicholas Foster, esq. son of an Irish baronet, and an officer in the army. She was blessed by nature with a beautiful person, and every shining talent, and had every advantage of education. She was the author of "The Old Maid," a novel, and some other works. But such is the instability of all human attainments, that by one false step, before she was sixteen, she so enraged her grandfather, that he disinherited her of 3000£ a year. Her last husband forsook and left her in extreme poverty. She supported herself by her pen and needlework for ten years past, and kept a day-school; but ill health, owing in part to exquisite sensibility and extreme poverty, lately reduced her to the greatest distress.

Gentleman's Magazine (1789)

Born Sylvia Brathwaite during the 1730s in South Carolina, she returned to England in 1740. A young child on the return voyage, she most likely witnessed her father's violent death—shot through the head by a French sailor. Raised by her determined and very strong mother, Sylvia Cole Brathwaite, who married The Reverend Thomas Winstanley in 1747, she grew up to become deeply religious and decidedly pessimistic. In 1764, she married Bonnell Thornton, who died four years later, and, in 1793, she died.

Like Susannah Dobson's letters, the two letters from Sylvia Thornton provide important exposition. While Dobson's letters belong to the domestic novel of manners centered on the lives of Lydia and John Clerke, Sylvia Thornton's reflect on the tragic consequences of Sylvia Brathwaite's sentimental romance. In particular, Thornton's second letter informs us that Sylvia's story has reached a crisis. She and her husband dwell in a "horrid prison."

27
From: Mrs. Thornton
To: Lady Clerke
Date: [1788?]
My dearest friend

I feel, greatly feel for you, alas. What must not a mind like yours suffer to see your Dear and affectionate Mother so changed? But What will not some disorders and accidents effect? Who that reflects how soon the finest faculties are impaired, and that the smallest obstruction in the brain can so impede every faculty, and prevents their exertion, Would be vain and be proud of superiour knowledge.

The great disposer of events, for reasons we cannot fathom, often permits the best and most humble of his creating to suffer calamity that seems only a proper punishment for the proud despisers of their fellow creatures. And was there no state but this we should be all astonishment, but in the land of promise all the evils we have suffered in our state of bondage will be amply repaid. I cannot flatter you or myself with hopes of your dear Mother's amendment, but hope time will enable you, My beloved friend, to bear your load of grief, and heaven grant that your spirits may not sink under your trial. Our blessed saviour was a man of sorrow and was despised, Which is very hard to bear. If the supreme being was in a state of suffering on earth We have reason to hope that it is not from the Anger of our Creator, that we have and do feel pain of body or <u>mind,</u> or both together, but for some wise and good purpose that must remain unknown While we continue in this state of Existence.

All my disorders, My dearest friend, increase daily, and the medicines failing of giving relief that Dr. Smith ordered, I have had the advice of Dr. Rigg, but have been if possible still worse so that he, conscious he cannot be of any service, has left me of himself, Which is a delicate way of informing me that I am too far gone for relief. Should I in any degree recover it will be quite a Miracle, and What I do not expect. Those days I am not confined to My bed, an airing of three or four miles is thought proper for me. When the weather is very fine, Mrs Dobson is here and, by the <u>greatest art</u>, got I may say into the house. Once in two or three days, she came into my room, and every time told me that my life depended upon air and gentle exercise, and·that if I was carried into a Carriage, I ought to make the trial, that hers Was Warm and always at my service. But as soon as the Weather mended, she in order to avoid saying any thing on the subject never comes near me. I have not seen her in my room for More than a Month. Her conduct is such that every body in the house hates her. It would fill a sheet of paper were I to inform you of her dirt, meanness, deceit, and hypocrisy. She courts every person that has a Carriage, and sends to request to accompany them, and I suppose possibly pleads as an excuse, that she has lent hers to her rich friends, for I know it is thought by some persons here, that my sister airs continually and that most likely I accompany if able. Unless she is engaged to a party at cards, she always goes to London, is set down at Hyde Park Corner, and the Coachman at between ten and eleven waits at the corner of some street for her, but never hardly knows where she has been. She comes to him alone, and generally punctual in regard to time. She three or four days in a Week cuts off some of the Meat When she has dined, and carries it into a closet in her room, takes candles in the same way, to hoard up, and all disappears by degrees—She has an old Grizzled Wig Which I suppose cost her two pence, it has been a Man's, Which she Wears of a morning to save a female one the colour of her hair. An Old Handkerchief coloured is tied ... [the rest of this letter is missing].

28
From: Mrs. Thornton
To: Lady Clerke, Hungerford, Berkshire
Date: 7 January 1792
My dearest friend

I am concerned I cannot enjoy the heartfelt satisfaction of seeing you this Christmas and that your more than amiable husband's time was so occupied when in town that I was deprived of the pleasure of his Company at Isleworth. It is a long time to April but the happy prospect will chear the gloom of Winter, and Make it to Me a gladsome spring indeed.

I have been [but] very indifferent, or I woud not have let so much time pass away this season, without wishing yourself, Mr Townsend, and family many, very many happy returns of it. How pleasing must it be recalling to mind the years that are past, in which religious and domestic duties performed have been considered by you as the highest felicity. Often do I regret that the World in general does not reflect that happiness is never so much enjoyed as when they bestow it on others with whom they are nearly connected. What a contrast has your conduct ever been, my beloved friend, for in the most trying situations, you have never deviated from what was highly worthy of praise.

I hear very often from my poor Niece, Who acts I think in such a manner, as to merit in my Idea the highest attention from her family, for few woud I believe like her live entirely in a horrid prison, in a room hardly superiour to one we put our domesticks in, surrounded with persons in the greatest distress, Many of them with large families, Who pass at times for a Whole day without food. My poor Niece and Mr. Parkhurst for two months supp[ed with] a Dutch Merchant, his Wife, and Children, who would have been starved if they had not fed them. Indeed the unfortunate Man acknowledges their kindness in his case, which he sent me at my request. But, great as his distress is, it hardly equals Many Men in the same prison. My unfortunate Sylvia informs me her nerves are so weak from the melancholy scenes she is witness to, and the bad air, that she cannot read a melancholy article in the paper without tears. I have pressed her in consequence to come to me and that possibly breathing a pure air one or two days in a week might brace her nerves, so as to enable her better to bear the having her feelings so wounded. And that I shall receive her with the affection of a fond parent, and that I was certain Mr Parkhurst woud be happy to think she paid some attention to her health. In short, My dear friend, I have neglected no argument to induce her to come to an aunt Who most sincerely loves her, but all is Without effect. I cannot prevail upon her.

I have seen my friend Who got Mr Parkhurst into St Lukes and [have] requested to know of him Whether he was put on the incurable list. He promised me he woud enquire, but that if he was not when he left the house, it woud he feard be out of his power to get it done. I have this day received a letter informing me that Mr Parkhurst's name was not down, but that by using the greatest interest possible he had got his name entered on the day he left it. Therefore he now has a good chance of being admitted for life though the time cannot be ascertained at present.

Robert begs to be most gratefully remembered to you. He has received a very polite letter from Lord Howe but does not give us as much hope as we coud wish as he assures my Son that he has for sometime past been soliciting the removal of a person to a 3^d [suit] in commission and has yet not been able to succeed. We still hope that in time We may receive more pleasing intelligence from his Lordship. My son Robert has got a very bad Cold and is with me till better. He joins in affectionate respects to Mr Townsend and family. Whaley is come to England Was to pay Me a Visit. Yesterday he received a hurt in his side by being overturned and is attended by Mr Keats, but looks very well as does my Sister. They both enquired how you did and M^r T, Miss Forbes and M^r and M^{rs} O'Flanagan send their best respects to you, my beloved friend, with every wish possible for your health and happiness.

> your ever affectionate S Thornton

Trials and Tribulations

In two cantankerous and compassionate letters, Sylvia Thornton presents herself as upright, religious, sentimental, satiric. According to her own letters and to references about her in others' letters, she was often unwell. Several times her niece describes her as in poor, or "indifferent," health. Although she had a sense of humor and of the ridiculous, she rarely used it on herself or on those dear to her. When writing about herself, Lydia, or her niece and Mr. Parkhurst, she is invariably solemn and contemplative. And, like the *Gentleman's Magazine* writer above, she can only see tragedy when a young woman disobeys her family.

Although Mrs. Thornton's first letter is not dated, I have placed it after Sylvia Brathwaite's 31 March 1788 letter, since, like her niece, she dwells on Mrs. Hammond's deterioration. Reading these two letters successively presents an intriguing contrast in tone. While the niece's letter blends sympathy with cheerfulness, the aunt's is irredeemably gloomy. Nonetheless, the letters are surprisingly similar in content. Both women sincerely commiserate with Lydia, and both soon bring the topic of discussion back to themselves. While Sylvia narrates an unpleasant incident during which she is rescued by the Prince, Mrs. Thornton speculates about the purpose of suffering in the world and turns to her own complaints. Like Mrs. Hammond, she is on her death bed. The effusiveness of Mrs. Thornton's sympathy for Mrs. Hammond seems at least partly a result of her own need for consolation.

In her meditation on the causes and consequences of suffering, Mrs. Thornton gravely and eloquently declares her faith in a "great disposer of events," who mysteriously causes the humblest of his creation to suffer calamities in this world, but who rights injustice in the next: "in the land of promise all the evils we have suffered in our state of bondage will be amply repaid." She offers Lydia (and herself) the virtues of thoughtful stoicism. There is an unknown purpose behind the accidents and misfortunes of life in this world, which will hopefully be revealed to us in the next. Mrs. Thornton insists that our pain and suffering are not meaningless. While there is much injustice in the world, and the good too often suffer, there is, ultimately, redemption. Also, there are reasons for our misery that we cannot fathom. Even the savior was "despised" and "in a state of suffering on earth." How can we expect to avoid sorrow?

Mrs. Thornton's philosophical discourse about a world beyond this one dissolves abruptly into a humorous and abbreviated diatribe against that perpetual target—Susannah Dobson. Although Mrs. Thornton is ill, she cannot resist detailing the foibles of Susannah. Speaking with increasingly energetic and comic relish, she accuses the bluestocking of hypocritically pretending to care about her only in order to get as much from her as possible. When Mrs. Thornton was too ill to take advantage of the offer, the learned lady freely offered her carriage, but as soon as she and the weather mended, Susannah and her carriage were nowhere to be seen. In fact, Mrs. Dobson was busy ensnaring the carriages of others under false pretenses. It would seem that Dobson used the false excuse that having loaned her carriage to her rich friends (presumably Mrs. Thornton and her sister Caroline) she must now ask others for the loan of theirs.

It is hard to ascertain from where Mrs. Thornton's first letter was sent. It might have been sent from Isleworth, Mrs. Thornton's home near London. When she describes Susannah's mysterious comings and goings it would seem that she and Susannah are not far from the city: "Unless she is engaged to a party at cards, she always goes to London, is set down at Hyde Park Corner, and the Coachman at between ten and eleven waits at the corner of some street for her, but never hardly knows where she has been. She comes to him alone, and generally punctual in regard to time." As usual, whatever Susannah does, it is suspect. She travels alone at night, does not tell anyone where she is going, and makes efforts to be sure no one (not even the coachman) knows where she has been. Mrs. Thornton's censoriousness comes through clearly. If my dating of the letter (1788) is correct, then Susannah's unseemly behavior is even more dubious. Her husband Matthew has been dead for four years. A widow, she ought to act with more decorum. Looking at Susannah's behavior from the distance of more than 200 years and through the lens of queer theory, we might speculate, that, now alone, Dobson goes on clandestine excursions to find women who will consort with her in sexual relationships or romantic friendships. Then again, she might be meeting with family members or acquaintances considered disreputable by her genteel friends. Of course, it is impossible to know for sure where she is going and why.

In addition to lying and sneaking around, Susannah steals. She takes meat and candles away from the table to hoard them in her room "and all disappears by degrees." Clearly this is inappropriate behavior on the part of a guest. But, as I earlier suggested in the chapter on Dobson, Susannah may impose upon Mrs. Thornton because she thinks of her as a patron. Like other eccentric intellectuals of her day, she may have believed that the wealthy had a duty to support the work of scholars. If only Mrs. Thornton would accept graciously the role Susannah extends—of generous patron—then her thefts and boorish presumption would be seen as the amusing but harmless antics of an absent-minded scholar. While sometimes the rich may have resisted the role, there were times when they were quite willing to patronize eccentric writers and scholars. Perhaps the problem is not so much that Susannah's expectations are ill-founded as that Mrs. Thornton does not respect her, her learning, or her eccentricities. She can only treat Susannah as an object of contempt and ridicule.

Stubbornly refusing to accept Susannah's version of herself, Mrs. Thornton nonetheless insists that others see her as she sees herself. She is ill and suffers endlessly; she is, in fact, dying. But perhaps there is more than one way to estimate her situation. Consider once again her view of her traffic in doctors: "All my disorders, My dearest friend, increase daily, and the medicines failing of giving relief that Dr. Smith ordered, I have had the advice of Dr. Rigg, but have been if possible still worse so that he, conscious he cannot be of any service, has left me of himself, Which is a delicate way of informing me that I am too far gone for relief. Should I in any degree recover it will be quite a Miracle." Mrs. Thornton believes that Dr. Rigg refuses to continue caring for her because her case is hopeless. However, this interpretation may not have been the good doctor's, who might have felt that, in good conscience, he could no longer accept money for treating a hypochondriac. Considering how often she is described as unwell or indisposed in Sylvia's letters and how much she relishes anticipating her own death (almost as much as she relishes mocking Susannah), there is the possibility that Mrs. Thornton was a woman who indulged herself in illness. Perhaps Smith did not give up on her as quickly or as completely as Rigg because he was not as scrupulous as his colleague. I wonder if Lydia smiled as she read this narrative of doctors and medicines coming and going. Did she agree with Mrs. Thornton that the situation was desperate or did she doubt that her friend's death was imminent?

If Mrs. Thornton's first letter mixes high tragedy with low comedy, her second is more homogeneous in form and content. Pervasively gloomy, it presents a world of trouble. Beginning with an expression of concern that she will not see Lady Clerke this winter, she notes that her own health is "very indifferent." Since this letter is dated 7 January 1792, only one year before her death, she may indeed have been seriously ill by this time. Poignantly she considers the purpose and value of our earthly lives. She praises Lydia for her constancy in fulfilling her "religious and domestic duties" and for never deviating from correct conduct and vehemently disapproves of the selfishness of "the World." Oddly, praising Lydia's selflessness and invariable steadfastness reminds Mrs. Thornton of her niece. Her niece, unlike Lydia, has not always acted properly. Sylvia did not always think of others before herself and now suffers the consequences of her disobedience. She lives in poverty and obscurity. Nonetheless she deserves attention for she has learned to behave better.

Seeking to help her niece and her husband, Mrs. Thornton has urged Sylvia to come visit; When, a little over one year later, in March 1793, she writes her will, she leaves her niece £20 and various articles of clothing and unmade-up fabric. While this may not seem much, it is the largest bequest in her will. Moreover, she gives the money to her niece before she dies as if to be sure the legacy reaches her.[1] Even after Sylvia married a man of whom the family disapproved, her aunt remembered and succored her.

In so doing, Mrs. Thornton resists the censoriousness of the *Gentleman's Magazine* article that serves as epigraph to this chapter. But, nonetheless, her reading of her niece is very like the anonymous writer's view of Anne Emelinda Foster. Disobedience inevitably leads to disaster. She tried to protect Sylvia from making mistakes, but she failed. Her niece ran off with a man of whom her father and grandmother disapproved and she subsequently lost their favor. Like the young woman in the *Gentleman's Magazine* article, she must now reap the consequences of her indiscretion. If Mrs. Thornton is correct, and her niece's only hope is that her husband will be "entered" as an incurable at St Luke's, a hospital opened in 1751 to treat the insane,[2] then Sylvia is indeed in dire straits.

Mrs. Thornton reads her niece's story as a gloomy morality tale. Despite the fact that her niece took over six years to decide whom to marry, she still made the wrong choice. Defying her family and their desire that she marry a man able to provide for and protect her, she cast her lot with a poor soldier and now must live "in a room hardly superiour to one we put our domesticks in." Overlooking what Mrs. Thornton's choice of words says about the way servants were treated in the eighteenth century, we can hear her concern for her niece. She exerts herself to help Sylvia, but her efforts are unavailing. Sylvia will not listen to her. One senses the older woman's frustration. Her niece, and the world, are in very bad shape indeed. As she brings her letter to a close, she leaves us (and Lydia) with a series of small calamities: Lord Howe has not been able to help her son Robert; Robert has a very bad cold; her

---

[1]   PROB 11/1234, Family Records Centre.
[2]   Information about St Luke's Hospital for Lunatics can be found at the "Mental Health History Timeline" website.

nephew Whaley, who visited her while in England, received a hurt in his side. In such a world, we must indeed fortify ourselves with stoic resignation and a belief in a world beyond this fallen one.

In reading these two letters from Mrs. Thornton, we can see just how much Lady Clerke was the supportive and playful mother to Sylvia, while Mrs. Thornton was the sober and anxious one who could only see tragedy when a young girl married against the advice of her elders. We can begin to understand why Sylvia might have hesitated to visit her solicitous and censorious aunt. As we shall see, Sylvia Parkhurst did not see herself as her aunt did, and she may not have wanted to listen to her aunt's gloomy estimation of her situation.

Wife and Mother

Probably one of the most surprising revelations about Mrs. Thornton is the identity of her husband—Bonnell Thornton. Two people could hardly be more unalike. She is religious, grave, sometimes fearful; he witty, warm, sometimes irresponsible. The only thing they seem to share is a penchant for satire. But while Mrs. Thornton's picture of Susannah waxes mean-spirited, commentators agree that Thornton's wit was warm and kind-hearted.

Sylvia and Bonnell first met soon after the marriage of her mother (Sylvia Brathwaite the first) to Thomas Winstanley, which took place on 29 October 1747. In 1748, the Winstanleys moved to Orchard Street, next door to John Thornton, Bonnell's father.[3] Bonnell Thornton and Sylvia Brathwaite the second married on 3 February 1764. He was several years older than she. While we do not have Sylvia Thornton's exact birth date, we do know that she was born after 1730 (when her parents married) and before 1738 (for her brother was born in 1739 and her father died in 1740), and that Bonnell was born in 1724, so there may have been as many as 14 years difference between them (or as few as six). Interestingly, despite all the mourning rings and pictures of the dear departed circulating in Sylvia Thornton's will, there is not one mention of a mourning ring or picture in remembrance of her husband. However, this may not be significant, for there is a memorial tablet in Westminster Abbey, which notes that "very properly, amidst the great grief of herself and her family, [his wife] bore the cost of this marble."[4] While it might seem that such a monument underscores her grief at the loss of her husband, the words "very properly" suggest something else. Perhaps propriety rather than sadness motivated her to install a plaque in her husband's memory.

---

3   Betty Rizzo, email to the author, 16 February 2001.
4   *Westminster Abbey Registers* 523.

If we turn to *The Public Advertiser*, a paper in which Thornton's work frequently appeared, we find a surprising representation of Sylvia and Bonnell's courtship. Several occasional pieces, written during the year preceding his marriage to Sylvia, suggest a very different Sylvia than the one we see in her letters to Lydia.

On 1 February 1763, a poem praising Sylvia's pins appeared:

> Others may to the Milliner repair,
> But Sylvia deigns not to be furnish'd there:
> Cupid himself supplies her magazines,
> And works his pointed Arrows into Pins:
> No wonder every Look should confound a Heart
> Each Corkin that adorns her is a Dart.[5]

Unambiguously delightful, this poem must have pleased Sylvia. And we might wonder what characteristics in her elicited such a playful piece.

On Monday, 11 April 1763, a much longer "ODE" appeared and ended with the following lines:

> Tho' half mankind with toil pursue,
> With more than stoic ease I view
>   Such glitt'ring toys as these:—
> But when the maid I love appears,
> A thousand hopes, a thousand fears,
>   Distract my soul, and please.[6]

Signed "H.P." the poem nevertheless seems linked to Thornton and Sylvia for all of the italicized words in it (Delia, Arabia, Sicilia, Britannia, India) end with "ia." Did Thornton write this and other anonymous pieces in *The Public Advertiser* in order to win Sylvia? Did she welcome or shun his advances? Did his sallies please or annoy her?

On 20 May, a long letter "To Sall Scribbler," which verges on the pornographic, appeared. Its author, identified as "A Whisperer," writes of his upcoming marriage to Sylvia. If it does not take place, he envisions drowning himself in Rosamond's Park and being found with "a Love-Letter in his Pocket, directed to SYLVIA"; or he might be found hanging on a tree in the Willow Walk with nothing in his pockets. Whisperer tells Sall that there are many obstacles on his road to matrimonial happiness. The most persistent obstacle is Sall herself, who "has all the Accomplishments that Miss X..... X......... has, except one; which one is, and the only one, that she makes me love her better, though I cannot tell—WHY?" Other obstacles

---

[5]   *The Public Advertiser*, 1 February 1763: 2.
[6]   *The Public Advertiser*, 11 April 1763: 2.

take the shape of comical rivals: a lap dog, a cat, and a canary bird. Whisperer tries to get the better of these competitors to Sylvia's affection: *"Poodle* I am not at all jealous or afraid of. She stroaks her,—so do I. I stroak her, because *It* is in HER Lap, and *It* gives me an Opportunity of touching HER Paw." How did Sylvia take these sly insinuations? Did she enjoy being mocked, however gently, however salaciously, in the public press? As Whisperer brings his tale of frustrated intentions to an end, he seems to prefer Sall to Sylvia: "I have something MY DEAR SALL, to say,—but that shall be in your Own Ear Only." Although he pleads that Miss X X (whose name contains the same number of letters as Sylvia's) is his love, he prefers whispering sweet nothings into Sall Scribbler's ear.[7]

Three days later Sall replied to Whisperer, mocking in turn:

> Sall Scribbler presents her Compliments to Sylvia's Monkey, Whisperer, and would advise him, by all Means, to be content in sharing his dearest Mistress's Favour with her other Animals, and not endeavour to monopolize that Fondness which seems now to be parcell'd out with the utmost Justice ... Sall declares she envies Miss X......X.....'s Conquest no more than she desires to be possessed of her Dog or Cat—If either Dog, Cat, or Monkey were to molest her, she would administer Materials for hanging with the greatest pleasure or conduct them to Rosamond's Pond, for she has an utter Aversion to all Animals void of sense.[8]

Who was Sall? Did Thornton take both sides of the dialogue? Or did Sylvia adopt a pseudonym and write back? Or did another journalist take the opportunity to display her (or his) wit? And, most important, who was this Sylvia who would marry a man with such lustful leanings?

While Whisperer looks forward to marrying in October 1763, Sylvia and Bonnell did not marry until February 1764. Was the marriage delayed because she (or he) had misgivings? Or were their reasons for delaying just such ordinary ones as illness or accident? As confusing, ironic, and coded as Thornton's journalistic epistles to Sylvia are, they are all we have to go on if we seek to understand their lives together, both before and after marriage. That, and Lance Bertelson's terse commentary: "For the next three years, Thornton lived in a state of domestic tranquility."[9] Was their domesticity tranquil or were there difficulties? Three children were born in almost as many years, and one died soon after birth. Thornton himself died young, at 43 years of age in 1768. Did Sylvia blame her husband for not taking better care of himself and his family and for dying young? Sylvia never married again. This could be a sign of

---

[7]   *The Public Advertiser*, 20 May 1763: 1.

[8]   *The Public Advertiser*, 23 May 1763: 2.

[9]   Lance Bertelson, *The Nonsense Club* (Oxford, 1986) 117. The most thorough biography to date of Bonnell Thornton appears in Bertelson's study. Information about him can also be found in *Alumni Oxiensis* 1414; *The Record of Old Westminsters* 2: 917; and *DNB*.

her abiding respect for and love of her husband. It could also, of course, be a sign of how little she cared for the conjugal state. Nonetheless, the droll yet equivocal poems and letters that passed between Sylvia and Bonnell during their courtship suggest that at least for a brief period there was much humor and good cheer circulating around them.

Sylvia and Bonnell's three children did not fare well. Their oldest son, Bonnell George Thornton, born in 1765, married Catherine Anne Bannerman at St Mary's Marylebone Parish Church in 1787. Three years later, at 25 years of age, he was dead. As they did for his father Bonnell and his cousin Thomas Ralph, his family placed a memorial tablet in the cloister of Westminster Abbey to commemorate his untimely death. Unfortunately, unlike the other two tablets which can still be seen, Bonnell George's decayed and was removed in 1950.[10] His obituary in the *Gentleman's Magazine* tells us that he died at Bristol of consumption, having spent his last months studying the scriptures.[11] While his cousin Sylvia castigated him for wasting his life ("Poor Bonnell goes on sadly I mean in <u>Nothingness</u>—if the Emperor Titus wept a lost day what torrents should He shed for a lost Life"), his mother obviously felt differently about this son who died young. His piety must have pleased her. He seems to have been her favorite child. In her will Sylvia bequeaths a picture of "my beloved Bonnell" to her nephew George Brathwaite. She also sends a copy of this picture to Lady Clerke. When a person dies young, he can never grow up to disappoint friends and family; parents cannot help but remember the absent child as the more perfect one. In her will, Sylvia Thornton also gives "Mrs. Dorway late Mrs. Ann Thornton five pounds of the money due to me from Samson and my Grey Silk Gown and Dimity long Gown likewise two Guineas." Is this a sign that Sylvia did not like her son's widow? Although Catherine Anne's legacy is small, the amount is in keeping with other bequests; only Sylvia Parkhurst receives anywhere near a larger amount (twenty pounds) and that, as already noted, even before her aunt's death. But if Mrs. Thornton did dislike Ann, perhaps the source of her dislike might be found in her wording: "Mrs. Dorway late Mrs. Ann Thornton." Did the doting mother resent the fact that her daughter-in-law remarried? Sylvia Thornton never did, and perhaps considered a lonely widowhood a sign of devotion to a dead husband. Given her penchant for pious interpretations, she probably preferred to think of herself as not remarrying out of a sense of duty and thus might have disapproved vehemently of her daughter-in-law's decision to do otherwise.

Sylvia and Bonnell's second son, Robert John, was born two years after his brother, in 1767. At 16 he entered Trinity College, Cambridge, being intended for the church. However, fascinated with botany, he decided to pursue a medical career. As part of a long and full life, he acted as physician to the Marylebone dispensary. He

---

[10]   *Westminster Abbey Registers* 523.
[11]   *Gentleman's Magazine*, April 1790: 378.

also lectured on medical botany at the united hospitals of Guy and St Thomas. He is perhaps most famous for his lavishly published *New Illustration of the Sexual System of Linnaeus*. When he died on 21 January 1837, he left his family very poor. His son, christened Bonnell Thornton on 16 October 1794, went on to lecture in astronomy and geography. He also had a daughter whose name we do not know.[12]

As we read the different documents about Robert John Thornton it is hard to determine what sort of man he was. In the biographical sketch published in the 1802/03 edition of *Public Characters*, he is described in glowing terms. Altogether the sketch presents a picture of a successful Renaissance man:

> His "Medical Extracts" contain a variety of information respecting the new discoveries in chemistry and medicine; and the perfections of each writer being selected with care and judgment, he has thus formed a most complete body of medical facts and rational reasoning.
>
> His "Politician's Creed," in two volumes, is equally the result of much reading and a retentive memory; and by interweaving his own remarks, and often drawing his own conclusions, he has given to both publications an air of originality. The first of these, which is to be found in the library of every man of taste and knowledge, has already gone through three editions and a fourth is preparing for the press.[13]

Likewise, his mother is treated with great respect. She is set forth as "the fondest of parents" and credited with providing her son with the education he needed to become the promising writer and physician he was.

While the *Public Characters* sketch is uniformly laudatory and presents the picture of a man to be envied and admired, his *Dictionary of National Biography* entry emphasizes his recklessness, misfortune, and final penury. Typical of its pique is the following assertion: "Almost at the outset of his career Thornton ruined himself by the lavish scale on which he published his 'New Illustration of the Sexual System of Linnæus.'" These two very different stories of Robert John's career suggest how carefully we must weigh the judgments of the past. While the exuberant eighteenth century praised Robert for his exuberance, the more restrained Victorian age condemned him for his excess.

The story of Sylvia and Bonnell Thornton's daughter is a sad one. According to the Parish Register of St James Piccadilly, their daughter Sylvia was born and baptized on 13 July 1766. Ordinarily Church of England babies might wait months or even years to be baptized. When a child was born and baptized on the same day, this was a sign that the child was sickly and not likely to live long. It is likely that Mrs. Thornton's daughter died in infancy. When, in 1769, John Brathwaite departed

---

[12]   *Gentleman's Magazine*, January 1837: 93; and *DNB*.
[13]   *Public Characters of 1802–1803* (London, 1803) 222.

for India and left his daughter Sylvia with his sister, Sylvia Thornton might have seen the young child as replacing the daughter she had lost.

Who Was Sylvia?

Sylvia Thornton is not an easy woman to know. Perhaps the best we can do, in summing her up, is return to her will for some final insights.

She is a good friend. In her will, she remembers not only Lydia Clerke but also Charlotte Lennox. By 1793, most of the world had forgotten the impecunious author, but not Sylvia. She leaves Mrs. Lennox "my grey Cabinet, my Black Cloak not trimmed, my White Dimity Cloak, and five guineas." In addition, there are numerous small bequests to other women, friends and servants, the wife of the carpenter at Isleworth, and many affectionate mentions of her mother, her sister, and her sons living and dead.

She is a good daughter. When she leaves money to "the poor French Emigrants" and "to the French Emigrant priests," it is as if she were returning a kindness her mother must have often told her about. In her will, Sylvia alludes to this family story: "my little Gold knife with Silver case I give to you in full confidence it may never go out of the family. It was my Grandfather's. He had it in his pocket when he fled from France in the time of persecution. It was his father's." Just as her great grandfather must have received help when he left his native land in times of persecution, just so people now fleeing from France and its revolutionary terrors need aid. Her family may have fled because they were Protestants persecuted in a Catholic country, but she is ready to support fleeing Catholics. There is something very satisfying in this bequest.

Most surprising of all, we learn from her will that she may not have always behaved as circumspectly as she should have. At least once in her life she may have risked impropriety.

Periodically throughout her will Sylvia alludes to money due her from a Lieutenant John Samson. At one point, she clarifies the situation (and, at the same time, further obscures it) by insisting that the sums due out of the moneys he owes her should be paid from her bank account even before the debt is settled and that he need only return to her the amount of money necessary to cover those sums: "and John Samson Lieutenant in the India Company who is in my debt more than one hundred and fifty pounds but I only demand that sum I have disposed of ... but previous to its being retrieved it must be paid out of the Money I have at Mr. Damon Banker." Clearly, Sylvia feared this debt might never be paid so she asks that standing funds be used to pay all the legacies due from it. She goes on to explain her fear in greater detail: "Samson when he went to India promised to pay me and previous to it never gave me a written agreement but I have never had a line from him." It is almost as if she uses the will to vindicate herself. He promised to pay me, but he never wrote anything down and has not written to me since. Don't expect much from this quarter. We never learn who this mysterious John Samson is. Is he a family friend? Is he her particular friend? Does Sylvia Thornton regret lending him money? When she did so, was her behavior all that it should have been? Tantalizing questions, but, ultimately, unanswerable.

Chapter 14

Sylvia Parkhurst

... sentimental stories, and books of mere entertainment ... should be sparingly used, especially in the education of girls. This species of reading cultivates what is called the heart prematurely, lowers the tone of the mind, and induces indifference for those common pleasures and occupations which, however trivial in themselves, constitute by far the greatest portion of our daily happiness ... . We know, from common experience, the effects which are produced upon the female mind by immoderate novel-reading. To those who acquire this taste every object becomes disgusting which is not in an attitude for poetic painting; a species of moral picturesque is sought for in every scene of life, and this is not always compatible with sound sense, or with simple reality.

Maria Edgeworth, *Practical Education* (1798)

If Lydia Hammond's story begins when she marries John Clerke, then Sylvia Brathwaite's ends when, on 25 April 1789, she marries Charles Parkhurst in St Mary's Marylebone Parish Church. She dwindles into a wife. Or does she?

Asserting in her final letter her power as the author of her own life, Sylvia gives a very different ending to her story than her aunt. While Mrs. Thornton puts her niece in a prison, Sylvia puts herself in Paradise.

29
From: Sylvia Parkhurst, Abergeley, Wales
To: Lady Clerke, Hungerford, Berkshire
Date: 13 November 1797
Can you tell me who a M^{rs} & Miss Harley are   Abergely November the 13th
who lived near Gosport.

My dear Friend

I am very sorry that you have been so unwell. I hope this warm fine weather for the time of year will have quite recovered you—I fear I have little chance of seeing you soon. We came here not for pleasure but economy and if we could meet with a House should probably settle here, but that is very difficult to meet with. And we are so miserably lodged for Winter that it is only People who have been used to as much inconvenience as we have who could put up with it.

Mr Parkhurst has been very ill treated about his Corps—not by the Duke of York for he would do anything to serve Him but by the <u>real Rulers</u> of the Army—for the

Duke has the name without power. We lived in London at much expence for such poor People. M^r P went abroad and took long Journeys when there—in short, spent money that would have been of material use—and all to no purpose, for not having the number of Men He was to have in three months, He lost the Corps, tho he had been <u>officially</u> assured the fixed time was a mere form and never kept strictly to. The fact is Mr Dundass is My Father's fixed Enemy and Troubles everything that belongs to Him. We have no comfort but that the Duke of York thinks M^r P hardly dealt with, and, we have reason to believe, intends at some time to make up for it. I tell you all this because I know you are sincerely interested for me. Be assured at any time when I do not mention My affairs it is because they are so perplexing that I wish to forget them, and from no want of confidence.

You will be glad, My dear friend, to hear that My Father has sent Me a Miniature Picture of Himself and a very fine Pearl Necklace. He ordered the best that could be found to be bought, which cost two hundred & forty pounds, & not content when He saw it—bought two rows of much longer. I am very happy at the affection this marks for Me, and tho God knows ornaments are what I am the least anxious about, and our affairs stand in need of very different assistance from Him, yet I feel that He is returning to His former love for Me, & that gives Me hope that He will do something to take us out of our Embarrassments, which would make me quite happy, for I am convinced Mr Parkhurst would live upon my Income now, as He is perfectly weaned from all extravagance. You will be glad also to know that I have written kindly to My Grandmother. While My Father took no notice but giving me money and but little of that, I could not prevail upon Myself to make it up with Her, because I knew it might be attributed to seeking Her Influence with My Father, but now that I want no service from Her, I have written and, if I have not forgotten Her unkindness, the memory of it is a little faded before Her great age and her former kindness to Me.

Here is a letter quite full of Myself and against all rules of anything but friendship. I am grieved I cannot see Mr Townsend's Books. I am not sure that I think much about the virtue of the Eastern Nations. In the very little knowledge I have of Them I find much dissimulation, revenge, and ambition, and that they seek the good things of this World at what we should call the total loss of the Next. The Hindus I am partial to, from the foolish whim I have of not putting any creature to death, which makes me a very bad Country Lady, where every Mistress of the Family is the Robber prince of Her unfortunate Poultry Yard.

My Brother whom you are good enough to ask after has been at Bognor Bocks Sea bathing. It has been of great service to Him. He is grown fat and is almost well, and has a very true pleasure in Mr Townsend's society, and will be very vain of His good opinion. You will see at Bath Mrs Macleod. She has no shining Talents to amuse, but has good and undeviating principles. The patient spirit with which She has lived an unpleasant life even from her childhood till now give her claims upon good minds, and Her being my friend from our childhood will make you like her. She is very much delighted with you, and will be a good chaperone for your charming daughters when you will not go with Them because she is of good Faschion and good conduct.

My little Boy is grown fat and is very happy in the Country. He thinks a dunghill quite as good as a hothouse—He is as yet perfectly without <u>taste</u>, which is the ruin or discontent of all the World. You will see My dear friend by this letter that I can be as dull and stupid as anybody living. Notwithstanding which we do pretty well living like the first Pair quite alone, or <u>better</u> than they did, for I have no mind to go looking for apples alone and we never upbraid Each other. M^r P joins me in compliments to Mr Townsend—accept them to Yourself also—and desire Miss Townsend not to forget Me & believe me Ever Yours affectionately

Sylvia Parkhurst.

Paradise Regained?

While Mrs. Thornton can only view her niece's story as tragic (there is no other way to structure a prodigal child's story), Sylvia refuses such an unmixed vision. She insists that her ending is a new beginning. When she writes five years after her aunt, she describes herself as contented. While her aunt can only see her niece's marriage to Parkhurst as a trap, Sylvia prefers to view it as an escape. In her last letter, the only one we have from her as a married woman, she writes in a tragicomic vein. Her father is not quite so inexorable as the grandfather in the *Gentleman's Magazine* account, and her ending not quite so mournful as Anne Foster's: "My Father has sent Me a Miniature Picture of Himself and a very fine Pearl Necklace .... I am very happy at the affection this marks for Me." Although her father's gifts are inadequate and inappropriate, they are signs of his love and returning favor. She can regain paradise. She may be poor and married to a man who is sometimes extravagant, but he has learned to curb his expensive tastes. More important, she, like her son, is free to arrange her world to her own liking and turn her piece of earth into a Garden of Eden and her potentially tragic story into a comedy.

Sylvia refuses to end up anywhere other than where she wants to be—in Paradise. The image of the first garden and couple crops up often in Sylvia's letters. It appears in the early letter about "The Royal Party" where Sylvia allows the ambivalent connotations of Eden and its dangerous fruit to suggest the rottenness at the core of the world she is entering and the care with which one must taste its pleasures. In letter #16, Sylvia raises her "Ideal Kingdom," creating not only a New Eden but recreating the Old World as well: "Fancy should adorn it with Inhabitants of her own Creation—There should be no rank but that of merit—no laws but those of honor—No marriages but of love—no cont[ribu]tions but in generosity—the souls of All our favorites should live again—Rouseau should rise again the child of nature and sensibility, Rouseau who felt more than Stern feigned—whose writings never called a tear where the Author had not shed a hundred—Sidney should charm another World—Our Essex should awake without those few faults that cost him so dear—& our Mary should rise unblushing cleared of all the guilt envy heaped upon her." Sylvia, who prefers the honest Rousseau to the feigning Laurence Sterne, prefers a world where Sir Philip Sidney could produce another arcadia and Mary Stuart be free of any taint of sin. She wants a world without rank or rancor, a world where love would be true and not feigned, a world where women could love without fear of ill repute. She wants a world where merit rules rather than money, nature rather than art, feeling rather than self-interest. But she knows such a world is nowhere, so, in the same letter, she playfully erects a dystopia of strange reversals: "if he [Sir Yelverton] comes and does not call upon us I will wish all the Ill things I can think of. First that he may be out of your favor and that he may read his favorite Mary defamed in every Book he takes up, and that the faschion of stooping may grow more universal [so] that upright People may be considered as Monsters—and that elegance and goodbreeding may be considered crimes in which case he will be found remarkably guilty, and, as my last wish—may he make the tour of Europe and visit Rouseau's tomb with no Companion but Mrs Kinderrly." We will probably never learn the identity of Mrs. Kinderrly, but, without doubt, she was someone who despised Rousseau and his ideals and thus would make the least likely companion for such a journey as Sylvia proposes.

In her last letter, Sylvia presents her most buoyant image of Eden. Married and living in Abergele, away from pomp and circumstance and royal parties of all sorts, she dwells with her Adam in a paradise of their own making: "we do pretty well living like the first Pair quite alone, or <u>better</u> than they did, for I have no mind to go looking for apples alone and we never upbraid Each other." When Sylvia was at the center of her world, she condemned its puppet shows, endless parades, empty frivolities, and shallow insincerity. Now at its margin, living in Wales, she is happy. She, like her son who "thinks a dunghill quite as good as a hothouse," has learned Milton's lesson: that the mind is its own place, and in itself can make a heaven of hell, a hell of heaven. Sylvia not only redeems the "lost" Mary Robinson, the flirtatious Miss James/ Mrs. Parkyns, and the misunderstood Mary Stuart, but she also redeems herself and writes herself into her own happy ending.

While many of her male contemporaries represented paradise as having access to all the naked, willing women they could possibly want and living without labor in a land where even a poor white man could become the master of others, Sylvia found paradise otherwise. She preferred Voltaire's solution. Not only does she end cultivating her own garden, but she rewrites Genesis in such a way that her garden can retain its beauty and freshness.

It is curious how completely Sylvia's life reflects the lives of Lydia Clerke and Charlotte Lennox. Like them, she married an improvident man with extravagant expectations and habits. Charles has even, like John, traveled to distant places to enhance his prospects. Nevertheless, Sylvia insists on giving her story a happy ending. Unlike Charlotte Lennox, who freely upbraided her husband for his inability to provide her or her daughter with necessaries, and unlike Lydia, who feared poverty and had much to forgive her first husband, Sylvia refuses to condemn the man she has chosen. Capable (like her Aunt Sylvia) of finding a species of moral picturesque in every scene of life she paints, she vehemently rejects her aunt's dismal perspective. She regards herself as an unfallen woman in a garden of her own devise with a deserving man as mate. The reader has to decide for herself if Sylvia's end is comic or tragic or if it is an end at all. Her life does, after all, go on, to close we know not when or how. Her ultimate fate remains, as it should in any good picaresque novel, unknown.

Chapter 15

Sarah Clerke

To the Memory of JOSEPH CLERKE Esq.
Who died July 24, 1790 A.E.T.
For more than half a Century an Inhabitant of this Village
And in the Commiſsion of the Peace;
He was regarded as an Uſeful Magiſtrate,
and a Man of Singular Benevolence;
in whom the Poor and Indigent ever found a Friend;
in the ſame Grave lie the Remains of Anne his Wife,
who died in Child bed of her 12ᵗʰ child, Feb 14, 1747.
Four of their children died in their Infancy, and of those
who attained mature Years; Sir JOHN CLERKE, Knt. their elder
Son, was a Captain in the Royal Navy & died at Madras,
September 1776. JOSEPH, their 2ⁿᵈ Son, Died at Abington, Cambridgeshire
April 18, 1784. WILLIAM their 3ʳᵈ Son, died Jan 2, 1753 and is
buried near this Stone. CHARLES, their 4ᵗʰ Son, was a Captain in the Royal Navy, who, after having, with equal Honour
to himſelf & his Country, completed three Voyages round
the World, died in attempting a fourth with Captain James Cook,
and was buried at Kamtſchatka August 29, 1779. THOMAS
their 5ᵗʰ Son was ſome time Chaplain to the English Factory
at Surat, and died there, 1773.
Reader, in this Example of a Father living to lament
over five Sons, who had brighten'd the Proſpect of his
advancing Years, see the Vanity of Human Hopes, and
look for permanent Felicity beyond the Grave.

Near this Stone lieth Enterr'd also the Body of Sarah Clerke
The last survivor of the family of JOSEPH & ANNE CLERKE
who departed this life the 16ᵗʰ Febʸ 1818; Aged 74 Years.
Who by Will left to the Trustees of M. Dorothy Motts School of this
Place, the Reversion of L360 in Furtherance of that Charity.
                                    The Clerke Family Memorial Plaque

They found it sufficiently furnished, and in such good order, that they settled in it without trouble. The condition of the poor soon drew their attention, and they instituted schools for the young, and alms-houses for the old. As they ordered every thing in their own family with great œconomy, and thought themselves entitled only to a part of their fortunes, their large incomes allowed them full power to assist many, whose situations differed very essentially from theirs. The next expence they undertook, after these establishment of schools and alms-houses, was that of furnishing a house for every young couple that married in their neighbourhood, and providing them with some sort of stock, which by industry would prove very conducive towards their living in a comfortable degree of plenty. They have always paid nurses for the sick, sent them every proper refreshment, and allow the same sum weekly which the sick person could have gained, that the rest of the family may not lose any part of their support, by the incapacity of one.

Sarah Scott, *A Description of Millenium Hall* (1762)

Sarah Clerke (1744?–1818) contributes two brief yet eloquent and thoughtful letters to *Circle*. The only two letters not addressed to Lady Clerke, they advise us of her death and give the "novels" formed by the letters their strong sense of an ending. Not sent to Lydia Clerke but to an anonymous other, their appearance in the collection is mysterious. Lydia Clerke saved the bulk of the letters, but who saved these two? When were they added to the collection? And, more important, why?

Sarah's letters are also important in that, closing both novels as they do, they remind us just how intricately intertwined the two texts and the two families are. The Clerke family may dominate the first book and the Brathwaites the second, but ties of kinship and friendship turn what might otherwise be two linear narratives into one circle of acquaintance.

30
From: Sarah Clerke, Castle Hedingham
To: My Dear Madam
Date: 27 October 1815

My Dear Madam,   Castle Hedingham Octo^{er}: 27th: <u>1815</u>

I take <u>shame</u> to <u>myself</u> in not having acknowledged the Receipt of yours, announcing the Death of my beloved Sister Clarke, but which the publick had long before Informed me of. I felt much at the Change & Particularly for Mr Townsend in the loss of so valuable a friend & <u>most</u> <u>agreeable</u> <u>Companion</u>, but did not <u>know</u> the picture of my Dear Brother was assigned me, till yesterday when it was mentioned in a letter from Miss Mullins of Southampton to a Mrs Bowles of this place, that you were at a loss how to convey it. That I much wishd to have it you will not doubt, but as it was not mentioned in yours, I <u>thought</u> it too <u>much</u> to ask from so slight an acquaintance. My Love & best regards will ever attend Mr Townsend, & if you will have the <u>goodness</u> to Draw a <u>Veil</u> over my <u>neglect</u> & <u>infirmity</u>; & give me a line, saying you <u>forgive</u> the <u>past</u>, and let me know how he does, you will confer a lasting obligation, & highly gratify your

Most obliged <u>Sarah Clarke</u>

[Written in the left-hand margin of the letter perpendicular to the above:] PS If you will have the goodness to convey the picture to Mrs Dyer No 95 Park Street Grosvenor Square I shall receive it Safe.

31
From: Sarah Clerke, Castle Hedingham
To: My Dear Madam
Date: 11 December 1816
My Dear Madam,

The Receipt of your most Kind letter, had not Remained unacknowledged so long, but your saying you hoped in a few Days to send the pictures according to my direction which was to Mrs Dyer 95 Park Street Grosvenor Square, as I have heard nothing of them, I think some mistake must have occurd. As to Dear Mr. Townsend, I shall ever think myself obliged by his kind intentions. As to <u>me</u> they woud be most <u>Invaluable</u> Relics. I have expected with great anxiety to hear of their arrival from Mrs Dyer. I am happy in the possession of my beloved and admirable Friend Lady Clerke, I much value it, but if Mr Townsend has not a picture of her, I shall with great pleasure present him with it.

I am much gratified, to hear your Dear Father is gradually recovering [from] his irreparable Loss, for such it must be, so good and amiable a Companion and in the Evening of Life when we have need of a friend's support. I have Buried all my near Connections, & sometimes feel as in the world alone. I am in my seventy second year, with its Infirmities, but am very thankful for the past, & for the Health I now enjoy. Will you have the goodness to give me some account of my Dear Sister's latter days. I hope they were not attended with much suffering, & pray give me the pleasure of hearing how my good friend Mr Townsend does, to whom I beg you will present my Love & best Regards and accept the same from your,

Most Obliged Friend
<u>S.Clerke</u>

Epistolary Mysteries

Sent from Castle Hedingham, a small village near Wethersfield, the letters from Sarah Clerke are at once the most transparent and the most opaque of all the letters in the Lydia Clerke collection. Informing us that Lady Clerke is dead, they also let us know that Sarah Clerke is the lone survivor of the Clerke family. Her brother John died in Madras in 1776, her brother Charles at sea in 1779. Her brother-in-law Paul Henry Maty died in 1787, and her father Joseph in 1790. We do not know when Hannah Maty died but, since she is mentioned in her husband's will but not in her father's, it was probably between 1787 and 1790. And Ann presumably died after her father but before Sarah, for her name does not appear in her sister's will (but does in her

CASTLE HEDINGHAM, ESSEX.

15.1 George Virtue print of Castle Hedingham, 1831. Reproduced by courtesy of the Essex Record Office.

father's). On 3 June 1814, Lydia Clerke died,[1] and, soon after Sarah Clerke wrote the two letters we have, she departed this life.

Sarah's letters are written in the shaky, fragile handwriting of an older person. Her orthography is old-fashioned. She still uses the long *f*, which was, by 1815, disappearing. Deferential yet stately, tentative yet persistent, her letters are brief and instrumental. She writes to retrieve a picture she has been "assigned" and to provide directions for its safe delivery. All is simple and self-evident. Or is it?

While on the surface Sarah's letters appear straightforward, if we look more closely at them, we discover troubling perplexities. First, it is not entirely clear whose picture Sarah has been given. In her first letter, she describes it as a picture of her "Dear Brother." We might assume it is a picture of John Clerke, Lady Clerke's first husband, a picture that she kept even after she remarried. However, it might also be a picture of Charles Clerke, who was, as is clear from his letters to Lydia, very dear to her. Sarah does not clarify whose portrait she is to receive, but, of course, this is the nature of epistolary discourse. We are entering into a conversation that has already begun; our comprehension is always partial; we cannot know what transpires in the letters we do not read. We can only surmise. Not only is it unclear whose picture has been left to Sarah, but it is also unclear how many pictures she is to receive. In the first letter she refers to "picture" in the singular; however, in the second she refers to "pictures" and tells "My Dear Madam" that "they woud be most <u>Invaluable</u> Relics." It would seem that in the interval between the first and second letter, Sarah received some indication that Mr. Townsend wanted to give her more than one picture. Perhaps

---

[1]   MISC 3/33/DF, 222B, Wiltshire & Swindon Record Office.

she was to receive pictures of both brothers. Perhaps she forgot that she was receiving only one.

In her second letter, Sarah expresses concern at the delay in receiving her bequest from Lydia. She offers Mr. Townsend a picture of Lady Clerke as if in compensation for the safe and timely delivery of what Lydia gave her, implying that he might not otherwise send it. Even in her first letter, where she explains how she learned of Lydia's gift to her, there are intimations of perhaps unconscious rebuke. Not only does she find it necessary to remind the Townsends of their obligation to her, but she subtly hints that they failed to tell her about the pictures in their letter to her announcing the death of Lydia. Also, in letting them know that she learned of Lady Clerke's death "long before" their letter arrived, she underscores their dilatoriness a second time.

When she uses the word "assigned" to describe Lydia's gift of the pictures, Sarah uses the language of eighteenth-century wills. She must have believed the pictures were a part of Lydia's formal will. Such a bequest was typical of the wills of her day. However, there is no such bequest in Lydia's will. Perhaps, as she lay dying, she remembered personal belongings left out of her written will and orally assigned them to appropriate recipients. Or, perhaps as her husband and step-children went through her effects, they decided to give some of her belongings to others. I wonder if it was at this time that someone came upon the cache of letters. What went through that person's mind as she or he read the letters that Lydia must have read many times?

The second mystery presented by these two letters concerns their dates. It would seem that fourteen months passed before Sarah Clerke wrote a second letter. However, I do not believe she would have waited that long before writing again, and I question the validity of the second letter's December 1816 date, even though it is written in Sarah's hand. If the October 1815 date of the first letter is correct, then why would Sarah wait more than a year before writing again? By the beginning of the nineteenth century, mails were regular and even packages of considerable size moved rapidly. Moreover, Sarah is not asking the Townsends to send the picture to her but to Mrs. Dyer in London, presumably because it would be easier and faster to send packages to London rather than to Castle Hedingham. Also, in her second letter, she writes that she had hoped the picture would be sent "in a few Days" and has waited for them "with great anxiety." It seems highly unlikely that she would wait fourteen months before writing again. In her second letter, Sarah expresses a fear that the earlier letter was lost ("I think some mistake must have occurd"), which would explain the delay, so, just to be safe, she sends the address again. In addition, she refers, in her second letter, to Joseph Townsend's "irreparable Loss" in such a way that it seems still fresh: "I am much gratified, to hear your Dear Father is gradually recovering [from] his irreparable Loss, for such it must be, so good and amiable a Companion and in the Evening of Life when we have need of a friend's support." And when she asks about Lady Clerke's "latter days" ("I hope they were not attended with much suffering") again she writes as if the event were recent. My most compelling reason for doubting the date on the second letter is the irrefutable fact that Mr. Townsend died on 6 November 1816.[2] Why would Sarah write as if he were alive in a letter sent one month later? Of course, it is possible that Sarah might not have known of Townsend's death when she wrote her second letter. But, given her age and her father's history of senile dementia, I wonder if she was not, in her second letter, misremembering the year. Another possibility is that the date is correct, many letters passed back and forth between October 1815 and December 1816, and Sarah, exasperated over the reluctance of the Townsends to forward the picture(s), finally, in desperation, offers her picture of Lydia in order to expedite matters. But, if there had been many letters in the interim of the two we have, wouldn't Sarah be more aware of Joseph Townsend's death and of the details of her sister-in-law's last moments?

Even more significant than the mystery of their dating is the mystery of their presence in the collection. Why were these two letters, the only ones not addressed to Lydia Clerke and the only ones written in the nineteenth century, included?

The first 29 letters were probably saved by Lydia for many different reasons over the course of 30 years. All of us have saved some of our letters. Few of us have saved all of them. But who adds letters to other people's collections? Why would anyone do such a thing? The person who placed Sarah Clerke's two letters among the letters in the Lydia Clerke collection must have had good reasons. Perhaps she inserted them intentionally as if to complete the stories the letters tell. With information about the death of the woman at the center of the collection of letters, we have narrative closure.

But there is still one more question we need to ask. Who did it? Although there is no way to know for sure, I suspect it was a step-daughter, perhaps the one to whom Sarah Clerke wrote, who gracefully and silently helped transform a sheaf of letters into fiction.

Unearthing Women's Stories

I do not need to reiterate just how much history is his story. But perhaps it is worth repeating once more how hard it is to get women's stories because this is so irrefutably the case. Although now I wonder how I could have missed it, I was long in coming to the realization that Lady Clerke remarried. Because she remained Lady Clerke even after she married Mr. Townsend, I was for years confused by the references to him. When I first read Mrs. Thornton's 1792 letter, I never connected the name Townsend to the role husband. I thought Townsend was simply a mutual acquaintance and the letter misdated (or that I was somehow misreading the numbers),

---

[2]   MISC 3/33/DF, 222B, Wiltshire & Swindon Record Office.

for she referred to a living husband ("your more than amiable husband's time was so occupied when in town that I was deprived of the pleasure of his Company at Isleworth"), and I knew John Clerke had died in 1776. How could Mrs. Thornton have been deprived of his company in 1792 (anymore than she already was by the fact of his death)? When I read Sarah's letters I was likewise at first confused. Who was Mr. Townsend? Again, I assumed he was a mutual acquaintance of Sarah's and the addressee's. Although the second Sarah Clerke letter made it clear that Mr. Townsend was the addressee's father, I still could not figure out his relation to Lady Clerke. It was years later, acting on a hunch and on a brief allusion in Sylvia's last letter ("I am grieved I cannot see Mr Townsend's Books"), that I read the *Dictionary of National Biography* entries for "Townsend," and found the entry for Joseph Townsend, who, it turned out, married Lydia Clerke, the widow of John Clerke, in 1790.

Women's stories are too often buried in the gaps of men's stories. Not only is Lady Clerke's marital history obscured because, as was customary, she kept her title after her husband died and she remarried, but I only found out about her second marriage because her second husband published several books and thus rated an entry in the *DNB*. What does it take for a woman to gain a niche of her own in history?

We find at least a few answers to this question if we turn to the Clerke family plaque in the Wethersfield Church, where the names of three women are engraved. Primarily memorializing the fate of Joseph Clerke, the epitaph opens with the date of his death and a testament to his importance as patriarch of a village and a family. Five lines describe his presence in the life of his community. One line identifies his wife Anne, who died in childbed of their twelfth child. So, if one married a prosperous, public-spirited man one might be remembered as his helpmate. After a brief mention of four children who died in infancy without gender and without name, the plaque goes on to identify five male children who reached maturity (and, of course, gender): John, Joseph, William, Charles, and Thomas. Their various deaths become an example of the moral picturesque: "Reader, in this Example of a Father living to lament/ over five Sons, who had brighten'd the Pro*∫*pect of his/ advancing Years, see the Vanity of Human Hopes, and/ look for permanent Felicity beyond the Grave." When a patriarch dies, we hope his sons will carry on his name, but if his sons die before him, we mourn their loss along with their father's for a line is now erased from history.

In his will, Joseph Clerke expended the sum of £100 to pay for "erecting a monument for myself and my most dear wife in the chancel in the church of Wethersfield aforesaid or in the church yard of that fair parish as they shall think fit."[3] We do not know who composed the words that were carved into the plaque, but obviously he or she (Ann or Sarah might have composed it) was most concerned with remembering the men of the family. Even though Joseph depended heavily on his

---

[3]   D/DU/423/21, Essex Record Office.

daughter Ann in his later years, her work and existence remain invisible, for she cannot carry on the family name. Hannah Maty's name is also absent from the family plaque. Although she married and bore a child, her life goes unnoted, for a daughter's children will not carry her father's name into futurity. Of the three sisters, only Sarah's name is mentioned. In her will, Sarah requested that her name be inscribed on the family monument and that her body be interred in the Chancel of the Parish Church of Wethersfield "as near to the remains of my late dear father Joseph Clerke Esquire deceased as may be."[4] As the last survivor of the family, Sarah can give herself a place in history. Tribute must be paid to her longevity. Also, she leaves £360 to a village institution. If a woman leaves a large bequest, she has a chance of being remembered. And, finally, if she establishes a school in her name, as her friend and sister townswoman Miss Dorothy Mott did, her name will live on at least for a short while.

15.2   Clerke family monument in Wethersfield Parish Church. Photo: Author's Collection

---

4   PROB 11/1602, Family Records Centre.

The Economic Power of Women

The actions of Sarah Clerke and Dorothy Mott offer compelling evidence of the limited but remarkable extent of women's economic power in the eighteenth century. While laws made it difficult for women to inherit property or to keep it once married, women could, by drawing on intertwined woman-to-woman liaisons, matrilineal inheritance patterns, and the growing need for charitableness and attention to the poor, circumvent patriarchy and its insistence on male inheritance. Especially if she were single, a woman might exercise considerable power.

In 1759, Dorothy Mott set up a charitable trust to provide a school for poor girls and to otherwise provide for Wethersfield's poor. According to the terms of her trust, the Vicar of Wethersfield was to distribute 20 shillings per annum among the poor of Wethersfield; pay a schoolmistress 12 pounds per year to teach 20 girls of the poorest persons of Wethersfield; as well as provide fuel for the schoolroom and prayer books, and gowns for the scholars.[5] In 1770, when she wrote her will, she set up a second charitable trust. Out of the rents of one of her properties, ten pounds was to be paid yearly to Ann Clerke, and, on her death, to Sarah Clerke, to be distributed to the poor of Wethersfield. At first, Mott stipulated that the money be paid at least half the time to people who went to church. However, she changed her mind and later scored through the words making this a condition. In the end, she decided that her money should go to those who were "Religious People" and attended divine worship whether at church or meeting.[6] Mott's terms are generous and, considering all the obstacles we still put in the way of giving money to the poor, freely extended. We begin to get a picture of women coming together to help the poor, considering seriously the best ways to do so, and trying to help the less fortunate of their own sex.

Three years after Dorothy Mott established her school, Sarah Scott's *A Description of Millenium Hall* appeared. Scott's novel is a utopian vision of wealthy spinster women philanthropists providing for the poor (but especially the female poor) of their village in many ways, with schools, alms, homes, and remunerative work. The novel reflected the work of Scott and her companion Barbara Montagu in Batheaston, near Bath, where they established a school for poor girls and boys. Reading and writing were taught to those who were capable, but much time was spent making linen and clothes for the poor of the neighborhood. According to Betty Rizzo, altruism was an important part of eighteenth-century women's lives: "After having studied combinations of eighteenth-century women for several years, it is my opinion that, more than men, women were by the second half of the century likely to come together for tacitly or avowedly altruistic purposes, that combinations of women, unable to meet for aggressive purposes (as in regiments), unlikely to meet for overtly

---

[5] D/P 119/25/145–7, Essex Record Office.
[6] D/P 119/25/148, Essex Record Office.

deliberative purposes (as in judicial or governmental bodies), condemned to meet only for social purposes, had begun to discover in charitable societies and purposes a challenging as well as acceptable use for their talents."[7] Rizzo's insights highlight the power of women to make small changes in their worlds. Women like Sarah Scott and Barbara Montagu, and Dorothy Mott, Ann Clerke, and Sarah Clerke did much to ameliorate the privations of others.

In our own day, some dismiss such women as "Ladies Bountiful," wealthy women who gave money grudgingly and only to those who fit their concept of "deserving poor." Seen as selfishly keeping the poor in their place with small amounts of support (just enough to stave off outright revolution), they are often represented as making no attempt to understand the world from the poor person's point of view. While Montagu, Scott, Mott, and Ann and Sarah Clerke may have looked at the world from their own genteel perspective, they must have pondered often and long the best ways to help those who were less fortunate than themselves. Their solutions may not be ours, but they could be liberal, heartfelt, carefully thought out, and generous.

Sarah Clerke and Dorothy Mott helped not only the poor of Wethersfield. Their wills make it clear that they passed on large amounts of money to other women like themselves. While Virginia Woolf lamented that women seldom left money to their daughters and nieces, sisters and friends, for women were too poor or too confined by patriarchal law to accumulate and bequeath significant amounts of money ("What had our mothers been doing then that they had no wealth to leave us?"[8]), the wills of Sarah Clerke and Dorothy Mott suggest that they were able to pass on significant amounts of money to members of their own sex. While Dorothy was only partly successful (and even then due to chance), Sarah was spectacularly so.

Sarah Clerke's will, written in 1817, contains an extraordinarily long list of large bequests to women, primarily spinsters, widows, unmarried daughters, and female servants. Sometimes the money was given outright; sometimes it was to be invested for the benefit of the legatee; sometimes, especially when giving money to a young girl, Sarah stipulates that the inheritor must marry to her mother's satisfaction if she is to receive her inheritance. Altogether Sarah left more than £32,800 in varying amounts to more than 30 women. Clearly some women were able to transfer large amounts of money to friends, family members, and servants.

Sarah also leaves £600 for the continuance of "Miss Dorothy Mott's Charity in Wethersfield." However, a codicil to her will reduces the amount to 400 pounds, which suggests that it was not always easy for women to spend money as they might have preferred. While we cannot rule out the possibility that the decrease was Sarah's own decision, we also cannot rule out the possibility that it was someone else's. Moreover, even the 400 is further reduced to 360 by the time the amount is engraved

---

[7]   Rizzo 23.
[8]   Virginia Woolf, *A Room of One's Own* (1929; New York, 1981) 21.

on the family plaque. Women could make inroads and even bequests, but their generosity could always be curbed by patriarchal law.

If history and journalism are gendered male, telling us more often than not the stories of men's feats and foibles, then letters (and novels) are gendered female, telling us the stories of women's inner and outer lives. While the absence of sisters Ann and Hannah from the family plaque memorializes once again women's absence from history, the letters of the Lydia Clerke circle remind us how full and significant women's lives can be. Women are the bearers of social history. But the documents of their lives are easily lost. Often they do not become part of the archive. Luckily, chance rescued the Lydia Clerke letters. In them, we learn much about women's desires and regrets and their very real accomplishments. We become acquainted with the myriad ways in which they helped one another. They could form a network for conveying precious mementoes from one end of the country to the other to insure that a woman's will be done; they could provide education and hope for the poor of their parishes; and they could offer one another solace, entertainment, and philosophical advice.

The retrospective and meditative tone of the plaque gracing the north wall of the church of St Mary Magdalene in Wethersfield echoes the melancholy tone of Sarah Clerke's letters. In both letter and stone, a woman's voice, however distanced, however disguised, however unknowingly, lets us know that a world of men has passed with no successor and that a single woman outlived her kin, and, when she died, she left some money to educate the poor. Sarah's will also gives us a glimpse into a world where women prospered and controlled their destiny, nurtured and protected one another, and worked together to help those less fortunate than themselves.

15.3 The Lydia Clerke letters at the Society of Antiquaries. Photo: Author's Collection. Reproduced by permission of the Society of Antiquaries of London

I admire Sara's love for and desire to hold on to the past. Her relationship to her portrait of Lady Clerke is both touching and haunting: "I am happy in the possession of my beloved and admirable Friend Lady Clerke, I much value it, but if Mr Townsend has not a picture of her, I shall with great pleasure present him with it." To give up a picture is to give up much. Possessing a picture is not only possessing the absent person but a piece of the past as well. In Sarah's world pictures were not easily obtained. They were costly and few. We can understand why she is eager to possess the pictures she believes she has been assigned, and prepared to do something generous in return.

As we come to the end of the Lydia Clerke letters and the novel(s) they serendipitously construct, once again we are surrounded by copies of copies and shadows of shades. Waiting for the picture of her "Dear Brother," tenderly anticipating the loss of her picture of Lady Clerke, Sarah leaves us haunted by the images of the people she once knew. Surrounded by ghostly presences of long-dead people, we, like Sarah Clerke, would do anything to get our hands on those pictures of the irrecoverable past.

Post/Crypt:
Closing the Circle ...

Such is the Power of Interest over almost every Mind, that no one is long without Arguments to prove any Position which is ardently wished to be true, or to justify any Measures which are dictated by Inclination.

By this subtil Sophistry of Desire, I have been persuaded to hope, that this Book may, without Impropriety, be inscribed to Your Lordship; but am not certain, that my Reasons will have the same Force upon other Understandings.

Charlotte Lennox, *The Female Quixote* (1752)

Like virtually every other source material historians ransack, [captivity narratives] are not writings that can be swallowed whole, but they can—and should—be sampled and sieved. For I do not accept the argument that sifting for accuracy in such texts is a fruitless enterprise, or that these and other European writings on encounters with non-Europeans are revealing only about the observers and writers, and never of the observed. No historical source should be automatically discounted on the basis of where its writers come from, or on the grounds of what their presumed ethnic group happens to be. Captivity narratives are fractured, composite sources, but it is inappropriate—indeed it is something of a cop-out—to analyse them textually but not contextually. Too much gets lost along the way.

Linda Colley, *Captives* (2002)

It is to burn with a passion. It is never to rest, interminably, from searching for the archive right where it slips away.

Jacques Derrida, *Archive Fever* (1996)

The easy possibility of letter writing must—seen merely theoretically—have brought into the world a terrible disintegration of souls. It is, in fact, an intercourse with ghosts, and not only with the ghost of the recipient but also with one's own ghost which develops between the lines of the letter one is writing.

Letter from Franz Kafka to Mrs. Milena Jesenská (1922)

He too has the power of raising from the Grave its Inhabitants how and by what means was but darkly Spoken. But so much they learned—the spirits having once been called had a perpetual Right to appear to the Person who so disturbed Them—& that they frequently did haunt the Beds and Feasts of These Noblemen. Further, that any one who would say from his heart—My God I abjure Thee—oh devil I worship Thee should see a Familliar & possess this power.

Letter from Sylvia Brathwaite to Lydia Clerke (1785)

Post/Crypt:
Closing the Circle ...

As *Circle* draws to a close, I would like to end where I began, where fiction and fact meet and where what Charlotte Lennox called "this subtil Sophistry of Desire" casts its inexorable spell. In looking for the real, we cannot avoid the seductive wiles of the imaginary. If we decide something is true we will find evidence to support our belief, even if we have to make it up.

In *Captives: The story of Britain's pursuit of empire and how its soldiers and civilians were held captive by the dream of a global supremacy, 1600–1850*, a brilliant and provocative study of the underbelly of imperialism, Linda Colley writes of the care we must take when approaching documents from the past. Historical documents are not immediately transparent. They are not neutral go-betweens. They are motivated and compromised; however, they still give us access to the past. We just need to read them carefully and contextually.

In presenting her arguments, Colley gives us many examples of the ways in which historical documents have been misread. Her most interesting cautionary tale, I believe, is her story about the journal of one Robert Drury. When Drury's captivity narrative about his life as a slave on the southern coast of Madagascar first appeared in London in 1729, readers questioned its authenticity. Although in his Preface Drury insisted that his tale was plain fact and not a romance like *Robinson Crusoe*, "some contemporary readers declined to believe Drury's story."[1] In 1943, a scholarly monograph proved to the author's and to many others' satisfaction that the book was a fiction and actually written by Daniel Defoe himself. Libraries reclassified the book and the *Encyclopedia Britannica* downgraded it "from respectable anthropological notice to a romantic fiction." What was first presented as fact had now unequivocally become fiction. Colley next turns her attention to Mike Parker Pearson, a marine archaeologist, who in 1991 not only validated the wreck of Drury's ship but also authenticated the biological details of his journal, and declared it to be "a largely accurate historical document." According to Pearson, Drury supplies too many accurate details for his work to be categorized as fiction. Colley agrees with Pearson and concludes her narration with an assertion that Drury's narrative is "real."

---

[1]   The full story of Robert Drury's journal can be found on pp. 14 to 15 of Linda Colley's *Captives* (New York, 2002).

However, I would like to argue the possibility that even though the details are accurate, the "journal of Robert Drury" is a fiction. Wouldn't it have been possible for Defoe, or even Robert Drury himself, to consult other sources to give a fictional story greater verisimilitude? Perhaps Drury spent time in Madagascar, enough time to take extensive notes about the flora and fauna, but never served as a slave. Perhaps in another hundred years another researcher will "discover"—once again—the book's "essential" fictionality.

In recent history, a far more disturbing example of the ease with which a fiction can become a fact occurred during a trial when a woman's life was at stake. In 2001, Andrea Yates drowned her five young children in a bathtub and then called police to her home. During her trial, several mental health experts for the defense testified that when she committed the crime she was insane, which is identified as not knowing right from wrong. One health professional, Park Dietz, a forensic psychiatrist and consultant to the TV show *Law and Order*, testified that Yates knew what she was doing: she killed her children because she had found a way of avoiding punishment for her crime after watching an episode of *Law and Order* during which a woman who killed her children was found innocent by reason of insanity. Claiming that Yates watched this TV show regularly and that the episode aired shortly before she committed the crime, Dietz argued that this show gave the mother her opportunity. At the time he testified, Yates faced a possible death penalty. Later, before the sentencing phase of the trial, it was discovered that there was no such *Law and Order* episode. In the end, Yates was not sentenced to death, but the story of the TV show that provoked a crime by providing an alibi becomes, like the story of Robert Drury's journal, a study of how easily truth can be manufactured out of the imagination.[2] While we might forgive Drury—after all, a good story is a good story whether it's true or untrue—Dietz's fictionalizing is far more reprehensible. A woman's life was at stake.

We need to be cautious and humble as we report on what we have discovered about the past or the present. Truth is elusive. Nevertheless, I would agree with Colley that it is not "a fruitless enterprise" to plumb historical documents for information about the past. They do help us, but for every story we learn, there are many others we miss, stories which might compromise or at least change the stories we currently hold true. And we can never be sure that the stories we find are true.

---

[2]   There are many articles about the trial and its aftermath. The following three are typical in the information provided and the doubts raised: "Prosecution Witness in Yates Trial Assailed" by Carol Christian (*Houston Chronicle*, 30 April 2002: B3); "Court Reverses Yates' Child-Murder Conviction" by Michael Graczyk (*The Philadelphia Inquirer*, Friday, 7 January 2005: A2); and "Who's Babysitting The Kids?" by Dirk Johnson and Carol Rust (*Newsweek*, 17 January 2005: 37).

When I first read the *Gentleman's Magazine* account of John Brathwaite's death in July 1740, I read it as unalloyed truth:

The *Baltic* Merchant, of near 300 Tons, 16 Guns, and 20 Men, laden chiefly with Rice, was taken within view of *Scilly* on the *English* Coast, after a Fight of 4 Hours, by a *Spanish* Privateer of 16 Guns, commanded by a *Frenchman*, and manned with 70 *Frenchmen*, and 56 *Spaniards*. Two *English* Sailors were killed in the Fight, and others wounded, and Col Braithwait, who with his Lady, two Children, and two other Ladies, passengers for *England*, after Boarding and Quarter given, was barbarously shot through the head by a French Sailor, who was clapt in Irons for it, and committed Prisoner to the Castle of St Sebastian.[3]

This narrative gives us a lively account of how John Brathwaite died in 1740 on his way home to England. It is an exciting and tragic story. To be within sight of home, after many years away, and never arrive—what could be more dramatic—and mythic—than that? It is also traumatic. It must have affected his wife, perhaps calling forth or reinforcing her sense of strict righteousness. Also, two of Brathwaite's children witnessed his violent death. His son John was only an infant when his father died so it is hard to know how or if he was affected. Perhaps his peripatetic life as an adult spent away from England betokens a deep-seated fear of going home. When he did finally return to England in December 1802, he died only eight months later, in August 1803. Sylvia (Brathwaite) Thornton was a few years older than her brother. She might have witnessed the event and remembered it vividly. Perhaps it contributed to her pessimism and religious austerity. Over the years she must have thought about the event—perhaps the most dramatic in her life—and pondered its significance. What did it have to tell her and others about the instability of life on this earth? It is also possible that Sylvia Thornton told this story to her friends. And since one of her dear friends was Charlotte Lennox, she might have told the story to her. If she did, might not Lennox have used it to give verisimilitude to *Harriot Stuart*, her first novel, which was published in 1750, ten years after the event?

On the way from America to England, the ship on which Harriot sails with her governess Mrs. Blandon is attacked by a Spanish privateer. Made prisoners, she and her governess hope that they will receive favorable treatment at St Sebastian, where they fear they will be imprisoned. Fortunately rescued by English sailors, Harriot is then assaulted by the English Captain who attempts to rape her. Grabbing his sword, she successfully fends him off, and is, in turn, rescued from the irate crew by his nephew, who also finds her attractive. An outrageous story, full of romance and improbability, but the more I thought about it, perhaps containing some truth. The detail in the novel and in the *Gentleman's Magazine* story that gave me greatest pause as I debated the truth of Harriot's unlikely adventures was the mention of St

---

[3]   *Gentleman's Magazine*, July 1740: 355.

Sebastian. While in the novel, Harriot and Mrs. Blandon fear incarceration there, in the *Gentleman's Magazine* narrative the French sailor who shot Col Brathwaite was indeed committed to the Castle of St Sebastian.

Once I saw the connection between *Harriot Stuart* and the news story, I then began to wonder about the "two other Ladies, Passengers for *England*." Who might these two ladies be and might their presence on the ship alert us to the possibility that Lennox's relationship with Mrs. Thornton began even earlier than I previously suspected? Might they have known one another as children in the American Colonies? Might the two ladies accompanying the Brathwaites to England be Charlotte and her governess? We do not know exactly when Charlotte left America for England. Her three biographers believe she sailed after her father's death, and if her father died in 1742, then the two other ladies could not have been Lennox and a traveling companion. But it is possible that Lennox, unlike Harriot Stuart, sailed before her father's death. By insisting that Lennox left the American Colonies after her father's death, as her fictional heroine did, we are tricked into misreading the author's biography, so ready are we—by the subtle sophistry of desire—to find Lennox's real story in Harriot's imaginary one.

I have tried to close *Circle*, to end my long examination of the thirty-one letters at its center, but I know there are stories I have left out, mostly because I have not been able to find them. I would like to know more about Sylvia Brathwaite. Did she ever receive any of her inheritance from her father? Did she give birth to any more children? When did she die? She is not mentioned in Lydia Clerke's will and given that Lydia named so many women friends and relations in her will, it is difficult to believe that she would have left out her young friend if she were alive. Then again, Sylvia might have traveled to another country, and the two women might have lost touch with one another. But this does not seem likely; they were both such inveterate letter writers. I would also like to know more about Ann Clerke. When did she die? Did she ever consider marriage? Did she ever try to leave her father's house? Likewise, there are still lingering questions about the life of John and Lydia. Will we ever find proof of his adultery? Or of something more shocking (perhaps a second, Anglo-Indian family)? I am also curious about the identity of "Mrs. B" in Susannah's second letter: "I am truly sorry to find your amiable friend M^{rs} B is so poorly. I pray God she may get better if He sees it best." Is this mysterious Mrs. B Sylvia's mother, and is she "poorly" because she has discovered she is pregnant by William Phillips? And, finally, who is the "Miss Palmer" Sylvia Brathwaite mentions in two of her letters? Evidently Lydia did not particularly like this woman. Why not? And wouldn't it be wonderful if one day we discovered that Sylvia's Miss Palmer was Charlotte Palmer, author of *It Is and It Is Not a Novel*?

Haunting the Archive

In *Archive Fever*, Jacques Derrida describes the utopian dream of the archivist: "An archive without archive, where, suddenly indiscernible from the impression of its imprint, Gradiva's footstep speaks by itself!"[4] An archive without archive: an immediate encounter with the past. Such is the dream of the errant researcher wandering in the mazes of records and documents that endlessly interconnect with one another. We seek to move in a direct line from one moment to the next; however, attempting to move in one direction, we are inevitably seduced into another. Perusing dusty papers and haunting libraries in order to enter worlds we can never know, we ironically increase the distance between us and the ghosts of the past. Producing more and more archive, we become better acquainted with long-ago worlds, but, paradoxically, we also become increasingly estranged. Gaps and discontinuities remain. We can never know the past completely and we are always left with frustrating and unanswerable (for the moment) questions. But then, this is our position with regard to the present. We can never know the present completely. The future will give us not only different answers to the questions we now have about past and present worlds but also different questions. The archive, as Derrida insists, "opens out of the future."

Like the archive, letters have a fragile yet indestructible relationship to the past. When we write letters we incorporate the past and textualize it. When we post letters, we send the present at once into both the past and the future. What was/ is immediately present irrevocably becomes past, and hopefully the epistolary tale of that disappearance bears that piece of the past into the future. When, in writing to Lady Clerke, Charlotte Lennox breathlessly affirms that she must finish her letter in order to make that day's post or risk her letter's untimely delivery, her frantic haste becomes a paradigm for the trajectory of all letters: "Mr. Lennox this moment tells me that if I send my letter now, you will get it before you leave Buxton, I have not a moment to lose—I will send it away—remember my dear Lady Clerke you must come directly here—I shall die with grief if you go to a lodging. For heaven's sake spare me this mortification—adieu my dearest friend I must not add another word for fear of delay." The exigencies of the postal system create the style of the letter: its hurry, its immediacy, its intensity, its ever-present fear of missing the mark, its obsessive self-reflexivity.

This immediacy and intensity create a strong sense of reality. When we read letters, we believe we are reading the thing itself—we witness the movement of the moment as it transpires. We are reading an archive without archive. But this is not so. Letters do not contain unmediated truth. "Letters and diaries," as Cynthia Ozick

---

4   Derrida, *Archive Fever* 98.

insists, "are not necessarily less fraudulent than works of fiction."[5] Like any other text, letters are constructed. When writing letters we do not always tell the truth. Sometimes we fabricate. Constantly making decisions about what to include and what to leave out, we can never tell our addressee the whole truth.

Although we assume the present is transparently present to us, everywhere available, always around us and accessible, paradoxically the immediacy of the present makes it untouchable. We are constrained to use literary forms to give shape to the shapelessness of existence. This is perhaps the reason why Lydia Clerke's letters form themselves so easily into novels. The impalpable present slips into the past as letters capture and memorialize the passing moment. The heterogeneousness of women's discourse, which lends itself to the capturing of the ephemeral, becomes a powerful instrument for grasping what is disappearing even as it is written about.

The Ghosts of the Past

To seek to know the past is, sooner or later, to disturb ghosts. "To read the letters of the long dead is to summon up a veritable army of apparitions," writes Amanda Vickery.[6] "The retrieving of these forgotten things from oblivion in some sort resembles the art of the conjuror," suggests John Aubrey, "who makes those walk and appear that have been in their graves many hundreds of years: and represents as it were to the eye the places, customs, and fashions that were of the old time." Lawrence Stone found these words of John Aubrey, a citizen of the seventeenth century, in a nineteenth-century book, and used them to meditate on his role as a twentieth-century historian.[7] From the seventeenth century to the present, we have felt the power of the past. The living dead prey upon us even as we prey upon them. They haunt us even as we insist that we are engaged in a rational study of the past.

In her letter about a ghost story, Sylvia Brathwaite ponders what happens when you disturb the dead. She tells her twice-told tale in her usual sprightly manner, and the ironic tone of her concluding comments—"read it and smile at Macbeth" and "tell Me if your head is not filled with fancy raised Specters, Your lights burning bleu, and the fatal winding sheet rolling round your Candle"—suggests that she did not entirely believe this "tale of spirits—from an Old German officer." However, the letter within which she imbedded the story and the news with which she surrounded it suggest it impressed her deeply. She too becomes haunted by ghosts, including her own.

---

[5]   Cynthia Ozick, "Portrait of the Artist as a Bad Character," *A Cynthia Ozick Reader* (Bloomington, 1996) 313.

[6]   Vickery 1.

[7]   Lawrence Stone, *Broken Lives: Separation and Divorce in England, 1660–1857* (Oxford, 1993) 4.

In her letter, bringing back the dead proves perilous, for the ghosts that you call forth may take over your life. "The Relater" of the story is now himself a haunted man who is always ill after telling his tale. Not only is he, like the ancient mariner, doomed to tell and retell a story that enthralls and enervates him, but the spirits can now haunt him with or without his summons. They have a perpetual right to appear to the person or persons who once disturbed them. Their power is as formidable as it is irrevocable. Though incorporeal and insubstantial as air, they cannot be banished. Once they have been called up, they pass into the being of all who are so foolhardy as to speak their names. Their spirits pass into the bodies of their hosts.

Bodies are better off without such spirits. And, it would seem, spirits are better off without such bodies. As Sylvia writes about disembodied visions with all their carnal habits (shrouds and decaying flesh) and about young girls with lingering illnesses ("You will I know be sorry to hear that Harriot Lenox is supposed to be dying"), she appears ready to part from her own body: "I am not able to fetch one breath out," she tells Lydia, "and have a cough that tears my breast to pieces." Sylvia's symptoms —fighting for breath and continual, painful coughing—are not to be taken lightly. The breath that animates her could easily fail. She is only a breath away from death, at which point she could become a ghost herself, forced to appear at the will of a living sorcerer or familiar or anyone willing to abjure God and worship the devil. In her own body she incorporates the pain and the resistance of the ghosts she has heard about and of the ghost she might become, forced to return again and again to a world well lost: "but I think as my health grows worse my spirits are better." As the body weakens, spirit strengthens. Spirit is not only separate from the body, but better off so. Her mortality does not frighten Sylvia. In fact, her spirits have become so lively as she reaches the end of her letter, that she is quite prepared to write off Lady Clerke's unhappiness: "I am sorry you are so Unhappy—but you was made to be so." Insensitively cheerful or cheerfully insensitive, Sylvia willingly pays the price of telling tales of ghosts and death and dying: indifference to a beloved friend's pains and her own. Loosening the bonds that tie our spirits to our bodies and our bodies to our spirits disrupts ordinary human relations. Our disembodied spirits laugh at all misfortunes.

Considering the curious doubling in Sylvia's ghost letter where she becomes as haunted as the relater she writes about—visited by the possibility of her own death and ghostly return to a world to come—I find Kafka's fear, as expressed in a letter to Milena Jesenská, oddly explanatory of the dilemma Sylvia faced at least once in her life: "The easy possibility of letter writing must—seen merely theoretically—have brought into the world a terrible disintegration of souls. It is, in fact, an intercourse with ghosts, and not only with the ghost of the recipient but also with one's own ghost which develops between the lines of the letter one is writing."[8] Sylvia is the most prolific writer in *Circle*. She obviously enjoyed writing letters. Her tone is almost always sprightly, engaging, humorous. She rarely pines or frets. But, in her ghost letter, she begins to experience what Kafka called "a terrible disintegration of souls." Conjuring up ghosts makes her aware of her own fragile hold on life. Ghosts call to ghosts.

The most surreal letter in the Lydia Clerke collection, Sylvia's oddly pertinent, indeed overdetermined, ghost letter also represents the dilemma of the dweller in the archives, never resting, eternally haunted by the spirits s/he has raised, unable to escape from the labyrinthine speculative caves s/he explores, until her own body separates from its spirit.

Freud argued that ghost stories are the return of our repressed knowledge of our own death. "It is true that the statement 'All men are mortal' is paraded in textbooks of logic as an example of a general proposition," he writes in his essay "The 'Uncanny,'" "but no human being really grasps it, and our unconscious has as little use now as it ever had for the idea of its own mortality."[9] Our fascination with the uncanny, with what is at once familiar and frightening, is kin to our fascination with ghost stories. Believing in unbelievable ghost stories is a way of holding on to a disbelief in our own permanent irrevocable absence.

We remain haunted by the possibility of immortality. "A Letter always feels to me like immortality because it is the mind alone without corporeal friend. Indebted in our talk to attitude and accent, there seems a spectral power in thought that walks alone—." So wrote Emily Dickinson in a letter to Thomas Wentworth Higginson.[10] If letters from our living friends assume spectral power, then what about letters written hundreds of years ago? Reading letters written by people long dead makes us even more aware how indebted we are to attitude and accent in understanding insubstantial words. To understand the letters of people we do not know, we begin by trying to imagine the people who indited the words. We walk with them in their thoughts and try to catch glimpses of them in their worlds. But we cannot see them. Nor can we enter their worlds. They become ghosts with the power to haunt and inhabit those who disturb them, and the letters they wrote become the signs of their absence.

When reading texts from the past, we cannot avoid double-consciousness. While we try to understand past wor(l)ds from their own remote perspectives, we cannot help measuring them against our modern (and postmodern) sensibilities. This is the

---

[8]   Qtd in Bernhard Siegert, *Relays: Literature as an Epoch of the Postal System* (Stanford, 1999) 4.

[9]   Sigmund Freud, "The 'Uncanny,'" *The Standard Edition of the Complete Psychological Works of Sigmund Freud* (London, 1955) 17:242.

[10]   Emily Dickinson, *Selected Letters* (Cambridge, 1994) 196. Letter #330.

only way we can encounter the past. We cannot enter the past or become one with it. If we were ever to succeed in totally disappearing into the past, we would probably be as full of horror as if ghosts had materialized before us.

A story about the past is always a story about ghosts. It is always a captivity narrative, captivating and holding readers in thrall to the dead.

Appendices

Appendices

APPENDIX A: BIOGRAPHICAL SKETCHES OF THE LETTER WRITERS AND OF PERSONS AND PLACES MENTIONED IN THEM

Abington, Frances (1737–1815)–an actress. According to *A Biographical Dictionary of Actors*, she sold flowers and sang in the streets as a child. She also worked as a servant before becoming an actress in 1755. Her marriage to Mr. Abington proved unhappy and they separated. She played mainly comic roles and was last seen upon the stage on 12 April 1799.

Almacks–a fashionable gambling club.

Armitage, Caroline (Brathwaite) (1740–99)–daughter of John Brathwaite and aunt of Sylvia (Brathwaite) Parkhurst. Married to Robert Armitage on 28 February 1766.

Armitage, Robert (1736–87)–merchant of Liverpool, married Caroline Brathwaite.

Armitage, Whaley (1767–1855)–son of Robert and Caroline Armitage, admitted to Trinity College, Cambridge on 13 December 1785. Called to the bar in 1794 and practiced in the court of Chancery.

Banks, Joseph (1743–1820)–a naturalist. In May 1766 he was elected fellow of the Royal Society. He and his friend Dr. Daniel Solander accompanied Cook and Clerke's 1768–71 expedition, bringing back a large collection of plants. President of the Royal Society for over forty years, he dispatched collectors abroad for the enrichment of the gardens at Kew and exerted enormous influence both inside and outside the scientific community.

Beckford, William (1759–1844)–author of *Vathek*. Originally written in French, an English version was published anonymously and surreptitiously in 1784.

Brathwaite, George-Charles (1762–1810)–brother of Sylvia Brathwaite and son of John Brathwaite and Elizabeth Browne. Took the surname and arms of Boughton when he married Eliza-Davis Boughton, the natural daughter of Sir Edward Boughton, in June 1801. He died nine years later without a will.

Brathwaite, Sir John (1739–1803)–father of Sylvia Brathwaite. Spent most of his career in India. Rose to become a Major-General. Created a baronet on 18 December 1802. Died in London on 22 August 1803, a wealthy man.

Browne, Elizabeth (?–?)–wife of John Brathwaite. Before they were divorced, she bore him four children, including Sylvia and George-Charles. Gave birth to four natural children by William Phillips. After Phillips died, she married Reverend Angus Macaulay.

Camden, Lord (Charles Pratt) (1714–94)–a reformist and a Whig. He worked to extend the Habeas Corpus Act to civil cases and maintained that taxation without representation was robbery. He also worked on behalf of authors to oppose the Booksellers' Copyright Bill, which limited an author's copyright to fourteen years.

Carlton House–built at the beginning of the eighteenth century and purchased by the royal family in 1732. In 1783, George III granted the use of the house to his eldest son, the Prince of Wales, who subsequently spent thirty years refurbishing it.

Carmarthen, Marquis of (Francis Osborne) (1751–99)–elected to the House of Commons in 1774. In 1776 he was called to the House of Lords. He was appointed Secretary of State for Foreign Affairs under Pitt in December 1783.

Carnac, John (1716–1800)–served in the East India Company and as a Member of Parliament. In 1776 he was appointed member of council at Bombay.

Casamajor, James Henry (1745?–1815)–a lover of Sylvia. According to his *Gentleman's Magazine* obituary, he died in his 70th year, on 23 January 1815, after serving over forty years in the East India Company.

Clerke, Ann (1738 –?)–sister of Charles and John Clerke, friend of Lydia. Spent most of her life in Essex, the site of the Clerke family estate. Took care of her father Joseph in his old age.

Clerke, Charles (1741–79)–younger brother of John Clerke; brother of Ann and Sarah Clerke and Hannah Maty; brother-in-law of Lydia. He sailed around the world three times. His fourth voyage ended in tragedy. Six months after Captain Cook was killed, Charles died and was buried off the coast of Russia.

Clerke, John (1734–76)–husband of Lydia Clerke. An adventurous and improvident man, he joined the navy and traveled far, to the Americas, Africa, and India. Became a friend of William Hastings before he died in Madras in 1776.

Clerke, Lady Lydia (1740–1814)–the absent presence at the heart of the circle of acquaintance. Wife of John Clerke, sister-in-law of Charles Clerke, she was the friend and confidante of many women, including Sylvia (Brathwaite) Parkhurst and Charlotte Lennox. Married to John Clerke for fourteen years and then a widow for fourteen more, she married Joseph Townsend in 1790.

Clerke, Sarah (1744?–1818)–the last survivor of the Clerke family. She was in her seventy-second year when, by writing two letters after the death of Lydia Clerke, she gave the Lydia Clerke collection its strong sense of an ending. Sarah died two years later, in 1818.

Cook, James (1728–79)–the son of an agricultural laborer, he was bound apprentice to a shipowner. In 1759, at the age of 31, he was appointed master of the *Mercury*, on which he sailed for North America. In 1768, he commanded the *Endeavour* on a three-year expedition to the Pacific to observe the transit of Venus. In 1772, he began a second three-year expedition to explore the Pacific. In 1776, he undertook an expedition into the North Pacific to search for a passage round the north of America. When, on 13 February 1779, he was killed by natives in Karakakoa Bay, Charles Clerke assumed command.

Craven, Lady Elizabeth, Margravine of Anspach (1750–1828)–married in 1767, when she was seventeen years old, to William Craven, she gave birth to six children. According to her memoirs, Lord and Lady Craven separated in 1783. She was rumored to have eloped with her footman, but she accuses her husband and his mistress of filling the newspapers with fake rumors. Upon the death of Lord Craven, in 1791, she married the Margrave of Anspach.

Cumberland, Duke and Duchess of–Henry Frederick, the Duke of Cumberland (1745–96), was an uncle of the Prince of Wales. His marriage to Mrs. Anne Horton (1743–1808), a commoner, was one of the circumstances that led George III to introduce the Royal Marriages Act of 1772. From all accounts, the Duke and Duchess were not good influences on the Prince. Their circle of acquaintance included the Duchess's brother and sister, Colonel Luttrell and Lady Elizabeth Luttrell.

Cumberland House–a Pall Mall mansion built in the early 1760s for Edward Augustus, Duke of York and Albany, brother of George III. It became Cumberland House when it passed to the Duke and Duchess of Cumberland and was refurbished by Robert Adams in the 1780s.

Devonshire, Duchess of (1757–1806)–born Georgiana Spencer and married, in 1774, to William Cavendish, fifth Duke of Devonshire, a wealthy nobleman, she was a confidante and supporter of Charles James Fox and a leader of the bon ton. A fashionable woman, her hats were notorious.

Dobson, Matthew (1732–84)–husband of Susannah Dobson, a medical doctor, and author of several medical treatises. He attended Hester Thrale in Bath and recommended that she reunite with Gabriel Piozzi. On the day Thrale and Piozzi married in Bath (25 July 1784), Dobson died of a chill caught by sitting on damp grass.

Dobson, Susannah (Dawson) (1742–95)–a learned lady and friend of Lydia Clerke. She published a life of Petrarch and translated Saint-Palaye's *Literary History of the Troubadours* and *Memoirs of Ancient Chivalry* as well as Petrarch's *View of Human Life* from the Latin. She also wrote *A Dialogue on Friendship and Society*.

Duncannon, Lady Harriet (1761–1821)–sister of Georgiana, Duchess of Devonshire. Like her sister, a great beauty and a compulsive gambler. She married Frederick Ponsonby, Viscount Duncannon, on 27 November 1780.

Dundas, Henry, lst Viscount Melville (1742–1811)–elected member of Parliament for Midlothian in 1774. In the early 1780s he became involved in Indian affairs, reporting on the war in the Carnatic and condemning the mismanagement of the Indian presidencies. He consequently brought forward a bill to regulate the government of India. From 1794 to 1801, he was secretary of war under Pitt.

Eliot, Lady Harriot (Pitt) (1758–86)–the youngest sister of William Pitt. Married Edward James Eliot, one of her brother William's intimate friends, and died tragically of puerperal fever on 25 September 1786 at 28 years of age.

Ferrers, Lady Anne (?–1791)–daughter of John Eliot and wife of the 5th Earl Ferrers, who died in 1778. Lady Ferrers died in 1791 at Hampton Court.

Fitzherbert, Maria, or Fritz (1756–1837)–"wife" to the Prince of Wales. A widow, she resisted the persistent Prince until he faked a suicide attempt and on his "deathbed" made her promise to marry him. Their marriage, which took place on 15 December 1785, became the open state secret of the age. They were together ten years when, under pressure from George III, the future George IV was forced to marry

Caroline of Brunswick, his first cousin, on 8 April 1795. After Caroline was removed to Blackheath, he resumed his intimacy with Mrs. Fitzherbert. The Prince only broke with her in 1811, when he was made regent.

Frederick II, King of Prussia (1712–86)–King of Prussia from 1740–86. During his reign, he was considered among the most notable of enlightened despots. In his *Antimachiavell*, which was published by Voltaire, he opposed the political doctrines of Machiavelli and supported peaceful and enlightened rule. He was sympathetic to the American Revolution and patronized the arts and sciences throughout his life.

Garrick, David (1717–79)–an actor. He played many roles throughout his career, comic as well as tragic, and eventually became part owner of Drury Lane. A contentious person, he offended many: theater managers, other actors and actresses, critics, and even old friends. He was buried with exceptional pomp at Westminster Abbey on 1 February 1779.

George III (1738–1820)–grandson of George II, he became Prince of Wales when his father died in 1751. High-principled and religious, he succeeded to the throne in 1760 determined to break the Whig oligarchy. His reign became a series of party maneuvers while he tried to find a minister who would carry out his conservative political views. In the last years of his life, he suffered from bouts of a debilitating illness, which was misdiagnosed as madness.

George IV (1762–1830)–eldest son of George III and Queen Charlotte. He and his father were at odds almost from the moment of his birth. He attached himself to the Whigs, his father's enemies. His youth was marked by many excesses, and, in defiance of the Royal Marriage Act of 1772, he secretly married Mrs. Fitzherbert in 1785. His official marriage to Princess Caroline, which took place in 1795, was a failure. In 1823, he withdrew from public view. He died in 1830.

Greville, Harry (1760–1816)–son of Frances Macartney and Fulke Greville. After the defeat of the British at Yorktown, he was taken prisoner. He wrote a letter to his mother about a lottery, in which he participated, to select an Englishman to be hung in retaliation for the death of an American. The letter, sent on 29 May 1782, was circulated widely by his mother. He was back in England by November 1782.

Hammond, Lydia (Isgar) (1700–?)–mother of Lydia Clerke. A Nonconformist.

Hardy, Sir Charles (1716?–80)–an admiral, who, in 1779, took over the Channel fleet. By anchoring at Spithead, he was able to foil an invasion by the French and Spanish. He died one year later on 18 May 1780.

Hastings, Warren (1732–1818)–governor general of India. Landing at Calcutta in October 1750, he rose rapidly through the ranks. Articles of impeachment were brought against him when he returned to England in 1785. His trial began in 1788 and lasted until 1795, when he was acquitted on St George's Day. He died 22 August 1818.

Howe, Lord (Richard Howe) (1726–99)–a career naval officer. In spring 1782, he was appointed commander-in-chief in the Channel; in January 1783, he became first lord of the admiralty; in May 1790, he was given the command of the fleet in the Channel.

Hyder Ali, or Haidar Ali (1722–82)–born a peasant, he acquired great power and much territory in eighteenth-century India. By 1761 he was the virtual ruler of Mysore. He invaded the Carnatic in 1780 and routed a British force, but, in 1781, he was defeated near Madras by Sir Eyre Coote; his son Tippu Sultan continued the war. He died on 7 December 1782.

Johnson, Samuel (1709–84)–writer, biographer, lexicographer. Born at Lichfield in 1709, he left Oxford after two years without a degree. In 1737, he and David Garrick set out together for London. In 1763, he met James Boswell, his future biographer, who helped make him the most important writer of his day. He died in 1784.

Lord Kames, Henry Home (1696–1782)–a judge and writer. Born in Scotland, son of an impecunious border laird, he pursued a career in the law. In 1747 his *Essays upon Several Subjects Concerning British Antiquities* appeared. In 1751 he published his *Essays on the Principles of Morality and Natural Religion*. In 1762 *Elements of Criticism* appeared.

Kemble, John Philip (1757–1823)–two years younger than his sister Sarah Siddons, he made his first appearance at Drury Lane as Hamlet on 30 September 1783. That season, there were five members of the Kemble family performing on the London stage.

King, James (1750–84)–friend of Charles Clerke. In 1776, he joined Cook's third voyage as an astronomer. Appointed to the *Resolution* as second lieutenant, he recorded Charles Clerke's dying words and wishes and succeeded to the command of the *Discovery* on his death. He prepared Cook's journal of the third voyage for the press, and wrote its conclusion.

Kingston, Duchess of (Elizabeth Chudleigh) (1720–88)–secretly married to Augustus John Hervey in 1744. In 1750, she entered into a liaison with Evelyn, second Duke of Kingston. In 1769, she married him. Four years later he died. Her sensational trial for bigamy, launched in an effort to dispute the late Duke's will, lasted one week, from 15 April to 22 April 1776. She was found guilty, but, pleading benefit of peerage, discharged.

Lennox, Alexander (?–?)–husband of Charlotte (Ramsay) Lennox. They were married on 6 October 1747. At that time, he worked for William Strahan, a London printer. He served as a Deputy King's Waiter in the Customs from 1773 to 1782. An abusive and inconstant husband, he and his wife often lived apart.

Lennox, Charlotte (Ramsay) (1729?–1804)–author of novels, plays, essays. A well-known writer in her day, her most famous and most controversial work was *Shakespear Illustrated*. Her first and last novels fictionalized the story of her life in the American Colonies.

Lennox, Henrietta Holles (1765–85?)–the daughter of Alexander and Charlotte Lennox.

Luttrell, Colonel Henry (1737–1821)–a member of the circle of the Duke and Duchess of Cumberland. An army officer and politician, he began his military career in 1757 and by 1782 was a major-general. He began his political career as member for the Cornish borough of Bossiney. On 25 June 1776 he married Jane Boyd. He died on 25 April 1821, survived by his wife and his only known child, a natural son, Henry Luttrell.

Maty, Hannah (Clerke) (1735?–?)–the oldest Clerke sister. On 18 September 1775, at the age of 40, she married Paul Henry Maty and later gave birth to a son, but, according to her sister Ann, remained childlike all her life.

Maty, Paul Henry (Harry) (1744–87)–the husband of Hannah Clerke; brother-in-law of Lydia Clerke. Upon his father's death in July 1776, he obtained the situation of an assistant-librarian in the British Museum, and, in 1782, was promoted to under-librarian in the department of natural history and antiquities. Elected a member of the Royal Society on 13 February 1772, he became its foreign secretary in 1776.

Melbourne, Lady (1751?–1818)–a political hostess. Born Elizabeth Milbanke, she married Sir Peniston Lamb 13 April 1769. From 1782 to 1786, satirists linked her with the Prince of Wales.

Meredith, Sir William (1724?–90)–member of Parliament for Wigan from 1754 to 1761 and for Liverpool from 1761 to 1780.

Montagu, Elizabeth (Robinson) (1720–1800)–essayist, critic, and letter writer. In 1760, she anonymously contributed three dialogues to Lord Lyttelton's *Dialogues of the Dead*, and, in 1769, her essay on Shakespeare appeared. Along with her friends Elizabeth Carter, Catherine Talbot, Sarah Fielding, Hester Chapone, and Hester Mulso, and her sister Sarah Scott, she formed a supportive network of women intellectuals which became known as "the Bluestocking Circle."

Parkhurst, Charles (?–?)–husband of Sylvia Brathwaite. They were married on 25 April 1789, and their son Charles was born in Northampton in March 1790.

Parkhurst, Sylvia (Brathwaite) (?–?)–a young girl when we first meet her, she bewitches all the men around her, including the Prince of Wales. Marries a "poor soldier" and, the last we hear of her, is destitute but still sprightly.

Parkyns, Thomas Boothby, Elizabeth-Anne James, and Lady James–Thomas Boothby Parkyns (1755–?) and Elizabeth-Anne James (?–?) married 24 December 1783, at St Mary's Church Marylebone. Elizabeth-Anne was the daughter and heiress of Sir William James, whose third wife was Miss Goddard (otherwise known in the letters as Lady James). Lady James died 9 August 1789.

Pennant, Richard, and Anne Susannah (Warburton) Pennant –Richard Pennant (1737–1808) was a member of Parliament and Liverpool merchant. His family had been associated with the sugar-making industry and the slave trade of the West Indies from the mid-seventeenth century. In 1765, he married the heiress Anne Susannah Warburton (1745–1816).

Peyton, Sir Yelverton, Lady Peyton, and Mr. Calvert–Sir Yelverton Peyton (?–1815) was a captain in the Royal Navy and a long-time resident of Southampton. Lady Peyton (?–1813?) was his wife. Widow of Felix Calvert, Lady Peyton had a son by her first marriage who went to India to make his fortune.

Phillips, William (1731–81)–pursued a long and active military career. In 1758, he was sent to Germany. In 1762, he returned to England and was stationed at Woolwich in command of a company of royal artillery. In 1776, he served in Canada under Carleton and Burgoyne. Saw action at Saratoga, and was second in command at the Council of War on 13 October 1777, when Burgoyne surrendered. Taken prisoner, he did not regain his freedom until four years later, in March 1781. He was then ordered to Virginia where he became seriously ill with a fever and died two months later.

Pitt, William (1759–1806)–prime minister of Great Britain from 1783 to 1801 and from 1804 to 1806. Born in Hayes in Kent, on 28 May 1759, Pitt, known as the Younger, was the second son of William Pitt, 1st Earl of Chatham. He entered Parliament in 1781 and linked himself with William Petty, Earl of Shelburne. In 1782, Shelburne took office with Charles Wentworth, Marquess of Rockingham, and became prime minister when Rockingham died three months later. Pitt became Chancellor of the Exchequer under Shelburne and left office with Shelburne in April 1783. In December of that year, King George III named him prime minister.

Reynolds, Sir Joshua (1723–92)–a portrait painter. Born the son of a schoolmaster in 1723, he became one of the most famous and wealthy painters of his age. The first President of the Royal Academy, he sought, in his *Fifteen Discourses*, to encourage history painting as the most noble form of art. Nevertheless, he remains most famous for his portraits.

Robinson, Mary (Darby), or Perdita (1758?–1800)–actress, author, and mistress of Prince of Wales. Her first poetry collection was published in 1775. In 1776, she debuted at Drury Lane as Juliet. In 1779, in the role of Perdita, she captivated the Prince of Wales. The Prince's affections, however, were short-lived and soon transferred to another. She subsequently formed an intimacy with Colonel Banastre Tarleton. After becoming disabled, possibly as a result of a miscarriage or of acute rheumatic fever or of a combination of the two, she was, at first, tenderly cared for by Tarleton, but by 1788, he was occupying himself with politics, gambling, and other women. Nursed by her daughter, Robinson died on 26 December 1800.

Rochford, Lord (William Henry Zuylestein) (1717–81)–a patron of John Clerke. Given many different political and diplomatic posts, he served at different periods as envoy extraordinary and plenipotentiary to the King of Sardinia and as British ambassador at Paris. In 1768, he cast the deciding ballot against repealing the controversial American duties. His personal extravagance was very great.

Rousseau, Jean-Jacques (1712–78)–a philosopher, social and political theorist, and novelist. Born in Geneva on 18 June 1712, he was apprenticed at the age of 13 to an engraver. In 1742, he went to Paris, where he earned his living as a music teacher, copyist, and secretary. He went on to become one of the great French writers. Ultimately, his writings spurred republicanism and romanticism, revolutionary movements in the worlds of politics and literature.

St Luke's Hospital for Lunatics–founded in 1750, opened in 1751. Taking its name from the parish of St Luke's and devoted almost exclusively to the treatment of insanity, it was located in Upper Moorfields (near present-day Finsbury Square). Upon entering, patients were identified as "curable" or "incurable." In 1754 and for some time after the numbers were 50 curable and 20 incurable patients. By 1812, there were three hundred patients, about half incurable.

Siddons, Sarah (Kemble) (1755–1831)–born into an acting family, the Kembles, she was brought to the stage as an infant phenomenon. David Garrick brought her to Drury Lane where she made her first appearance, on 29 December 1775, as Portia. Her first London season was a dismal failure. In the following years, she performed in Manchester, Liverpool, and Bath, where she became all the rage. After she returned to Drury Lane in 1782, her career took off.

Sidney, Sir Philip (1554–86)–author and courtier. Most famous for *Astrophel and Stella*, a sonnet sequence, and *A Defence of Poetry*, his *Arcadia*, written to entertain his sister, the countess of Pembroke, was not published until 1590.

Sterne, Laurence (1713–68)–author, most famous for *The Life and Opinions of Tristram Shandy*. Born in 1713, he went to Cambridge, where he took orders and became vicar of Sutton-on-the-Forest in 1738. Samuel Johnson, Samuel Richardson, Horace Walpole, and others denounced *Tristram Shandy* on moral and literary grounds.

Sydney, Lord (Thomas Townshend) (1733–1800)–a significant political figure during the 1780s.

Tarleton, Sir Banastre (1754–1833)–a cavalry officer and a member of parliament. Educated at Oxford University, he accompanied Lord Cornwallis as a volunteer to North America, where he took part in several battles. Returning to England in 1782, he lived on half-pay as lieutenant-colonel. Elected to the House of Commons in 1790, he sided with the opposition, but still managed to hold his seat without interruption until 1806. In his maiden speech to Parliament, he spoke against the abolition of slavery.

Thornton, Bonnell (1724–68)–husband of Sylvia Thornton. Journalist, translator of Plautus, humorist and editor of *The Connoisseur*, he was part of the Johnson Circle.

Thornton, Bonnell George (1765–90)–older son of Sylvia and Bonnell Thornton, he died young and was deeply mourned by his mother.

Thornton, Robert John (1768?–1837)–younger son of Sylvia and Bonnell Thornton. Was probably born in 1768, the year of his father's death. Entered Trinity College, Cambridge. Studied at Guy's Hospital medical school. Most famous for his edition of "A New Illustration of the Sexual System of Linnæus."

Thornton, Sylvia (Brathwaite) (?–1793)–aunt of Sylvia (Brathwaite) Parkhurst; member of Lydia Clerke's circle of acquaintance. Wife of Bonnell Thornton and mother of their three children, Bonnell George, Robert, and Sylvia.

Tippu Sultan (1753–99)–son of Hyder Ali. At the age of fifteen he accompanied his father Hyder Ali on different military campaigns. He took over the kingdom of Mysore after his father's death in 1782. He was defeated in Srirangapattana on 22 March 1792.

Townsend, Joseph (1739–1816)–geologist and author; second husband of Lady Clerke. Educated at Clare Hall, Cambridge, he subsequently studied medicine in Edinburgh. He took orders and eventually became rector of Pewsey, Wiltshire. Authored many works, including *Every True Christian a New Creature*, *Free Thoughts on Despotic and Free Governments*, *A Dissertation on the Poor Laws*, and *The Character of Moses Established*. By his first wife Joyce Nankivell (who died in 1785), he had four sons and two daughters.

Winstanley, Thomas (1716?–89)–rector of the Church of St Dunstan-in-the-East, London, and a prebendary of Peterborough. Husband of Sylvia (Cole) Brathwaite, and father of Thomas Ralph Winstanley, who died young.

York and Albany, Duke of (Frederick Augustus) (1763–1827)–second son of George III and Queen Charlotte. On 1 November 1780, he was appointed a colonel in the army. He became commander-in-chief of the army in 1798. In 1809 he was forced to retire from his post as commander-in-chief because his mistress Mary Anne Clarke was found guilty of receiving money in exchange for promoting officers. Two years later, he was reinstated.

APPENDIX B: CHRONOLOGY

1700	Lydia Isgar, mother of Lydia (Hammond) Clerke, born
1729	Charlotte Ramsay born
1734	John Clerke born
1735	Hannah Clerke born
1738	Ann Clerke born
1739	Joseph Townsend born
1740	Lydia Hammond born; John and Sylvia (Cole) Brathwaite travel with their children from the American Colonies to England
1741	Charles Clerke born
1742	Susannah Dobson born
1744	Sarah Clerke born; Paul Henry Maty born
1747	On 14 February, Anne Clerke (mother of John, Hannah, Ann, Charles, and Sarah) dies in childbed of her twelfth child; Charlotte Ramsay marries Alexander Lennox in October; in November Lennox's *Poems on Several Occasions* published; Thomas Ralph Winstanley dies on 21 May
1748	John Clerke serves as midshipman aboard the *Lion* in North America
1750	In December, Lennox's *Harriot Stuart* published
1751	Prince Frederick dies; his son, George, George II's grandson, becomes Prince of Wales (the future George III)
1752	*The Female Quixote* published on 13 March
1753	*Shakespear Illustrated*, volumes one and two published
1754	*Shakespear Illustrated*, volume three published
1755	Lennox publishes a translation of the *Memoirs of Maximilian de Bethune, Duke of Sully*; John Clerke serves as lieutenant on the *Kent* in the West Indies; Charles Clerke enters navy
1756	The Seven Years' War begins; the *Kent*, with John Clerke on board, captures the *Ceriah*, a French ship
1759–60	John Clerke serves as commander on the *Baselisk*; participates in the bombardment of Le Havre
1759	On 5 February, Susannah Dawson marries Matthew Dobson
1760	On 25 October, George II dies; the Prince of Wales becomes George III
1761	On 13 August, the *Bellona*, with Charles Clerke on board, captures the *Courageux*; John Clerke serves as post captain on the *Melampe* off the coast of Africa; in April Elizabeth Browne marries John Brathwaite; Charlotte Lennox, assisted by Samuel Johnson, Lord Corke, and others, translates *The Greek Theatre of Father Brumoy* and serializes *The History of Harriot and Sophia* in *The Lady's Museum*
1762	On 19 April, Lydia Hammond marries John Clerke, who is afterwards ordered to the coast of Africa for three or four years

1763	The Seven Years' War ends
1764	In February 1764, Bonnell Thornton marries Sylvia Brathwaite; Charles Clerke sails with John Byron on a voyage round the world in the *Dolphin* (1764–66)
1765	Birth of Henrietta Holles Lennox (baptized 28 April)
1766	In February 1766, Caroline Brathwaite marries Robert Armitage
1767	Charles Clerke reads his paper about the Patagonians before the Royal Society on 12 February
1768	On 20 November, John Clerke writes from Paris; Bonnell Thornton dies; Elizabeth Browne and John Brathwaite return to London from Gibraltar
1768	Charles Clerke appointed master's mate to the *Endeavour*, and, with Captain Cook, makes his second voyage round the world (1768–71)
1769	*The Sister*, a comedy by Lennox based on *Henrietta*, withdrawn after its first performance (18 February) at Covent Garden; Mrs. Elizabeth Montagu publishes *An Essay on the Writings and Genius of Shakespear*; John Brathwaite sails to India
1771	Birth of George Louis Lennox
1772	John Clerke made a knight on 31 January; ordered to the East Indies in the *Prudent* to protect East India Company trade; Charles Clerke sails as second lieutenant of the *Resolution* on his third and Cook's second voyage round the world (1772–75); *The Rambles of Mr. Frankly* by Mrs. Elizabeth Bonhote published (in four volumes from 1772 to 1776)
1775	Susannah Dobson publishes her *Life of Petrarch, collected from Mémoires pour la vie de Petrarch*; on 18 September, Hannah Clerke and Paul Henry Maty marry
1776	The trial of the Duchess of Kingston opens 15 April and concludes 22 April; Charles Clerke appointed to command the *Discovery* during Cook's third expedition; John Clerke dies on 11 October, in Madras; the battles of Lexington and Concord mark the beginning of the American War of Independence
1777	The English defeated at Saratoga; William Phillips placed under house arrest; John Brathwaite divorces Elizabeth Browne
1778	Elisa Dobson, Susannah Dobson's daughter, dies; in October, Charlotte Lennox, Henrietta Holles Lennox, and Hannah Davis indicted in Middlesex for riotous assembly, disturbing the peace of Nicholas Hancock, and assaulting Ann Brown
1779	When Cook dies on 14 February, Charles Clerke takes command of the expedition; six months later, on 22 August, he dies; seven days later, he is buried at Kamchatka; Dobson translates Sainte-Palaye's *Literary*

History of the Troubadours; fear of a French invasion upon Portsmouth; on 3 December, Mary Robinson plays Perdita by royal command, and subsequently becomes the mistress of the Prince of Wales

1781   Major-General William Phillips dies on 13 May; Cornwallis surrenders to Washington on 19 October

1782   Banastre Tarleton and Harry Greville return to England from the American Colonies; in February, Tippu Sultan (Hyder Ali's son) attacks, defeats, and takes John Brathwaite prisoner; on 7 December, Hyder Ali dies

1783   By signing the Treaty of Paris on 3 September, Great Britain recognizes the independence of the former colonies; Pitt leaves office with Shelburne in April, but, in December, King George III names him prime minister, a post he will hold for 18 years; on 24 December, Thomas Boothby Parkyns marries Elizabeth-Anne James

1783–84   Poems by George Louis appear in periodicals

1784   In April, John Brathwaite obtains release from prison on the conclusion of peace with Tippu Sultan; Dobson translates Sainte-Palaye's *Memoirs of Ancient Chivalry*; in Bath, on 25 July, Hester Thrale marries Gabriel Piozzi and Matthew Dobson dies; on 13 December, Samuel Johnson dies in London

1785   Death of Henrietta Holles Lennox [?]; on 15 December, the Prince of Wales marries Maria Fitzherbert in a secret and illegal ceremony

1786   Impeachment charges brought against Hastings; a pirated English translation of *Vathek* appears; in August, Frederick II, King of Prussia, dies

1787   William Beckford publishes *Vathek* in French; *Victim of Fancy* by Elizabeth Sophia Tomlins published; on 16 January, Paul Henry Maty dies

1789   In February, Reverend Thomas Winstanley dies; on 25 April, Sylvia Brathwaite marries Charles Parkhurst

1790   *Euphemia* published; in March in Northampton, Charles Parkhurst born; on 26 March, Lydia Clerke marries Joseph Townsend; Joseph Clerke, the patriarch of the Clerke family, dies on 24 July

1791   Dobson translates Petrarch's *View of Human Life*

1792   Lennox begins to receive financial assistance from the Royal Literary Fund

1793   George Louis, Lennox's son, forced to leave England, emigrates to America [?]; Sylvia (Brathwaite) Thornton dies

1795	On 8 April, the Prince of Wales and the future George IV marries Caroline of Brunswick, his first cousin; on 30 September, Susannah Dobson dies
1799	Sylvia (Brathwaite) Winstanley dies
1804	On 4 January, Lennox dies, penniless, in Dean's Yard, Westminster
1811	The Prince of Wales becomes regent; makes final break with Mrs. Fitzherbert
1814	On 3 June, Lydia Clerke dies
1815	On 18 June, Wellington and Blücher defeat Napoleon at Waterloo
1816	On 6 November, Joseph Townsend dies
1818	On 16 February, Sarah Clerke dies
1820	George III dies
1824	Lady Vincent (Augusta Elizabeth Herbert), collector of the Lydia Clerke letters and daughter of the Hon. Charles Herbert, 2nd son of Henry, 1st Earl of Carnarvon, and Bridget, daughter of John (Byng), 5th Viscount Torrington, marries Sir Francis Vincent, 10th Bart
1830	George IV dies
1871	Lady Vincent's daughter, Blanche, marries John Raymond Cely-Trevilian
1876	Lady Vincent dies
1881	Blanche inherits the estate of Debden Hall, Essex, from her father
1915	Blanche Cely-Trevilian bequeaths the Cely-Trevilian collection to the Society of Antiquaries

Bibliography

Manuscript Sources

Beinecke Rare Book and Manuscript Library, Yale University, The James Marshall and Marie-Louise Osborn Collection.

Bodleian Library, MS Montagu d.8, fols. 124–6.

British Library. Manuscript Collections: Althorp Collection, Thomas Birch Papers (ADD MS 4303), Hastings Papers (Add MS 29,136; ADD MS 29,137; ADD MS 29,141), Newcastle Papers, Royal Literary Fund Records (Microfilm M1077, Reel #1), and Thomas Edgar Masters's "Journal of a Voyage" (ADD MS 36,528). Major-General William Phillips's letters (ADD MS 21,807; ADD MS 21,834; ADD MS 24,320; ADD MS 35,510; ADD MS 38,213; ADD MS 38,214; ADD MS 38,215; ADD MS 38,307; ADD MS 38,308) and Bonnell Thornton's letters (ADD MS 27,780; ADD MS 30,869; ADD MS 36,593). Burney Index. India Office Records (0/6/9 MSS EurB 392, MSS EurB 392).

City of Westminster Archives Centre, Parish Record Books.

Essex Record Office, Papers: D/DU/423/21; D/DFyP1; D/P 119/1/2; D/P 119/25/145–47; D/P 119/25/148; Q/RAq4, f. 78; Q/RSq4.

The Family Records Centre: PROB 11/1102, PROB 11/1128, PROB 11/1150, PROB 11/1176, PROB 11/1234, PROB 11/1328, PROB 11/1398, PROB 11/1563, PROB 11/1602.

Greater London Record Office. Indictments, Middlesex: MJ/SP 1778, f. 29; MJ/SR 3358/9. Sundry Papers: OB/SP 1782 Ap/41, OB/SP 1789 Jy/24.

Hampshire Record Office, Parish Register.

The Houghton Library, The Lennox Collection.

House of Lords Record Office, HL/PO/JO/10/7/520.

The Huntington Library, The Montagu Papers, Box 29, MO5754.

John Rylands University Library of Manchester, Letters from Charlotte Lennox to Samuel Johnson.

Liverpool Record Office, Antiquarian notes, Ref 942 WAK 7(9).

Public Record Office, Army List of 1745: WO 64/10; PRO 355.3/WOD.

Royal College of Surgeons of England, Hunter-Baillie Letters: one letter from Charlotte Lennox to Dr. William Hunter.

The Royal Hospitals NHS Trust Archives and Museum.

Society of Antiquaries, The Cely-Trevilian Collection. 444/19 (the Lydia Clerke letters); 444/18 (letter from Warren Hastings to John Clerke).

Society of Genealogists, PCC Wills Index. July 352, Nov 508.

Southampton Archives Office.

Victoria and Albert Museum, Pressmark Forster 48 (letters from Charlotte Lennox to David Garrick).

Westminster Abbey Muniment Room & Library.

Wiltshire and Swindon Record Office, 493/84 (a booklet about Joseph Townsend); MISC 3/33/DF,222B.

Online Sources

Chawton House Library and Study Website
Gathering the Jewels (Casglu'r Tlysau)
International Genealogical Index
Mental Health History Timeline
Oxford Dictionary of National Biography

Printed Sources

Reference Works

Admissions to Trinity College, Cambridge. Eds N.W. Rouse Ball and J.A. Venn. Vol. 3. London: Macmillan, 1911.

Alphabetical List of the Officers of the Indian Army. Eds Dodwell and Miles. London, 1838.

Alumni Cantabrigienses: A Biographical List of all Known Students, Graduates, and Holders of Office at the University of Cambridge, from the Earliest Times to 1900. Compiled by J.A. Venn. Cambridge: Cambridge University Press, 1940.

Alumni Oxonienses: The Members of the University of Oxford, 1715–1886. Ed. Joseph Foster. Nendeln/ Liechtenstein: Kraus Reprint, 1968.

The Annual Register, or a View of the History, Politics, and Literature, for the Year 1772. The Third Edition. London, 1780.

The Baronetage of England or the History of the English Baronets, and such Baronets of Scotland as are of English Families; with Genealogical Tables, and Engravings of their Armorial Bearings. Compiled by The Reverend William Betham. 5 vols. Ipswich, 1805.

Biographia Navalis. Ed. John Charnock. 6 vols. London, 1794–98.

A Biographical Dictionary of Actors, Actresses, Musicians, Dancers, Managers and Other Stage Personnel in London, 1660–1800. Eds Philip H. Highfill, Jr, Kalman A. Burnim, and Edward A. Langhaus. 16 vols. Carbondale: Southern Illinois University Press, 1973.

British Women Writers: A Critical Reference Guide. Ed. Janet Todd. New York: Continuum, 1989.

Catalogue of Political and Personal Satires. Ed. Mary Dorothy George. Vol. 3. London, 1877.

The Complete Peerage of England, Scotland, Ireland, Great Britain, and the United Kingdom, extant, extinct, or dormant. Compiled by George E. Cokayne. 6 vols. New York: St Martin's Press, 1984.

The Correspondence of George, Prince of Wales, 1770–1812. 8 vols. Ed. A. Aspinall. London: Cassell, 1963–71.

Diary of Col Cromwell Massy, Late of Hon'ble East India Company's Service Kept While a Prisoner at Seringa Patam Bangelore. Reprinted by Higginbotham & Co., 1912.

Dictionary of National Biography. Eds Leslie Stephen and Sir Sidney Lee. London: Smith, Elder & Co., 1885–1901.

An Encyclopedia of British Women Writers. Eds Paul Schlueter and June Schlueter. 2nd edn. New Brunswick: Rutgers University Press, 1998.

Gentleman's Magazine

History of the Royal Regiment of Artillery. Compiled by Francis Duncan. 2nd edn. Vol. 1. London, 1874.

Journals of the House of Commons

Journals of the House of Lords

The Knights of England: A Complete Record from the Earliest Times to the Present Day of the Knights of all the Orders of Chivalry in England, Scotland, and Ireland, and of Knights Bachelors. Compiled by W.A. Shaw. Vol. 2. London: Sherratt & Hughes, 1906.

The London Encyclopaedia. Eds Ben Weinreb and Christopher Hibbert. 2nd edn. Papermac: 1983.

The London Stage: 1660–1800: A Calendar of Plays, Entertainments and Afterpieces together with Casts, Box-Receipts and Contemporary Comment. Part 4 ed. George Winchester Stone, Jr. Carbondale: Southern Illinois University Press, 1962. Part 5 ed. Charles Beecher Hogan. Carbondale: Southern Illinois University Press, 1968.

Miscellanea Genealogica et Heraldica. Ed. Joseph Jackson Howard. 2 vols. London, 1888.

Public Characters of 1802–1803. London, 1803.

The Record of Old Westminsters: A Biographical List of all those who are known to have been educated at Westminster School from the earliest times to 1927. Compiled by G.F. Russell Barker and Alan H. Stenning. 2 vols. London: Chiswick Press, 1928.

Synopsis of the Extinct Baronetage of England. Compiled by William Courthope. London, 1835.

Westminster Abbey Registers. Ed. J.L. Chester. London, 1876.

Books and Journal Articles

Adams, Percy G. *Travel Literature and the Evolution of the Novel*. Lexington: University Press of Kentucky, 1983.
———. *Travelers and Travel Liars, 1660–1800*. Berkeley: University of California Press, 1962.
Alliston, April. *Virtue's Faults: Correspondences in Eighteenth-Century British and French Women's Fiction*. Stanford: Stanford University Press, 1996.
Altman, Janet Gurkin. "Postscript: Epistolary Acts and Literary Careers in the Eighteenth Century: Permutations of Public Sphere and Private Persona among Writers." In *Sent as a Gift: Eight Correspondences from the Eighteenth Century*. Ed. Alan T. McKenzie. Athens: The University of Georgia Press, 1993.
Anstey, Christopher. *The New Bath Guide*. 1766; Kensington: Cayme Press, 1927.
Armstrong, Nancy. *Desire and Domestic Fiction: A Political History of the Novel*. New York: Oxford University Press, 1987.
———. "The Rise of Feminine Authority in the Novel." *Novel* 15 (1982): 127–45.
Auerbach, Nina. *Communities of Women: An Idea in Fiction*. Cambridge: Harvard University Press, 1978.
Backscheider, Paula R., ed. *Revising Women: Eighteenth-Century 'Women's Fiction' and Social Engagement*. Baltimore: The Johns Hopkins University Press, 2000.
———. "Women Writers and the Chains of Identification." *Studies in the Novel* 19 (1987): 245–62.
Ballaster, Ros. *Seductive Forms: Women's Amatory Fiction from 1684 to 1740*. Oxford: Clarendon Press, 1992.
Bannet, Eve Tavor. *The Domestic Revolution: Enlightenment Feminisms and the Novel*. Baltimore: The Johns Hopkins University Press, 2000.
Bass, Robert D. *The Green Dragoon: The Lives of Banastre Tarleton and Mary Robinson*. New York: Henry Holt, 1957.
Beaglehole, J.C., ed. *The Journals of Captain James Cook on his Voyages of Discovery*. 4 vols and a portfolio. Cambridge: The Hakluyt Society, 1955.
Beasley, Jerry C., ed. "Women and Early Fiction." *Studies in the Novel* 19 (1987): 239–44.
Beattie, J.M. *Crime and the Courts in England, 1660–1800*. Princeton: Princeton University Press, 1986.
Beebee, Thomas O. *Epistolary Fiction in Europe, 1500–1850*. Cambridge: Cambridge University Press, 1999.
Bell, Susan Groag, and Marilyn Yalom, eds. *Revealing Lives: Autobiography, Biography, and Gender*. Albany: State University of New York Press, 1990.

Benstock, Shari, ed. *The Private Self: Theory and Practice of Women's Autobiographical Writings*. Chapel Hill: University of North Carolina Press, 1988.

Berg, Temma F. "Charlotte Lennox and Lydia Clerke: Reflecting on Letters." In *Eighteenth-Century Women: Studies in Their Lives, Work, and Culture*. Ed. Linda V. Troost. Vol. 2. New York: AMS Press, 2002.

———. "Getting the Mother's Story Right: Charlotte Lennox and the New World." *Papers on Language and Literature* 32 (1996): 369–98.

Bertelsen, Lance. *The Nonsense Club: Literature and Popular Culture, 1749–1764*. Oxford: Clarendon Press, 1986.

Bickerton, Thomas H. *A Medical History of Liverpool from the Earliest Days to the Year 1920*. London: John Murray, 1936.

Blewett, David, ed. *Reconsidering the Rise of the Novel*. Special Issue of *Eighteenth-Century Fiction*. 12:2–3 (2000).

Bloom, Edward A. *Samuel Johnson in Grub Street*. Providence: Brown University Press, 1957.

Boaden, James, ed. *Memoirs of Mrs. Inchbald: including her Familiar Correspondence with the Most Distinguished Persons of Her Time, to which are added* The Massacre *and* A Case of Conscience; *now first published from her autograph copies*. 2 vols. London, 1833.

Boswell, James. *The Life of Samuel Johnson*. 2 vols. London: Everyman's Library, 1973.

———. *The Ominous Years, 1774–1776*. Eds Charles Ryskamp and Frederick A. Pottle. New York: McGraw-Hill, 1963.

Boucé, Paul-Gabriel, ed. *Sexuality in Eighteenth-Century Britain*. Manchester: Manchester University Press, 1982.

Bradfield, Nancy Margetts. *Historical Costumes of England, 1066–1968*. New York: Costume and Fashion Press, 1977.

Brewer, John. *The Pleasures of the Imagination: English Culture in the Eighteenth Century*. London: HarperCollins, 1997.

Briggs, Nancy. *Georgian Essex*. Chelmsford: Essex Record Office, 1989.

Broadley, A.M., and Lewis Melville, eds. *The Beautiful Lady Craven: The Original Memoirs of Elizabeth Baroness Craven afterwards Margravine of Anspach and Bayreuth and Princess Berkeley of the Holy Roman Empire (1750–1828)*. 2 vols. London: John Lane, The Bodley Head, n.d.

Brophy, Elizabeth Bergen. *Women's Lives and the Eighteenth-Century English Novel*. Tampa: University of South Florida Press, 1991.

Brown, A.F.J. *Prosperity and Poverty: Rural Essex, 1700–1815*. Chelmsford: Essex Record Office, 1996.

Browne, Alice. *The Eighteenth-Century Feminist Mind*. Detroit: Wayne State University Press, 1987.

Brownstein, Rachel M. *Becoming a Heroine: Reading about Women in Novels*. New York: Viking Press, 1982.

Buck, Anne. *Dress in Eighteenth-Century England*. New York: Holmes & Meier, 1979.

Burney, Frances. *Diary and Letters of Madame D'Arblay (1778–1840)*. Ed. Charlotte Barrett. 6 vols. London: Macmillan, 1904–1905.

———. *The Early Journals and Letters of Fanny Burney*. General Ed. Lars E. Troide. Vols 1 & 2 ed. Lars E. Troide. Vol. 3 ed. Lars E. Troide and Stewart J. Cooke. Vol. 4 ed. Betty Rizzo. Kingston: McGill-Queen's University Press, 1988–2003.

———. *The Journals and Letters of Fanny Burney (Madame d'Arblay)*. Eds Joyce Hemlow, Curtis D. Cecil, and Althea Douglass. 12 vols. Oxford: Clarendon Press, 1972.

———. *The Wanderer*. Eds Margaret Anne Doody, Robert L. Mack, and Peter Sabor. 1814; Oxford: Oxford University Press, 2001.

Butler, Judith. "Imitation and Gender Insubordination." In *Inside/ Out: Lesbian Theories, Gay Theories*. Ed. Diana Fuss. New York: Routledge, 1991.

Byrne, Paula. *Perdita: The Literary, Theatrical, Scandalous Life of Mary Robinson*. New York: Random House, 2004.

Cannon, John. *Aristocratic Century: The Peerage of Eighteenth-Century England*. Cambridge: Cambridge University Press, 1984.

Carr, David. *Time, Narrative, and History*. Bloomington: Indiana University Press, 1986.

Carter, Elizabeth, and Catherine Talbot. *A Series of Letters between Mrs. Elizabeth Carter and Miss Catherine Talbot, from the year 1741 to 1770*. London, 1819.

Case, Alison A. *Plotting Women: Gender and Narration in the Eighteenth- and Nineteenth-Century British Novel*. Charlottesville: University Press of Virginia, 1999.

Castle, Terry. *The Apparitional Lesbian: Female Homosexuality and Modern Culture*. New York: Columbia University Press, 1993.

Centlivre, Mrs. *The Work of the Celebrated Mrs. Centlivre in Three Volumes*. London, 1761.

Clarke, Norma. *Dr. Johnson's Women*. London: Cambridge University Press, 2000.

Clerke, Charles. "An Account of the very tall Men, seen near the Streights of Magellan, in the Year 1764, by the Equipage of the Dolphin Man of War, under the Command of the Hon. Commodore Byron; in a Letter from Mr. Charles Clerke, Officer on board the said Ship, to M. Maty, M.D. Sec. R.S." *Philosophical transactions, giving some account of the present undertakings, studies, and labours of the ingenious, in many considerable parts of the world*. 12 February 1767: 75–9.

Clifford, James L. "Johnson's First Club." In *Evidence in Literary Scholarship*. Eds René Wellek and Alvaro Ribeiro. Oxford: Clarendon Press, 1979.

Cole, W.A. "The Arithmetic of Eighteenth-Century Smuggling: Rejoinder." *The Economic History Review*. New Series 28 (1975): 44–49.

———. "Trends in Eighteenth-Century Smuggling." *The Economic History Review*. New Series 10 (1958): 395–410.

Colley, Linda. *Captives: The story of Britain's pursuit of empire and how its soldiers and civilians were held captive by the dream of global supremacy, 1600–1850*. New York: Pantheon Books, 2002.

Collins, A.S. *Authorship in the Days of Johnson: Being a Study of the Relation between Author, Patron, Publisher and Public, 1726–1780*. London: Robert Holden & Co., Ltd, 1927.

Cook, Elizabeth Heckendorn. *Epistolary Bodies: Gender and Genre in the Eighteenth-Century Republic of Letters*. Stanford: Stanford University Press, 1996.

Cook, Captain James, F.R.S., and Captain James King, LL.D. and F.R.S. *A Voyage to the Pacific Ocean Undertaken, by the Command of his Majesty, for Making Discoveries in the Northern Hemisphere. To Determine the Position and Extent of the West Side of North America; its Distance from Asia and the Practicality of a Northern Passage to Europe. Performed under the Direction of Captains Cook, Clerke, and Gore. In His Majesty's Ships the Resolution and Discovery. In the Years 1776, 1777, 1778, 1779, and 1780*. In 3 vols. Vols I and II written by Captain James Cook, F.R.S. Vol. III written by Captain James King, LL.D. and F.R.S. London, 1784.

Cowley, Gordon, and Les Deacon. *In the Wake of Captain Cook: The Life and Times of Captain Charles Clerke, R.N., 1741–79*. Boston: Richard Kay, 1997.

Cox, Jane. *Hatred Pursued Beyond the Grave: Tales of our Ancestors from the London Church Courts*. London: HMSO, 1993.

Craft-Fairchild, Catherine. *Masquerade and Gender: Disguise and Female Identity in Eighteenth-Century Fictions by Women*. University Park: Penn State University Press, 1993.

Davidson, Cathy N. *Revolution and the Word: The Rise of the Novel in America*. Oxford: Oxford University Press, 1986.

Davis, Lennard J. *Factual Fictions: The Origins of the English Novel*. New York: Columbia University Press, 1983.

Davis, Robert P. *Where a Man Can Go: Major General William Phillips, British Royal Artillery, 1731–1781*. Westport, CT: Greenwood Press, 1999.

Day, Robert Adams. *Told in Letters*. Ann Arbor: Michigan University Press, 1963.

Derrida, Jacques. *Archive Fever: A Freudian Impression*. Trans. Eric Prenowitz. Chicago: The University of Chicago Press, 1996.

————. *Glas*. Trans. John P. Leavey, Jr and Richard Rand. Lincoln: University of Nebraska Press, 1986.

————. *The Post Card: From Socrates to Freud and Beyond*. Trans. Alan Bass. Chicago: The University of Chicago Press, 1987.

Dickinson, Emily. *Selected Letters*. Ed. Thomas H. Johnson. Cambridge: The Belknap Press, 1994.

Dobson, Austin. "The Female Quixote." *Eighteenth-Century Vignettes*. 3 vols. London: Chatto and Windus, 1982.

Dobson, Susannah. *A Dialogue on Friendship and Society*. London, 1777.

————. *Historical Anecdotes of Heraldry and Chivalry*. Worcester, 1795.

Donoghue, Emma. *Passions between Women: British Lesbian Culture 1668–1801*. London: Scarlet, 1993.

Doody, Margaret Anne. "Introduction." *The Female Quixote*. 1752; London: Oxford University Press, 1970.

————. "Shakespeare's Novels: Charlotte Lennox Illustrated." *Studies in the Novel* 19 (1987): 296–310.

————. *Frances Burney: The Life in the Works*. New Brunswick: Rutgers University Press, 1988.

————. *The True Story of the Novel*. New Brunswick: Rutgers University Press, 1996.

Duffy, Ian. *Women and Society in the Eighteenth Century*. Bethlehem, PA: Lawrence Henry Gipson Institute, 1983.

Eaves, T.C. Duncan, and Ben D. Kimpel. *Samuel Richardson: A Biography*. Oxford: Clarendon Press, 1971.

Edgeworth, Maria, and Richard Lovell Edgeworth. *Practical Education*. 2 vols. 1798; New York: Garland Publishing Inc., 1974.

Ellis, Kenneth. *The Post Office in the Eighteenth Century: A Study in Administrative History*. London: Oxford University Press, 1958.

Ellison, Julie. *Delicate Subjects: Romanticism, Gender and the Ethics of Understanding*. Ithaca: Cornell University Press, 1990.

Erskine, David, ed. *Augustus Hervey's Journal*. 2nd edn. London: W. Kimber, 1954.

Evans, Eric J. *William Pitt the Younger*. London: Routledge, 1999.

Ezell, Margaret J.M. *Writing Women's Literary History*. Baltimore: The Johns Hopkins University Press, 1993.

Faderman, Lillian. *Surpassing the Love of Men: Romantic Friendship and Love Between Women from the Renaissance to the Present*. New York: Morrow, 1981.

Favret, Mary A. *Romantic Correspondence: Women, Politics, and the Fiction of Letters*. Cambridge: Cambridge University Press, 1993.

Feather, John. "The Publishers and the Pirates: British Copyright Law in Theory and Practice, 1710–1775." *Publishing History* 22 (1987): 5–16.

————. *A History of British Publishing*. London: Croom Helm, 1988.

Feiling, Keith. *Warren Hastings*. London: Macmillan, 1954.

Ferguson, Moira, ed. *First Feminists: British Women Writers, 1578–1799*. Bloomington: Indiana University Press, 1985.

Ferris, Ina. *The Achievement of Literary Authority: Gender, History, and the Waverley Novels*. Ithaca: Cornell University Press, 1991.

Fielding, Henry. Rev. of *The Female Quixote*. In *The Covent Garden Journal*, Tuesday, 24 March 1752. Reprinted in *The Covent Garden Journal*. Ed. Gerhard Edward Jensen. Vol. 1. New Haven: Yale University Press, 1915.

Finke, Laurie A. *Feminist Theory, Women's Writing*. Ithaca: Cornell University Press, 1992.

Foreman, Amanda. *Georgianna, Duchess of Devonshire*. New York: Random House, 1998.

Forster, George. *A Voyage Round the World, in His Britannic Majesty's Sloop, Resolution, Commanded by Captain James Cook during the Years 1772, 1773, 1774, and 1775*. Eds Nicholas Thomas and Oliver Berghof. 2 vols. 1777; Honolulu: University of Hawai'i Press, 2000.

Foucault, Michel. "What Is an Author?" In *Contemporary Literary Criticism: Literary and Cultural Studies*. 2nd edn. Eds Robert Con Davis and Ronald Schleifer. New York: Longman, 1989.

Freud, Sigmund. "The 'Uncanny'." *The Standard Edition of the Complete Psychological Works of Sigmund Freud*. Trans. James Strachey. Vol. 17. London: The Hogarth Press, 1955.

Gilmore, Leigh. *Autobiographics: A Feminist Theory of Women's Self-Representation*. Ithaca: Cornell University Press, 1994.

Gilroy, Amanda, and W.M. Verhoeven, eds. *Epistolary Histories: Letters, Fiction, Culture*. Charlottesville: University Press of Virginia, 2000.

Goldsmith, Elizabeth C., ed. *Writing the Female Voice: Essays on Epistolary Literature*. Boston: Northeastern University Press, 1989.

Graves, Richard. *The Spiritual Quixote, or, The Summer's Rambles of Mr. Geoffry Wildgoose: A Comic Romance*. 3 vols. London, 1792.

Gray, James. "Dr. Johnson, Charlotte Lennox, and the Englishing of Father Brumoy." *Modern Philology: A Journal Devoted to Research in Medieval and Modern Literature* 83 (1985): 142–50.

Greenberg, Janelle. "The Legal Status of the English Woman in Early Eighteenth-Century Common Law and Equity." *Studies in Eighteenth-Century Culture* 4 (1975): 171–81.

Grundy, Isobel. "Samuel Johnson as Patron of Women." In *The Age of Johnson: A Scholarly Annual*. Ed. Paul J. Korshin. Vol. 1. New York: AMS Press, 1987.

Guillim, John. *A Display of Heraldrie*. London, 1638.

Gunning, Henry. *Reminiscences of the University, Town, and Country of Cambridge from the Year 1780*. 2 vols. London, 1854.

Halsband, Robert, ed. *The Complete Letters of Lady Mary Wortley Montagu*. 3 vols. Oxford: Clarendon Press, 1967.

———. "Editing the Letters of Letter-Writers." *Studies in Bibliography* 55 (1958): 25–37.

———. *The Life of Lady Mary Wortley Montagu*. Oxford: Clarendon Press, 1956.

Hawkins, Laetitia M. *Anecdotes*. 2 vols. London, 1824.

Haywood, Eliza. *The History of Miss Betsy Thoughtless*. Ed. Christine Blouch. 1751; Ontario: Broadview Press, 1998.

———. *Selections from* The Female Spectator. Ed. Patricia Meyer Spacks. 1742–44; New York: Oxford University Press, 1999.

Heilbrun, Carolyn G. *Writing a Woman's Life*. New York: Norton, 1988.

Hendy, John G. *The History of the Early Postmarks of the British Isles from their Introduction Down to 1840*. New York: Charles Scribner's Sons, 1905.

Hickey, William. *Memoirs of William Hickey*. Ed. Alfred Spencer. 4 vols. London: Hurst & Blackett, 1925.

Hill, Bridget. *Eighteenth-Century Women: An Anthology*. London: Allen & Unwin, 1984.

———. *Women Alone: Spinsters in England, 1660–1850*. New Haven: Yale University Press, 2001.

———. *Women, Work, and Sexual Politics in Eighteenth-Century England*. Oxford: Basil Blackwell, 1989.

Hill, George Birkbeck, ed. *Boswell's Life of Johnson*. Rev. and Ed. L.F. Powell. Oxford: The Clarendon Press, 1934.

Hirsch, Marianne. *The Mother/Daughter Plot: Narrative, Psychoanalysis, Feminism*. Bloomington: Indiana University Press, 1989.

Hitchcock, Tim. *English Sexualities, 1700–1800*. New York: St Martin's Press, 1997.

Hoh-Cheung, and Lorna H. Mui. "'Trends in Eighteenth-Century Smuggling' Reconsidered." *The Economic History Review*. New Series (28): 28–43.

Home, J.A., ed. *Letters and Journals of Lady Mary Coke*. 4 vols. Edinburgh, 1889–96.

Honan, Park. "Eighteenth and Nineteenth Century English Punctuation Theory." *English Studies* 41 (1960): 92–102.

How, James. *Epistolary Spaces: English Letter Writing from the Foundation of the Post Office to Richardson's* Clarissa. Aldershot: Ashgate, 2003.

Hunter, J. Paul. *Before Novels: The Cultural Contexts of Eighteenth-Century English Fiction*. New York: Norton, 1991.

Isles, Duncan. "Johnson and CL." *New Rambler* 19 (1967): 34–8.

———. "The Lennox Collection." *Harvard Library Bulletin* 18 (1970): 317–44; 19 (1971): 36–60, 165–86, 416–35.

Jay, Ricky. *Learned Pigs & Fireproof Women*. New York: Farrar, Straus and Giroux, 1986.

Jenkins, Annibel. *I'll Tell You What: The Life of Elizabeth Inchbald*. Lexington: The University Press of Kentucky, 2003.

Johnson, Claudia L. *Equivocal Beings: Politics, Gender, and Sentimentality in the 1790s: Wollstonecraft, Radcliffe, Burney, Austen*. Chicago: The University of Chicago Press, 1995.

Johnson, Nichola. *Eighteenth Century London*. London: HMSO, 1991.

Jones, Mary. *Miscellanies in Prose and Verse*. Oxford, 1750.

Jones, Vivien, ed. *Women in the Eighteenth Century: Constructions of Femininity*. London: Routledge, 1990.

Kames, Henry Home, Lord. *Elements of Criticism*. Ed. Rev. James R. Boyd. New York, 1857.

Kaplan, Benjamin. *An Unhurried View of Copyright*. New York: Columbia University Press, 1966.

Kaplan, Deborah. *Jane Austen Among Women*. Baltimore: The Johns Hopkins University Press, 1992.

Kauffman, Linda. *Discourses of Desire: Gender, Genre, and Epistolary Fictions*. Ithaca: Cornell University Press, 1986.

———. *Special Delivery: Epistolary Modes in Modern Fiction*. Chicago: The University of Chicago Press, 1992.

Keener, Frederick M., and Susan E. Lorsch, eds. *Eighteenth-Century Women and the Arts*. New York: Greenwood Press, 1988.

Kelly, Gary, ed. *Bluestocking Feminism: Writings of the Bluestocking Circle, 1738-1785*. 6 vols. London: Pickering & Chatto, 1999.

Kelly, Linda. *The Kemble Era: John Philip Kemble, Sarah Siddons, and the London Stage*. New York: Random House, 1980.

Kenyon, Olga. *800 Years of Women's Letters*. Phoenix Mill, Gloucestershire: Alan Sutton, 1992.

Keymer, Tom. *Richardson's Clarissa and the Eighteenth-Century Reader*. Cambridge: Cambridge University Press, 1992.

Kirkham, Margaret. *Jane Austen, Feminism and Fiction*. New York: Methuen, 1986.

Lamb, Jonathan. "Minute Particulars and the Representation of South Pacific Discovery." *Eighteenth-Century Studies* 28 (1995): 281–94.

Langbauer, Laurie. "Romance Revised: Charlotte Lennox's *The Female Quixote*." *Novel: A Forum on Fiction* 18 (1984): 29–49.

Langford, Paul. *Public Life and the Propertied Englishman, 1689–1798*. Oxford: Clarendon Press, 1991.

Lanser, Susan Snaider. *Fictions of Authority: Women Writers and Narrative Voice*. Ithaca: Cornell University Press, 1992.

Leavis, Q.D. *Fiction and the Reading Public*. New York: Russell & Russell, 1965.

Ledyard, John. *A Journal of Captain Cook's Last Voyage*. 1783; Chicago: Quadrangle Books, 1963.

Lennox, Charlotte Ramsay. *Euphemia*. Ed. Mary Anne Schofield. 1790; Delmar, NY: Scholars' Facsimiles and Reprints, 1989.

———. *The Female Quixote, or the Adventures of Arabella*. Ed. Margaret Dalziel. "Introduction" by Margaret Anne Doody. Chronology and Appendix by Duncan Isles. 1752; London: Oxford University Press, 1970.

———. *The Lady's Museum*. By the author of *The Female Quixote*. 11 Numbers. London, [1760/61].

———. *The Life of Harriot Stuart, Written by Herself*. 2 vols. London, 1751. (Microfilm. New Haven, Conn. © Research Publications, 1975 [History of Women, Reel 55, no. 344]).

———. *Memoirs of Maximilien de Bethune, Duke of Sully, Prime Minister to Henry the Great*. 3 vols. London, 1756.

———. *Shakespear Illustrated: or the Novels and Histories, on which the Plays of Shakespear are founded, Collected and Translated from the Original Authors, with Critical Remarks*. 1753; New York: AMS Press, 1973.

———. *The Sister: A Comedy*. London, 1769.

Lenta, Margaret. "Form and Content: A Study of the Epistolary Novel." *University of Cape Town Studies in English* 10 (1980): 14–29.

Lonsdale, Roger, ed. *Eighteenth-Century Women Poets*. Oxford: Oxford University Press, 1989.

Lovell, Terry. *Consuming Fiction*. London: Verso, 1987.

Lowenthal, Cynthia. *Lady Mary Wortley Montagu and the Eighteenth-Century Familiar Letter*. Athens: The University of Georgia Press, 1994.

Lynch, James J. "Romance and Realism in Charlotte Lennox's *The Female Quixote*." *Essays in Literature* 14 (1987): 51–63.

MacArthur, Elizabeth J. *Extravagant Narratives: Closure and Dynamics in the Epistolary Form*. Princeton: Princeton University Press, 1990.

Maynadier, Gustavus Howard. *The First American Novelist?* Cambridge: Harvard University Press, 1940.

McKenzie, Alan T., ed. *Sent as a Gift: Eight Correspondences from the Eighteenth Century*. Athens: The University of Georgia Press, 1993.

McKeon, Michael. *The Origins of the English Novel, 1600–1740*. Baltimore: The Johns Hopkins University Press, 1987.

McLachlan, H., ed. *Transactions of the Unitarian Historical Society*. Vol. 9. London: The Lindsey Press, 1950.

Melville, Lewis, ed. *The Trial of the Duchess of Kingston*. Edinburgh: William Hodge & Co., Ltd, 1927.

"Memoirs of Mrs. Lenox, the Celebrated Author of the Female Quixote, and other works." *The Edinburgh Weekly Magazine*, 9 October 1783: 33–6.

Miles, Rosalind. *The Female Form: Women Writers and the Conquest of the Novel*. London: Routledge & Kegan Paul, 1987.

Misra, B.B. *The Central Administration of the East India Company, 1773–1834.* New York: Barnes & Noble, Inc., 1959.

Monod, Paul. "Dangerous Merchandise: Smuggling, Jacobitism, and Commercial Culture in Southeast England, 1690–1760." *The Journal of British Studies* 30 (1991): 150–82.

Montagu, Elizabeth Robinson. *An Essay on the Writings and Genius of Shakespear, compared with the Greek and French dramatic poets.* 3rd edn. London, 1772.

———. *"The Queen of the Bluestockings": Her Correspondence from 1720 to 1761.* Ed. Emily J. Climenson. London: Murray, 1906.

de Montolieu, Élisabeth Jeanne Isabelle Pauline. *Caroline of Lichtfield: A Novel.* Trans. Thomas Holcroft. 3 vols. London, 1786.

Moon, Penderel. *Warren Hastings and British India.* New York: Macmillan, 1949.

Murray, Judith Sargent. *The Gleaner.* 1789–95; Schenectady: Union College Press, 1992.

Myers, Mitzi. "Reform or Ruin: 'A Revolution in Female Manners.'" *Studies in Eighteenth-Century Culture* 11 (1982): 199–216.

Myers, Sylvia H. *The Bluestocking Circle: Women, Friendship, and the Life of the Mind in Eighteenth-Century England.* Oxford: Clarendon Press, 1990.

Nichols, John. *Literary Anecdotes of the Eighteenth Century.* 7 vols. London, 1812–16.

Nussbaum, Felicity A. *The Autobiographical Subject: Gender and Ideology in Eighteenth-Century England.* Baltimore: The Johns Hopkins University Press, 1989.

———. "'Savage' Mothers: Narratives of Maternity in the Mid-Eighteenth Century." *Eighteenth-Century Studies* 16 (1992): 163–84.

———. *Torrid Zones: Maternity, Sexuality, and Empire in Eighteenth-Century English Narratives.* Baltimore: The Johns Hopkins University Press, 1995.

Obeyesekere, Gananath. "'British Cannibals': Contemplation of an Event in the Death and Resurrection of James Cook, Explorer." *Critical Inquiry* 18 (1992): 630–54.

Olsen, Kirstin. *Daily Life in Eighteenth-Century England.* Westport, CT: Greenwood Press, 1999.

Owens, John B. *The Eighteenth Century, 1714–1815.* New York: Norton, 1976.

Palmer, Charlotte. *It Is and It Is Not a Novel.* 2 vols. London, 1792.

Parkes, M.B. *Pause and Effect: An Introduction to the History of Punctuation in the West.* Berkeley: University of California Press, 1993.

Patterson, A. Temple. *The Other Armada: The Franco-Spanish Attempt to Invade Britain in 1779.* Manchester: Manchester University Press, 1960.

Peace, John. *A Descant on the Penny Postage.* London, 1841.

Pearson, Jacqueline. *Women's Reading in Britain, 1750–1835: A Dangerous Recreation.* Cambridge: Cambridge University Press, 1999.

Pennington, Lady Sarah. *An Unfortunate Mother's Advice to her Absent Daughters in a Letter to Miss Pennington*. 5th edn. London, 1770.

Perry, Ruth. "Bluestockings in Utopia." In *History, Gender & Eighteenth-Century Literature*. Ed. Beth Fowkes Tobin. Athens: The University of Georgia Press, 1994.

———. "Colonizing the Breast: Sexuality and Maternity in Eighteenth-Century England." *Eighteenth-Century Studies* 16 (1992): 185–213.

———. *Novel Relations: The Transformation of Kinship in English Literature and Culture, 1748–1818*. Cambridge: Cambridge University Press, 2004.

———. *Women, Letters, and the Novel*. New York: AMS Press, 1980.

Pilkington, Laetitia. *Memoirs of Mrs. Laetitia Pilkington*. 3 vols. 1749–54; Dublin, 1770.

Planché, J.R. *British Costume: A Complete History of the Dress of the Inhabitants of the British Islands*. London, 1839.

Plant, Marjorie. *The English Book Trade: An Economic History of the Making and Sale of Books*. 1939; London: George Allen & Unwin, 1965.

Pohl, Nicole, and Betty A. Schellenberg, eds. *Reconsidering the Bluestockings*. San Marino, CA: Huntington Library, 2003.

Poovey, Mary. *The Proper Lady and the Woman Writer: Ideology as Style in the Works of Mary Wollstonecraft, Mary Shelley, and Jane Austen*. Chicago: The University of Chicago Press, 1984.

Porter, Roy. *English Society in the Eighteenth Century*. Rev. edn. London: Penguin, 1990.

Quinlan, Maurice J. "The Rumor of Dr. Johnson's Conversion." *The Review of Religion* 12 (1948): 243–61.

"Reconsidering the Rise of the Novel." Ed. David Blewett. Special issue of *Eighteenth-Century Fiction* 12 (2000). Numbers 2 and 3.

Redford, Bruce. *The Converse of the Pen: Acts of Intimacy in the Eighteenth-Century Familiar Letter*. Chicago: The University of Chicago Press, 1986.

Rennie, Neil. *Far-Fetched Facts: The Literature of Travel and the Idea of the South Seas*. Oxford: Clarendon Press, 1995.

Reynolds, Myra. *The Learned Lady in England, 1650–1760*. 1920; Gloucester, MA: Peter Smith, 1964.

Ribeiro, Aileen. *The Art of Dress: Fashion in England and France, 1750 to 1820*. New Haven: Yale University Press, 1995.

———. *Dress in Eighteenth-Century Europe, 1715–1789*. New York: Holmes & Meier, 1985.

Ribeiro, Alvara, and James G. Basker, eds. *Tradition in Transition: Women Writers, Marginal Texts, and the Eighteenth-Century Canon*. Oxford: Clarendon Press, 1996.

Ricoeur, Paul. *Oneself as Another*. Trans. Kathleen Blamey. Chicago: The University of Chicago Press, 1992.

Rizzo, Betty. *Companions Without Vows: Relationships among Eighteenth-Century British Women*. Athens: The University of Georgia Press, 1994.

Roberts, William, ed. *Memoirs of the Life and Correspondence of Mrs. Hannah More*. 2nd edn. 4 vols. London, 1834.

Robertson, Joseph. *An Essay on Punctuation*. 1785; Menston, Yorkshire: The Scholar Press, 1969.

Robinson, Howard. *Britain's Post Office: A History of Development from the Beginnings to the Present Day*. London: Oxford University Press, 1953.

———. *The British Post Office: A History*. Westport, CT: Greenwood Press, 1948.

Robinson, Mary. *Perdita: The Memoirs of Mary Robinson*. Ed. M.J. Levy. London: Peter Owen, 1994.

Rodger, N.A.M. *The Admiralty*. Lavenham, Suffolk: Terence Dalton Ltd, 1979.

———. *The Wooden World: An Anatomy of the Georgian Navy*. Annapolis: Naval Institute Press, 1986.

Rogers, Katherine M. *Feminism in Eighteenth-Century England*. Urbana: University of Illinois Press, 1982.

Rose, Mark. *Authors and Owners: The Invention of Copyright*. Cambridge: Harvard University Press, 1993.

Ross, Deborah. "Mirror, Mirror: The Didactic Dilemma of *The Female Quixote*." *Studies in English Literature, 1500–1900* 27 (1987): 455–73.

Rudé, George. *Hanoverian London, 1714–1808*. Berkeley: University of California Press, 1971.

Rupp, Gordon. *Religion in England, 1688–1791*. Oxford: Clarendon Press, 1986.

Scheuermann, Mona. *Her Bread to Earn: Women, Money, and Society from Defoe to Austen*. Lexington: University Press of Kentucky, 1993.

Schnorrenberg, Barbara Brandon. "The Blue Stocking Assembly: A Comment on Women's Lives in Eighteenth-Century England." In *Views of Women's Lives in Western Tradition: Frontiers of the Past and the Future*. Ed. Frances Richardson Keller. Lewiston, ME: The Edwin Mellen Press, 1990.

Schofield, Mary Anne, and Cecilia Macheski, eds. *Fetter'd or Free?: British Women Novelists, 1670–1815*. Athens: Ohio University Press, 1986.

Scott, Sarah. *A Description of Millenium Hall*. Ed. Gary Kelly. 1762; Ontario: The Broadview Press, 1995.

Séjourné, Philippe. *The Mystery of Charlotte Lennox: First Novelist of Colonial America (1727?–1804)*. Aix-en-Provence: Publications des Annales de la Faculté des Lettres, 1967.

Sherman, Sandra. *Finance and Fictionality in the Early Eighteenth Century: Accounting for Defoe*. Cambridge: Cambridge University Press, 1996.

Shevelow, Kathryn. "Charlotte Lennox." *A Dictionary of British and American Women Writers, 1660–1800*. Ed. Janet Todd. Totowa, NJ: Rowman and Littlefield, 1987.

———. "'C– L–' to 'Mrs. Stanhope': A Preview of Charlotte Lennox's *The Lady's Museum*." *Notes and Queries* 1 (1982): 83–6.

———. *Women and Print Culture: The Construction of Femininity in the Early Periodical*. London: Routledge, 1989.

Siegert, Bernhard. *Relays: Literature as an Epoch of the Postal System*. Trans. Kevin Repp. Stanford: Stanford University Press, 1999.

Simpson, D.H. *The Twickenham of Laetitia Hawkins, 1760–1835*. Twickenham: Local Historical Society Paper, 1978.

Simpson, David. *Romanticism, Nationalism, and the Revolt Against Theory*. Chicago: The University of Chicago Press, 1993.

Small, Miriam Rossiter. *Charlotte Ramsay Lennox: An Eighteenth Century Lady of Letters*. 1935; Archon Books, 1969.

Smith, Charlotte. *The Romance of Real Life*. 3 vols. London, 1787.

Smith, E.A. *George IV*. New Haven: Yale University Press, 1999.

Smith, Graham. *King's Cutters: The Revenue Service and the War Against Smuggling*. London: Conway Maritime Press, 1983.

Smithers, Henry. *Liverpool, Its Commerce, Statistics, and Institutions with a History of the Cotton Trade*. Liverpool, 1825.

Spacks, Patricia Meyer. *Imagining a Self: Autobiography and the Novel in Eighteenth-Century England*. Cambridge: Harvard University Press, 1976.

———. "The Subtle Sophistry of Desire: Dr. Johnson and *The Female Quixote*." *Modern Philology* 85 (1988): 532–42.

Spear, Percival. *The Nabobs: A Study of the Social Life of the English in Eighteenth-Century India*. London: Oxford University Press, 1963.

Spence, Joseph. *Observations, Anecdotes, and Characters of Books and Men, Collected from Conversation*. Ed. James Marshall Osborn. 2 vols. Oxford: Clarendon Press, 1966.

Spencer, Jane. *The Rise of the Woman Novelist from Aphra Behn to Jane Austen*. New York: Basil Blackwell, 1986.

Spender, Dale, ed. *Living by the Pen: Early British Women Writers*. New York: Teachers College Press, 1992.

———. *Mothers of the Novel: 100 Good Women Writers Before Jane Austen*. London: Pandora, 1986.

Staff, Frank. *The Penny Post, 1680–1918*. London: Lutterworth Press, 1964.

Stanley, Liz. *The auto/biographical I: The theory and practice of feminist auto/biography*. Manchester: Manchester University Press, 1992.

Stanton, Judith. "Statistical Profile of Women's Writing in English from 1660 to 1800." In *Eighteenth-Century Women and the Arts*. Eds Frederick M. Keener and Susan E. Lorsch. Westport, CT: Greenwood Press, 1988.

Steer, F.W., F.S.A. "Stories in Porcelain: The Clerke Service." *The Essex Countryside*, April 1960: 145–6.

Stewart, Maaja A. *Domestic Realities and Imperial Fictions: Jane Austen's Novels in Eighteenth-Century Contexts*. Athens: The University of Georgia Press, 1993.

Stone, Lawrence. *Broken Lives: Separation and Divorce in England, 1660–1857*. Oxford: Oxford University Press, 1993.

———. *The Family, Sex and Marriage in England, 1500–1800*. New York: Harper & Row, 1977.

———. *Road to Divorce: England, 1530–1987*. Oxford: Oxford University Press, 1990.

———. *Uncertain Unions: Marriage in England, 1660–1753*. Oxford: Oxford University Press, 1992.

Suleri, Sara. *The Rhetoric of English India*. Chicago: The University of Chicago Press, 1992.

Tadmor, Naomi. *Family and Friends in Eighteenth-Century England: Household, Kinship, and Patronage*. Cambridge: Cambridge University Press, 2001.

Taylor, John Tinnon. *Early Opposition to the English Novel: Popular Reaction from 1760 to 1830*. New York: King's Crown Press, 1943.

Thomson, Helen. "Charlotte Lennox's *The Female Quixote*: A Novel Interrogation." In *Living by the Pen: Early British Women Writers*. Ed. Dale Spender. New York: Teachers College Press, 1992.

Thornton, Bonnell, and George Colman the Elder, eds. *Poems by Eminent Ladies*. 2 vols. London, 1755.

Thrale, Hester Lynch. *Thraliana: The Diary of Mrs. Hester Lynch Thrale (Later Mrs. Piozzi), 1776–1809*. Ed. Katharine C. Balderston. 2 vols. Oxford: Clarendon Press, 1942.

Tillyard, Stella. *Aristocrats: Caroline, Emily, Louisa, and Sarah Lennox, 1740–1832*. New York: The Noonday Press, 1994.

Tobin, Beth Fowkes, ed. *History, Gender, and Eighteenth-Century Literature*. Athens: The University of Georgia Press, 1994.

Todd, Janet. *Feminist Literary History*. New York: Routledge, 1988.

———. *The Sign of Angellica: Women, Writing and Fiction, 1660–1800*. New York: Columbia University Press, 1989.

———. *Women's Friendship in Literature: The Eighteenth-Century Novel in England and France*. New York: Columbia University Press, 1980.

Tomlins, Elizabeth Sophia. *The Victim of Fancy*. 2 vols. London, 1787.

Tompkins, J.M.S. *The Popular Novel in England, 1770–1800*. Lincoln: University of Nebraska Press, 1961.

Townsend, Joseph. *A Dissertation on the Poor Laws*. London, 1787.

————. *Etymological Researches; wherein Numerous Languages Apparently Discordant Have Their Affinity Traced, and Their Resemblance is Manifested as to Lead to the Conclusion that All Languages Are Radically One*. Bath, 1824.

————. *Observations on Various Plans Offered to the Public, for the Relief of the Poor*. London, 1788.

Traub, Valerie. *The Renaissance of Lesbianism in Early Modern England*. Cambridge: Cambridge University Press, 2002.

Turner, Cheryl. *Living by the Pen: Women Writers in the Eighteenth Century*. New York: Routledge, 1992.

Turner, Thomas. *The Diary of Thomas Turner, 1754–1765*. Ed. David Vaisey. New York: Oxford University Press, 1984.

Uphaus, Robert W. "Jane Austen and Female Reading." *Studies in the Novel* 19 (1987): 334–45.

————, and Gretchen M. Foster, eds. *The Other Eighteenth Century: English Women of Letters, 1660–1800*. Lansing, MI: Colleagues Press, 1991.

Veyne, Paul. *Did the Greeks Believe in Their Myths?: An Essay on the Constitutive Imagination*. Trans. Paula Wissing. Chicago: The University of Chicago Press, 1988.

Vickery, Amanda. *The Gentleman's Daughter: Women's Lives in Georgian England*. New Haven: Yale University Press, 1998.

Wakefield, Gilbert. *Memoirs of the Life of Gilbert Wakefield, B.A.* 2 vols. London, 1804.

Walpole, Horace. *The Yale Edition of Horace Walpole's Correspondence*. Ed. W.S. Lewis. 48 vols. New Haven: Yale University Press, 1937–83.

————. *Memoirs of the Reign of King George the Third*. Ed. Sir Denis le Marchant. 2 vols. Philadelphia, 1845.

Warner, William B. *Licensing Entertainment: The Elevation of Novel Reading in Britain, 1684–1750*. Berkeley: University of California Press, 1998.

Warren, Leland E. "Of the Conversation of Women: *The Female Quixote* and the Dream of Perfection." In *Studies in Eighteenth-Century Culture*. Ed. Harry C. Payne. Madison: University of Wisconsin Press, 1982.

Watson, Nicola J. *Revolution and the Form of the British Novel, 1790–1825: Intercepted Letters, Interrupted Seductions*. Oxford: Clarendon Press, 1994.

Watt, Ian. *The Rise of the Novel: Studies in Defoe, Richardson, and Fielding*. 1957; Berkeley: University of California Press, 1971.

Weisser, Susan Ostrov. *A Craving Vacancy: Women and Sexual Love in the British Novel, 1740–1880*. New York: New York University Press, 1997.

Wheeler, Roy. *A Postal History*. Hassocks, West Sussex: Pier Point, 1996.

Whitmore, Clara H. *Women's Work in English Fiction: From the Restoration to the Mid-Victorian Period*. New York: G.P. Putnam's Sons, 1910.

Williams, E.N. *Life in Georgian England*. London: B.T. Batsford Ltd, 1962.

Williams, Raymond. *Culture and Society: 1780–1950*. London: Chatto & Windus, 1958.

Wilson, Mona. *They Were Muses*. London: Sidgwick & Jackson, Ltd, 1924.

Winstanley, Thomas, D.D. *A Sermon Preached on Occasion of the Clamours against the Act of Naturalizing the Jews*. London, 1753.

Wolf. A. *A History of Science, Technology, and Philosophy in the Eighteenth Century*. 1938; London: George Allen & Unwin, 1952.

Wollstonecraft, Mary. *A Vindication of the Rights of Woman*. Ed. Charles W. Hagelman, Jr. 1792; New York: Norton, 1967.

Woodmansee, Martha, and Peter Jaszi, eds. *The Construction of Authorship: Textual Appropriation in Law and Literature*. Durham, NC: Duke University Press, 1994.

Woolf, Virginia. *A Room of One's Own*. 1929; San Diego: A Harvest/HBJ Book, 1957.

Yarwood, Doreen. *English Costume from the Second Century BC to 1950*. New York: Crown Publishers, 1952.

Young, Arthur. *A Six Weeks' Tour through the Southern Counties of England and Wales*. London, 1772.

Zimmerman, Everett. *The Boundaries of Fiction: History and the Eighteenth-Century Novel*. Ithaca: Cornell University Press, 1996.

Index